Language, Vision, and Music

'S

Advances in Consciousness Research

Advances in Consciousness Research provides a forum for scholars from different scientific disciplines and fields of knowledge who study consciousness in its multifaceted aspects. Thus the Series will include (but not be limited to) the various areas of cognitive science, including cognitive psychology, linguistics, brain science and philosophy. The orientation of the Series is toward developing new interdisciplinary and integrative approaches for the investigation, description and theory of consciousness, as well as the practical consequences of this research for the individual and society.

Series B: Contributions to the development of theory and method in the study of consciousness.

Volume 35

Language, Vision, and Music: Selected papers from the 8th International Workshop on the Cognitive Science of Natural Language Processing, Galway, Ireland 1999
Edited by Paul Mc Kevitt, Seán Ó Nualláin and Conn Mulvihill

Language, Vision, and Music

Selected papers from the 8th International Workshop on the Cognitive Science of Natural Language Processing, Galway, Ireland 1999

Edited by

Paul Mc Kevitt
University of Ulster (Magee)

Seán Ó Nualláin
Nous Research, Dublin

Conn Mulvihill
National University of Ireland, Galway

John Benjamins Publishing Company
Amsterdam / Philadelphia

TM The paper used in this publication meets the minimum requirements of American National Standard for Information Sciences – Permanence of Paper for Printed Library Materials, ANSI Z39.48-1984.

Library of Congress Cataloging-in-Publication Data

International Workshop on the Cognitive Science of Natural Language Processing (8th : 1999: Galway, Ireland).

Language, vision and music: selected papers from the 8th International Workshop on the Cognitive Science of Natural Language Processing, Galway, Ireland 1999 / edited by Paul Mc Kevitt, Seán Ó Nualláin and Conn Mulvihill.

p. cm. (Advances in Consciousness Research, ISSN 1381–589X ; v. 35)

Includes bibliographical references and index.

1. Computational linguistics--Congresses. 2. Visual communication--Congresses. 3. Music and language--Congresses. I. Mc Kevitt, Paul. II. Ó Nualláin, Seán. III. Mulvihill, Conn. IV. Title. V. Series.

P98.I583 2002
410'.285--dc21 2001056597
ISBN 90 272 5155 X (Eur.) / 1 58811 109 1 (US) (Hb; alk. paper)

John Benjamins Publishing Co. · P.O. Box 36224 · 1020 ME Amsterdam · The Netherlands
John Benjamins North America · P.O. Box 27519 · Philadelphia PA 19118-0519 · USA

This book is dedicated to:

Professor Gerry McKenna
Vice-Chancellor & President
University of Ulster
Northern Ireland

and

Professor John Hughes
Pro Vice-Chancellor (PVC), Research & Development
University of Ulster
Northern Ireland

Contents

About the Editors

Professor Paul Mc Kevitt is 38 and from Dún Na nGall (Donegal), Ireland on the Northwest of the EU. He is Chair in Intelligent MultiMedia at the School of Computing & Intelligent Systems, Faculty of Informatics, University of Ulster (Magee College), Derry (Londonderry), Northern Ireland. Previously, he was Associate Professor (Senior Lecturer) in the School of Computer Science at The Queen's University of Belfast, Northern Ireland. He has been Visiting Professor of Intelligent MultiMedia Computing in the Institute of Electronic Systems at Aalborg University, Denmark and a British EPSRC (Engineering and Physical Sciences Research Council) Advanced Fellow in the Department of Computer Science at the University of Sheffield, England. The Fellowship, commenced in 1994, and released him from his Associate Professorship (tenured Lectureship) for 5 years to conduct full-time research on the integration of natural language, speech and vision processing. He completed a Master's degree in Education (M.Ed.) at the University of Sheffield in 1999. He completed his Ph.D. in Computer Science at the University of Exeter, England in 1991. His Master's degree in Computer Science (M.S.) was obtained from New Mexico State University, New Mexico, USA in 1988 and his Bachelor's degree in Computer Science (B.Sc., Hons.) from University College Dublin (UCD), Ireland in 1985. His primary research interests are in Natural Language Processing (NLP) including the processing of pragmatics, beliefs and intentions in dialogue. He is also interested in Philosophy, MultiMedia and the general area of Artificial Intelligence.

Seán Ó Nualláin holds an M.Sc. in Psychology and a Ph.D. in Computer Science from Trinity College, Dublin, Ireland. He is associate professor at Dublin City University, where he initiated and directed the B.Sc. in Applied Computational Linguistics, and the director of Nous Research. Seán is currently a visiting scholar at Stanford University. He is the author of a book on the foundations of Cognitive Science: "The Search for Mind" (1995) and the co-editor of "Two sciences of Mind" (1997). Intellect (England) just published a second edition of "The Search for Mind" (2002) and a follow-up "Being Human" is due soon. John Benjamins published "Spatial Cognition" in 2000, the proceedings of Mind-3. The Mind and CSNLP conferences are held in Ireland.

Conn Mulvihill holds B.Sc. and Ph.D. degrees from University College Dublin, Ireland. He holds a Lectureship in Computing Science at the National University of Ireland, Galway. His research interests are centred on creativity, complex systems and security.

Introduction

Paul Mc Kevitt, Seán Ó Nualláin, Conn Mulvihill
University of Ulster (Magee), Northern Ireland / Nous Research and Cognitive Science Society of Ireland / National University of Ireland, Ireland

1. Introduction

Occurring during the solar eclipse of 1999, The Eighth International Workshop on the Cognitive Science of Natural Language Processing (CSNLP-8) with the theme "Language, vision and music" has been a tremendous success. The delegates enjoyed themselves, and particularly not only the academic content but also the feast of social events, and expressed their congratulations on the programme and organisation. CSNLP-8 attracted a large number of delegates and papers from abroad including many from Britain, Europe, the USA and Asia.

CSNLP-8 was hosted by the Information Technology (IT) Centre at The National University of Ireland, Galway (NUI Galway), Ireland, The Cognitive Science Society Of Ireland (CSSI) and Nous Research, Ireland in cooperation with IntelliMedia 2000+, Aalborg University, Denmark. It was run just before "MIND-IV: Two Sciences Of Mind", The Annual Conference of the Cognitive Science Society of Ireland (CSSI), at Dublin City University, Dublin, Ireland (August 15th–18th), organised by Seán Ó Nualláin.

CSNLP-8 was advertised internationally to mailgroups and on usenet as well as by placing information at the Information Technology (IT) Centre, NUI Galway on WWW. Paul Mc Kevitt was Programme Chair for CSNLP-8 with Conn Mulvihill and Micheál Colhoun as Local Organisation Chairs and Seán Ó Nualláin is the General Chair for CSNLP. More details on the Workshop are available on http://www.it.ucg.ie/csnlp8.

A full workshop report can be found in Mc Kevitt et al. (2000).

2. The programme

The programme for CSNLP-8 contained a balanced set of papers from both Humanities and Engineering in response to the following Call for Papers:

Language, vision & music:
What common cognitive patterns underlie our competence in these disparate modes of thought? Language (natural & formal), vision and music seem to share at least the following attributes: a hierarchical organisation of constituents, recursivity, metaphor, the possibility of self-reference, ambiguity, and systematicity. Can we propose the existence of a general symbol system with instantiations in these three modes or is the only commonality to be found at the level of such entities as cerebral columnar automata? Also, we invite papers which examine cross-cultural experience of these modalities.

What can Engineering of software platforms for integrated Intelligent MultiModal & MultiMedia processing of language/vision/music/etc. tell us?

Topics include:
- combinations: language and music; language and vision; music and vision.
- What can Engineering of software platforms (e.g. AAU CHAMELEON) for integrated Intelligent MultiMedia processing of language/vision/etc. tell us?
- Metaphor: For example: the use of terms like "interval" and "range" in music.
- Rhythm: How is Rhythm important for language, vision and music?
- Acoustics: What role does it play in the three modalities?
- The roles of embodiment and culture in the formation of symbolic apparatus; For example: the use of gesture in face-to-face communication.
- Emotions: what role do they play in the three modalities?
- Synesthesia
- What the visual, musical and linguistic arts can tell us.
- What is the developmental relationship between prosody and music? What is the cognitive evidence for the dependence of music on language?
- Can we speak meaningfully about a semantics of music?
- Architectures for integration of language, vision and music; what aspects are conscious and what automatic? What aspects are common and what are specific to each?
- What is the role of modelling creativity? Are the creative processes similar or in what way are they different?

Special session on creativity: In AI we have failed to get much handle on creativity. Conn Mulvihill will Chair a special session on creativity looking at writing, poetry, painting, and music composition. Irish Nobel Prize Laureate Seamus Heaney is composing a translation of Beowulf at present with special attention to the sound — reminiscent of movement in a longship type craft and there are those that claim that music is central to any hope of understanding Joyce. We think also of the likes of Kandinsky here. Is Joyce prose or music? Is Kandinsky art or music? What is Picasso? What are the links between language, vision and music? Is creativity the same for each? and by the way, What is creativity? It is intended to involve Writers-in-Residence at NUI, Galway Pat McCabe ("The Butcher Boy") & Paula Meehan (Poet).

- Are recent trends towards integrating ideas in the Arts/Humanities and Sciences/Engineering important here? (cf. http://www.futurehum.uib.no/ & http://tn-speech.essex.ac.uk/tn-speech/)
- Why are there many arts and not just one?

The Programme Committee for CSNLP-8 consisted of around eighty members from Ireland and abroad including a large number of internationally renowned researchers:

Elisabeth André (DFKI, Saarbrücken, Germany)
Tom Brøndsted (Aalborg University, Denmark)
Liam Bannon (University of Limerick & Xerox PARC, Stanford, US)
John Barnden (University of Birmingham, England)
Bill Barry (University of Saarbrücken, Germany)
David Bell (University of Ulster, Jordanstown)
Niels Ole Bernsen (Odense University, Denmark)
Mike Brady (Oxford University, England)
Derek Bridge (University College Cork)
Harry Bunt (Tilburg University, The Netherlands)
Jon Campbell (University of Ulster, Magee)
Norman Creaney (University of Ulster, Coleraine)
Michel Denis (LIMSI-CNRS, Paris, France)
Koenraad de Smedt (University of Bergen, Norway)
Daniel Dennett (Tufts University, US)
Charles Fillmore (University of California, Berkeley, US)
Mikael Fernstrom (University of Limerick)
John Fitch (University of Bath, England)
James Flanagan (Rutgers University, US)
John Gammack (Murdoch University, Perth, Australia)
Erik Granum (Aalborg University, Denmark)
Niall Griffith (University of Limerick)
ChengMing Guo (NTT, Kyoto, Japan)

Steven Harnad (University of Southampton, England)
Jerry Harper (National University of Ireland, Maynooth)
Douglas Hofstadter (Indiana University, US)
Mike Holcombe (University of Sheffield, England)
Stephen Isard (University of Edinburgh, Scotland)
Brian Karlsen (Aalborg University, Denmark)
Mark Keane (University College Dublin)
Shalom Lappin (King's College London, England)
Margaret Leahy (Trinity College Dublin)
Chin-Hui Lee (Lucent Technologies' Bell Laboratories, US)
Bernard Levrat (LERIA, University of Angers, France)
James Martin (University of Colorado, US)
Mark Maybury (MITRE, Massachusetts, US)
Tony McEnery (Lancaster University, England)
Paul Mc Kevitt (Aalborg University, Denmark & University of Sheffield, England)
Peadar Mc Kevitt (Global Information Partnership (GIP) Ltd., Dublin)
Barry McMullin (Dublin City University)
MURPHY (ANDROID [M]) (University of Sheffield, England)
Alex Monaghan (Dublin City University)
Andrew Morris (IDIAP, Martigny, Switzerland)
Conn Mulvihill (National University of Ireland, Galway)
Fergal Murray (The Melanie O Reilly Band, Dublin)
Fionn Murtagh (Queen's University Belfast)
Stephen Nachmanovitch (Free Play Productions, Los Angeles, US)
Yoshiki Niwa (Hitachi Limited, Tokyo, Japan)
John Nolan (The Melanie O Reilly Band, Dublin)
Diarmuid O'Donoghue (National University of Ireland, Maynooth)
Greg O'Hare (University College Dublin)
Seán Ó Nualláin (Dublin City University)
Melanie O'Reilly (The Melanie O Reilly Band, Dublin)
Padraig Ó Seaghdha (Lehigh University, US)
Douglas O'Shaughnessy (INRS-Telecom, University of Quebec, Canada)
Ryuichi Oka (RWC P, Tsukuba, Japan)
Naoyuki Okada (Kyushu University, Japan)
Derek Partridge (University of Exeter, England)
Gert Rickheit (University of Bielefeld, Germany)
Jonathan Rowe (De Montford University, England)
Gérard Sabah (LIMSI-CNRS, Paris, France)
Noel Sharkey (University of Sheffield, England)
Noel Sheehy (Queen's University Belfast)
SINEAD (ANDROID [F]) (University of Sheffield, England)
Arnold Smith (NRC, Ottawa, Canada)
Humphrey Sorensen (University College Cork)
Mark Steedman (University of Edinburgh, Scotland)
Keith Stenning (University of Edinburgh, Scotland)
Oliviero Stock (IRST, Trento, Italy)
Mark Tatham (University of Essex, England)
Kris Thórisson (MIT Media Lab., Cambridge, US)

Peter Todd (Max Planck Institute for Human Development, Germany)
Jun-Ichi Tsujii (University of Tokyo, Japan & UMIST, England)
David Vernon (National University of Ireland, Maynooth)
Walther von Hahn (University of Hamburg, Germany)
Ipke Wachsmuth (University of Bielefeld, Germany)
Paul Whelan (Dublin City University)
Mary McGee-Wood (University of Manchester, England)
Michael Zock (LIMSI-CNRS, Paris, France)

CSNLP-8 had four invited speakers with thirty papers split into nine oral sessions (multimodal communication interfaces, multimodal communication and music, multimodal system formalisms and architectures, language & vision, language & music, language & music (semantics), synaesthesia, creativity I & II), panel session (on creativity), and five posters. We had a distinguished group of invited speakers from both Europe and the US: Sheldon Klein (Computer Sciences Department & Linguistics Department, University of Wisconsin, Madison, USA), Stephen Nachmanovitch (Free Play Productions, Los Angeles, USA), Gérard Sabah (LIMSI-CNRS, Orsay, France), and Ipke Wachsmuth (Faculty of Technology, University of Bielefeld, Germany). Sheldon Klein's presentation was during a creativity session from 10.50 AM until 11.40 AM on Wednesday, August 11th, at the maximum of a solar eclipse, which was 90% in Galway, occurring at 11.10 AM during his presentation.

During his presentation, Seán Ó Nualláin hastened to add that none of the music associated with the Riverdance dance show is Irish traditional music! During his, Paul Mc Kevitt introduced his presentation by showing a postcard from his mother which had a picture of the "Brian Boru" harp, a 15th or 16th century harp which is the oldest surviving Irish harp and on which the national government seal of Ireland (the harp) is based, and noted that many countries have birds or animals rather as their government seals. He also showed a picture of the Irish IR 10 pounds note on which there is a picture of James Joyce (1882-1941). Finally, Paul blessed the workshop proceedings with some sprinklings of Irish whiskey in what he called a pre-christian blessing which was appropriate during this time of solar eclipse and also since the meeting was being held in St. Anthony's College Oratory.

This book addresses the call for papers and programme with part I focussing on "language & vision", part II on "language & music" and part III on "creativity" (including a summary report of the panel session on creativity). We hope that the book conveys some of the excitement of the event. Some papers by leading experts included here, which were not presented at the workshop, are accepted by the committee due to valid reasons. For a fuller understanding on the genesis of the inspiration for the theme of this workshop and book the reader is directed towards recommended readings on philosophical works and engineering systems published in Mc Kevitt (1994, 1995/96, 1999), Ó Nualláin (1995/2000, 2000, 2002), Ó Nualláin and Smith (1995) and Ó Nualláin et al. (1997). Also of relevance are Ascott (1999, 2000), Dalsgaard et al. (1999), Friberg et al. (1994), Friberg and Sundberg (1995), Griffith and Todd (1999), Hofstadter (1999), Roth (1990) and Wallin et al. (2000).

3. Local organisation

Local organisation was coordinated by Conn Mulvihill and Micheál Colhoun who together with Josephine Griffith and Colm O'Riordan comprised the Local organising committee. Conn and Micheál took responsibility for social events whilst Micheál also focussed on equipment and web pages and Conn on accounts. Josephine dealt with registrations and accommodation and Colm worked on the proceedings and the participants list. The Registrar and Deputy President (now the President) of NUI Galway, Iognáid Ó Muircheartaigh, started off the workshop by welcoming all delegates in both the Irish and English languages with a light hearted introduction. He noted that the times are a changing and sprinting times for the 100 metres had reduced considerably over the years, that when he heard we were having a creativity session he thought that was interesting, but when he heard we were going to Aran he had an entirely different idea of what we might be doing, and he hoped that everyone enjoyed themselves.

This workshop was very international with many coming from Britain, Europe, the USA and Asia. We hope that this trend will continue so that CSNLP remains an international meeting. We had around 50 delegates for CSNLP-8, a large number for a focussed workshop, which has made this the largest CSNLP meeting ever. We were glad that delegates such as Glorianna Davenport, Paul Nemirovsky, and Kris Thórisson from the MIT Media Lab. who are world leaders in Intelligent MultiMedia were able to come and now with MIT MediaLabEurope established in Dublin, Ireland with first students started in September 2000 and funded initially with IR 28 million pounds by the Irish government (see http://www.mle.ie). A full picture gallery for the workshop is available at http://www.it.ucg.ie/csnlp8 and clips from Glorianna's camcorder are on: http://wwwic.media.mit.edu/About_IC/Gid-Iceland/.

A related meeting organised by Seán Ó Nualláin, "Mind-IV: Two sciences of mind", the Fourth Annual Meeting of the Cognitive Science Society of Ireland was held at Dublin City University (August 15–18) and had a focus on (1) outer and inner empiricism in consciousness research and (2) foundations of cognitive science with speakers Bernard Baars, David Galin, Stuart Hameroff, Katie McGovern, Stephen Nachmanovitch and Karl Pribram and this meeting was also very successful (see http://www.compapp.dcu.ie/~tdoris/mind4.html).

Acknowledgements

We would like to take this opportunity to thank Maxim Stamenov of the Bulgarian Academy of Sciences and Göttingen University, Germany, series editor for Advances in consciousness research and Ms. Bertie Kaal, Editor at John Benjamins Publishing Company for their helpful suggestions during the production of this volume. Seán Day is due a special thanks for editing and preparing the Russian paper herein.

Recommended reading

Ascott, Roy (Ed.) (1999). *Reframing consciousness: art, mind and technology.* Bristol, England: Intellect Books.

Ascott, Roy (Ed.) (2000). *Art, technology, consciousness.* Bristol, England: Intellect Books.

Dalsgaard, Paul, Paul Heisterkamp and Chin-Hui Lee (Eds.) (1999). Proc. of the ESCA Tutorial and Research Workshop on Interactive Dialogue in MultiModal Systems (IDS-99). Kloster Irsee, Germany, June.

Friberg, A, J. Iwarsson, E. Jansson and J. Sundberg (Eds.) (1994). Proceedings of the Stockholm Music Acoustics Conference (SMAC-93), July 28–August 1, Publication Nr. 79. Stockholm, Sweden: Royal Swedish Academy of Music.

Friberg, A and J. Sundberg (Eds.) (1995). *Grammars for music performance.* Proceedings of a KTH Symposium, May, 1995. Stockholm, Sweden: KTH, Dept. of Speech Communication and Music Acoustics.

Griffith, Niall and Peter M. Todd (Eds.) (1999). *Musical networks: Parallel distributed perception and performance.* Cambridge, Mass.: MIT Press.

Hofstadter, Douglas R. (1999). *Gödel, Escher, Bach: An eternal golden braid.* New York, USA: Basic Books.

Mc Kevitt, Paul (1994). "Visions for language". In *Proceedings of the Workshop on integration of natural language and vision processing.* Twelfth American National Conference on Artificial Intelligence (AAAI-94), Seattle, Washington, US, August, 47–57.

Mc Kevitt, Paul (Ed.) (1995/96). *Integration of natural language and vision processing (Vols. I–IV).* Dordrecht, The Netherlands: Kluwer-Academic Publishers.

Mc Kevitt, Paul (1999). *Ideas for universities. Master's of Education* (M.Ed.) Dissertation, University of Sheffield, Sheffield, England.

Mc Kevitt, Paul, Seán Ó Nualláin and Conn Mulvihill (2000). Workshop Report on The Eighth International Workshop on the Cognitive Science of Natural Language Processing (CSNLP-8) In *AI Review,* 14(6), 591–613.

Ó Nualláin, Seán (1995/2000). *The search for mind: A new foundation for cognitive science.* Norwood, New Jersey: Ablex Publishing Corporation, Also as new edition with Intellect Books, Bristol, England, 2000.

Ó Nualláin, Seán (Ed.) (2000). *Spatial cognition: Foundations and applications.* Amsterdam/Philadelphia: John Benjamins.

Ó Nualláin, Seán (Ed.) (2002). *Being human: The search for order.* Bristol, England: Intellect Books.

Ó Nualláin, Seán and Arnold Smith (1995). An investigation into the common semantics of language and vision. In *Integration of natural language and vision processing* (Vol. I), *computational models and systems,* Mc Kevitt, Paul (Ed.), 21–30 and *Artificial Intelligence Review,* Vol. 8 (2–3), 113–122. Dordrecht, The Netherlands: Kluwer-Academic Publishers.

Ó Nualláin, Seán, Paul Mc Kevitt and Eoghan Mac Aogain (Eds.) (1997). *Two sciences of mind: readings in cognitive science and consciousness.* Amsterdam/Philadelphia: John Benjamins.

Roth, Dennis Morrow (1990). *Rhythm vision: A guide to visual awareness.* Texas, USA: College Station.

Wallin, Nils L., Björn Merker and Steven Brown (Eds.) (2000). *The origins of music.* Cambridge, Mass., USA: MIT Press

Part I
Language & vision

Paul Mc Kevitt
University of Ulster (Magee), Derry, Northern Ireland

Inspiration for this book and preceding workshop comes in part from the efforts of Paul Mc Kevitt to catalyse the integration of natural language and vision processing (Mc Kevitt 1994, 1995/96, 1999). It was obvious that although there had been much work in each of these fields there had been little or no work on their integration and there was so much to be gained by doing so. Work reported therein (95/96) included that of Mc Kevitt and Gammack (1996) investigating the maximisation of communication between users and computers with a philosophy of interface design where the computer analyses the intentions of users through verbal and nonverbal media will result in optimum communication. Also, Mc Kevitt and Hall (1996) looked at the interpretation of angiograms or X-rays of human blood vessels. The idea is that 3-D vision reconstruction techniques can be applied to angiograms and can reconstruct a model of the vasculature of an individual. Medical reports are produced by doctors on an individual's vasculature and natural language processing (NLP) can be applied to these to aid the reconstruction process. A medical report usually specifies the location of a lesion on the vasculature and applying NLP to the report can aid the vision system to locate lesions more effectively. Ó Nualláin and Smith (1995) reported on a system called SI (spoken image) which incrementally reconstructs a visual scene from descriptions spoken by a human user. The work is based on the sound philosophical work of Vygotsky (1962) and Wittgenstein (1963) and on Ó Nualláin's theories themselves (Ó Nualláin 1995/2000, 2000, Ó Nualláin et al. 1997). They use SI to investigate two of the most interesting problems in integration of language and vision: (1) the relation between a semantics for each, and (2) the notion of symbol grounding. They point to the fact that a shift from neat to scruffy which Wittgenstein (1961, 1963) and Schank (1972, 1977) had gone through reaching Vygotsky (1962) may be crucial for a common semantics for language and vision. Much of this work can be grounded in, and can learn from, unsolved and related psychological and philosophical questions about how language and vision are different and similar and how their integration can solve one of the most stinging problems in the field of artificial intelligence, Searle's Chinese Room Problem (extrapolated as Harnad's Symbol Grounding Problem), in the form of an Irish Room (see Mc Kevitt and Guo, 1997). Mc Kevitt (1995/96) notes that spatial relations appear to be the key to integration (see also, Mc Kevitt 2000, Ó Nualláin 2000). Since 1994 there has been a large upsurge of interest in the area, otherwise known as MultiModal Systems or Intelligent MultiMedia. Three of the contributions in this section are based on work emanating from the establishment of IntelliMedia 2000+, a research and education programme at Aalborg University, Denmark resulting in over thirty students on average graduating annually with Master's degrees in Intelligent MultiMedia (see Mc Kevitt 1999).

First, with respect to computational aspects, John Connolly, using the example of a rail map, looks at how different media can be combined into a coherent whole and how this can be achieved using some fundamental principles of General System Theory (GST). The next three papers investigate a variation of applications of multimodal integration. Carson-Berndsen and Gibbon show how prosodic representations for speech technology applications can be visualised. John Gurney et al. describe a software agent that uses simulated perception to perform spoken language navigation in a natural language and virtual reality project (NLVR) where the user interface simulates the look and flow of movement through terrain and sky operating in real-time presenting a detailed, photographic quality landscape. Cohen-Rose and Christensen discuss a system called *The Guide* which answers natural language queries about places to eat and drink with relevant stories generated by storytelling agents from a knowledge base containing previously written reviews of places and the food and drink they serve. *The Guide* is based on the electronic guide to Life, the Universe and Everything in Douglas Adams' "Hitch Hikers Guide to the Galaxy" science fiction story (see Adams 1979) and is now the basis of a product from Adams' company, The Digital Village (TDV).

The next five contributions focus on computer applications, targetted mainly at the human-computer interface, general architectures and platforms, models and theories which have been developed to integrate modalities, with particular focus on speech and gesture. The first two contributions are from IntelliMedia 2000+, Aalborg University, Denmark. Brøndsted et al. discuss the exchange of affect/emotions in human-computer interaction and classify a user's input based on basic emotional attitudes from traditional media (eye-tracker, gesture recognition, speech-to-text recognition) and also signals communicated through extra-linguistic features (prosodic mode). The user interacts with an autonomous dog-like 3D agent called Bouncy. Next, Brøndsted et al. present the CHAMELEON system which is a general platform for performing the integration of speech and image processing with an application incorporating spoken dialogue and gesture where people can ask questions like "Whose office is this?" and "Show me the route from Paul Mc Kevitt's office to Paul Dalsgaard's office" about 2D building plans. Thorissón presents the perceptual mechanisms of an embodied, human-like agent called Gandalf which is capable of perceiving natural-language, prosody and free form gesture, and produces natural, unconstrained turn-taking in real-time, task-oriented multimodal dialogue with a human. Gandalf is implemented in the Ymir architecture — a computational model of psychosocial dialogue that integrates perception, knowledge, decision and action in a modular way. Wachsmuth investigates the fundamental role that rhythms apparently play in speech and gestural communication among humans. He focusses on how multimodal interfaces are conceptualised on the basis of timed agent systems and how multiple agents are used to poll presemantic information from different sensory channels (speech and hand gestures) and integrated into multimodal data structures that can be processed by application systems. Wachsmuth motivates and presents work which exploits rhythmic patterns in the development of biologically and cognitively motivated mediator systems between humans and machines. Wachsmuth is co-directing the large SFB-360 project "Situated Artificial Communicators" (see Rickheit and Wachsmuth 1996) focussing on the integration of speech, vision and robotics, demonstrating the importance of rhythm in systems. Poggi and Pelachaud look at the meaning of gaze in animated faces. They analyse gaze from both a signal side (physiological state and muscular actions of eye region) and on the meaning side (type of information conveyed) and a formal representation is proposed for each possible meaning. Their interest is in creating conversational agents with expressive and communicative behaviours where the relationship between the agents' communicative intentions and their expression in a coordinated verbal and nonverbal message is defined. Work on speech and gesture modelling in systems is popular and clearly because this is one area where people integrate language and vision processing naturally. All of the latter computational approaches from general architectures to applications, mainly focussing on speech and gesture, are not only invaluable in themselves as useful engineering results but are also fundamental to investigating how people conduct language, vision and music integration.

Next, Ahlsén reports on a study which demonstrates the influence of verbal vocal focus versus nonverbal visual focus and their consequences for the "constitution" of a person having a severe communication handicap such as aphasia. It is hoped that our investigations on multimodal integration can help the handicapped. The next three contributions discuss synaesthesia, the general name for a set of cognitive states where stimuli to one sense, e.g. smell, are involuntarily simultaneously perceived as if by one/more other senses, such as sight and/or hearing. For example, we can have people hearing colours or tasting shapes. Gammack notes that recent years have seen a resurgence of interest in synaesthesia. He focusses in particular on the integration of colour imagery with language or musical notes and points to an explanation suggested by an esoteric understanding of mental phenomena with linkages to a noetic quality or the nature of human knowing. Sean Day, a synaesthete himself, where sounds from various musical instruments make him see certain colours, gives an overview of current scientific views of synaesthesia attempting to correct misunderstandings and answer common questions. Sean proposes that research on synaesthesia will give useful insights into brain and language evolution and functions and can be a useful tool towards exploring new artistic media.

Finally, Galeyev considers synaesthesia as one of the forms of interaction in polysensorial perception where normal synaesthesia is considered to be "intersensational association" with manifestation of non-verbal thinking connected with intersensational comparison and hence concluding that synaesthesia is not a psychic anomaly but a form of non-verbal thinking. It must certainly be true that synaesthesia can throw some light on how we can integrate the processing of language, vision and music by machines but also experiments with the latter may explain and demonstrate what synaesthetes experience.

References

Adams, Douglas (1979). *The hitchhiker's guide to the galaxy.* London, England: Pan Books.

Mc Kevitt, Paul (1994). Visions for language. In Proceedings of the Workshop on integration of natural language and vision processing. Twelfth American National Conference on Artificial Intelligence (AAAI-94), Seattle, Washington, US, August, 47–57.

Mc Kevitt, Paul (Ed.) (1995/96). *Integration of natural language and vision processing* (Vols. I–IV). Dordrecht, The Netherlands: Kluwer-Academic Publishers.

Mc Kevitt, Paul (1999). *Ideas for universities.* Master's of Education (M.Ed.) Dissertation, University of Sheffield, Sheffield, England.

Mc Kevitt, Paul (2000). CHAMELEON meets spatial cognition, In *Spatial cognition: foundations and applications*, Ó Nualláin, Seán (Ed.), 149–170. Amsterdam/Philadelphia: John Benjamins.

Mc Kevitt, Paul and Peter Hall (1996). Automatic interpretation of angiograms In *Integration of natural language and vision processing (Vol. IV), Recent advances*, Mc Kevitt, Paul (Ed.), 81–98, Dordrecht, The Netherlands: Kluwer-Academic Publishers. Also in *Artificial Intelligence Review*, Vol. 10 (3–4), 235–252. Dordrecht, The Netherlands: Kluwer-Academic Publishers.

Mc Kevitt, Paul and John Gammack (1996). The sensitive interface. In *Integration of natural language and vision processing* (Vol. IV), *Recent advances*, Mc Kevitt, Paul (Ed.), 121–144. Also in *ArtiWcial Intelligence Review*, Vol. 10 (3–4), 275–298. Dordrecht, The Netherlands: Kluwer-Academic Publishers.

Mc Kevitt, Paul and Guo Chengming (1997). From Chinese rooms to Irish rooms: New words on visions for language. In *Two sciences of mind: readings in cognitive science and consciousness*, Seán Ó Nualláin, Paul Mc Kevitt and Eoghan Mac Aogáin (1997) (Eds.), 179–196, Amsterdam/Philadelphia: John Benjamins. *Also in Integration of natural language and vision processing* (Vol. III), *Theory and grounding representations.* Mc Kevitt, Paul (Ed.), 151–165 and *Artificial Intelligence Review*, Vol. 10 (1–2), 49–63. Dordrecht, The Netherlands: Kluwer-Academic Publishers.

Ó Nualláin, Seán (1995/2000). *The search for mind: A new foundation for cognitive science.* Norwood, New Jersey: Ablex Publishing Corporation, Also as new edition with Intellect Books, 2000.

Ó Nualláin, Seán (Ed.) (2000). *Spatial cognition: Foundations and applications*, Advances in Consciousness Research" (AiCR 26). Amsterdam/Philadelphia: John Benjamins.

Ó Nualláin, Seán and Arnold Smith (1995). An investigation into the common semantics of language and vision In *Integration of natural language and vision processing* (Vol. I), *Computational models and systems*, Mc Kevitt, Paul (Ed.), 21–30 and *Artificial Intelligence Review*, Vol. 8 (2–3), 113–122. Dordrecht, The Netherlands: Kluwer-Academic Publishers.

Ó Nualláin, Seán, Paul Mc Kevitt and Eoghan Mac Aogáin (Eds.) (1997). *Two sciences of mind: Readings in cognitive science and consciousness.* Amsterdam/Philadelphia: John Benjamins.

Rickheit, Gert and Ipke Wachsmuth (1996). Collaborative Research Centre "Situated Artificial Communicators" at the University of Bielefeld, Germany. In *Integration of Natural Language and Vision Processing* (Vol. IV), *Recent Advances*, Mc Kevitt, Paul (ed.), 11–16. Also in *Artificial Intelligence Review*, Vol. 10 (3–4), 165–170. Dordrecht, The Netherlands: Kluwer Academic Publishers

Schank, Roger C. (1972). Conceptual dependency: A theory of natural language understanding. *Cognitive Psychology* 3(4): 552–631

Schank, Roger C. and Robert P. Abelson (1977). *Scripts, plans, goals and understanding: An inquiry into human knowledge structures.* Hillsdale, NJ: Lawrence Erlbaum Associates.

Vygotsky, L.S. (1962). *Thought and language.* Cambridge, Mass.: MIT Press.

Wittgenstein, Ludwig (1961). *Tractatus logico-Philosophicus* (translated by D.F. Pears and B.F. Mc Guinness). London: Routledge and Kegan Paul (Original work published 1921).

Wittgenstein, Ludwig (1963). *Philosophical Investigations* (translated by G.E. Anscombe) Oxford: Blackwell.

Multimedia integration

A system-theoretic perspective

John H. Connolly
Loughborough University, England

1. Introduction

The problem of multimedia integration — that is to say, the problem of combining different media of communication into a single, coherent whole — is one which can be approached from a variety of angles. However, the aim of the present paper is to consider this issue particularly from the point of view of General System Theory (GST).

As its name suggests, GST is concerned with providing an account of the nature and properties of systems of all kinds, among which multimedia systems constitute an example. Indeed, as we shall see, several ideas that are central to GST have already been taken up in existing work on multimedia systems. Nevertheless, an explicit treatment of multimedia integration from the standpoint of GST would seem to be worthwhile at this point, not least for the reason that the approach raises particular kinds of question which might not otherwise come into sharp focus.

GST, like Cognitive Science, is an interdisciplinary field. Of course, it does not share Cognitive Science's goal of developing a computational model of the mind. But nevertheless, insofar as it may provide a possible common framework for the integration of linguistic and non-linguistic media of communication, the GST-based approach is undoubtedly germane to the field of Cognitive Science.

GST is, perhaps, better regarded as consisting, primarily, not in a body of knowledge but in an particular approach to scientific description, an approach which is known, appropriately, as 'systems thinking'; see, for example, Checkland (1993: 3). The approach in question has been translated into a number of principles and precepts which are too numerous to enumerate here; see Skyttner (1996) for a fairly comprehensive account, or Blanchard and Fabrycky (1981: chapter 1) for a briefer (but still useful) summary. However, we shall consider what seem, in the present context, to be the most salient points.

2. Holism and emergent properties

Let us begin by enumerating five important principles of GST:

(1) A system is an integrated whole which is, in some sense, greater than the sum of its component parts.
(2) A system has emergent properties which belong to the whole and not to any subset of the components.
(3) Each constituent of the system has an effect upon the whole.
(4) No constituent of the system has an independent effect upon the whole.
(5) Optimality within a component may be sacrificed, if this is in the best interests of the system as a whole.

In order to appreciate a system as such, therefore, it is essential to view it holistically. Analysing it into its constituent elements will not reveal the synergy that results from the interaction of these components with one another.

Let us consider the above five principles in relation to a familiar multimedia entity, namely a railway map. Such a map can be regarded as a system, whose constituents include both linguistic components (such as the names of the stations) and non-linguistic components (notably the network of lines representing the rail routes, marked with symbols indicating the location of the stations). The various components form an integrated whole, the integration being dependent on the textual labels bearing the names of the stations being placed next to the relevant cartographic symbols. This integrated whole possesses a crucial emergent property, namely that it can serve as a useful guide for someone planning a train journey, in a way that neither the linguistic nor the non-linguistic components could if taken separately. Hence, the whole is more than merely the sum of the parts. Moreover, if any of the textual labels, the station symbols or the lines representing rail routes were unintentionally deleted, then the functionality of the map as a whole would be impaired. This shows that each component has an effect on the whole. However, the effect is not independent of all the other components. For instance, the deletion of a textual label would leave a station symbol devoid of an indication as to the associated name, while the deletion of a route line would leave a pair of station symbols without a connection. Nevertheless, if the rail network depicted by the map is dense, then it may be necessary for textual labels to over-write small segments of route lines. Careful design can ensure that this will not impair the usefulness of the map as a whole, thus illustrating the principle that optimality within one component (here, the integrity in the representation of the rail network) may be sacrificed for the benefit of the system as a whole (the functionality of which would be jeopardised if the textual labels could not all be fitted in).

The obvious corollary that follows from the above is the following:

- The successful design of an integrated multimedia system will depend on defining the system's overall purpose and then choosing an appropriate blend of media in order to achieve it. Each component of the overall system will need to be designed in such a way as to take into account the presence, and the characteristics, of the other constituents. These points are also relevant to the analysis of existing systems.

Of course, this corollary is easy enough to state, but in practice it calls for a mode of thinking in which the analysis of the whole into its component parts is combined with a complementary, holistic appreciation of the entire blend. This balance of opposites is by no means easy for the human mind to achieve, and is perhaps even more difficult to model computationally.

It thus becomes apparent that what at first sight appears to be an obvious corollary actually raises a distinctly non-trivial problem for Cognitive Science. Indeed, several quite difficult scientific questions emerge. For instance:

- How do we develop a computational model of holistic thinking, at least sufficient to account for multimedia integration?
- How do we predict the emergent properties of a multimedia system, given a knowledge of its components and how they interrelate? Conversely, given the definition of the overall function of a multimedia system, how do we predict a necessary and sufficient set of components and interrelations?
- How might we measure the synergy among the components of a multimedia system?

Moreover, these questions have practical consequences for the engineering of computer-based multimedia systems. For example:

- A software system designed to create multimedia displays should take into account the holistic aspects of the presentations which it delivers. This principle is implicit in, for example, Maass (1995) and Srihari (1995a, 1995b).
- A software system designed to interpret multimedia data ought to be designed to be sensitive to the synergy among the different component media. Compare, for instance, Herzog and Wazinski (1995) or Mc Kevitt and Hall (1996).

The better we understand the underlying scientific problems, the better chance we have of designing systems with such capabilities.

3. Systems and components

As stated above, a system contains a set of interrelated components. Some further principles, pertinent to this fact, are as follows:

(6) A component of a given system may be:
  a. Either a system in its own right (in which case it will be a subsystem of the larger system, the latter being termed the suprasystem)
  b. Or an element not comprising a system in its own right.

(7) In general, any system will be a component subsystem of some larger system. Normally, systems do not exist in isolation from one another.

(8) Components within a given system may:
  a. Either have no overlap in function
  b. Or have a partial overlap in function
  c. Or have a total overlap in function.

Within a map, the network of lines, in association with the station symbols which they connect, together constitute a system, which is therefore a subsystem of the labelled map, the latter being the suprasystem in which it is embedded. However, each individual station symbol is an atomic element and therefore cannot be regarded as a system, given that it contains no components.

The principle that any system is normally part of a larger system might seem to imply that there exists a great hierarchy of systems in the universe. For instance, a rail map display could be part of a computer-based rail information system, which could be part of a larger computing system, which could be part of a network (the latter being a kind of distributed system), and so on. However, it is obvious that the universe does not consist of a neat and tidy hierarchy. Among other things, it is possible to identify overlapping subhierarchies, and to find that a given system has a place within more than one of these. For instance, the rail information system could also conceivably be a component of a travel agent's information system, based partly on computers but partly on non-computer-based materials.

With regard to the various possibilities in relation to the functional overlap of components, we can again look to our rail map for exemplification. Station symbols and station names have no overlap in function, but complement each other. However, station symbols and route lines have a partial overlap in function. Both of them serve to indicate which parts of the country are served by the rail network, and in that respect they overlap. On the other hand, the map reader requires both the symbols and the lines in order to know exactly where the trains may stop and which pairs of stations are directly connected, and so in this respect the two types of information complement one another. An example of a total overlap in function would arise if a station at the end of a route line were redundantly labelled as a terminus. Redundancy is, of course, not to be equated with pointless repetition. On the contrary, it is very well known in the area of communications as a source of robustness in the transmission of messages. (See Martin and Béroule (1995) for a somewhat similar approach.)

Again, a straightforward corollary follows from the above principles:

When designing or analysing a particular system, it can be instructive to ask:
- How do the system's internal components interrelate, particularly with regard to functional overlap?
- What is the relevant suprasystem (or suprasystems), and what are the latter's other subsystems?
- How do the suprasystem's internal components interrelate, particularly with regard to functional overlap?

These questions lead to a homogeneous view of each system in relation both to its interior and exterior environment. This homogeneity helps towards an integrated overall picture of the systems concerned.

However, as before, we are faced with scientific questions of a less straightforward character. Examples:

- Given a system embedded within a suprasystem, is there a reliable method of identifying all of the other components of the suprasystem involved? (For example, besides natural language, what other components of a multimedia system can express negative meaning? How do we know when we have identified all such components?)
- Is there a reliable method of identifying all three degrees of functional overlap among the components of a multimedia system? (Example: the partial overlap mentioned in the rail map example might have been overlooked.)

Associated points relating to the engineering of multimedia systems include the following:

- A software system designed to create multimedia displays should take into account and exploit appropriately the various degrees of functional overlap among components. For instance, an important item of information might be highlighted through being expressed (in a sense, redundantly) in two media simultaneously.
- A software system designed to interpret multimedia data should integrate non-overlapping and partially overlapping information-sources and take advantage of any redundancy. This kind of approach has been adopted in, for example, the CUBRICON system, in relation to the coordination of natural language and gesture input; see Neal and Shapiro (1991).

4. Function and internal organisation

A further principle will now be enunciated, the first part of which has, in fact, already been implied in the previous section:

(9) A system manifests:
  a. Internal organisation.
  b. Purpose.
  c. Continuity of identity.

The interior structure of a system may be hierarchical or otherwise, but every system must have some kind of internal organisation. An essential property of this internal organisation is a coordinated division of function among the components. In the rail map example the nature of this division is manifest: the station symbols show the location of the stations, the lines show the routes, and the labels give the names of the stations. However, the point at issue is that if the components had all somehow duplicated each other's function, then they would not have together formed a system. In other words, although a certain amount of redundancy is deemed to be possible within a system, total redundancy is not. As for the coordination, this would be destroyed if, for example, the station symbols were not displayed as lying on the lines, or the textual labels were not near enough to the appropriate station symbols for it to be clear which applied to which. Silly as such states-of-affairs may sound, it is by no means impossible for them to come about unintentionally in practice. Plainly, they militate against the intended integration of components within the overall system.

Just as the individual components of a system have their own particular functions, so too does the system as a whole. In GST, an integrated whole which is greater than the sum of its component parts is, nevertheless, generally not regarded as being of interest unless it can be seen to have some purpose. Providing information to potential travellers, as our example rail map is able to do, would, of course, qualify as a suitable purpose for a system.

The continuity of identity exhibited by a system refers to its ability to preserve its function, and also at least part of its internal organisation, over time and in the face of change. In other words, adjustments to a system should not result in its disintegration, or else it should not have been described as a system in the first place. In the case of our rail map example, the system as a whole would be expected to survive a modification such as the addition of a symbol representing a newly-opened station.

Some straightforward corollaries of the above are as follows:

– A system should be designed in such a way that it can fulfil its function through periods of both stability and change.
– The internal organisation of the system should enable each component to fulfil its own function in such a way as to integrate with the functions of the other components and the function of the system as a whole.

Some less straightforward academic questions are:

– What factors keep a system from disintegrating?
– What, precisely, confers continuing identity upon a changing system?

The latter question touches on a well-known philosophical issue, but it has not been treated comprehensively in relation to GST.

5. Drawing on semiotics

We can take our analysis of intra-system organisation a step further if we borrow some concepts from Semiotics. Admittedly, Semiotics has both enthusiasts and detractors. However, because it offers a common vocabulary which is applicable to both linguistic and non-linguistic communication, it has a useful part to play in the treatment of multimedia; see, for instance, Purchase (1998).

Within a multimedia display, every component (be it an image, a piece of text or whatever) can be regarded as a semiotic entity. This means that, despite the differences that exist between the distinct media, we nevertheless have available to us a level of analysis at which all the elements can be treated as being entities of the same type. Semiotic entities are normally termed signs. A sign can be one of three types:

- An index. (In this case, there is a direct, and possibly causal, relationship between the sign and what it signifies, as for example when the glow from the screen of a computer monitor is taken as a sign that it is switched on.)
- A symbol. (In this case, the relationship between the sign and what it signifies is arbitrary and a matter of social convention. For instance, the Irish word iarnród and the English word railway both have the same meaning, but neither of these two sequence of sounds or letters has any better claim than the other as a suitable symbol for the entity concerned. Or a red circle may represent a station on a map, but a green square would do just as well, provided that there was general agreement on this.)
- An icon. (In this case there is a perceptible resemblance between the sign and the entity signified. For example, a blue line on a map can denote the course of a river.)

Importantly, these three categories can, between them, accommodate any medium of communication in common use.

If we thus regard a multimedia system as a semiotic system, then we can draw on the literature on semiotics for some useful analytical concepts. An example is the distinction between paradigmatic and syntagmatic relations. When a display is designed, its author has available a variety of choices in terms of (a) what to include and (b) how to arrange whatever is included. The alternative choices at any point are said to be paradigmatically related, while the co-occurring components that have actually been chosen are said to be syntagmatically related.

Given its Saussurean origin, this terminology is especially commonplace in Linguistics, where sophisticated treatments of both the (paradigmatic) dimension of choice and the (syntagmatic) dimension of combination have been developed. The syntagmatic axis is fundamental to all theories of syntax, including those of Chomsky and other authors in the field of generative grammar, and furthermore, much linguistic work on discourse is concerned with the sequential structure of text. As for the paradigmatic axis, this has received special attention in the work of M.A.K. Halliday and other exponents of the Systemic Functional approach. Attempts have also been made to apply comparable ideas to non-linguistic media. A particularly interesting example is Kress and van Leeuwen's (1996) treatment of the organisation of images in terms of paradigmatic choices and syntagmatic arrangements.

It has to be borne in mind that multimedia systems are often also hypermedia systems, a very well-known example being provided by the world-wide web. The non-linear character of hypermedia inevitably complicates the treatment of the syntagmatic axis, but does not fundamentally alter the nature of the semiotic systems involved.

6. Semiotic systems and subsystems

If a multimedia system can be regarded as a semiotic system, then equally well, its subsystems can be treated as semiotic subsystems. This is a very useful view when we are seeking to appreciate multimedia systems as integrated wholes.

With regard to the paradigmatic axis, much of Kress and van Leeuwen's work is relevant here. For instance, following Halliday (1985), they state (1996: 127–130) that verbal communication involves (inter alia) a choice among four functions:

- Offering information. (Example: 'The Irish word for system is córas.')
- Offering goods-and-services. (Example: 'Would you like a glass of poitín?')
- Demanding information. (Example: 'Have you kissed the Blarney Stone?')
- Demanding goods-and-services. (Example: 'Lend me a map of Galway!')

However, Kress and van Leeuwen propose that in images there are basically two choices:

- Offering information. (For example, this is the function of a rail map.)
- Demanding goods-and-services of a specific kind, namely a particular type of social response. (Example: a face smiling at the viewer invites a degree of (imaginary) social connection between the viewer and the smiling person.)

This kind of analysis is helpful in the present context for two reasons. Firstly, the two functions which are shared between the linguistic and pictorial media provide one possible means of integrating those media within a common framework. Secondly, an explicit account of the capacity of each medium to communicate particular types of information is useful in deciding which medium to select for the purpose of expressing the various aspects of the message-content, with a view to achieving a coherent multimedia presentation.

With regard to the syntagmatic axis, the combination of semiotic components can be rather complex, but is amenable to representation by means of a graph showing the concurrence and sequence of the constituents (such as pieces of text, images and so on). An element of recursivity is also possible, inasmuch as a video component of a multimedia display may itself be considered as a relatively self-contained multimedia system.

It should be noted that single-medium components of a multimedia semiotic system may themselves be systemic in nature. For instance, a text is a whole (composed of components such as words) which has emergent properties (for instance, coherence) not found in its ultimate constituents. Similarly, images possess emergent properties (for example the depiction of scenes) not found in their ultimate constituents (such as lines).

All semiotic systems and subsystems following a syntax of some kind, all have a semantics, and all are subject to pragmatic constraints. However, these are not necessarily well understood.

The corollary that follows straightforwardly from the above is:

– Multimedia systems and subsystems can usefully be analysed as signs.

However, once more, there are more challenging questions that lie behind this. Examples:

– Can we develop a common, or at least compatible, syntax, semantics and pragmatics for the various kinds of media that can go to make up a multimedia system?
– Can we find an optimal way of allocating the presentation of information to the various available media?

Solving these problems would result in self-evident benefits to designers of multimedia systems. Relevant previous work is reported in, for example, Mc Kevitt (1995–1996), but much more research is needed.

7. System and environment

The last of the system-theoretic principles which we shall include in the present paper is as follows:

(10) a. A system exists within an environment.
  b. It is separated from its environment by a boundary.

The environment (or context) can be viewed as broadly or narrowly as is appropriate to the investigator's interests and purposes. If the system is a component of a suprasystem, then that suprasystem, including all of its other components, constitutes an essential part of the environment of the system in question.

The boundary is important to the identity of the system which it encloses, given that it serves to distinguish what is part of the system from what lies outside of it; compare Arens and Hovy (1995). However, a system will generally interact with its context, and therefore the boundary should not be seen as insulating the system from its environment.

In any communication system there is a strong interrelationship between the system and its environment. On the one hand, the context exerts a crucial influence both on what is communicated and how it is presented. For example, the background knowledge that the author of a message ascribes to the intended audience is a contextual factor which normally has a significant effect upon the composition of that message. On the other hand, the interpretation of the message also generally owes much to the context. A familiar example is found in the interpretation of deictic expressions like 'here' or 'now'.

In the case of our rail map example, the audience will be assumed to be familiar with the idea of maps and of rail systems, with the result that little in the way of an explanatory key is likely to be included. The name of the country served by the rail system may well not be stated either, but might be inferred from the place where the map was situated (in which case it would probably be taken by default to represent the local rail system) or from the outline shape of the country (if clearly shown) or from the location of the named stations, both of which might reasonably be assumed to form part of the user's background knowledge.

Yet again, we find a straightforward corollary concealing some difficult questions. The corollary is:

- Context should be taken fully into account in the design of multimedia systems. This implies a degree of integration between the context and the actual system whose environment it forms.

The underlying scientific questions include the following:

- How do we model context in respect of multimedia systems? In particular how do we formalise it rigorously and in sufficient detail for it to be usable in AI systems? See McCarthy and Buvac (1998) for a possible starting point.
- Is there a reliable method for establishing the boundary between system and environment? (In some ways this problem is akin to distinguishing between figure and ground. This is not always straightforward in a multimedia display, as ostensibly background material can have substantive content.)

Again, achieving answers to these questions would have practical consequences. For instance:

- A software system designed to create multimedia displays should take context into account when deciding on both content and form.
- A software system designed to interpret multimedia data should take context into account when deciding on the meaning and pragmatic effects of the input.

However, until we have better models of context, computer-based systems with a thorough capability in such respects will remain just an ambition.

8. Conclusion

In conclusion, it appears that the system-theoretic perspective, with its emphasis on wholes and on understanding how parts interrelate within wholes, has a distinctive contribution to offer in the quest for a possible integrative framework for multimedia systems. This is especially so if we regard multimedia systems and their components as semiotic entities.

Up to a certain point, system-theoretic concepts seem to be capable of reasonably straightforward application to multimedia. Beyond that point, the system approach serves to interesting questions, some of them very challenging, which provide an agenda for future research.

References

Arens, Y. & E. Hovy (1995). The design of a model-based multimedia interaction manager. In Mc Kevitt (1995), volume 2, 95–116.

Blanchard, B.S. & W.J. Fabrycky (1981). *Systems engineering and analysis.* Englewood Cliffs: Prentice-Hall.

Checkland, P. (1993). *Systems thinking, systems practice.* Chichester: Wiley.

Halliday, M.A.K. (1985). *An introduction to Functional Grammar.* London: Arnold.

Herzog, G. & P. Wazinski (1995). VIsual TRAnslator: linking perceptions and natural language descriptions. In Mc Kevitt (1995), volume 1, 83–95.

Kress, G. & T. van Leeuwen (1996). *Reading images: The grammar of visual design.* London: Routledge.

Maass, W. (1995). From vision to multimodal communication: incremental route descriptions. In Mc Kevitt (1995), volume 1, 67–82.

McCarthy, J. & S. Buvac (1998). Formalising context (expanded notes). In Aliseda, A., R. van Glabbeek & D. Westerståhl (Eds.), *Computing natural language* (13–50). Stanford, CA: CSLI Publications.

Mc Kevitt, P. (Ed.) (1995–1996). *Integration of natural language and vision processing.* 4

volumes. Dordrecht: Kluwer.

Mc Kevitt, P. & P. Hall (1996). The sensitive interface. In Mc Kevitt (1996), volume 4, 121–144.

Martin, J.-C. & D. Béroule (1995). Temporal codes within a typology of cooperation between modalities. In Mc Kevitt (1995), volume 2, 23–30.

Neal, J.G. & S.C. Shapiro (1991). Intelligent multi-media interface technology. In Sullivan, J.W. & S.W. Tyler (Eds.), *Intelligent user interfaces* (11–43). Reading, MA: Addison-Wesley.

Purchase, H.C. (1998). Defining multimedia. *IEEE Multimedia*, 5, no. 1, 58–65.

Skyttner, L. (1996). *General Systems Theory: An introduction.* Basingstoke: Macmillan.

Srihari, R.K. (1995a). Computational models for integrating linguistic and visual information: a survey. In Mc Kevitt (1995), volume 1, 185–205.

Srihari, R.K. (1995b). Use of captions and other collateral text in understanding photographs. In Mc Kevitt (1995), volume 1, 245–266.

Visualising lexical prosodic representations for speech applications

Julie Carson-Berndsen and Dafydd Gibbon
University College Dublin, Ireland / Universität Bielefeld, Germany

1. Introduction

This paper presents a technique for generic lexical representation of phonological, in particular prosodic properties in the lexicon (cf. Gibbon 1998), which can have applications in various areas of speech technology. The relevance of this work to language and vision lies in the visualisation of feature geometry and multilinear representations of prosodic phonologies such as autosegmental phonology. Multilinear phonological representations were originally proposed in the theory of autosegmental phonology by Goldsmith (1976) in order to cater for tonal phenomena which could not be integrated into a purely segmental system. Multilinear representations consist of separate tiers (e.g. tonal tier, nasality tier) each of which has its own synchronisation function and melody (similar to the musical score of an orchestra). Furthermore, feature geometry introduces the dimension of the internal organisation of sounds into a multilinear representation.

The approach presented in this paper combines work on prosodic inheritance (cf. Reinhard & Gibbon 1991, Gibbon 1991) with a recent proposal to use nonsegmental phonological representation in lexical description in order to compile lexica for specific speech applications from a more general lexical representation (cf. Cahill et al. 2000) using the notion of *time maps* as defined in Carson-Berndsen (1998). The generic lexicon is modelled in the DATR lexical representation language and generates a range of representations, including graphical objects.[1] The proposal in this paper differs from previous work in that it uses feature geometry as a basis for the representation rather than autosegmental inheritance (Gibbon 1991) or the multivalued feature vectors proposed in Carson-Berndsen (1998). The advantage of this over feature vectors is that the generic lexicon can then be used not only for those applications suggested in

Cahill et al. (2000) but also in connection with a testbed for phonological descriptions in more theoretical work and in connection with web-based tutorials for students of phonology and phonetics. This paper will present the generic lexical description and the graphical visualisations.

2. Prosodic inheritance: A DATR model

Prosodic inheritance is a theory of generalisations about prosody expressed as a connected system of implications conforming to the structure of an inheritance graph, rather than as individual implication rules or constraint sets. In line with developments in computational phonology, the computational core of the generic lexicon is based on finite state transducers.

The representation language which has been chosen for the generic lexicon is DATR (cf. Evans & Gazdar 1989 and more recently the discussion in Evans & Gazdar 1996). DATR is a language which has been specifically designed for the representation of lexical entries and generalisation hierarchies over these entries. The language permits definition of nonmonotonic inheritance hierarchies using path/value equations, allowing lexical regularities, subregularities and idiosyncrasies to be captured in a principled manner. DATR is not restricted to nonmonotonic inheritance, and subsumption-style hierarchies can also be represented if required. Numerical, string-processing and file-handling extensions to DATR have been added in the *Zdatr* implementation used in the present study (Gibbon & Strokin 1998); with these extensions quantitative information, such as duration, frequency and weightings can be included in the lexicon and numerical functions of these can be defined. In Gibbon & Ahoua (1991), phonological features are explicitly used in a prosodic framework where default inheritance is used to model both phonological markedness and the extraction of autosegmental tiers. In Cahill et al. (2000), *time maps* from autosegmental structures to phonetic coordinates are defined, allowing symbolic and numerical representations of tier melodies to be calculated from a general lexicon representation using finite state transducers. This work has been extended to include enhancements permitting numerical and symbolic representations which are suitable for use in speech systems (cf. Carson-Berndsen (1999a, b)), and graphic visualisation techniques. This paper concentrates on the graphic visualisation techniques.

The work presented in this paper has been implemented and tested using the *Zdatr* implementation described in Gibbon & Strokin (1998). The graph visualisation system **daVinci**, an X-Window visualisation tool for drawing directed graphs which is being developed at the University of Bremen,[2] is used for the visualisation of the feature geometry structures in a more user-friendly format.

Queries to the *Zdatr* lexicon control the extraction of the following kinds of information:

- standard segmental phonemic representations with/without temporal annotations;
- standard segmental feature bundle representations with/without temporal annotations;
- tier melodies with precedence constraints ('relative time map');
- tier melodies with temporal annotations ('absolute time map');
- inter-tier overlap constraints;
- syllable structure;
- **daVinci** objects in tree-structured feature geometry graphs, with a post-processor for defining re-entrancies.

3. An inheritance hierarchy for feature geometry

The feature geometry description used here is based primarily on Clements and Hume (1995) but also uses some conventions from Pullyblank (1995). A feature geometry representation is a graph with the following clearly distinguished components:

1. Rooted trees which are isomorphic up to depth 3 for each C or V segment in a sequence, labelled with articulatory features, and representing constraints on the articulation of speech sounds;
2. Operations over nodes in successive trees, for example generating re-entrancies between segments in order to represent assimilations and other phonological relations.

The following shows general definitional statements for consonants formulated in DATR, together with specific definitions for the consonants /t/, /d/, /s/, /f/ and /v/.

```
C:
   <>              == Null
   <rootfeats>     == "<sonorant>" "<approximant>" "<vocoid>"
   <sonorant>      == [-sonorant]
   <approximant> == [-approximant]
```

```
    <vocoid>       == [-vocoid]
    <laryngeal>    == [spreadglottis]
    <oral_cavity> == [-continuant]
    <nasal>        == [-nasal]
    <atr>          == [-atr]
    <place>        == [coronal] "<[coronal]>"
    <[coronal]>    == '(' [+anterior] ')' '(' [-distributed]')'
    <featural>     == '(' root "<rootfeats>"
                      '(' laryngeal '(' "<laryngeal>" ') )'
                      '(' "<nasal>" ')'
                      '(' oral cavity '(' "<oral_cavity>" ')'
                      '(' c_place '(' "<place>" ') )' ')' ')'
    <davinci>      == Davinci_Node:<name_root lightgreen>.

C_t: <> == C
     <segmental>    == t.
C_d: <> == C
     <laryngeal>    == [voice]
     <segmental>    == d.
C_s: <> == C
     <oral_cavity> == [+continuant]
     <segmental>    == s.
C_f: <> == C_s
     <place>        == [labial]
     <segmental>    == f
C_v: <> == C_f
     <laryngeal>    == [voice]
     <segmental>    == v.
```

An individual consonantal segment such as /d/ defined above inherits everything which is not specified at C_d from the more general C node. Vowels are defined similarly with each specific vowel inheriting from a more general V node.

The <featural> and <davinci> paths in these general definitions refer to the feature geometry. The <featural> path refers to the text representation of the feature geometry description in terms of bracketed structures. From these node definitions, we can now infer the following feature representations for the segment /t/, for example:

```
C_t:  <featural> =
   ( root [-sonorant] [-approximant] [-vocoid]
     ( laryngeal ( [spreadglottis] ) )
```

```
( [-nasal] )
( oral cavity ( [-continuant] )
( c_place     ( [coronal]      ( [+anterior] )
                               ( [-distributed] ))))).
```

The <davinci> path inherits the graph structure from Davinci_Node in a format which can be read by the **daVinci** interpreter. The **daVinci** format defines nodes and edges which can be specified with respect to name, colour and pattern attributes. In the <davinci> path of the C node definition, the root level nodes are defined to be lightgreen. However, since the details of the **daVinci** representation are not relevant to the discussion which follows, let it suffice to say that in addition to the generation of the text format, other information must be inherited which is used to define nodes. For example, **daVinci** does not allow two nodes to have the same name; therefore, it is not sufficient to say that a segment /t/ has a laryngeal node and that another segment /m/ also has a laryngeal node but we must define these in the **daVinci** notation to be laryngeal_t and laryngeal_m. These extensions are inherited using global inheritance via the <segmental> path of the individual segments. The part of the Davinci_Node node definition which defines the graph from the root down is therefore as follows:

```
Davinci_Node:
<>              ==  Null
<name_root $C>  ==  Davinci_Edge:<dashed>
                    'l("root_' "<segmental>" '" ,
                    n("Node",[a("OBJECT","'
                     root "<rootfeats>" '"),
                     a("COLOR","' $C '")], ['
                    Davinci_Edge
                     <name_laryngeal lightyellow> ']))),'
                    Davinci_Edge
                     <nasal lightyellow> ','
                    Davinci_Edge
                     <name_oral_cavity
                        lightyellow>'])))]))'.
```

This node also contains paths for <name_laryngeal lightyellow>, <nasal lightyellow> and <name_oral_cavity lightyellow>. $C is a DATR variable representing any colour. The syllable entries are defined, in line with those given in Cahill et al. (2000), as follows:

```
S_mIt:
   <>                    ==  Syllable
   <phn onset first>     ==  "C_m:<>"
   <phn peak first>      ==  "V_I:<>"
   <phn coda first>      ==  "C_t:<>".
```

This node definition for the syllable /mɪt/ states that the first position of the syllable onset inherits specific properties from the consonant definition for /m/, the first position in the syllable peak inherits from the vowel definition for /ɪ/ and the first position in the syllable coda inherits from the consonant definition for /t/. All other information is inherited from the `Syllable` node.

From the node definitions for the syllable entries, taken together with the axioms for syllable structure, we can now infer the following **daVinci** graph representation of the feature geometry representations for the syllable /mɪt/ (only a subsection of the complete graph is given in Figure 1).

As can be seen from Figure 1, this is a purely segmental representation of the feature geometry of the syllable /mɪt/ in the sense that the synchronisation function is the same across tiers. In order to move to a nonsegmental description, information on tier melodies is required.

In the DATR representation we have information about the individual tiers and their melodies. We can, therefore, use this information to generate a

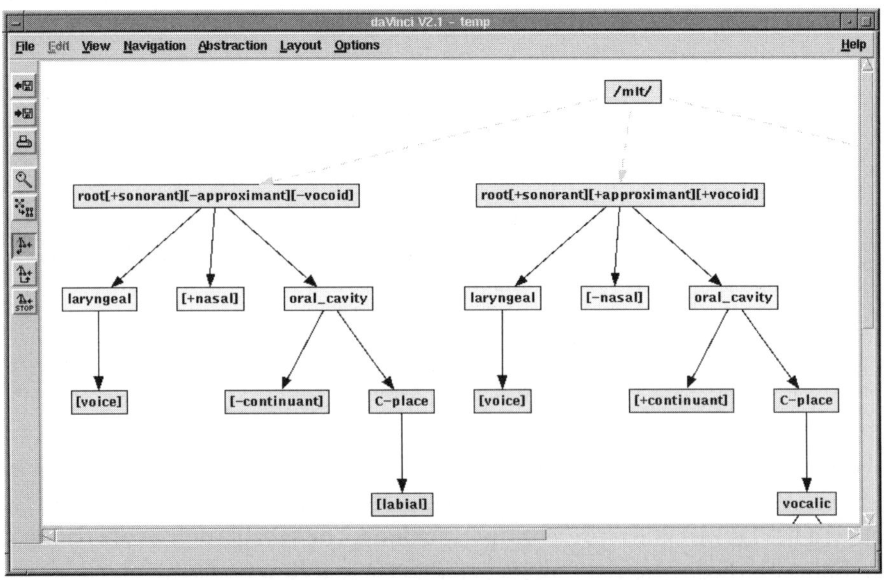

Figure 1. A subsection of the DaVinci representation for the syllable /mɪt/

new graph description for the tier and feature values which can be substituted in the graph representation format. Individual tier melodies are represented in DATR using finite state transducers. These provide a *smoothing function* modelling Leben's *Obligatory Contour Principle (OCP)* over feature value trajectories on specific tiers. As demonstrated in Cahill et al. (2000), such finite state transducers can be represented elegantly by variables in DATR.

The approach taken in this paper is similar in that variables are also used. For example, in the syllable /mɪt/, the melody on the `laryngeal` tier consists of the feature value [voice] preceding the feature value [spreadglottis]. For the graph visualisation, however, information about the melody alone is not sufficient and information about the feature geometry of the individual segments is also required.

We therefore want to construct a representation like the following for the laryngeal tier: `[voice]` m ɪ/ `[spreadglottis]` `t`. This determines that the arc from the root of the segment /ɪ/ to the node `laryngeal` is the one which must be manipulated. The actual substitution in the graph representation format is performed on the output from the *Zdatr* component currently using a postprocessor UNIX script with regular expression substitutions; this postprocessor will be replaced by *Zdatr* operations. The graph representation in Figure 2 is generated by specifying that smoothing should be applied on the `laryngeal` tier.

The new arc, from the `root` node of /ɪ/ to the `laryngeal` node, which has been inserted into the feature geometry representation, is highlighted using the colour red (although this is not apparent in the greyscale representation). The second `laryngeal` node from Figure 1 has been deleted.

In the current experimental model, the `laryngeal` tier and the `[continuant]` branch of the `oral_cavity` tier can be processed in this way. As already noted, in contrast to the treatment of melodies in Cahill et al. (2000), where the feature values are assumed to be simplex in the phonological domain (cf. Carson-Berndsen 1998), feature geometry representations assume a more complex internal organisation of speech sounds (cf. Clements & Hume 1995). We must, therefore, distinguish in this context between simplex and complex nodes; the `oral_cavity` node, as can be seen in the representation in Figure 1 dominates the `C_place` and the [±continuant] nodes. We cannot simply replace the arc to the `oral_cavity` node unless the complete subtree is identical. Currently one level of node complexity has been integrated: it is recognised that `oral_cavity` is a complex node and therefore only the `[continuant]` branch undergoes the nonlinearity constraint.

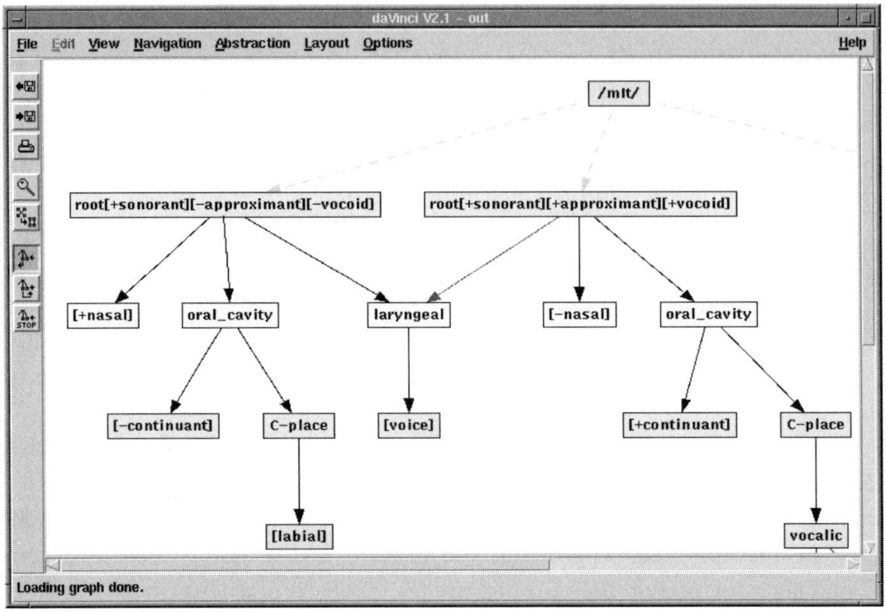

Figure 2. A subsection of the DaVinci representation for the syllable /mIt/ with smoothing over laryngeal tier

Applying smoothing to the `oral_cavity` tier in the syllable /ʃoːn/ currently results in the representation defined in Figure 3. Here a new arc is inserted from the `oral_cavity` node of the feature geometry representation of /oːn/ to the [`+continuant`] node since both /ʃ/ and /oːn/ have the same [continuant] values but the further internal organisation of their `C_place` nodes differ and thus smoothing cannot be applied here.

By incorporating temporal annotations based on average durations of context-dependent phonological segments, this representation can be used to model speech variants and to provide coarticulation models for speech technology applications as suggested in Carson-Berndsen (1999a, b).

4. Conclusion

This paper has presented a nonsegmental feature geometry based lexical description of syllables within the framework of a generic lexicon representation. In line with developments in computational phonology, the computational core

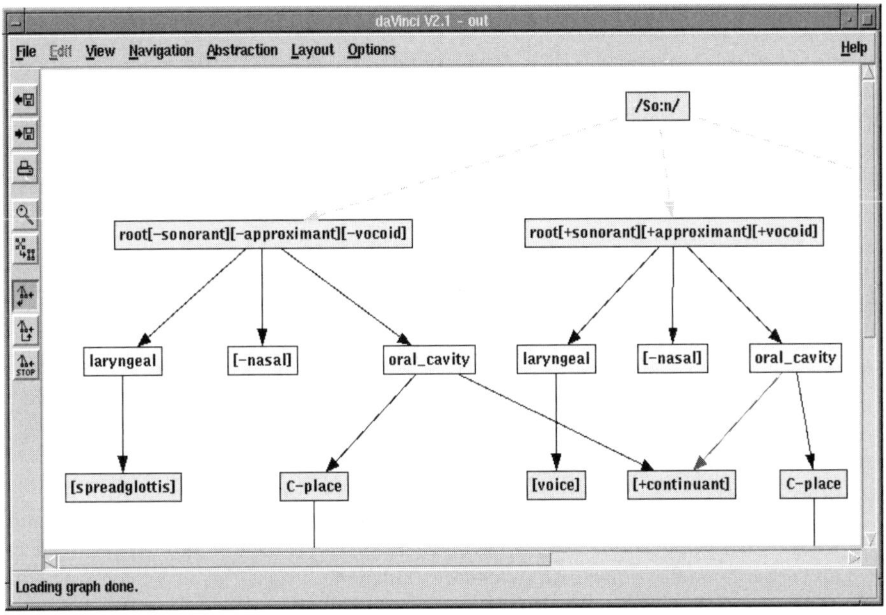

Figure 3. A subsection of the DaVinci representation for the syllable /ʃoːn/ with smoothing over `oral_cavity` tier

of the generic lexicon is based on finite state transducers. The lexicon, implemented in DATR, can be queried so as to output a range of types of information required both in linguistic analysis (for example, different phonological structures) and in speech research (for example, duration information for signal annotation). Any of these information types can be visualised on the fly, providing both feature geometry representations and temporal annotations for the individual features. The main emphasis of this paper was on generating graphical visualisations and text representations of the feature geometry descriptions in terms of bracketed structures for the lexical entries. However, the generic techniques described here could also be applied to complex multimodal tasks, for example that of integrating lexical information with the visual synthesis of articulatory movements synchronised with acoustic output.

The relationship of this work to speech applications lies in the representation of nonlinear phonology in highly structured lexica allowing modelling of coarticulation phenomena and temporal interpretation of spoken forms. These aspects are discussed further with respect to a linguistic word recognition system in Carson-Berndsen (1999a, b).

Note

1. The language described in this application is German. Phonemic representations are in SAMPA and typewriter font for machine readable examples and in conventional IPA roman font in the text.

2. daVinci is now available as a commercial product at http://www.davinci-presenter.de.

References

Cahill, L., J. Carson-Berndsen & G. Gazdar (2000). Phonology-based Lexical Knowledge Representation. In: van Eynde, F. & D. Gibbon (Eds.), *Lexicon Development for Speech and Language Processing* (77-114). Dordrecht: Kluwer Academic Publishers.

Carson-Berndsen, J. (1998). *Time Map Phonology: Finite State Models and Event Logics in Speech Recognition.* Dordrecht: Kluwer Academic Publishers.

Carson-Berndsen, J. (1999a). A Generic Lexicon Tool for Word Model Definition in Multimodal Applications. *Proceedings of EUROSPEECH 99, 6th European Conference on Speech Communication and Technology*, Budapest.

Carson-Berndsen, J. (1999b). A Feature Geometry Based Lexicon Model for Speech Applications. *Proceedings of IDS 99, Interactive Dialogue in Multimodal Systems*, ESCA Tutorial and Research Workshop, Kloster Irsee.

Clements, G. N. & E. V. Hume (1995). The Internal Organization of Speech Sounds. In: Goldsmith, J. A. (Ed.), *The Handbook of Phonological Theory* (245-306). Cambridge, MA: Blackwell Publishers.

Evans, R. & G. Gazdar (1989). Inference in DATR. *Proceedings of the Fourth Conference of the EACL*, 66-71.

Evans, R. & G. Gazdar (1996). DATR: A language for lexical knowledge representation. *Computational Linguistics*, 22,2, 167-216.

Gibbon, D. (1998). German Intonation. In: Hirst, D. & A. Di Cristo (Eds.), *Intonation Systems; A Survey of Twenty Languages* (78-95). Cambridge: Cambridge University Press.

Gibbon, D. & F. Ahoua (1991). DDATR: un logiciel de traitement d'heritage par defaut pour la modelisation lexicale. *Cahiers Ivoiriens de Recherche Linguistique* (CIRL) 27, 5-59.

Gibbon, D. & G. Strokin (1998). *ZDATR Version 2.0 Reference Manual Version 1.0.* University of Bielefeld.

Goldsmith, J. A. (1976). *Autosegmental Phonology.* Bloomington: Indiana University Linguistics Club.

Pullyblank, D. (1995). Feature geometry and underspecification. In: Durand, J. & F. Katamba (Eds.), *Frontiers of Phonology* (3-33). London and New York: Longman.

Reinhard, S. & D. Gibbon (1991). Prosodic Inheritance and Morphological Generalisations. *Proceedings of the ACL European Chapter Conference*, Berlin.

A simulated language understanding agent using virtual perception

John Gurney, Elizabeth Klipple, and Robert Winkler
Adelphi Laboratory Center, Adelphi, MD, USA

1. Introduction

We introduce a new kind of software agent as the human computer interface (HCI) in virtual reality (VR) environments. This agent uses virtual perception to perform what we call the Spoken Language Navigation Task in our virtual world. We motivate this agent-based approach to HCI by comparing the performance of our agent to a more traditional database type of HCI. The comparison uses a few key examples of natural language imperatives (e.g., *keep looking at the tree, stay here*) that occur during our Spoken Language Navigation Task. The four navigation problems we will discuss are:

Problem 1: Recovering from misadventures while navigating;
Problem 2: Respecting the distinction between telic and atelic actions (i.e., temporally bounded *vs.* temporally unbounded actions);
Problem 3: Tracking and following moving objects;
Problem 4: Respecting the distinction between staying somewhere and simply stopping.

Our discussion focuses on the following key points: (1) a geographical information system (GIS) database model often fails to perform our Spoken Language Navigation Task in dynamic, changing virtual environments; (2) our new software agent model succeeds by simulating virtual perception of objects in the virtual world; (3) we simulate perception for our agent in a novel way that is inspired by the flow of information theory of human perception; (4) ultimately and essentially, our agent succeeds by tying its virtual perception (along with simulated robot-like reactive behavior) *systematically* to its interpretation of the sentences it hears during the navigation task (see Gurney et al. 1998).

After briefly describing the NLVR system in the next section we show how problems arise for the GIS database method. Following this, we first motivate and then explain our novel method for simulating perception. We finish by showing how our new agent uses virtual perception to overcome the above problems and perform our Spoken Language Navigation Task correctly in dynamic virtual environments.

2. The NLVR System

The NLVR system is an independent natural language understanding system that provides an HCI to our Virtual Graphic Information System (VGIS).[1]

VGIS is a 3D version of a GIS. It does a good job of simulating the look and flow of movement over terrain. Through a menu interface or by writing programs that use the VGIS Navigation Application Program Interface (API) one can simulate continuous motion, relative position, and point of view and all this is realistic; it operates in real time, presenting a detailed, photographic quality landscape.

The NLVR system replaces the VGIS menu interface with a spoken language interface. It is an example of a useful, much desired HCI to a 3D VR decision aid like VGIS. It also serves as a testbed for our attempts to understand and simulate some aspects of human language understanding. It seems ideal for simulation of the interplay between language and vision just because what you see is artificial; in VGIS we have a mathematical model of the ground truth (terrain, buildings, vehicles, etc.) that the VGIS Rendering Engine uses to paint pixels on the display screen. Our NLVR software accesses this ground truth in order to manipulate and/or retrieve information about the VR scene; so the VGIS model is a stand-in for the mental model in human perception.

3. Simulation

The Spoken Language Navigation Task amounts to this: You need to move about in the virtual world presented by VGIS at various speeds and altitudes, to various locations, along various paths, and at various positional attitudes. But the only way you can communicate with the system is by talking. Moving around in this virtual world is equivalent to moving the VGIS View Point (see Figure 1).

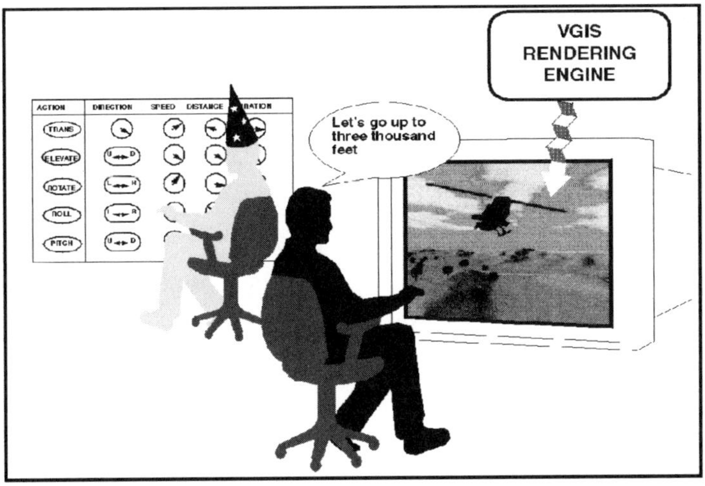

Figure 1. Wizard's virtual control panel

If we deal with this problem as a 3D GIS database access problem, it is as if you were talking to a wizard who: (a) knows where everything is in your virtual world, but (b) is limited to only adjusting dials and pushing buttons on the control panel to move you about in response to what you say: *go south for five kilometers, look straight down, ascend slowly to fifty meters, zoom off to Bicycle Lake.*[2]

The simulated database wizard

To show how this simulated wizard and control panel work and how problems arise for it, we will step through this first example:

(1) *fly to the top of the Tiefort Mountains.*

We talk to the wizard who uses the control panel shown in Figure 1. Upon detecting sentence (1), the wizard:

(A) Parses (1);
(B) Reads off the Logical Form (LF) from the parse tree: [3]

```
[v:fly:X1,
  [[d:the:X2,[[d:the:X3, [n:multiword([tiefort, mountains]):X3]],
             [n:top:X2:X3]]],
   [p:to:X1:X2]]].
```

(C) Omnisciently resolves the reference of the three unbound variables (`X1`, `X2`, and `X3`) in the above LF to find a coherent interpretation:

```
[v:fly:translate,
 [[d:the:top(mt5),
  [[d:the:mt5,[n:multiword([tiefort,mountains]):mt5]],
   [n:top:top(mt5):mt5]]],
  [p:to:translate:top(mt5)]]].
```

(where `mt5` is the internal database name for the mountains and `translate` is a linear horizontal motion action) and, finally,

(D) Looks up and then executes appropriate actions for this interpreted LF; that is, sets two dials on the control panel and then pushes the `translate` button for linear motion:

```
EXECUTE: setbearing(translate, 40.0),
EXECUTE: setdistance(translate, 66.0),
EXECUTE: translate.
```

At step (D), above, the wizard can look up the latitude and longitude (Lat:Lon) of the top of the Tiefort Mountains, `top(mt5)`, by consulting the VGIS ground truth data. This is like a database for him, so he is omniscient regarding all such names and definite descriptions. The wizard also knows about the available action buttons on the panel and which dials go with which actions. The choice of `translate` for the event `X1` was the only coherent choice of action for sentence (1).[4] Since speed was not mentioned, the speed dial on the control panel remains untouched, as do any other dials. [5] The action `translate` simply launches you on a path through the virtual world according to the dial settings.

Problems for the Wizard in Example 1

Now we can raise a few problems for the wizard. First, Problem 1, misadventures. If you are blown or bumped off course[6] you will not make it to those mountains, because the `translate` action that was executed will you keep moving on the same bearing but now along a parallel path. [7] This is the price we pay for treating the control panel settings and actions along the lines of database query actions. Once the action is performed the database wizard has nothing else it can do until a new action is called for because it has no perceptual knowledge of the evolving situation. The wizard can only execute actions as updates to its database. Changing speed and stopping for a rest while *en route* are also problematic. If you tell the wizard to *go slower* he needs to reset the speed dial and then execute a new `translate` action.

```
EXECUTE: setspeed(translate, 20.0),
EXECUTE: translate.
```

In designing this kind of control panel wizard, we have two clear choices. We can (a) make any selection of an execute action button automatically kill any current action *of the same kind* so that the old action can be replaced by the new action; or (b) simply let the new action add itself to whatever other actions are underway. Choice (b) will result in very bizarre and unacceptable behavior when the old and new actions happen to be in competition (e.g., moving north and moving south). This leaves us with choice (a); the wizard can only obey the command to slow down by killing off the current journey to the mountain and starting a new slower `translate` action. He will also leave the previous dial setting for distance as it was (and this would take you on past the mountains since you were already part way there!) In any case, the wizard cannot simply slow down without resetting the speed dial and pushing the `translate` button again, initiating an entirely new action.

It is interesting to note that you would not notice these problems if you had told the wizard, not to go to the mountains, but to just fly in some direction and then slow down: *fly south, now go slower.* Flying south is an atelic event (with indefinite extent) and flying to the mountains is a telic event (with definite extent). Telling the wizard to go slower while already flying south would result in the same control panel manipulation as before. After resetting the speed dial, the wizard would stop the current `translate` but immediately start a new indefinite `translate` in the same direction. Since these atelic actions have no end point or goal, when the wizard replaces the current southward `translate` with a new slower southward `translate` you will not miss or fly past your (non-existent) goal. It is apparent that the wizard and his control panel cannot get the difference between telic and atelic events right. Atelic actions can always be decomposed into sequences of similar atelic actions. This is not the case for telic actions.

Diagnosis

One source of trouble is that the wizard is too detached from the virtual context. He does not see the world from your point of view. By treating all actions on a par with database queries, he ignores the fine-grained, continuous dynamics of the Spoken Language Navigation Task. This is similar to database query problems for dynamic databases in those cases when a database entry can change after a query is sent but before an answer is returned. In our system, where values are changing continuously, poor performance is clear to the user, who *is* paying close attention to the dynamics of motion through the virtual world. We will try to show that if we simulate some aspects of perception, that will lead us to interesting solutions to all of the above natural language interpretation problems (Problems 1 through 4). In place of the wizard, we will be simulating a *companion* who must rely on virtual perception rather than database omniscience to move us about in response to what we say.

4. Reactive behavior with virtual perception

First consider the way navigation would be handled by a person operating a typical arcade game. There is no speech understanding, so you cannot talk to the game system, but you have a control stick for direction and you have another lever for speed. You want to fly over to the top of a mountain. You keep looking at your (virtual) goal, perhaps a flag planted at the summit, and you guide your way on over there. Here we have a typical case of hand-eye coordination.

Note that you do not have difficulty with some of the problems cited above. You can distinguish telic from atelic imperatives. For example, you can slow down and speed up while keeping your eye on that flag so you'll know when to stop. And, of course, you can catch up with and track a moving object (Problem 3). But you need to keep your eye on it!

This is what we want to simulate — the hand-eye coordinated software agent. You talk, just as before, but your companion now simulates what you would do in the arcade game, or in driving a car, or in piloting a helicopter. In order to make this work, we need to somehow simulate perception of both stationary and moving objects in the virtual world for the new agent. We have simulated some aspects of perception, which we explain in the next section, and we have simulated reactive, perception-governed behavior, which we explain in the section after that.

A general case could be made for implementing this kind of software agent based on an interest in human skills and methods. We want to make the point here that *our* reasons are more urgent and easily stated. We want to be able to simulate understanding of (i.e., adequately process) natural language sentences that we could not easily handle, if at all, using the database wizard. We believe that simulating perception in the NLVR system should be taken seriously as one possible solution.[8]

5. Perception as information from a source

To simulate perception we draw from the causal theory of perception and reference which we can introduce with a story: If Tom were out walking one evening with Mary and said *do you see that star?* and she said *yes, I see it,* Tom might assume she is both referring to and perceiving the same star as he. The most important question to ask here is: what makes it the case that Tom and Mary both are perceiving and referring to the same star? What are the criteria?

One of the few answers that comes close to saying something helpful is in terms of the source and flow of information. This theory is due to Dretske in (Dretske 1969) and (Dretske 1981). Tom and Mary perceive the same star simply because that star is causing their perceptions of it. They each have a mental representation (one in Tom's head and one in Mary's). It is necessary that both representations are caused by the same star and that the representations have a certain informational dependence on that star (as explained by Dretske). Otherwise they are *not,* in truth, perceiving the same star[9] — even though their complete internal mental states may differ in no significant way between this case and the case of mistakenly looking at two different stars.[10] If what Tom and Mary say (*that star, it*) originates in these information-tracking perceptions then Tom and Mary are both talking about the same star. Otherwise they may not be talking about the same star.[11]

This kind of causal tracking is what we want to partially simulate. We don't have real stars, mountains, and helicopters. After all, it's a simulation. So there are no real objects that both you and your simulated companion can see. But we do have causality. There is a process, the VGIS Rendering Engine, that paints the pixels on the VR display screen which you (the one doing all the talking) see. This Rendering Engine will be the surrogate cause of perception.

Figure 2 depicts how we simulate perception for your simulated companion who is now metaphorically turned toward the display screen so she can "see" what you see and only that.[12] This is how it works: The Rendering Engine paints a cluster of helicopterish pixels at a bearing of about 340.0 degrees on the VR screen as in Figure 2. This is what you see. It simultaneously sends a message

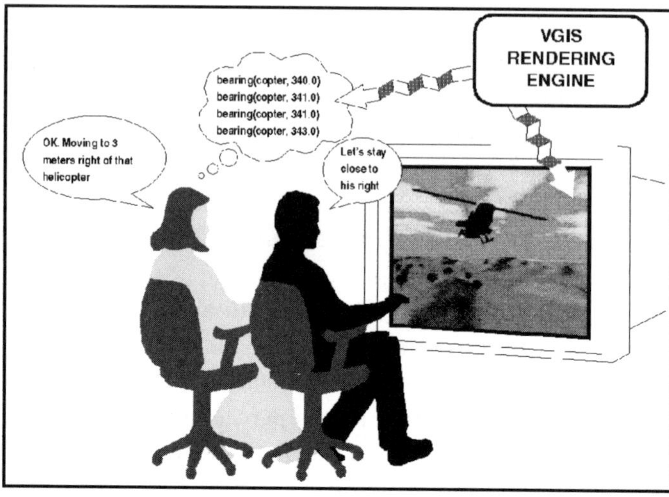

Figure 2. Virtual perception for your simulated companion

stream to your companion (which is a client process) giving the bearing of the helicopter (340.0). It doesn't send pixels to the companion or create another VR screen for her to "look" at! She only needs to "see" that the helicopter is currently at a bearing of 340.0. In the NLVR system we represent this message as `bearing(copter3, 340.0)`. The companion is continuously getting this stream of information from the Rendering Engine. She is, however, only getting information about what we want her to be "looking at" at the time.

As the helicopterish pixels move across the VR screen the message stream carries new numbers for bearing, etc. to the companion. Now we have a parallel to the case of Tom and Mary. When you see the helicopterish pixels move across the screen you interpret this as a moving helicopter; your vision system can track it and you can talk about it and refer to it as the same moving helicopter. The companion can now understand all this talk (as we will explain in the section on simulated behavior) because the message stream gives it the information that the same helicopter is changing its relative location (bearing). All of this captures what is essential to human perception of the same object by two people; they get information that originates from the same source.

We only want the companion to be perceiving one thing at a time. What we need for this is some sort of analog to looking at and noticing one thing rather than another. We must avoid some interesting issues here about how humans are able to quickly and easily look from one object to another. (Deixis is important here; see (Klipple and Gurney 1999) and our work on eye tracking in (Voss *et al.* 1997)). But given some object that the companion should be looking at, we simulate the act of turning one's visual attention to that object by sending a request message from the companion process to the Rendering Engine process, upon which the latter begins sending back a message stream of information simulating perception of that VR object.

It might be thought that the companion knows the bearing of the helicopter with too much precision (our messages give the bearing of an object to 0.1 degrees). This is not obvious. We cannot adequately discuss the matter here other than to point out that people are very good at resolving *relative* angles in the visual field. The fact that they may not be able to say what the magnitudes of those angles are is not relevant to whether they can visually discriminate them as required for the particular examples of language understanding we introduced above and will discuss below.

6. Simulated reactive behavior

How is virtual perception used? Here is where we simulate the eye-coordinated hand on the stick of the arcade game.

Flying to a perceived mountain

Recall the problems (Problem 1: misadventures and Problem 2: telic actions) that the wizard had with the following telic sentence:

(1) *fly to the top of the Tiefort Mountains.*

The companion can deal with the following sort of telic sentence without encountering those problems:

(2) *fly to the top of that mountain.*

This is a variant of example (1) where the definite description or name *the Tiefort Mountains* has been replaced with the deictic expression *that mountain.* Parsing and finding the LF (steps (A) and (B)) are just like before:

```
[v:Xy:X1,
 [[d:the:X2,[[d:that:X3,[n:mountain:X3]],
             [n:top:X2:X3]]],
 [p:to:X1:X2]]].
```

Step (C) deals with the binding of variables somewhat differently than before:

(C) Resolve the references by binding the free variables `X2` and `X3` by using perception (rather than looking up their referents in a database); and resolve the reference to the action by binding the event `X1` to a process of reactive behavior (rather than the `translate` function which resembled a database query):

```
[v:fly:advance,
  [[d:the:top(index3),[[d:that:index3,[n:mountain:index3]],
                      [n:top:top(index3):index3]]],
   [p:to:advance:top(index3)]]].
```

Here the companion uses virtual perception to determine `X3`. As a convenience we use the index `index3` to stand for that mountain that your companion has perceived.

Step (C) simulates understanding of what was said and that requires knowing what has been referred to. We are simulating perception of the mountain by the companion. In this context this underlies the simulated coming to know (by the companion) what the noun phrase *that mountain* refers to.[13]

The virtual perceiving is brought off in the manner we explained above. This simply means that, at step (C), the companion is receiving a stream of messages from the Rendering Engine, i.e., "from" the mountain. If the companion does not receive the message stream the companion is not perceiving the mountain and therefore does not know what you are talking about when you say *fly to the top of that mountain.* [14]

Step (D) is where the companion decides what to do. She is already perceiving the mountain. She needs to home in on `top(index3)`. Of course, there are many ways one could do this. The companion is limited to, but good at, perception. So she starts perceiving and getting a message stream "from" `top(index3)`.

Now she needs to start moving. The LF clause `[p:to:advance:top (index3)]` requires a process of rotation to the direction of `top(index3)`, while the LF clause `[v:go:advance]` simply requires moving in whatever direction is forward: [15]

```
PROCESS: rotateto(DIRTOP3),
PROCESS: advance(SPEED).
```

These are simple asynchronous control processes of the type discussed in

(Brooks 1991a, 1991b), and Kortenkamp et al. 1998). The first process simulates the hand on the stick in the arcade game that keeps you always turning to the direction `DIRTOP3` of your target. The second process simulates the speed control that keeps you moving forward at the current `SPEED` in meters per second. The control panel, with its default settings for direction, speed, and so on is no longer operable. In its place we have these two parallel processes.

Now we can easily speed up or slow down by resetting `SPEED`. Since `SPEED` is monitored by `advance` we can reset it without killing the whole set of processes. We will also easily recover from misadventures along the way since the message stream `bearing(top(index3), DIRTOP3)` will always report the *current* direction we should be moving. If blown off course we will automatically turn toward `DIRTOP3`. By using perception, the companion can perform the Spoken Language Navigation Task in a dynamic, changing virtual environment. It can also understand sentences that use demonstrative references like *that mountain*. Understanding demonstratives would be impossible for the wizard.

Staying with a moving object

Our third example will raise both the problem of moving objects (Problem 3) and the problem of staying at a position (Problem 4).

Verbs like *stay*, *sit*, *stand*, and *remain* are maintenance-of-state verbs. *Stay here* does not mean *stop here*. If a virtual wind begins to blow, staying at a place requires one to hold one's position and return to it if displaced.

The wizard using the control board would not be able to deal with:

(3) *stay to his right*

unless he simply executed a `stop`, which does not really capture or satisfy the meaning of *stay*. The point becomes sharper if the object referred to is not stationary but moving. Assume *he* is a helicopter, the one in Figure 2.

Now look at the interpreted LF for (3) which the companion gets at step (D) in the processing:

```
[v:stay:holdposition,
 [[[d:his:index2,[n:right:index2:rightpart(index2)]]],
  [p:to:holdposition:rightpart(index2)]]].
```

In this case `index2` is a place holder for that moving helicopter that the companion is now perceiving (i.e., getting a message stream `bearing(in-`

dex2, DIR2) from the Rendering Engine).

If the wizard tried to deal with (3), he could, at best, get one fix on the Lat:Lon of the helicopter at one instant in time. From this he could calculate the bearing from your viewpoint to that Lat:Lon at the same instant. This would prove to be inadequate when we come to step (D).

As before, step (D) is where the companion decides what to do. She is already perceiving the helicopter. She needs to home in on rightpart(index2). So she starts perceiving and getting a message stream from rightpart (index2). The messages in this stream have the form:

```
bearing(rightpart(index3), DIRRT2),
bearing(rightpart(index3), DIRRT2),
bearing(rightpart(index3), DIRRT2),
...
```

where the value of the variable DIRRT2 changes as the position of the helicopter changes.

Now she needs to holdposition at rightpart(index3). This task looks a lot like the one in example (2). In fact the same two control processes (with different parameters) will do the job:

```
PROCESS: rotateto(DIRRT2),
PROCESS: advance(SPEED).
```

These parallel processes will get you to the right side of the moving helicopter and keep you there by tracking the helicopter (using virtual perception) and by always moving you in the proper direction DIRRT2. When you finally catch up with the helicopter you will hold your apparent position there simply because as the helicopter moves your companion will perceive it in a new position; you will stay to its right. Notably, the staying is accomplished without planning or satisfying preconditions such as that one must be at a place to stay there! By contrast, the wizard would get you to the spot that was to the right of the helicopter at some instant in time. But the helicopter may have long since flown away.

7. Concluding remarks

The agent behaviors we have implemented for the companion are, in fact, simple control systems which are minimally adequate. They are cognitively reasonable responses in the examples above. This model can serve as a basis for future development of somewhat more sophisticated software agents that deal with further aspects of verb phrase meaning for other interesting examples of sentences such as: *look toward the lake*, *keep turning left*, *keep away from those camels*, and *drop to the ground when strangers appear.*

By simulating perception according to the causal, information-based theory of human perception we were able to create a navigation agent completely in software that simulates understanding of some non-trivial Spoken Language Navigation Task sentences.

Acknowledgment

We are happy to acknowledge Timothy Gregory for the VGIS Navigation API, Steve Choy for the Speech API, and Prof. Dekang Lin for his Minimalist GB parser, MINIPAR.

Notes

1. The VGIS software was created at the Georgia Institute of Technology and developed to its present form at the Army Research Laboratory.

2. An earlier version of our NLVR system implemented something similar to this wizard.

3. We discuss some reasons for using this sort of LF in (Klipple and Gurney, 1998) as well as lexical representation in (Gurney and Klipple, 1998). The notation is Prolog, where all variables are capitalized and all constants begin lowercased or are numbers. These quasi-logical forms retain syntactic labels because they have not been fully interpreted at this stage; e.g., references of definite noun phrases have not been resolved.

4. We explain how we use the lexical semantics of verb modification to properly represent and bind the event variables in (Klipple and Gurney, 1998).

5. This is how we implement some aspects of defaults without bothering to implement default reasoning. This is not intended to be a robust solution to any default problems that may arise in this project.

6. VGIS also simulates micro-scale weather in real time through an API.

7. Here, we will neither deal with nor mention again the additional problem of obstacles along your route.

8. There are other, equally practical, reasons for simulating perception, having to do with computational errors and real-time computing. We will leave discussion of these software issues for another occasion.

9. Whether and how they know they are, or are not, both perceiving and talking about the

same star, while an interesting topic, is an additional matter that we cannot discuss here.

10. The classic arguments that referring to and thinking about a particular physical thing requires your words and the thing to be directly related (perhaps causally related) appear in (Kripke, 1972) and (Putnam, 1975). The theory presented in (Dretske, 1981) is the flow of information variant of these causal theories.

11. If Mary's pronoun *it* is a discourse anaphor, perhaps she is referring to Tom's star. If the pronoun is deictic, then perhaps she is referring to her own star.

12. Mental maps, which retain representations of what one has seen in the past, are real and we can simulate them, but we will not discuss the matter at this time.

13. See (Kaplan, 1989) for the classic work in this vein.

14. There are things such as visual seeking by the companion involved here that we must deal with on another occasion.

15. `DIRTOP3` is a variable representing the current direction to the mountain's top.

References

Brooks, Rodney (1991a). Intelligence without reason. *A.I. Memo 1293.* Cambridge: MIT Artificial Intelligence Laboratory.

Brooks, Rodney (1991b). Intelligence without representation. *Artificial Intelligence*, 47(1–3):139–159.

Dretske, Fred (1969). *Seeing and Knowing.* Chicago: Chicago.

Dretske, Fred (1981). *Knowledge and the Flow of Information.* Cambridge, Massachusetts: MIT.

Gurney, John & Elizabeth Klipple (1998). Composing conceptual structure for spoken natural language in a virtual reality environment. *Proceedings of Mind III: Spatial Cognition.* Dublin: Cognitive Science Society of Ireland.

Gurney, John, Elizabeth Klipple, & Timothy Gregory (1998). The spoken language navigation task. *Proceedings of the AAAI Workshop on Representations for Multi-Modal Human-Computer Interaction.* Madison: American Association for Artificial Intelligence.

Kaplan, David (1989). Demonstratives. In J. Almog, J. Perry, and H. Wettstein, (Eds.), *Themes from Kaplan*, (481–563). New York: Oxford.

Klipple, Elizabeth & John Gurney (1998). Verb modification and the lexicon in the Natural Language and Virtual Reality system. *Proceedings of the Workshop on Lexical Semantic Systems.* Pisa.

Klipple, Elizabeth & John Gurney (1999). Deixis to properties in the NLVR system. *Proceedings of the ESSLLI Workshop on Deixis, Demonstration and Deictic Belief in Multimedia Contexts.* Utrecht: European Summer School for Language, Logic and Information.

Kortenkamp, David, R. Peter Bonasso, & Robin Murphy, (Eds.) (1998). *Artificial Intelligence and Mobile Robots: Case Studies of Successful Robots.* Menlo Park: American Association for Artificial Intelligence.

Kripke, Saul (1972). Naming and Necessity. In D. Davidson and G. Harman, (Eds.), *Semantics of Natural Language.* Dordrecht: Reidel.

Putnam, Hilary (1975). *Mind, Language and Reality.* Cambridge: Cambridge.

Voss, Clare, John Gurney, & James Walrath (1997). Exploration in a large corpus: Research on the integration of eye gaze and speech with visual information in a virtual reality system. *Proceedings of the AAAI Spring Symposium.* Stanford: American Association for Artificial Intelligence.

The Hitchhiker's Guide to the Galaxy

A.L. Cohen-Rose and S.B. Christiansen
Aalborg University, Denmark

> "In many of the more relaxed civilizations on the Outer Eastern Rim of the Galaxy, the Hitchhiker's Guide has already supplanted the great Encyclopedia Galactica as the standard repository of all knowledge and wisdom, for though it has many omissions and contains much that is apocryphal, or at least wildly inaccurate, it scores over the older, more pedestrian work in two important respects.
> First, it is slightly cheaper; and secondly it has the words DON'T PANIC inscribed in large friendly letters on its cover."
>
> *Douglas Adams, The Hitchhiker's Guide to the Galaxy (1979)*

1. Introduction

The *Hitchhiker's Guide to the Galaxy* is a science fiction story written by Douglas Adams that foresees an electronic guide to Life, the Universe and Everything. Together with *The Digital Village*, Douglas Adams's company, we define the capabilities of a modern version of *The Hitchhiker's Guide*: providing information in a contextual setting; using a third party interaction metaphor via software agents; and providing personality-based feedback to encourage the user to trust the agents.

Since a complete *Hitchhiker's Guide* is not possible with current technology, we prototype a Guide that can provide guidance over a more limited domain. Our *Guide* answers natural language queries about places to eat and drink with relevant stories. These stories are created by *Storytelling Agents* from a knowledge base containing previously written reviews together with more detailed information about the places and the food and drink they serve.

Providing information in context

The Internet could be viewed as similar to the fictional *Hitchhiker's Guide to the Galaxy*, at least in the apocryphal and wildly inaccurate senses. Unfortunately, it is missing the all-important, large friendly letters on the cover.

There are many Web sites that offer searching facilities. To use them, you type in some keywords and the search sites give you a list of sites that contain the words. The next stage is to flip to and from the list of links until you find the information you want. There are three problems occurring here:

1. There is no way to tell from the page of links which page contains the exact information you are looking for.
2. The information you are looking for might be spread across several pages.
3. The pages gathered by the search engine have no semantic links between them.

According to Roger Schank (Schank and Abelson 1977), the human mind operates in terms of context. We understand things only as they relate to experiences. Schank therefore proposed a model of human memory and understanding based on *scripts*, the stories we distill from our experiences. He suggested that we understand information by fitting it into scripts or by creating new ones. In order to do this, however, the information must be provided in context, not as lists of unrelated items.

Agent technology

Most current day software interfaces use the *direct manipulation* metaphor. This implies both that the user can see what choices are available at any time and that the user is entirely responsible for making those choices. This metaphor breaks down when the user must handle the large amounts of information available on the Internet.

An alternative metaphor was proposed by the Knowledge Navigator (Apple Computer 1992). This vision of future computing allowed the user to *delegate* his tasks to the computer: instead of conducting a search by carefully selecting keywords, dates and author names, the user said, "Find me the paper I read on deforestation published by uh Flemson or something." The resulting loss of direct control necessitates that the user *trusts* the agent to complete its tasks satisfactorily.

An agent can gain the user's trust by gradually learning from the user's actions and reactions. In this way the user can see the agent developing and is "given time to gradually build up a model of how the agent makes decisions, which is one of the prerequisites for a trust relationship" (Maes 1994). Software agents learn the user's habits by building up a model of how they expect the *user* to behave. Two of the problems associated with such models are:

1. The agent must be able to convey the state of its model to the user so that she can see how the agent is developing.
2. A model can never fully capture the user's decision making process. For example, if a restaurant guidance agent is familiar with the restaurants that *you* like, what happens when you want one that's suitable for your parents?

Personality-based expression

Communicating a complex internal model to the user is a difficult task. However, agents can harness people's expectations by using facial expressions to convey their internal state (how they "feel"). If done consistently, the user will quickly build a model of the agent's decision processes.

Naoko Tosa's *Neurobaby* (Tosa 1993) used neural networks to model an artificial baby that reacted in emotional ways to the sounds made by a user looking into its crib. *Neurobaby* was a fairly simple system, but because of the users' knowledge and expectations of a *real* baby, it was judged very convincing.

The concept of personalities can also counteract the second problem above. *Amalthaea* (Moukas 1996) is an information filtering and discovery system that makes use of evolving populations of genetically-based agents (each a separate "personality"). While the selection process ensures that the agents become customised to an individual user, the reproduction and mutation processes provide diversity in the population and in the resulting information.

Proposal

While there have been several thought experiments that combined the concepts in the previous three sections (for example, Apple's *Knowledge Navigator*), no one has yet come up with a satisfactory working product.

It is our belief that a successful presentation of information from varied sources must be both *relevant* and *easily understandable*. From our research we have discovered that these two criteria could be satisfied in a system that combines the three concepts of:

1. providing information in a contextual setting;
2. changing the interaction metaphor from direct to third party interaction;
3. and providing personality-based feedback to encourage the user to trust that third party.

Our primary aim in this project is to design and construct a *Guide* that successfully combines these three concepts.

2. Description of *The Guide*

The Digital Village's *Principles of Guidance* (TDV and AT&T 1997) was our main inspiration for this project. This uses an in-depth profile of the user to answer natural language queries; it works by itself while the user is doing something else; and it can even use several methods of communication to keep in contact with the user.

Our *Guide* is not so advanced. While it does accept natural language queries and does answer in the form of stories, it does not work offline and only uses a simple (but still effective) profile of the user. It also has an interface that combines the modalities of speech input, text and graphics display, pointing input (mouse-based in our case, but pen-based on a mobile device) and positional input (such as Global Positioning System signals). We designed this interface to be scaleable from a desktop computer to a mobile phone.

Information flow

Figure 1 summarises how the user's query is interpreted and processed by *The Guide*. Briefly, the syntax and semantics of the user's query are analysed to determine her intention. This intention is then sent to the Storytelling Agents, which select and order the information from the FramerD database. This process results in *smarticles* which are displayed to the user. The sections that follow provide more details on each part of the system.

FramerD Database

Since *The Guide* is a storytelling system, frames and scripts (Schank and Abelson 1977) provide a convenient way to represent its knowledge. FramerD (Haase 1996) is an object-oriented database designed to store and index frame-based information. It also comes with a large language knowledge base (KB) called *Brico*, consisting of the *WordNet* lexical thesaurus, the top-level *CYC* ontology (Cycorp 1999) and a semantic network of Roget's thesaurus. To this we added frames representing knowledge of the world (see the section on *Domain Knowledge* below).

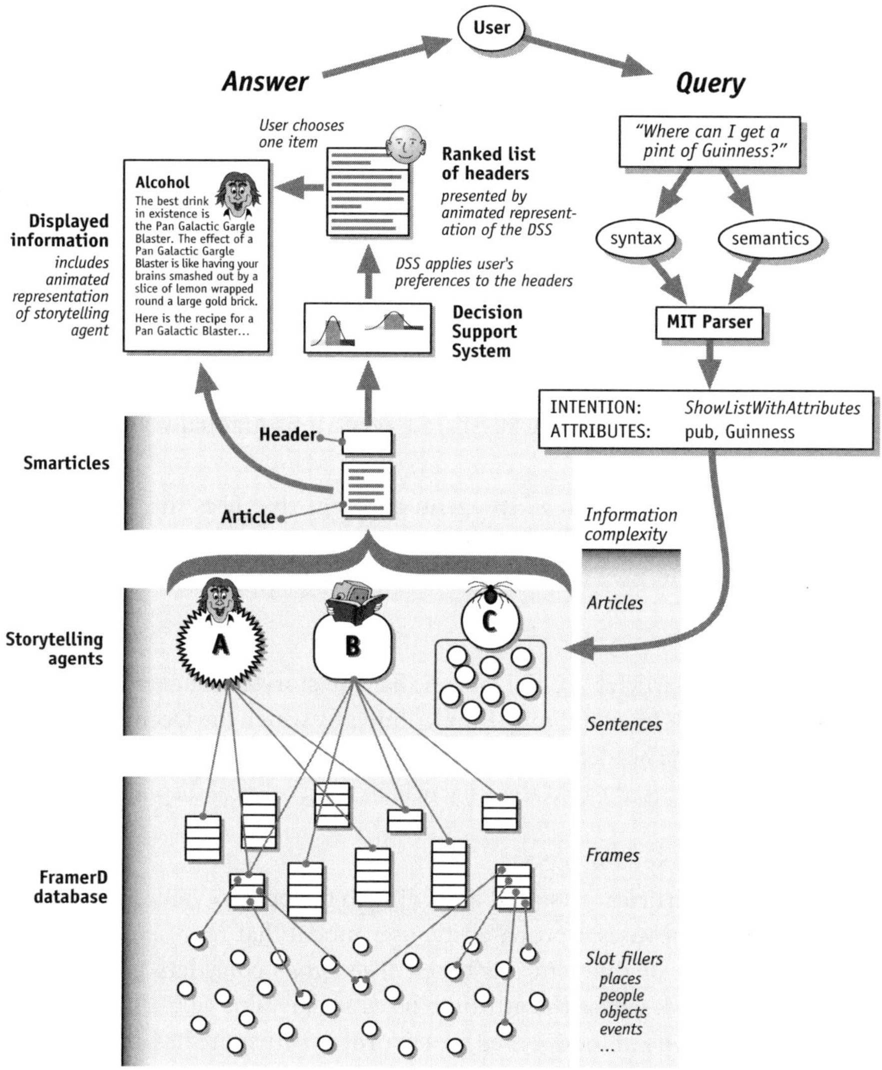

Figure 1. Information flow in *The Guide*

Storytelling agents

Having several storytelling agents provides *The Guide* with a greater diversity of information to present to the user. This counteracts the problem noted in the Introduction that the user model could never fully capture the user's decision process. All the agents can access the FramerD database to create their stories. Three possible types of storytelling agent are shown in Figure 1:

A. **Actual Human Being (AHB) agent:** could be a human operator writing smarticles to answer the user's queries or a software agent that selects smarticles from a database of human-written ones.
B. **Predefined agent:** has some fixed code that is executed to generate a smarticle each time it gets a query from the user.
C. **Genetically-based agent:** an evolving population of agents similar to those in *Amalthaea* (Moukas 1996). Each of the agents in the population has a genotype that determines how it creates smarticles. The genotypes evolve according to a selection process based on whether the user chooses to read the smarticles. The genetically-based agent thus gradually adapts to the user.

The Guide currently has an AHB agent; an agent that uses the *Dada engine* (Bulhak 1996) to talk feasible nonsense; and an agent that interprets the user's query in terms of its own bias and returns combinations of existing smarticles.

Smarticles

In *The Guide*, smarticles are the stories that the storytelling agents tell. Each smarticle has a header containing the attributes by which the Decision Support System rates it. The header also contains a title and a reference to the authoring agent — these are used to list the smarticle in the graphical display.

Decision Support System (DSS)

The available smarticles are sorted according to the penalty values they receive from the DSS. This uses a probabilistic user model that represents the user's likes and dislikes of different attributes. *The Guide* considers two kinds of attributes: ordered, where the attribute has a scalar value (e.g. distance); and unordered (e.g. type of food served). Each ordered attribute has an equivalent preference distribution in the DSS which represents how much the user dislikes that attribute. The unordered attributes are dealt with by a single preference distribution representing the user's least favourite unordered attribute.

The penalties are calculated using decision theory and the smarticles with the least penalties (those that best fit the current user model) are placed at the top of the list. The DSS updates the user model using Bayes's theorem each time the user chooses a smarticle to read. This probabilistic user model can quickly adapt to the user's preferences without the user having to provide any feedback other than choosing which smarticle she wants to read.

Graphical display
The Guide has two main displays for presenting information:

- the list of smarticles, presented by an animated representation of the DSS (the *Presentation Agent*)
- and the smarticle the user chooses, presented by the authoring agent.

The Presentation Agent has emotions that reflect the state of the user model. The greater the accuracy of the user model (as measured by the success of the DSS's prediction of the user's choice), the less confused and the more happy it gets. This change in facial expression can be seen in Figure 2.

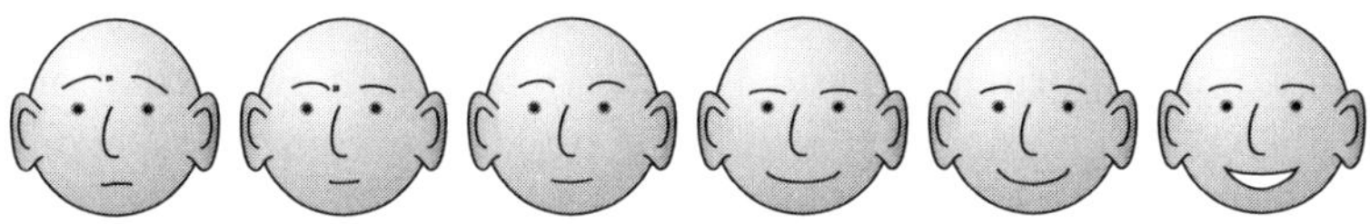

Figure 2. The expressions of the Presentation Agent, from "Hopeless" to "Happy"

Queries

TDV's *Principles of Guidance* (TDV and AT&T 1997) envisions complex natural language queries: if the user says he wants to sell Peril-Sensitive sunglasses, the Guide doesn't look for information about the glasses themselves but for people who would be interested in buying them. This involves the Guide understanding the user's *intention* rather than reducing the user's query to keywords.

However, intentions cannot be observed directly, but can only be inferred and recognised from the syntax, semantics and context of the communication. The system must have a deep knowledge of the world to be able to determine, for example, that Peril-Sensitive sunglasses might be worn by people interested in dangerous sports. It must also have a deep knowledge of language, since the same intention could be expressed in many different ways.

We use a parser developed by the Machine Understanding Group at MIT (Haase 1997) to help solve the second part of this problem. This parser uses the extensive language knowledge represented by *Brico* and is able to draw analogies between sentences.

Domain knowledge

Providing knowledge of the subject (the *domain* knowledge) is a much harder problem. A Guide that could answer questions on Life, the Universe and Everything would need to be able to reason about every possible subject in great detail and such a knowledge base is not available. A Guide that knows a large amount about a particular subject is possible, however, and we therefore limit *The Guide*'s domain to guidance on places to eat and drink.

To allow us to add new domains at a later stage, we designed a structure that could handle information on any subject, based on the Universal Context Model.[1] *The Guide*'s knowledge structure is based on Roger Schank's types (*Events, Places, People* and *Things*) and extends them to five categories of *Events, Entities, Places/Objects, Concepts* and *Relationships*. It also defines particular attributes for each type, including the attributes of *Trust* (the respect given to the source of the information) and *Veracity* (fact, fiction or speculation).

We then define frames within this structure to represent our specific world knowledge. The resulting world knowledge structure can be seen in Figure 3.

Intention analysis

Within a specific domain, people have specific intentions. Mc Kevitt (1991) has categorised several intention types relevant for the consultancy domain. However, *The Guide*'s domain of guidance is slightly different — a consultant is assumed to be telling the truth with respect to achieving some specific task. To

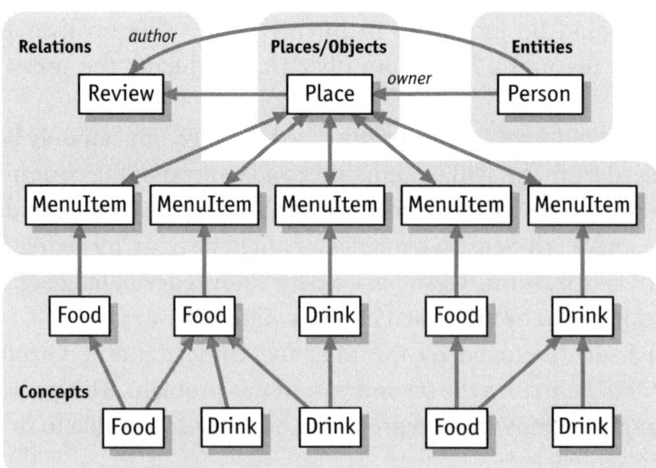

Figure 3. *The Guide*'s knowledge structure

discover some of the intention types in our domain, we conducted an informal survey of three people. We asked them to think of all the questions that they might ask a system that knew everything there was to know about restaurants and pubs. The subjects were familiar with spoken dialogue systems but we asked them to imagine that they were talking to a person.

Our survey did not include a conversational context: the subjects were asked to think of individual questions and were not presented with any answers on which they could follow up. Since our domain was different, we used Mc Kevitt's intention types as guidelines but not solutions. We then grouped the similar questions together and found there to be five main types of intention (Table 1).

Table 1.

Intention	Example
Show a list of places with specific attributes (*ShowListWithAttributes*)	"I want a free-range, organic meal in town."
Give details of a specific attribute at a specific place (*DetailAttribute*)	"What is the corkage price at *La Provence*?"
Give an opinion about a specific subject (*GiveOpinion*)	"What do you know about *Carlsberg Classic*?"
Show a list of places suitable for a specific situation (*ShowListForSituation*)	"I want to take my Grandma to a restaurant she'd like."
Generalisations (*Generalisation*)	"What percentage service do I have to pay in a Danish restaurant?"

Some of the intentions we found are similar to those in Mc Kevitt (1991) but there are significant differences due to the difference in domain. Notably, a guide does not provide a set of actions to achieve a goal, but instead provides opinions on possible actions that the user already knows about.

Because our survey did not include a conversational context, we did not find any discourse-related intentions such as *repetition* (repeated requests) or *elaboration* (requesting more information) (see Mc Kevitt 1991). This was a limitation of our survey and not of *The Guide* — it is designed to be able to notice and act upon sequences of intentions.

Restriction of user input

Initially, we have restricted the intentions that *The Guide* detects to the simpler ones: *ShowListWithAttributes*, *DetailAttribute* and *GiveOpinion*. We then specified the information that each of these intentions should carry by designing frames such the one for a *ShowListWithAttributes* intention (Table 2).

Table 2.

ShowListWithAttributes	
UTTERANCE:	"I want a quiet, French meal and I don't mind driving."
ATTRIBUTES:	quiet, French, drive
USERLOC:	(9.9872632 E, 57.0138211 N, 126.2923482 m)
USERTIME:	3/5/1999 11:23:23.091 am

3. Results

As of now, we have only conducted module and integration tests of *The Guide.* By putting the system together we have achieved the goals we set out in our Proposal of Section 1.

Providing information in a contextual setting: *The Guide* tells stories (albeit simple ones) in response to the user's queries rather than giving a list of unrelated information.
Third party interaction: the user interacts with the system via the presentation agent, delegating the search to the system rather than specifying keywords herself.
Providing personality-based feedback: the state of the system's probabilistic model of the user is conveyed back to the user by an animated humanoid face.

The following paragraphs decribe the operation of *The Guide* as seen in Figure 4:

Screen 1: When *The Guide* is started, the user is presented with a welcome screen. She can then either speak or type her question to the guide.
Screen 2: The Presentation Agent then indicates that the system is busy processing. Meanwhile, *The Guide* attempts to interpret the user's intention using a combination of the MIT parser and word-spotting. If the intention is recognised, *The Guide* builds an intention frame such as the *ShowListWithAttributes* frame on the previous page and passes it to the Storytelling Agents.
Screen 3: Each Storytelling Agent is free to operate in its own way, using all the information in the FramerD database. Once they have generated their smarticles, they pass them back to the user via the DSS. The DSS sorts the smarticles according to its probabilistic user model and indicates its current state using the Presentation Agent.

Screen 4: The user can choose either to read one of the smarticles or to cancel her question. Choosing one of the smarticles results in a graphical representation of the authoring Storytelling Agent presenting the chosen smarticle. The DSS then updates its user model to reflect the new information provided by the user's question and her choice of smarticle. At this point, the user can cancel and go back to the list of smarticles, ask another question straight away or use the pointer to indicate that she wants to ask another question.

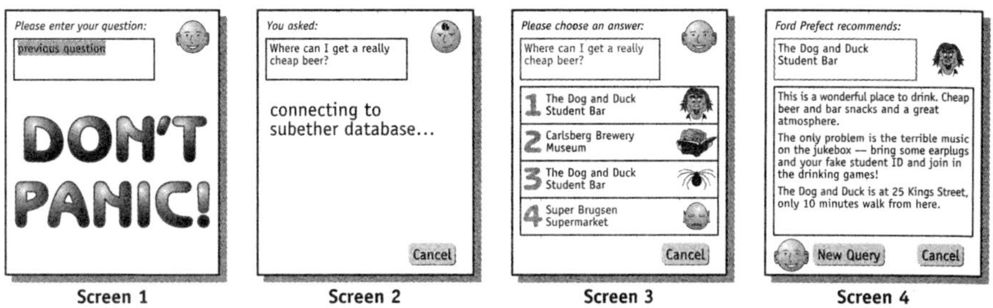

Figure 4. *The Guide*: what the user sees

4. Conclusion

Compared to many of the large research projects in the field of Intelligent MultiMedia, *The Guide* is a simple prototype. However, as Schank (1990) points out, "a computer that had thousands or hundreds of stories and carefully selected which ones to tell might well be considered to be not only intelligent but wise" (p.15). By using intention analysis and a probabilistic user model, *The Guide* can easily select relevant stories and only seems to lack a large collection of stories to be considered wise.

Possible future developments could include improving the storytelling capabilities of *The Guide*, perhaps by using a tailored version of the Dada engine to write believable reviews, or by using artificial life -based Storytelling Agents to provide a greater level of personalisation. The interface could be further personalised to the users by analysing the *sequence* of their intentions as well the intentions themselves.

Though there are many successful projects that provide guidance over limited domains, a Guide to Life, the Universe and Everything is still in the realm of science fiction. Fortunately, *The Guide* has the words DON'T PANIC inscribed in large friendly letters on its cover.

Acknowledgements

Richard Harris, Technical Director of *The Digital Village*, for providing us with the Universal Context Model and Principles of Guidance documents.

Prof. Ken Haase of the Machine Understanding Group at the MIT Media Lab for his help in compiling FramerD and for allowing us to use his unpublished parser software.

We would also like to thank our supervisor, Dr. Paul Mc Kevitt, for his invaluable advice, and Ruth Cohen-Rose, Adam's wife, for her support.

Note

1. © 1998 Richard Harris, TDV.

References

Adams, D. (1979). *The Hitchhiker's Guide to the Galaxy.* London: Barker.

Apple Computer (1992, May) Knowledge navigator. In B.A. Myers (ed.), *Conference on Human Factors in Computing Systems: Special Video Program*, Monterey, CA. ACM/SIGCHI.

Bulhak, A. C. 1996. On the simulation of postmodernism and mental debility using recursive transition networks. Technical Report 96/264, Dept Computer Science, Monash Univ., Melbourne, Australia.

Cycorp (1999, Apr). CYC ontology. http://www.cyc.com.

Haase, K. (1996). FramerD: Representing knowledge in the large. *IBM System Journal 35*, 381–397.

Haase, K. (1997, October). Chopper, an unprincipled parser. Kindly provided by Prof. Haase.

Maes, P. (1994, July). Agents that reduce work and information overload. *Communications of the ACM 37*(7), 31–40.

Mc Kevitt, P. (1991) *Analysing coherence of intention in natural language dialogue.* Ph. D. thesis, Department of Computer Science, University of Exeter, England.

Moukas, A. (1996). Amalthaea: Information discovery and filtering using a multiagent evolving ecosystem. In *Proceedings of the Conference on Practical Application of Intelligent Agents and Multi-Agent Technology*, London.

Schank, R. (1990). *Tell Me A Story: a new look at real and artificial memory.* Charles Scribner's Sons.

Schank, R. and R. Abelson (1977). *Scripts, Plans, Goals and Understanding.* Hillsdale, NJ: Lawrence Erlbaum Associates, Inc.

TDV and AT&T (1997, August). Principles of guidance. Commercial-in-confidence.

Tosa, N. (1993). Neurobaby. In *SIGGRAPH-93 Visual Proceedings. Tomorrow's Realities*, pp. 212–213. ACM SIGGRAPH.

Affective multimodal interaction with a 3D agent

Tom Brøndsted, Thomas Dorf Nielsen, Sergio Ortega
Aalborg University, Denmark

1. Introduction

The exchange of affect/emotions is continuous in human-human interaction and plays a key role in decision making. We propose a similar paradigm for human-computer interaction and describe a novel method for classifying a user's input to a computer system for some very basic emotional attitudes. The paradigm is based on multiple communication channels including not only traditional media (eye tracker, gesture recognition, conventional "speech to text" recognition) but also on signals communicated through extra-linguistic (or "non-textual") features of the oral mode (prosodic analysis). A strategy for fusion of concordant input is described, as we believe that affect is communicated through many channels simultaneously. Our experimental environment centres on an autonomous simpleminded dog-like 3D agent called Bouncy. Our evaluation of the agent-paradigm furnishes good grounds for believing that the proposed fusion strategy can be used also for revealing very complex attitudes like irony and certain kinds of humour realised as a contradiction between input channels (e.g. between what the user says and how he says it).

In normal communication between humans, the exchange of affect/emotions is continuous and plays a key role in decision making. Today's communication with computers is (mostly) affect impaired. Computers do not "care" whether the user is excited, sad or bored. However, as suggested in (Picard 1997) we can think of a computer recognising and expressing affect in terms of e.g. a tutor reacting to the user's emotional attitudes by individualising the teaching strategy or a robot "having" emotions enabling it to deal more effectively with the complex demands and uncertainty of its environment.

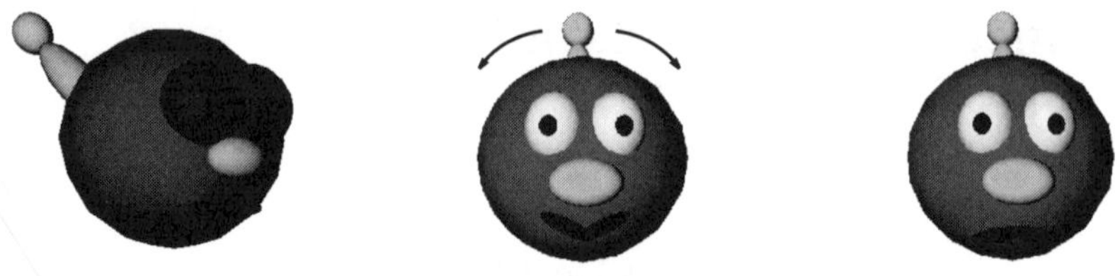

Figure 1. Bouncy sleeping, teasing and having the blues

For humans to relate to an agent, it should have a (virtual) spatial body, as Silas T. Dog (Blumberg and Galyean 1995) or *Swamped!* from the MIT media lab (Johnson et al. 1999). Both place a great emphasis on expressing affect but less on recognising it. The Bouncy agent (Pirjanian 1998, Pirjanian et al. 1998) was developed at the Laboratory of Image Analysis at Aalborg University. Bouncy has several behaviours and an expressive face (Figure 1) which enable him to communicate affect to the user. The enhancement of the Bouncy environment described in this paper includes a paradigm for recognising affect from multiple communication channels.

A novel approach is proposed to fuse the inputs obtained from a concordant environment, that is an environment where all inputs are used to provide estimates in the same dimension, namely estimating the user's emotion. Each input is assigned a negative/neutral/positive distribution complying with some basic human emotional attitudes (scolding, not addressing, praising). Three traditional media are used in the enhanced Bouncy paradigm: A head (eye) tracker device, a gesture recognition device & a speech recogniser. Further, two devices classifying the oral input based on an analysis of pitch contours and rate of speech have been added. Also the prosodic classification represents (at least to our knowledge) a novel approach to affective interaction and to recognition of emotional attitudes in speech.

Bouncy's world is a plane with only three walls to avoid loss of time running around corners. To provoke affective interaction between Bouncy and the user, Bouncy's world has good (healthy) food and bad (unhealthy) food. Bouncy has a naughtiness value that is influenced by the recognition of the user's inputs. When Bouncy feels naughty, he starts eating bad food (if hungry) or moving away from the user (if in an interacting state). Otherwise he will eat good food or stay with the user.

The Bouncy agent still has to be evaluated systematically. We plan an experimental set-up, where users are provided with different tasks such as preventing Bouncy from eating bad food (tasty, but unhealthy candy). This introduces a "conflict of interests" between the user and Bouncy. In this way we hope to be able to evaluate if and to which extent affective interaction has taken place following the guidelines from (Picard 1997). Further, we expect to be able to evaluate the reliability and usability of each device included in the system. Some first results are reported in Section 6.

2. The enhanced Bouncy paradigm

The enhanced Bouncy paradigm is based on a general blackboard architecture and a control panel for manipulating/simulating input and monitoring the system's state and behaviour. A blackboard organises all the inputs that it gets from the devices and makes them available to whichever modules might need them. Due to the fusion strategy described in Section 5, inputs are passed to a fusing module in a way that can be monitored via the control module (Figure 2).

As shown in Figure 2, the system currently employs five devices: *HEAD*: Head tracking (actually pseudo eye tracking) device determining if the user is looking at Bouncy or not; *GESTURE*: Data glove device enabling Bouncy to understand a limited number of hand signs like lifted finger, fist; *STT*: Conventional "Speech-To-Text" recogniser enabling Bouncy to understand a limited number of command-like phrases; *ROS*: A Rate of Speech estimator; *PITCH*: A pitch contour analyser.

In this paper, we concentrate on the latter two devices that represent a more novel approach to classification of emotional speech (Section 3). Bouncy's internal states and parameters can be monitored and manipulated via the

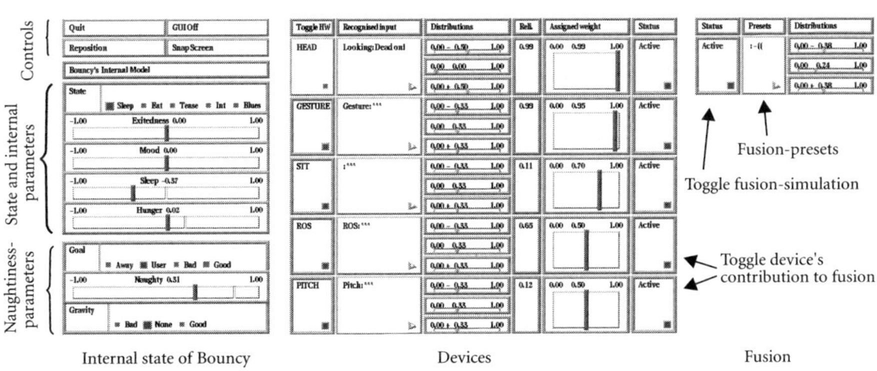

Figure 2. The control panel

control panel. Bouncy reacts due to internal preferences of his own, his "naughtiness-parameters" (Section 4) and to the fused input from the five devices (Section 5).

For further details on the enhanced Bouncy paradigm, refer to (Ortega and Nielsen 1999).

3. Emotional speech

Emotional speech has so far mostly been studied in the context of speech synthesis and/or human perception. The analysis is in most cases based on speech databases where professional actors pronounce semantically neutral sentences with certain intended emotions. A typical emotional speech database is reported in (Engberg et al. 1997). Most studies concentrate on between four and seven different emotions, e.g. neutrality, happiness, anger, sadness in (Carlson et al. 1992) and in (Montero et al. 1998), neutrality, surprise, happiness, anger, sadness in (Engberg et al. 1997), happiness, hot anger, cold anger, sadness in (Pereira and Watson 1998), neutrality, joy, boredom, anger, sadness, fear, indignation in (Mozziconacci 1998). The typical acoustic-phonetic correlates to emotions being discussed are pitch (intonation patterns), speech rate, rhythm, loudness, voice quality, intensity (root mean square). Currently, mainly pitch and speech rate are in focus. This is due to the fact that time/pitch scaling can easily be controlled in modern concatenative (diphone based) speech synthesis systems (Mozziconacci 1998: 15). Hence, the research normally focuses on finding optimal pitch and speech rate parameters for synthesising angry speech, happy speech etc.

Though these studies dealing with synthesis and human perception are of limited relevance to our task, we find that they furnish good grounds for believing that pitch and speech rate constitute useful parameters also for revealing basic emotional attitudes of humans when communicating with a pet-like agent.

Rate of speech

It is, in our opinion, doubtful whether the disapproval and approval attitudes in pet-directed speech can be associated directly with the anger and joy emotions discussed in the literature referenced above. Anger may in normal human-directed speech have varying rate of speech (henceforth ROS) correlates (fast or slow), but it is possible that speakers have a more consistent way of scolding their pets. Intuitively, we feel that "fast" ("hot anger") is a more useful feature for disapproval than "extreme". Further, the characteristic use of prolonged vowels in the approval attitude — in a cartoon-like notation: "Goooood boy!" — hardly ever occurs in the speech databases discussed in literature. Such long vowels could indicate that the ROS feature of approval is "slow" rather than "fast" or at least that such vowels could be an independent feature to look for.

A full phonemic segmentation and labelling of a speech signal can easily be extracted by a standard speech recogniser based on Hidden Markov Models modelling phonemes, diphones or triphones. However, to improve flexibility, a ROS estimation device based on a variable frame rate technique have been developed. In speech recognition, variable frame rates have been used as an alternative to standard fixed frame rates of typically 10 ms. The approach, described in e.g. (Flammia et al. 1992), aims at segmenting the speech into stable frames of variable length to be passed on to traditional acoustic matching using Hidden Markov Models. The approach presented here is based on the idea that the segmentation carried out in the preprocessor of such a recogniser results in phone-like units that can be used for ROS estimation. The main reason for using phone based ROS estimation in Bouncy is it's suitability for capturing prolonged vowels. Other units that can be considered relevant for ROS estimation (stress groups, syllables) are discussed in (Brøndsted et al. 2000).

The ROS estimation device developed for the Bouncy application consists of: (i) An acoustic analysis based on the program mfcc by (Huckvale 1997). The module processes the speech signal through a mel-scaled filterbank into 16th order mel-scaled cepstral coefficients. The result of this analysis is a feature vector for every 10 ms of the speech signal. (ii) A segmentation analysis calculating the Euclidean distance between the current feature vector and the feature vector at the start of the current segment. Whenever the distance exceeds a certain empirically defined threshold, the current feature vector is set to be the start vector of a new segment. The result of this analysis is a segmentation of the speech signal into stable regions with only small spectral variations. (iii) A heuristic based analysis of the derived segments resulting in a classification of the emotional attitude. The analysis only takes voiced segments larger than a certain threshold into account and calculates the standard deviation of this threshold. A great deviation is interpreted as an positive approval attitude ("goood boy, Bouncy") and a small deviation as a non-positive (neutral or negative) attitude. For further details, refer to (Brøndsted et al. 2000).

Pitch analysis

The relation between pitch level and protesting/scolding attitudes is indicated in expressions like "raise one's voice" (Danish "løfte stemmen", German "die Stimme erheben", French "élever la voix", etc.). (Mozziconacci 1998) shows that anger by speakers is expressed with a significantly higher mean pitch than neutrality: Unfortunately, the same is true for joy (p. 58). (Pereira and Watson 1998) have a high pitch for "hot anger" and "happiness" and a medium pitch for "neutrality" and "cold anger". However, we believe that these studies are dealing with speech samples where actors pretend to be "beside themselves" with "joy" (e.g. having won the lottery!). A speaker praising a dog will probably produce more "neutral" pitch level characteristics. Nevertheless, pitch level is difficult to apply in the Bouncy application where (in terms of the classical two level component intonation model) the "floor" and "ceiling" of the speaker is unknown. (Mozziconacci 1998), (Pereira and Watson 1998) and similar studies substitute pitch level with mean pitch. This makes sense only in a situation where utterances spoken by the same speaker with different intended emotions are compared.

Pitch range, or more precisely the declining top- and baseline on which pitch range depends (Brøndsted et al. 2000), is difficult two determine in natural speech. Hence, studies on emotional speech often substitute pitch range with the standard deviation of the mean pitch (henceforth SDPITCH). Further, SDPITCH is more expressive than pitch range because it gives you an idea of the variability of the F0-distribution. The analysis in (Mozziconacci 1998 shows a tendency towards a slightly higher SDPITCH in angry speech than in happy speech and, in both cases, a significantly greater deviation than in neutral speech (p. 58). (Pereira and Watson 1998) have a high pitch range for "hot anger", "cold anger", and "happiness". Again, presupposing that praising pet-directed speech has more neutral pitch characteristics than the joy/happiness emotion discussed in the literature, we find that the SDPITCH is the most promising parameter to be used in Bouncy. Unlike mean pitch (as substitute for pitch level), SDPITCH (as substitute for pitch range) is independent of sex and age (child, female adult, male adult). For further discussion, refer to (Brøndsted et al. 2000).

The SDPITCH estimation device developed for the Bouncy application consists of (i) A fundamental frequency estimation by cepstral analysis based on the program fxcep by (Huckvale et al. 1997). A 512 point FFT is performed on round 40 ms windows of the input speech to find the log spectrum, and then an FFT of that provides the cepstrum. Then the Noll rules are implemented to decide whether the input is voiced or unvoiced, and if voiced, a fundamental frequency value is determined. The result of this analysis is an F0 estimate for every 10 ms time frame of the speech signal (0 if the frame is unvoiced). (ii) A module continuously calculating the standard deviation based on the F0s from the start of the utterance to the current frame. An empirically defined threshold classifies the speech into two categories: (1) A disapproval attitude, (2) a non-disapproval (approval or neutral) attitude. For further details, refer to (Brøndsted et al. 2000).

4. The naughty approach

In the enhanced Bouncy paradigm, the naughtiness is a new concept reflecting the agent's willingness to react appropriately to the user's input. Naughtiness has an impact on which places Bouncy is going to in his virtual world. When Bouncy is nice, he goes to the good food (if in the hungry state)or approaches the user when called. When he is naughty, he goes to the bad food or away from the user. The naughtiness is updated proportionally to the largest negative/ neutral/positive value from the fusion distribution (see Section 5). The naughtiness updating algorithm is shown in Figure 3.

When the naughtiness is in an outer region, Bouncy is either naughty or nice. In the middle region, Bouncy has just left one of the outer regions due to the user's scolding him. In that case, Bouncy tends to approach one of the two outer regions. For instance, if Bouncy is in the middle region and has just been

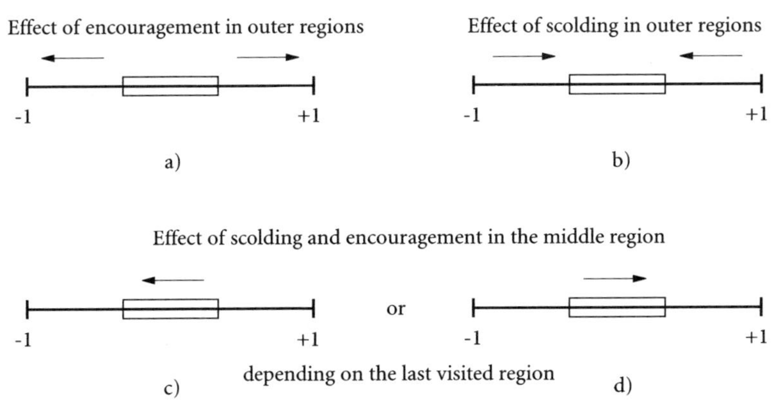

Figure 3. The effects of scolding and encouragement on naughtiness value

eating bad food, he now wants the good food due to the user having scolded him and the naughtiness having left the "bad end". In the middle region of the naughtiness-interval where Bouncy is changing his mind, he becomes "semi-deaf": He perceives the user's input, but does not pay attention to whether he is being scolded or encouraged. This implies that the user can both agree and disagree with what Bouncy is doing.

The naughty approach implies that Bouncy is not just trying to please the user. We have further provided him a preference of his own (to be a bad or good dog) by applying a "gravity" to the naughtiness: depending on the gravity settings, naughtiness slowly moves to good or bad even if the user gives him no input.

5. Fusing concordant input

The enhanced Bouncy paradigm involves a novel fusion strategy for dealing with concordant input-modalities. The SDPITCH and ROS input devices reported above are together with the other input-modes concordant in the sense that they provide estimates on the same thing, namely the user's emotional attitude. This situation is different from a multimodal dialogue application such as the IntelliMedia Workbench (Brøndsted et al. 1998) combining speech and pointing gestures as complementary media (where e.g. deictic demonstratives like "this" and "that" are accompanied by pointing). Our fusion-technique may even have the potential of revealing very complex emotional attitudes like irony and certain kinds of humour realised as a contradiction between what is said and how it is said (prosody) or certain signals communicated with eyes (upturned eyes) or fingers (crossed fingers).

However, the actual fusion module implemented in the enhanced Bouncy paradigm has to face the harsh fact that contradicting input is more likely to be due to erroneous classifications than to irony, humour etc. Both SDPITCH and ROS are uncertain devices based on digital signal processing techniques that are not 100% robust. Nor is the speech-to-text device 100% reliable, though the recognition process is constrained by a low-perplexity grammar network (Bouncy understands a limited number of command-like phrases like "come, Bouncy!", "bad boy, Bouncy!" etc.). Most notably, it is not possible to address the oral devices of the system in a manner that is optimal for all of them. Conventional speech recognition presupposes a controlled speech mode that contradicts with the spontaneous mode presupposed by SDPITCH and

ROS. Finally, Bouncy has been designed as a simpleminded dog-like 3D agent. Though we are no experts in animal psychology, we don't think dogs can perceive irony and humour! An approach introducing a confused state in Bouncy's personality dealing with contradicting input was given up in favour of the approach described below. The real problem in the system is the uncertainty of the oral input channel.

In our fusion approach, a "negative/neutral/positive"-distribution is assigned to all possible inputs from each device (Figure 2). The distributions are used in the calculation of the media fusion together with a weight denoting the extent to which the system should "believe" in the distribution. The formula for fusing the separate distributions and weights into a single and "global" distribution is shown in Figure 4, where all active devices *ad* contribute with their negative/neutral/positive parts; the result is normalised. This resolves any conflict between the devices. For further discussion of the fusing method, refer to (Ortega and Nielsen 1999).

In this environment, SDPITCH always returns the same "probability" for the approval and neutral attitude. The sum of these two probabilities is inversely proportional to the probability set for the approval attitude and calculated from the standard deviation of mean pitch. Also the "reliability" of SDPITCH is calculated by the device itself and estimated against the standard deviation. For instance, the higher the standard deviation the higher the estimation of the device that the emotional attitude is negative (not neutral and not positive) and that the system should "believe" in this estimation.

Similarly, ROS sets the same probability for the disapproval and the neural attitude. The higher the standard deviation of the short-threshold the higher the estimation that the emotional attitude is positive (not neutral and not negative) and that the system should "believe" in this estimation.

The control panel described in Section 2 allows direct manipulation of the fusion mechanism. Uncertain devices can be disabled or simulated manually. This panel eases the work with integrating and optimising new devices.

$$\begin{bmatrix} \text{fusion}_{neg} \\ \text{fusion}_{neu} \\ \text{fusion}_{pos} \end{bmatrix} = \left\| \begin{bmatrix} \sum_{ad} \text{device}_{ad_{neg}} * \text{weight}_{ad} \\ \sum_{ad} \text{device}_{ad_{neu}} * \text{weight}_{ad} \\ \sum_{ad} \text{device}_{ad_{pos}} * \text{weight}_{ad} \end{bmatrix} \right\|$$

Figure 4. Calculation of the fusion-distribution

6. Results

A user test was performed to evaluate whether the fusion method and the prosodic analysis techniques proposed in this paper enable a computer system to estimate a user's affective state thus giving affective communication. Each user was given the task to keep Bouncy away from the bad food and only let him eat from the good food. The users were then interviewed about their views on various aspects of the interaction and the system as a whole. Due to time constraints tests with a large volume of users still have to be carried out. However, the interviews provide indicators to future investigations.

In general the users succeeded in making Bouncy obey. They felt that it was possible to make Bouncy understand when they were encouraging or scolding him, and that Bouncy responded correspondingly. The user tests revealed a problem with seeing/interpreting Bouncy's facial expression when he was moving around and was far away from the user: In our setup, the user was "inside" Bouncy's world which made automatic camera-movement (as in *Swamped!* (Johnson et al. 1999)) less useful. Bouncy interacts with the user whereas the agents in *Swamped!* interact with each other.

The entire system was implemented and run on a single Silicon Graphics O_2, experiencing no speed problems. However, to implement a more immediate ROS and pitch estimation it would be necessary to use additional hardware, as the speech-to-text system did not allow other modules to use sound input on the same machine. As developers we found that a mechanism such as the control panel that allows online tracking and manipulation of the internal values in the agents is indispensable when developing autonomous agents.

7. Conclusion

In general, the approach has proven its feasibility. The user test proved it possible to use the proposed fusion-method to estimate the user's affective state from a number of multimodal inputs. The users enjoyed very much keeping an eye on Bouncy, trying to keep him away from the bad food. We also conclude that the prosodic analysis of speech is a valuable addition to traditional speech-to-text systems. The prosodic estimations tended to be more stable in case of more exaggerated speech input (in which case speech-to-text systems typically fail).

The estimation techniques presented in this paper still need some improvement. The prosodic modules can be optimised and other phonetic features revealing emotional attitudes (pause structure, intensity) can be taken into account. Systematic tests with large numbers of users will also provide a better understanding of the affective interaction and how it should be modelled. The decoding algorithms used in current speech technology (e.g. Viterbi or similar) imply that the text string being recognised can only be made accessible in speech pauses or after larger delays (using trace back). This collides with the request for immediate response when e.g. scolding. The prosodic devices are capable of — and should be used for — taking and giving continuous input/output. Also Bouncy should be equipped with learning abilities in order to make him able to adapt to a user. Some ability to calibrate his own internal parameters could also be considered. Finally, Bouncy is envisioned as a tool-like agent where he can put his emotion-recognising abilities to use for performing a task for or with a user. Hence, a natural follow-up to our approach would be to use Bouncy in some application.

Acknowledgments

We acknowledge Prof. Paul Mc Kevitt for his advice and extensive comments on this paper. We thank Flemming Fink of the Study Board of electrical engineering at Aalborg University who funded our participation at the CSNLP-8 conference. We thank Bosch Telecom Danmark A/S for supplying both equipment and funding for this project and finally we thank InterMedia Aalborg who provided the equipment on which Bouncy is running. Also we thank Det Obelske Familiefond for funding.

References

Blumberg, B. M. & T. A. Galyean (1995). Multi-level direction of autonomous creatures for real-time virtual environments. In *Proceedings of SIGGRAPH 95*, pages 47–54. Addison Wesley. ISBN 0–201–84776–0.

Brøndsted, T., P. Dalsgaard, L. B. Larsen, M. Manthey, P. Mc Kevitt, T. Moeslund, K. Olesen (1998). *A platform for developing intelligent multimedia applications.* Technical Report R-98–1004, Aalborg University.

Brøndsted, T., T. D. Nielsen, S. Ortega (2000). Classification of emotional attitudes in pet-directed speech. In *CST Working Papers no. 3*, Centre for Language Technology, Copenhagen, ISSN 1600–339X.

Carlson, R., B. Granstrøm, L. Nord (1992). Experiments with emotive speech: acted utterances and synthesized replicas. In *Proceedings ICSLP*, Volume 1, pages 671–674, BanV. http://www.speech.kth.se/info/emot.html.

Engberg, I., A. Hansen, O. Andersen, P. Dalsgaard (1997). Design, recording and verification of a danish emotional speech database. In *Eurospeech*, Rhodes.

Flammia, G., P. Dalsgaard, O. Andersen, B. Lindberg (1992). Segment based variable frame rate speech analysis and recognition using spectral variation function. In *Proceedings ICSLP*, Volume 1, pages 671–674, BanV.

Huckvale, M. (1997). *The Speech Filing System V 3.0 (mfcc)*. University College London. ftp://pitch.phon.ucl.ac.uk/pub/sfs.

Huckvale, M., L. Whitaker, D. Howard (1997). *The Speech Filing System V 3.0 (fxcep)*. University College London. ftp://pitch.phon.ucl.ac.uk/pub/sfs.

Johnson, M. P., A. Wilson, C. Kline, B. Blumberg, A. Bobick, (1999). Using a plush toy to direct synthetic characters. In *Conference on Human Factors in Computing Systems*, Pittsburgh, Pennsylvania, USA. ACM SIGCHI. http://lcs.www.media.mit. edu/groups/characters/swamped/.

Montero, J., J. Palazuelos, E. Enriques, S. Aguilera, J. Pardo (1998). Emotional speech synthesis: From speech database to tts. In *Proceedings ICSLP*, Volume 3, pages 923–926, Sydney.

Mozziconacci, S. (1998). *Speech Variability and Emotion, Production and Perception*. Eindhoven.

Ortega, S. & T. D. Nielsen (1999). Affective multimodal interaction with a 3D agent. Master's thesis, Intelligent MultiMedia, Aalborg University.

Pereira, C. & C. Watson (1998). Some acoustic characteristics of emotion. In *Proceedings ICSLP*, Volume 3, pages 927–930, Sydney.

Picard, R. W. (1997). *Affective Computing*. MIT Press.

Pirjanian, P. (1998). Behavior-based control of an interactive life-like character. http://www.vision.auc.dk/~paolo/staging/bouncy/html2/all.html.

Pirjanian, P., C. Madsen, E. Granum (1998). Bouncy: An interactive life-like pet. http://www.vision.auc.dk/~paolo/staging/bouncy/html/all.html.

CHAMELEON

A general platform for performing intellimedia

Tom Brøndsted, Paul Dalsgaard, Lars Bo Larsen,
Michael Manthey, Paul Mc Kevitt, Thomas B. Moeslund
and Kristian G. Olesen
Aalborg University, Denmark

1. Introduction

IntelliMedia, which involves the computer processing and understanding of perceptual input from at least speech, text and visual images, and then reacting to it, is complex and involves signal and symbol processing techniques from not just engineering and computer science but also artificial intelligence and cognitive science (Mc Kevitt 1994, 1995/96, 1997). With IntelliMedia systems, people can interact in spoken dialogues with machines, querying about what is being presented and even their gestures and body language can be interpreted.

People are able to combine the processing of language and vision with apparent ease. In particular, people can use words to describe a picture, and can reproduce a picture from a language description. Moreover, people can exhibit this kind of behaviour over a very wide range of input pictures and language descriptions. Although there are theories of how we process vision and language, there are few theories about how such processing is integrated. There have been large debates in Psychology and Philosophy with respect to the degree to which people store knowledge as propositions or pictures (Kosslyn and Pomerantz 1977, Pylyshyn 1973). Other recent moves towards integration are reported in Denis and Carfantan (1993), Mc Kevitt (1994, 1995/96) and Pentland (1993).

The Institute for Electronic Systems at Aalborg University, Denmark has expertise in the area of IntelliMedia and has established an initiative called IntelliMedia 2000+ funded by the Faculty of Science and Technology. IntelliMedia 2000+ coordinates research on the production of a number of real-time demonstrators exhibiting examples of IntelliMedia applications, a Master's degree in IntelliMedia, and a nation-wide MultiMedia Network (MMN) concerned with technology transfer to industry. A number of student projects related to IntelliMedia 2000+ have been completed and a number of student groups are enrolled in the Master's conducting projects on multimodal interfaces, billard game trainer, virtual steering wheel, audio-visual speech recognition, and face recognition. IntelliMedia 2000+ is coordinated from the Center for PersonKommunikation (CPK) which has a wealth of experience and expertise in spoken language processing, one of the central components of IntelliMedia, but also radio communications which would be useful for mobile applications (CPK Annual Report, 2001). IntelliMedia 2000+ involves four research groups from three Departments within the Institute for Electronic Systems: Computer Science (CS), Medical Informatics (MI), Laboratory of Image Analysis (LIA) and Center for PersonKommunikation (CPK), focusing on platforms for integration and learning, expert systems and decision taking, image/vision processing, and spoken language processing/sound localisation respectively. The first two groups provide a strong basis for methods of integrating semantics and conducting learning and decision taking while the latter groups focus on the two main input/output components of IntelliMedia, vision and speech/sound.

2. CHAMELEON and the IntelliMedia WorkBench

IntelliMedia 2000+ has developed the first prototype of an IntelliMedia software and hardware platform called CHAMELEON which is general enough to be used for a number of different applications. CHAMELEON demonstrates that existing software modules for (1) distributed processing and learning, (2) decision taking, (3) image processing, and (4) spoken dialogue processing can be interfaced to a single platform and act as communicating agent modules within it. CHAMELEON is independent of any particular application domain and the various modules can be distributed over different machines. Most of the modules are programmed in C++ and C. More details on CHAMELEON and the IntelliMedia WorkBench can be found in Brøndsted et al. (1998).

IntelliMedia WorkBench

An initial application of CHAMELEON is the *IntelliMedia WorkBench* which is a hardware and software platform as shown in Figure 1. One or more cameras and lasers can be mounted in the ceiling, microphone array placed on the wall and there is a table where things (objects, gadgets, people, pictures, 2D/3D models, building plans, or whatever) can be placed. The current domain is a *Campus Information System* which at present gives information on the architectural and functional layout of a building. 2-dimensional (2D) architectural plans of the building drawn on white paper are laid on the table and the user can ask questions about them. The plans represent two floors of the 'A' (A2) building at Fredrik Bajers Vej 7, Aalborg University.

Presently, there is one static camera which calibrates the plans on the table and the laser, and interprets the user's pointing while the system points to locations and draws routes with a laser. Inputs are simultaneous speech and/or pointing gestures and outputs are synchronised speech synthesis and pointing. We currently run all of CHAMELEON on a standard pentium PC which handles input for the Campus Information System in real-time.

The 2D plan, which is placed on the table, is printed out on A0 paper having the dimensions: 84x118cm. Due to the size of the pointer's tip (2x1cm), the size of the table, the resolution of the camera and uncertainty in the tracking algorithm, a size limitation is introduced. The smallest room in the 2D plan, which is a standard office, can not be less than 3cm wide. The size of a standard office on the printout is 3x4cm which is a feasible size for the system. The 2D plan is shown in Figure 2.

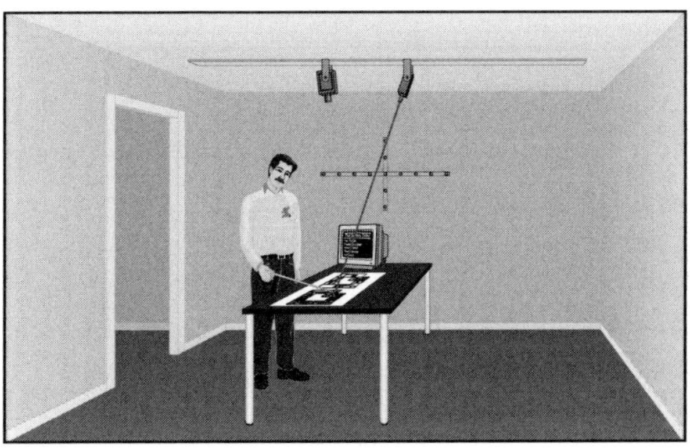

Figure 1. Physical layout of the IntelliMedia WorkBench

Sample interaction dialogue

We present here a sample dialogue which the current first prototype can process. The example includes user intentions which are instructions and queries, and exophoric/deictic reference.

USER: Show me Tom's office.
CHAMELEON: [points]
This is Tom's office.
USER: Point to Thomas' office.
CHAMELEON: [points] This is Thomas' office.
USER: Where is the computer room?
CHAMELEON: [points] The computer room is here.
USER: [points to instrument repair] Whose office is this?
CHAMELEON: [points] This is not an office, this is instrument repair.
USER: [points] Whose office is this?
CHAMELEON: [points] This is Paul's office.
USER: Show me the route from Lars Bo Larsen's office to Hanne Gade's office.
CHAMELEON: [draws route] This is the route from Lars Bo's office to Hanne's office.
USER: Show me the route from Paul Mc Kevitt's office to instrument repair.
CHAMELEON: [draws route] This is the route from Paul's office to instrument repair.
USER: Show me Paul's office.
CHAMELEON: [points] This is Paul's office.

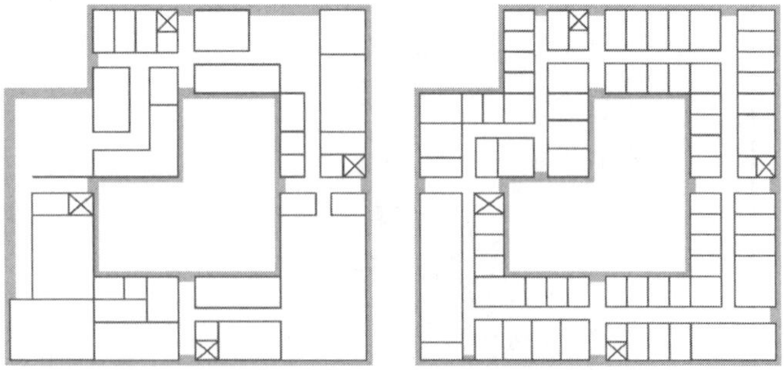

Figure 2. 2D plan of the 'A' building at Fredrik Bajers Vej 7, Aalborg University. Left: ground floor; Right: 1st floor.

Architecture of CHAMELEON

CHAMELEON has a distributed architecture of communicating agent modules processing inputs and outputs from different modalities and each of which can be tailored to a number of application domains. The process synchronisation and intercommunication for CHAMELEON modules is performed using the DACS (Distributed Applications Communication System) Inter Process Communication (IPC) software (see Fink et al. 1996) which enables CHAMELEON modules to be glued together and distributed across a number of servers. Presently, there are ten software modules in CHAMELEON: blackboard, dialogue manager, domain model, gesture recogniser, laser system, microphone array, speech recogniser, speech synthesiser, natural language processor (NLP), and Topsy as shown in Figure 3. Information flow and module communication within CHAMELEON are shown in Figures 4 and 5. Note that Figure 4 does not show the blackboard as a part of the communication but rather the abstract flow of information between modules. Figure 5 shows the actual passing of information between the speech recogniser, NLP module, and dialogue manager. As is shown all information exchange between individual modules is carried out using the blackboard as mediator.

As the intention is that no direct interaction between modules need take place the architecture is modularised and open but there are possible performance costs. However, nothing prohibits direct communication between two

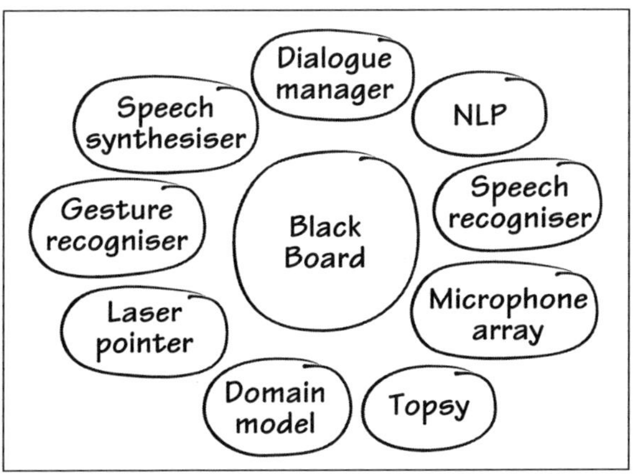

Figure 3. Architecture of CHAMELEON

or more modules if this is found to be more convenient. For example, the speech recogniser and NLP modules can interact directly as the parser needs every recognition result anyway and at present no other module has use for output from the speech recogniser. The blackboard and dialogue manager form the kernel of CHAMELEON. We shall now give a brief description of each module.

The **blackboard** stores semantic representations produced by each of the other modules and keeps a history of these over the course of an interaction. All modules communicate through the exchange of semantic representations with each other or the blackboard. Semantic representations are frames in the spirit of Minsky (1975) and our frame semantics consists of (1) input, (2) output, and (3) integration frames for representing the meaning of intended user input and system output. The intention is that all modules in the system will produce and read frames. Frames are coded in CHAMELEON as messages built of predicate-argument structures following the BNF definition given in Appendix A. The frame semantics was presented in Mc Kevitt and Dalsgaard (1997) and for the sample dialogue given in Section 2. CHAMELEON's actual blackboard history in terms of frames (messages) is shown in Appendix B.

The **dialogue manager** makes decisions about which actions to take and accordingly sends commands to the output modules (laser and speech synthesiser) via the blackboard. At present the functionality of the dialogue manager is to integrate and react to information coming in from the speech/NLP and gesture modules and to sending synchronised commands to the laser system and the speech synthesiser modules. Phenomena such as managing clarification subdialogues where CHAMELEON has to ask questions are not included at present. It is hoped that in future prototypes the dialogue manager will enact more complex decision taking over semantic representations from the blackboard using, for example, the HUGIN software tool (Jensen, F. 1996) based on Bayesian Networks (Jensen, F.V. 1996).

The **domain model** contains a database of all locations and their functionality, tenants and coordinates. The model is organised in a hierarchical structure: areas, buildings and rooms. Rooms are described by an identifier for the room (room number) and the type of the room (office, corridor, toilet, etc.). The model includes functions that return information about a room or a person. Possible inputs are coordinates or room number for rooms and name for persons, but in principle any attribute can be used as key and any other attribute can be returned. Furthermore, a path planner is provided, calculating the shortest route between two locations.

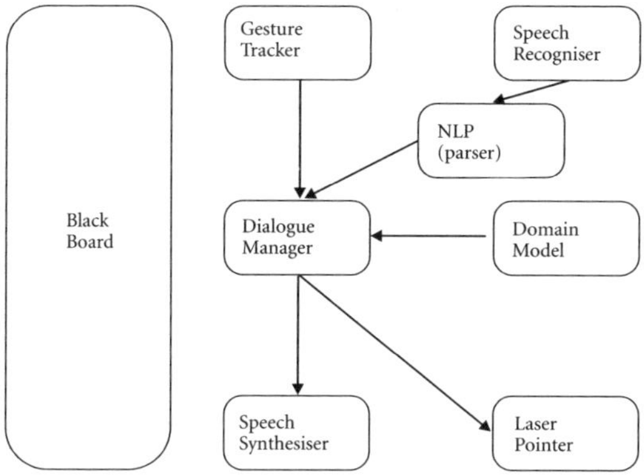

Figure 4. Information flow and module communication

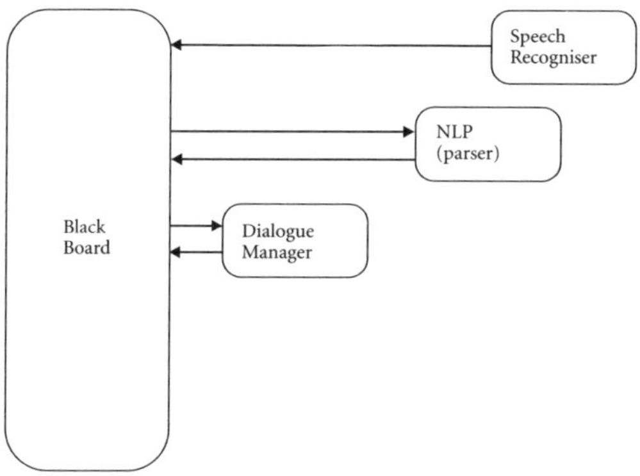

Figure 5. Information flow with the blackboard

A design principle of imposing as few physical constraints as possible on the user (e.g. data gloves or touch screens) leads to the inclusion of a vision based **gesture recogniser**. Currently, it tracks a pointer via a camera mounted in the ceiling. Using one camera, the gesture recogniser is able to track 2D pointing gestures in real time. Only two gestures are recognised at present: pointing and not-pointing. The recognition of other more complex kinds of gestures like marking an area and indicating a direction (with hands and fingers) will be incorporated in the next prototype.

The camera continuously captures images which are digitised by a frame-grabber. From each digitised image the background is subtracted leaving only the motion (and some noise) within this image. This motion is analysed in order to find the direction of the pointing device and its tip. By temporal segmenting of these two parameters, a clear indication of the position the user is pointing to at a given time is found. The error of the tracker is less than one pixel (through an interpolation process) for the pointer.

A **laser system** acts as a "system pointer". It can be used for pointing to positions, drawing lines and displaying text. The laser beam is controlled in real-time (30 kHz). It can scan frames containing up to 600 points with a refresh rate of 50 Hz thus drawing very steady images on surfaces. It is controlled by a standard Pentium PC host computer. The pointer tracker and the laser pointer have been carefully calibrated so that they can work together. An automatic calibration procedure has been set up involving both the camera and laser where they are tested by asking the laser to follow the pointer.

A **microphone array** (Leth-Espensen and Lindberg 1996) is used to locate sound sources, e.g. a person speaking. Depending upon the placement of a maximum of 12 microphones it calculates sound source positions in 2D or 3D. It is based on measurement of the delays with which a sound wave arrives at the different microphones. From this information the location of the sound source can be identified. Another application of the array is to use it to focus at a specific location thus enhancing any acoustic activity at that location. This module is in the process of being incorporated into CHAMELEON.

Speech recognition is handled by the grapHvite real-time continuous speech recogniser (Power et al. 1997). It is based on HMMs (Hidden Markov Models) of triphones for acoustic decoding of English or Danish. The recognition process focusses on recognition of speech concepts and ignores non content words or phrases. A finite state network describing phrases is created by hand in accordance with the domain model and the grammar for the natural language parser. The latter can also be performed automatically by a grammar converter in the NLP module. The speech recogniser takes speech signals as input and produces text strings as output. Integration of the latest CPK speech recogniser (Christensen et al. 1998) which is under development is being considered.

We use the Infovox Text-To-Speech (TTS) **speech synthesiser** which at present is capable of synthesising Danish and English (Infovox 1994). It is a rule based formant synthesiser and can simultaneously cope with multiple languages, e.g. pronounce a Danish name within an English utterance. Infovox takes text as input and produces speech as output. Integration of the CPK speech synthesiser (Nielsen et al. 1997) which is under development for English is being considered.

Natural language processing is based on a compound feature based (so-called unification) grammar formalism for extracting semantics from the one-best utterance text output from the speech recogniser (Brøndsted 1999). The parser carries out a syntactic constituent analysis of input and subsequently maps values into semantic frames. The rules used for syntactic parsing are based on a subset of the EUROTRA formalism, i.e. in terms of lexical rules and structure building rules (Bech 1991). Semantic rules define certain syntactic subtrees and which frames to create if the subtrees are found in the syntactic parse trees. The natural language generator is currently under construction and at present generation is conducted by using canned text.

The basis of the Phase Web paradigm (Manthey 1998), and its incarnation in the form of a program called **Topsy**, is to represent knowledge and behaviour in the form of hierarchical relationships between the mutual exclusion and co-occurrence of events. In AI parlance, Topsy is a distributed, associative, continuous-action, dynamic partial-order planner that learns from experience. Relative to MultiMedia, integrating independent data from multiple media begins with noticing that what ties otherwise independent inputs together is the fact that they occur simultaneously. This is also Topsy's basic operating principle, but this is further combined with the notion of mutual exclusion, and thence to hierarchies of such relationships (Manthey 1998).

DACS

DACS is currently the communications system for CHAMELEON and the IntelliMedia WorkBench and is used to glue all the modules together enabling communication between them. Applications of CHAMELEON typically consist of several interdependent modules, often running on separate machines or even dedicated hardware. This is indeed the case for the IntelliMedia WorkBench application. Such distributed applications have a need to communicate in various ways. Some modules feed others in the sense that all generated output from one is treated further by another. In the Campus Information System all modules report their output to the blackboard where it is stored. Although our intention is currently to direct all communication through the blackboard, we could just as well have chosen to simultaneously transfer output to several modules. For example, utterances collected by the speech recogniser can be sent to the blackboard but also sent simultaneously to the NLP module which may become relevant when efficiency is an important issue.

Another kind of interaction between processes is through remote procedure calls (RPCs), which can be either *synchronous* or *asynchronous.* By synchronous RPCs we understand procedure calls where we want immediate feedback, that is, the caller stops execution and waits for an answer to the call. In the Campus Information System this could be the dialogue manager requesting the last location to which a pointing event occurred. In the asynchronous RPC, we merely submit a request and carry on with any other task. This could be a request to the speech synthesiser to produce an utterance for the user or to the laser to point to some specific location. These kinds of interaction should be available in a uniform way in a heterogeneous environment, without specific concern about what platform the sender and receiver run on.

All these facilities are provided by the Distributed Applications Communication System (DACS) developed at the University of Bielefeld, Germany (Fink et al. 1995, 1996), where it was designed as part of a larger research project developing an IntelliMedia platform (Rickheit and Wachsmuth 1996) discussed further in the next section. DACS uses a communication demon on each participating machine that runs in user mode, allows multiple users to access the system simultaneously and does not provide a virtual machine dedicated to a single user. The demon acts as a router for all internal traffic and establishes connections to demons on remote machines. Communication is based on simple asynchronous message passing with some extensions to handle dynamic reconfigurations of the system during runtime. DACS also provides on top more advanced communication semantics like RPCs (synchronous and asynchronous) and *demand streams* for handling data parts in continuous data streams. All messages transmitted are recorded in a Network Data Representation which includes type and structure information. Hence, it is possible to inspect messages at any point in the system and to develop generic tools that can handle any kind of data. DACS uses POSIX threads to handle connections independently in parallel. A database in a central name service stores the system configuration to keep the network traffic low during dynamic reconfigurations. A DACS Debugging Tool (DDT) allows inspection of messages before they are delivered, monitoring configurations of the system, and status on connections.

3. Relation to other work

Situated Artificial Communicators (SFB-360) (Rickheit and Wachsmuth 1996) is a collaborative research project at the University of Bielefeld, Germany which focusses on modelling that which a person performs when with a partner he cooperatively solves a simple assembly task in a given situation. The object chosen is a model airplane (Baufix) to be constructed by a robot from the components of a wooden building kit with instructions from a human. SFB-360 includes equivalents of the modules in CHAMELEON although there is no learning module competitor to Topsy. What SFB-360 gains in size it may loose in integration, i.e. it is not clear yet that all the technology from the subprojects have been fitted together and in particular what exactly the semantic representations passed between the modules are. The DACS process communication system currently used in CHAMELEON is a useful product from SFB-360.

Gandalf is a communicative humanoid which interacts with users in MultiModal dialogue through using and interpreting gestures, facial expressions, body language and spoken dialogue (Thórisson 1997). Gandalf is an application of an architecture called *Ymir* which includes perceptual integration of multimodal events, distributed planning and decision making, layered input analysis and motor-control with human-like characteristics and an inherent knowledge of time. Ymir has a blackboard architecture and includes modules equivalent to those in CHAMELEON. However, there is no vision/image processing module in the sense of using cameras since gesture tracking is done with the use of a data glove and body tracking suit and an eye tracker is used for detecting the user's eye gaze. Yet, it is anticipated that Ymir could easily handle the addition of such a vision module if one were needed. Ymir has no learning module equivalent to Topsy. Ymir's architecture is even more distributed than CHAMELEON's with many more modules interacting with each other. Ymir's semantic representation is much more distributed with smaller chunks of information than our frames being passed between modules.

AESOPWORLD is an integrated comprehension and generation system for integration of vision, language and motion (Okada 1997). It includes a model of mind consisting of nine domains according to the contents of mental activities and five levels along the process of concept formation. The system simulates the protagonist or fox of an AESOP fable, "the Fox and the Grapes", and his mental and physical behaviour are shown by graphic displays, a voice generator, and a music generator which expresses his emotional states.

AESOPWORLD has an agent-based distributed architecture and also uses frames as semantic representations. It has many modules in common with CHAMELEON although again there is no vision input to AESOPWORLD which uses computer graphics to depict scenes. AESOPWORLD has an extensive planning module but conducts more traditional planning than CHAMELEON's Topsy.

The INTERACT project (Waibel et al. 1996) involves developing MultiModal Human Computer Interfaces including the modalities of speech, gesture and pointing, eye-gaze, lip motion and facial expression, handwriting, face recognition and tracking, and sound localisation. The main concern is with improving recognition accuracies of modality specific component processors as well as developing optimal combinations of multiple input signals to deduce user intent more reliably in cross-modal speech-acts. INTERACT also uses a frame representation for integrated semantics from gesture and speech and partial hypotheses are developed in terms of partially filled frames. The output of the interpreter is obtained by unifying the information contained in the partial frames. Although Waibel et al. present good work on multimodal interfaces it is not clear that they have developed an integrated platform which can be used for developing multimodal applications.

4. Conclusion and future work

We have described the architecture and functionality of CHAMELEON: an open, distributed architecture with ten modules glued into a single platform using the DACS communication system. We described the IntelliMedia WorkBench application, a software and physical platform where a user can ask for information about things on a physical table. The current domain is a *Campus Information System* where 2D building plans are placed on the table and the system provides information about tenants, rooms and routes and can answer questions like "Whose office is this?" in real time. CHAMELEON fulfills the goal of developing a general platform for integration of at least language/vision processing which can be used for research but also for student projects as part of the Master's degree education. Also, the goal of integrating research from four research groups within three Departments at the Institute for Electronic Systems has been achieved. More details on CHAMELEON and the IntelliMedia WorkBench can be found in Brøndsted et al. (1998).

There are a number of avenues for future work with CHAMELEON. We would like to process dialogue that includes examples of (1) spatial relations and (2) anaphoric reference. It is hoped that more complex decision taking can be introduced to operate over semantic representations in the dialogue manager or blackboard using, for example, the HUGIN software tool (Jensen (F.) 1996) based on Bayesian Networks (Jensen (F.V.) 1996). The gesture module will be augmented so that it can handle gestures other than pointing. Topsy will be asked to do more complex learning and processing of input/output from frames. The microphone array has to be integrated into CHAMELEON and set to work. Also, at present CHAMELEON is static and it might be interesting to see how it performs whilst being integrated with a web-based virtual or real robot or as part of an intellimedia videoconferencing system where multiple users can direct cameras through spoken dialogue and gesture. A miniature version of this idea has already been completed as a student project (Bakman et al. 1997).

Intelligent MultiMedia will be important in the future of international computing and media development and IntelliMedia 2000+ at Aalborg University, Denmark brings together the necessary ingredients from research, teaching and links to industry to enable its successful implementation. Our CHAMELEON platform and IntelliMedia WorkBench application are ideal for testing integrated processing of language and vision for the future of Super-informationhighwayS.

Acknowledgments

This opportunity is taken to acknowledge support from the Faculty of Science and Technology, Aalborg University, Denmark and Paul Mc Kevitt would also like to acknowledge the British Engineering and Physical Sciences Research Council (EPSRC) for their generous funded support under grant B/94/AF/1833 for the Integration of Natural Language, Speech and Vision Processing (Advanced Fellow).

References

Bakman, Lau, Mads Blidegn, Thomas Dorf Nielsen, and Susana Carrasco Gonzalez. (1997). *NIVICO — Natural Interface for VIdeo COnferencing* Project Report (8th Semester), Department of Communication Technology, Institute for Electronic Systems, Aalborg University, Denmark.

Bech, A. (1991). Description of the EUROTRA framework. In *The Eurotra Formal Specifications, Studies in Machine Translation and Natural Language Processing*, C. Copeland, J. Durand, S. Krauwer, and B. Maegaard (Eds), Vol. 2, 7–40. Luxembourg: Office for Official Publications of the Commission of the European Community.

Brøndsted, Tom (1999). The CPK NLP Suite for Spoken Language Understanding. Eurospeech, 6th European Conference on Speech Communication and Technology. Budapest, September, 2655–2658.

Brøndsted, T., P. Dalsgaard, L.B. Larsen, M. Manthey, P. Mc Kevitt, T.B. Moeslund, K.G. Olesen (1998). *A platform for developing Intelligent MultiMedia applications.* Technical Report R-98-1004, Center for PersonKommunikation (CPK), Institute for Electronic Systems (IES), Aalborg University, Denmark, May.

Christensen, Heidi, Børge Lindberg and Pall Steingrimsson (1998). *Functional specification of the CPK Spoken LANGuage recognition research system (SLANG).* Center for PersonKommunikation, Aalborg University, Denmark, March.

CPK Annual Report (1998). *CPK Annual Report.* Center for PersonKommunikation (CPK), Fredrik Bajers Vej 7-A2, Institute for Electronic Systems (IES), Aalborg University, DK-9220, Aalborg, Denmark.

Denis, M. and M. Carfantan (Eds.) (1993). *Images et langages: multimodalité et modelisation cognitive.* Actes du Colloque Interdisciplinaire du Comité National de la Recherche Scientifique, Salle des Conférences, Siège du CNRS, Paris, April.

Fink, G.A., N. Jungclaus, H. Ritter, and G. Sagerer. (1995). A communication framework for heterogeneous distributed pattern analysis. In *Proc. International Conference on Algorithms and Applications for Parallel Processing,* V. L. Narasimhan (Ed.), 881–890. IEEE, Brisbane, Australia.

Fink, Gernot A., Nils Jungclaus, Franz Kummert, Helge Ritter and Gerhard Sagerer (1996). A distributed system for integrated speech and image understanding. In *Proceedings of the International Symposium on Artificial Intelligence,* Rogelio Soto (Ed.), 117–126. Cancun, Mexico.

Infovox (1994). *INFOVOX: Text-to-speech converter user's manual (version 3.4).* Solna, Sweden: Telia Promotor Infovox AB.

Jensen, Finn V. (1996). *An introduction to Bayesian Networks.* London, England: UCL Press.

Jensen, Frank (1996). Bayesian belief network technology and the HUGIN system. In *Proceedings of UNICOM seminar on Intelligent Data Management,* Alex Gammerman (Ed.), 240–248. Chelsea Village, London, England, April.

Kosslyn, S.M. and J.R. Pomerantz (1977). Imagery, propositions and the form of internal representations. In *Cognitive Psychology.* 9, 52–76.

Leth-Espensen, P. and B. Lindberg (1996). Separation of speech signals using eigenfiltering in a dual beamforming system. In *Proc. IEEE Nordic Signal Processing Symposium (NORSIG).* Espoo, Finland, September, 235–238.

Manthey, Michael J. (1998). The Phase Web Paradigm. In *International Journal of General Systems, special issue on General Physical Systems Theories,* K. Bowden (Ed.).

Mc Kevitt, Paul (1994). Visions for language. In *Proceedings of the Workshop on Integration of Natural Language and Vision processing.* Twelfth American National Conference on Artificial Intelligence (AAAI-94), Seattle, Washington, USA, August, 47–57.

Mc Kevitt, Paul (Ed.) (1995/1996). *Integration of Natural Language and Vision Processing (Vols. I–IV).* Dordrecht, The Netherlands: Kluwer-Academic Publishers.

Mc Kevitt, Paul (1997). SuperinformationhighwayS. In "*Sprog og Multimedier*" (*Speech and Multimedia*). Tom Brøndsted and Inger Lytje (Eds.), 166–183, April 1997. Aalborg,

Denmark: Aalborg Universitetsforlag (Aalborg University Press).

Mc Kevitt, Paul and Paul Dalsgaard (1997). A frame semantics for an IntelliMedia TourGuide. In *Proceedings of the Eighth Ireland Conference on Artificial Intelligence (AI-97), Volume 1.* 104–111. University of Uster, Magee College, Derry, Northern Ireland, September.

Minsky, Marvin (1975). A framework for representing knowledge. In *The Psychology of Computer Vision.* P.H. Winston (Ed.), 211–217. New York: McGraw-Hill.

Nielsen, Claus, Jesper Jensen, Ove Andersen, and Egon Hansen (1997). *Speech synthesis based on diphone concatenation.* Technical Report, No. CPK971120-JJe (in confidence), Center for PersonKommunikation, Aalborg University, Denmark.

Okada, Naoyuki (1997). Integrating vision, motion and language through mind. In *Proceedings of the Eighth Ireland Conference on Artificial Intelligence (AI-97), Volume 1.* 7–16. University of Uster, Magee, Derry, Northern Ireland, September.

Pentland, Alex (Ed.) (1993). *Looking at people: recognition and interpretation of human action.* IJCAI-93 Workshop (W28) at The 13th International Conference on Artificial Intelligence (IJCAI-93), Chambéry, France, August.

Power, Kevin, Caroline Matheson, Dave Ollason and Rachel Morton (1997). *The grapHvite book (version 1.0).* Cambridge, England: Entropic Cambridge Research Laboratory Ltd.

Pylyshyn, Zenon (1973). What the mind's eye tells the mind's brain: a critique of mental imagery. In *Psychological Bulletin,* 80, 1–24.

Rickheit, Gert and Ipke Wachsmuth (1996). Collaborative Research Centre "Situated Artificial Communicators" at the University of Bielefeld, Germany. In *Integration of Natural Language and Vision Processing, Volume IV, Recent Advances.* Mc Kevitt, Paul (ed.), 11–16. Dordrecht, The Netherlands: Kluwer Academic Publishers.

Thórisson, Kris R. (1997). Layered action control in communicative humanoids. In *Proceedings of Computer Graphics Europe '97.* June 5–7, Geneva, Switzerland.

Waibel, Alex, Minh Tue Vo, Paul Duchnowski and Stefan Manke (1996). Multimodal interfaces. In *Integration of Natural Language and Vision Processing, Volume IV, Recent Advances.* Mc Kevitt, Paul (Ed.), 145–165. Dordrecht, The Netherlands: Kluwer Academic Publishers.

Appendix A

Syntax of frames

The following BNF grammar defines a predicate-argument syntax for the form of messages (frames) appearing on CHAMELEON's implemented blackboard.

```
FRAME          ::=  PREDICATE
PREDICATE      ::=  identifier(ARGUMENTS)
ARGUMENTS      ::=  ARGUMENT
                |   ARGUMENTS, ARGUMENT
ARGUMENT       ::=  CONSTANT
                |   VARIABLE
                |   PREDICATE
CONSTANT       ::=  identifier
                |   integer
                |   string
VARIABLE       ::=  $identifier
```

FRAME acts as start symbol, CAPITAL symbols are non-terminals, and terminals are lower-case or one of the four symbols `(` `)` `,` and `$`. An *identifier* starts with a letter that can be followed by any number of letters, digits or _, an *integer* consists of a sequence of digits and a *string* is anything delimited by two "'s. Thus the *alphabet* consists of the letters, the digits and the symbols `(` `)` `,` _ and `$`. A parser has been written in C which can parse the frames using this BNF definition.

Appendix B

Blackboard in practice

Here we show the complete blackboard (with all frames) as produced exactly by CHAMELEON for the example dialogue given in Section 2.

```
Received: nlp(intention(instruction(pointing)),location(person(tb),
type(office)),time(889524794))
which is passed on to dialog_manager
Received: dialog manager(output(laser(point(coordinates(249,623))),
speech_synthesizer(utterance("This is Toms office"))))
Calling laser: laser(point(coordinates(249,623)))
Calling speech_synthesizer:
speech_synthesizer(utterance("This is Toms office"))

Received: nlp(intention(instruction(pointing)),location(person(tbm),
type(office)),time(889524818))
```

```
which is passed on to dialog_manager
Received: dialog_manager(output(laser(point(coordinates(278,623))),
speech_synthesizer(utterance("This is Thomass office"))))
Calling laser: laser(point(coordinates(278,623)))
Calling speech_synthesizer:
speech_synthesizer(utterance("This is Thomass office"))

Received: nlp(intention(query(where)),location(place(a2_221)),
time(889524831))
which is passed on to dialog_manager
Received: dialog_manager(output(laser(point(coordinates(132,500))),
speech_synthesizer(utterance("computer room is here"))))
Calling laser: laser(point(coordinates(132,500)))
Calling speech_synthesizer:
speech_synthesizer(utterance("computer room is here"))

Received: nlp(intention(query(who)),location(this($Deixis),
type(office)),time(889524864))
which is passed on to dialog_manager
Received: dialog_manager(output(laser(point(coordinates(658,546))),
speech_synthesizer(
utterance("This is not an office, this is instrument repair"))))
Calling laser: laser(point(coordinates(658,546)))
Calling speech_synthesizer:
speech_synthesizer(
utterance("This is not an office, this is instrument repair"))

Received: nlp(intention(query(who)),location(this($Deixis),
type(office)),time(889524885))
which is passed on to dialog_manager
Received: dialog_manager(output(laser(point(coordinates(223,568))),
speech_synthesizer(utterance("This is Pauls office"))))
Calling laser: laser(point(coordinates(223,568)))
Calling speech_synthesizer:
speech_synthesizer(utterance("This is Pauls office"))

Received: nlp(intention(instruction(show_route)),
source(location(person(lbl),type(office))),
destination(location(person(hg),type(office))),time(889524919))
which is passed on to dialog_manager
Received: dialog_manager(output(laser(route(
coordinates(278,585,278,603,249,603,220,603,197,603,197,623))),
speech_synthesizer(
utterance("This is the route from Lars Bos office to Hannes office"))))
Calling laser:
laser(route(
```

```
coordinates(278,585,278,603,249,603,220,603,197,603,197,623)))
Calling speech_synthesizer:
speech_synthesizer
(utterance("This is the route from Lars Bos office to Hannes office"))

Received: nlp(intention(instruction(show route)),
source(location(person(pmck),
type(office))),destination(location(place(a2_105))),time(889524942))
which is passed on to dialog_manager
Received:
dialog_manager(output(laser(route(
coordinates(174,453,153,453,153,481,153,500,153,510,153,
540,153,569,153,599,153,603,184,603,197,603,220,603,249,
603,278,603,307,603,330,603,330,655,354,655,911,655,884,
655,884,603,810,603,759,603,717,603,717,570,696,570))),
speech_synthesizer(
utterance("This is the route from Pauls office to instrument repair"))))
Calling laser:
laser(route(coordinates(174,453,153,453,153,481,153,500,153,
510,153,540,153,569,153,599,153,603,184,603,197,603,220,603,
249,603,278,603,307,603,330,603,330,655,354,655,911,655,884,
655,884,603,810,603,759,603,717,603,717,570,696,570)))
Calling speech_synthesizer:
speech_synthesizer(
utterance(
"This is the route from Pauls office to instrument repair"))

Received: nlp(intention(instruction(pointing)),location(person(pd),
type(office)),time(889524958))
which is passed on to dialog_manager
Received: dialog_manager(output(laser(point(coordinates(220,585))),
speech_synthesizer(utterance("This is Pauls office"))))
```

Machine perception of real-time multimodal natural dialogue

Kristinn R. Thórisson
The Media Laboratory, Massachusetts Institute of Technology, USA[1]

1. Introduction

A machine capable of taking the place of a person in face-to-face dialogue needs a rich flow of sensory data. Moreover, its perceptual mechanisms need to support interpretations of real-world events that can result in real-time action of the type that people produce effortlessly when interacting via speech and multiple modes. The goal of the work described here has been to create such a machine.

Most of human actions are goal-oriented (Waltz 1999) — avoid hitting that light post, reach for the pen to write, look to see who entered. It is a fair assumption that dialogue is no different from other human activity in this respect. If we couldn't move, act, or communicate, there would be no reason to perceive; perception is the servant of action. In dialogue perception serves the goal of keeping conversants on track, to match the overall plan of the communication. Endowing an artificial agent with multimodal perception gives it a solid foundation to base its actions on (Aloimonos 1993). The approach taken here to perception — and indeed to the general problem of multimodal interpretation — is that it based on highly opportunistic processes, using whatever cues possible to determine the meaning of a communicative act. This view has been voiced by others in the context of natural language interpretation (Pols 1997, Cullingford 1986).

This paper presents the perceptual mechanisms of a computational model of psychosocial dialogue skills called Ymir.[2] Ymir encompasses a layered, modular perception system that allows any embodied, computer-controlled humanoid to participate in natural, multimodal communication with a human. It proposes new ways for achieving real-time performance in language-capable systems. Ymir is constructed with a holistic view on the dialogue process, modeling human-human conversation as a single dialogue system (Thórisson

1999, 1996, 1995). The architecture is also holistic in the sense that it takes into account all types, and time scales, of multimodal behavior perceived and produced in a typical free-form dialogue, and distinguishes itself from a lot of other related research on these grounds (e.g. Heinz & Grobel 1997, Sparrell & Koons 1994, Wahlster 1991). The work described here also distinguishes itself from that of others in that real-time turn-taking is modeled and implemented for multiple modes (cf. Heinz & Grobel 1997, Frölich & Wachsmuth 1997, Rigoll et al. 1997, Wren et al. 1997, Essa et al. 1994, Sparrell & Koons 1994, Bolt 1980), and that high-level knowledge and natural language is included in the interaction (cf. Blumberg & Galyean 1995, Brooks & Stein 1993, Wilson 1991, Maes 1990).

Gandalf, the first character created in this architecture, is capable of fluid turn-taking and unscripted, task-oriented dialogue (Thórisson 1999, 1996); he perceives natural language, natural prosody and free-form gesture and body language, and conducts natural, multimodal dialogue with a human. Computer-naïve users have rated him highly on believability, language ability and interaction smoothness (Thórisson 1998, 1996).

Here we will focus on the mechanisms for multimodal perception prescribed by Ymir and realized in Gandalf, emphasizing spatial representation and prosody analysis, and explain how top-down and bottom-up perception is organized in the Ymir architecture. Other aspects of Ymir are discussed elsewhere: Real-time decision making in (Thórisson 1998); real-time motor control in (Thórisson 1997); an overview of Ymir can be found in (Thórisson 1999).

The paper is organized as follows: First we give an overview of Ymir, with an emphasis on its general perceptual mechanisms. Then we give a summary of Gandalf and the dialogue skills exhibited by this agent. The final section explains how these perceptual mechanisms are implemented in the Gandalf prototype using particular examples. Related work is referenced throughout the paper.

2. Perceptual mechanisms in Ymir

Ymir is a computational model of psychosocial dialogue skills that addresses the main characteristics of face-to-face dialogue. It is also a very malleable structure to test models of various mental mechanisms. In Ymir the perceptual abilities of an agent are assumed to be grounded in knowledge about the interaction — knowledge about participants, body parts, turn taking, etc. — via situational indexing. This knowledge is provided through symbolic and

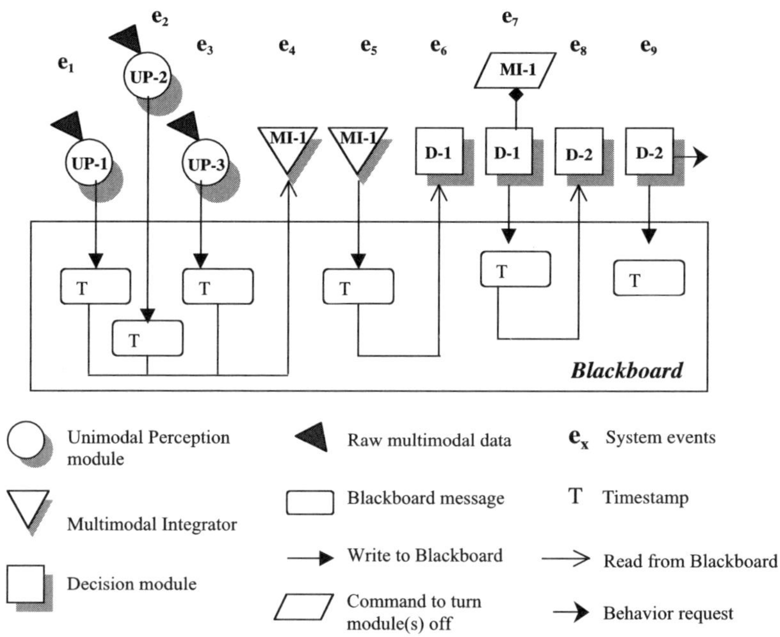

Figure 1. Internal events involving perceptual processing and decision making. Events e1, e2, e3: Raw data from sensing devices streams in to dedicated Unimodal Processors (UP), which process each mode separately and post the results of this processing on one of two blackboards (CB and FSB in Figure 3). e4: Multimodal Integrators (MI) combine the data from two or more UPs and/or MIs and process further, again posting results (e5). e6, e8: Deciders read data from UPs, MIs and other deciders to issue overt and covert decisions. e7: An overt decision is made to turn a perceptual module off, and this decision is posted. e9: A decision is made to issue an overt behavior request.

spatial representations. Ymir also borrows several features from prior blackboard (Dodhiawala 1989) and behavior-based artificial intelligence architectures (Maes 1990, Wilson 1991), but goes beyond these in the amount of communication modalities and performance criteria it addresses.

Ymir has four types of processing modules: *perceptual*, *decision*, *knowledge* and *behavior-motor*, in four process collections, (1) a *Reactive layer* (RL), (2) a *Process Control layer* (PCL), (3) a *Content layer* (CL), and an (4) *Action Scheduler* (AS). The four process collections give Ymir a hierarchical structure for dealing with *time* and *complexity*. Multimodal user behavior is collected through chosen tracking mechanisms and separated into significant segments (e.g. *hands, arm, trunk* for the body; *intonation* and *words* for speech; see below). This data streams into all three layers (Figure 3), which contain Perception and Decision modules. The output of the Perception modules provides input to Decision modules (see Figure 1). Perception modules with particular cycle times process the raw data to various degrees and output their results to one of two blackboards, supporting decisions with corresponding perceive-act cycle times (Thórisson 1998). Interpretation can be driven, or triggered, based on any perceptual data — speech, prosody, gesture, gaze, internally generated decisions and knowledge, or any combination of these. These principles serve as the foundation for perceptual data handling and integration, and support real-time decision making, planning, and interpretation throughout the architecture.

The relationship between Perception modules and Decision modules in Ymir is the relationship between bottom-up and top-down processing: (1) Bottom-up processing works by having Perception and Decision modules in one layer process *only data from modules in the same layer or the layer below.* Economical use of computation is thus gained through bottom-up "value-added" data flow, modules in each successive layer add information to the results from the layer below. (2) Top-down control is implemented by having Perceptual modules in one layer *turned on and off by Decision modules in the layer above and sometimes in the same layer* (but never below). A goal produced by planning algorithms in the Content Layer (CL) can trigger a Decision module to turn on or off a Perception module (or a group of them) in the Process Control Layer. Interweaving top-down and bottom-up processing in this way is powerful enough for a broad range of dialogue mechanisms, and is easy to manage.

```
MODULE TYPE: dir-Unimodal-Perceptor
NAME: user-looking-at-me?
DATA-1: user-gaze-direction-vector
DATA-2: my-head-position
INDEX-1: get-users-gaze-direction
INDEX-2: get-my-head-position
FUNCTION: user-looking-at-me?
BLACKBOARD-DEST: FSB
TIMESTAMP: 203948
STATE: TRUE
```

Figure 2. Example of an implemented spatio-directional Unimodal Perceptor. The process *user-looking-at-me?* computes the intersection of a cone and a plane using spatial representations (see Figures 5 and 6). The state of the module changes based on whether its function returns true or false.

Perceptual modules and perceptual integration

The two main types of Perception modules are Unimodal Perceptors (UP) and Multimodal Integrators (MI). UPs process data from only a single mode or a subset of a mode (e.g. speech, manual gesture, prosody); these are relatively simple processes (Figure 2). A total of 26 Perception Modules were created for Gandalf; 16 Unimodal Perceptors (4 prosody, 3 speech, 9 body), and 10 Multimodal Integrators describing the user's turn-giving, manual gesture activity, back-channel activity and completeness (syntactic, grammatical, and pragmatic) of the utterance/multimodal act. Unimodal Perceptor modules are classified into groups based on their function. These have been implemented in the Gandalf prototype: (1) *spatio-positional*, (2) *spatio-directional*, (3) *speech*, (4) *prosody*. The MIs aggregate information from the UPs, and other MIs, to compute multimodal descriptions of the user's behavior. An example is a collection of MIs that determine in concert whether the user is giving the turn. Perceptual modules can also be *static* or *dynamic*. Static modules look at a state in time, regardless of history; dynamic modules integrate data over time.

The use of time-stamped symbolic tokens, e.g. (User-Speaking, TRUE, 9394), (Intonation-Going UP, 9672), as the main format of the perceptual system output proved to be very useful. It is easy to work with and is directly digestible by automatic decision processes using first-order or fuzzy logic — two obvious candidates for use in decision mechanisms. Significant results in the classification of cue phrases have been achieved by Litman (1996) using similar logical combinations of features gleaned from natural language and speech.

Ymir presents an inherent symmetry between perception, decision, and action, inspired by behavior-based AI (cf. Wilson 1991). For example, the representation and distribution of Perceptual modules in the layers are complementary to the Decision modules: In the RL both have a relatively low accuracy/speed trade-off; the PCL contains more sophisticated perceptual processing — and more sophisticated decision making; and so on in the CL. The Action Scheduler mirrors this symmetry: The layer from which an incoming behavior requests comes determines its priority, reactive decisions having the highest. An action such as turning the head toward a sudden sound is thus always guaranteed the shortest and most appropriate route through the system, from the perceptual cue, to the decision to turn, to the process that pulls the muscles (Thórisson 1998).

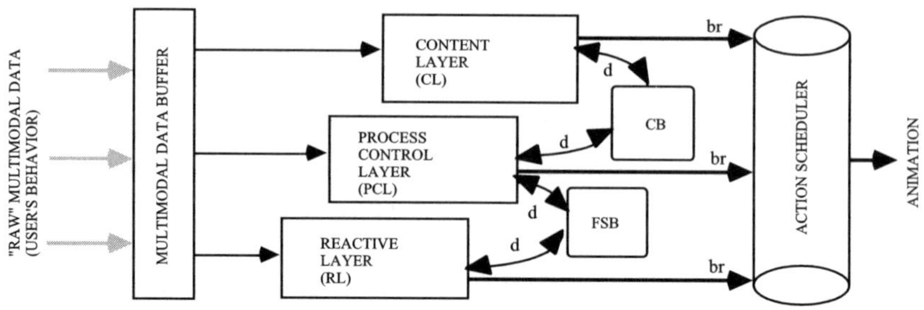

Figure 3. The Ymir architecture is composed of four process collections, each which is made up of several modules for perception, knowledge, decision and action. Multimodal data streams in from the left and is stored in a buffer. From this buffer perception, decision and knowledge modules fetch the data they need to produce their output. This output (d) is posted in blackboards (Content Blackboard and Functional Sketchboard). When a decision is made a behavior request (br) is sent to the Action Scheduler, and usually an animation action results, controlling one or more muscles of the agent's body. Not depicted is a Motor Feedback blackboard, used for tracking motor state.

3. Gandalf: Summary of capabilities

To construct Gandalf's dialogue skills, data from the psychological and linguistic literature was modeled in Ymir's layered, modular structure (cf. McNeill 1992, Rimé & Schiaratura 1991, Clark & Brennan 1990, Pierrehumbert & Hirschberg 1990, Groz & Sidner 1986, Kleinke 1986, Goodwin 1981, Duncan 1989, Sacks et al. 1974, Yngve 1970, Effron 1941). This enables Gandalf to participate in *collaborative, task-related activities* with users, perceiving and manipulating a three-dimensional graphical model of the solar system: Via natural dialogue a user can ask Gandalf can manipulate the model, travel to any of the planets, and tell about them (Figure 4).

Gandalf's perception extracts the following kinds of information from a conversational partner's behavior: (1) Eyes: *Attentional and deictic functions* of conversational partner, during speaking and listening. (2) Hands: *Deictic gesture* — pointing at objects, and *iconic gesture* illustrating tilting (in the context of 3-D viewpoint shifts). (3) Vocal: *Prosody* — timing of partner's speech-related sounds, and intonation, as well as *speech content* — words produced by a speech recognizer. (4) Body: *Direction of head and trunk* and *position of hands in body space.* (5) *Turn-taking signals:* Various feature-based analyses of co-dependent and/or co-occurring multimodal events, such as intonation, hand

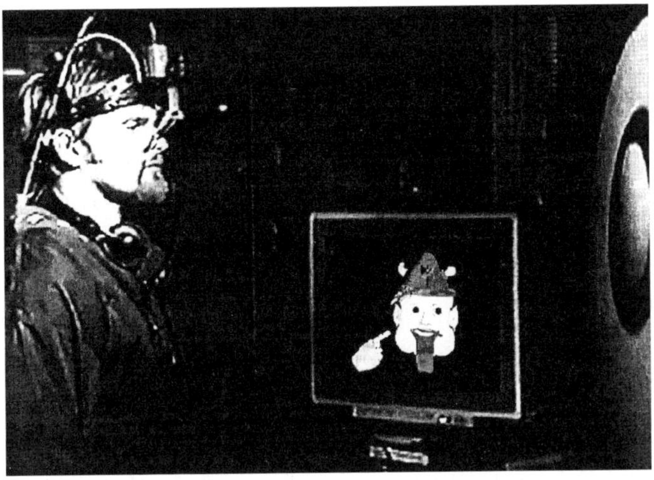

Figure 4. Gandalf appears on his own monitor, the large monitor (right) displays a model of the solar system. Here Gandalf (viking helmet) points (using a manual gesture) as he answers the author's (eye tracking helmet) question "What planet is that?" with the utterance "That is a top view of Saturn".

position and head direction, and combinations thereof. These perceptions (1–5) are interpreted in context to conduct real-time dialogue. For example, when Gandalf takes turn he may move his eyebrows up and down quickly (a common turn-taking signal in the western world) in the same way as humans, typically 2–300 msec after user gives turn. This kind of precision is made possible by making timing a core feature of the architecture. Gandalf will also look (with a glance or by turning his head) in the direction that a user points. The perception of such gestures is based on data from multiple modes; where the user is looking, shape of the user's hand, and data from intonation. The result is that Gandalf's behavior is highly relevant to the user's actions, even under high variability and individual differences.

Gandalf uses these perceptual data and interpretations to produce real-time multimodal behavior output in the all of the above categories, with the addition of: (6) Hands: *Emblematic gesture* — e.g. holding the hand up, palm forward, signaling "hold it" to interrupt when the user is speaking, and *beat gestures* — hand motion synchronized with speech production. (7) Face: *Emotional emblems* — smiling, looking puzzled, and *communicative signals*–e.g. raising eyebrows when greeting, blinking differently depending on the pace of the dialogue, facing user when answering questions, and more. (8) Body: *Emblematic body language*—nodding, shaking head. (9) Speech:[3] *Back channel feedback.* These are all inserted into the dialogue by Gandalf in a free-form way, to support and sustain the dialogue in real-time. While the perception and action processes are highly time-sensitive and opportunistic, the Ymir architecture allows Gandalf to produce completely coherent behavior.

4. Implementation

We will now look at the implementation-specific details of Gandalf's visual, speech, and prosody perception.

In any efficient perception system the world is sampled at a rate of 20–30 Hz. In the Gandalf prototype an eye tracker, body tracking suit and gloves[4] produce over 60 floating point numbers at this rate (Bers 1996); the prosody analyzer reports (filtered) changes in intonation *during* speech at 3–4 Hz, and the speech recognizer delivers words *after* speech. As mentioned before, Ymir deals with timing explicitly — all perceptual events are time-stamped as they are received through transducers, and every time they are re-processed and re-posted to a blackboard by a module. Time-stamps for each successive improvement in a perception's detail and/or accuracy are carried through, such that the history of raw data processing towards full interpretation can be traced back to its origins at any point in the processing, from perception of raw data to a potential action resulting from it.

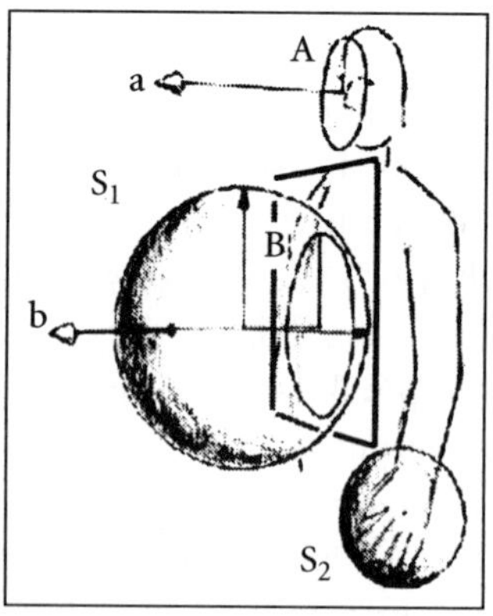

Figure 5. Geometric definitions of gesture volume (S1), face plane (A) and hand volume (S2), along with normals showing direction of head (a) and trunk (b). Plane B is an offset of S1 from the trunk.

Vision in situated dialogue

All visual perception in the Gandalf prototype happens through geometric representations of the world, an approach shared by others (Wren et al. 1997). Gandalf's real-world environment — the user, position of screens — is mapped out using the same geometric technique. A large, flat-screen monitor is used to display a 3-D model of the solar system; planets appearing on this monitor are mapped to the screen's 2-D projection in real space, so that the agent can point its gaze and hand at them. High-frequency, high-reliability measurement of body movements allows high-frequency user behavior such as fixations to be tracked and integrated in real-time in a realistic manner. An example of this is Gandalf glancing to the big screen, mirroring a user's gaze towards an object, in less than 300 ms (Figure 4). When combined with real-time prosody tracking, the analysis of the geometric representation described was sufficient to support the realistic production of reactive, interactive dialogue behaviors such as fluid turn-taking (Thórisson 2001), back channel feedback (Yngve 1970) and gaze control (Kleinke 1986), behaviors which require perception-action loops of 250 ms or less.

Information spaces

Space is divided into volumes, planes and points, for perceptual processing. Three spatial features are critical to conversants in multimodal dialogue: (1) *Gesture volumes*, (2) *Face planes*, (3) *Work volume(s)*. These features mark the (somewhat fuzzy) boundary in which events, objects or sources of information can be located during interaction. Knowing the sizes and shapes of these is not enough, however, one needs to know the positions of these volumes and planes, and, in particular, objects within them. The following coarse positional data are essential to embodied dialogue: (1) *Position of work volume*, (2) *Position of gesture volumes*, (3) *Position of face planes*, and (4) *Position of hands* (or hand volumes).

In the Gandalf prototype volumes are mapped out as shown in Figure 5. Work space and faces are simply three-dimensional planes with an orientation — a circular one for the face and a square one for the work space display (not shown). Position is given by the planes' centers. In the prototype, objects within these volumes and planes (other than hand and face) can be treated as 2-D and 3-D points — a useful (but not always completely accurate) simplification. The user's hands are surrounded by a 20 cm diameter sphere, in order to give their position a larger margin. Coarse body movements can be generated on the basis of coarse spatial knowledge — e.g. the boundaries of a volume. For example, orienting your body towards a person requires only rough knowledge of where the person is located relative to you. Fine motion, such as gaze, requires very accurate pinpointing of objects in space.

Directional data
When is a person "facing" someone? When is a person "turned to" something? These questions need to be answered by participants in any embodied, face-to-face conversation, if they want the interaction to succeed. The directional features extracted in Gandalf are: (1) *Direction of gaze*, (2) *Direction of head*, (3) *Direction of trunk*, (4) *Direction of deictic gestures*. Figure 5 shows the two normals used for head and trunk. The head, gaze and trunk normals are made into cones so that their interception with other spaces, such as the agent's face space, is broader: Interception happens if the inside of the cone overlaps the area or point in question (Figure 6). The angle of the cones is graded such that gaze has the narrowest (a 20° cone), then the head (35°), and lastly the trunk (40°). These were chosen based on the frequency of movements of these body parts to the amount of error in measuring them, and the size of the objects of interest (Gandalf's face for example). The user is *looking at point p* if p falls within the boundary of the gaze cone; the user is *facing point p* if p falls within the boundary of the head cone (Figure 6); and the user is *turned to point p* if p falls within the boundary of the body cone. Saccades provide an excellent basis for gaze segmentation: We filter eye movements into saccades, fixations and blinks, and use only data from the fixation when estimating the gaze vector (Koons & Thórisson 1993).

Gesture recognition
Ymir goes beyond most recent efforts in co-verbal gesture recognition, which typically are limited to only one of the gesture types, do not allow their free mixture, do not consider other contextual factors like gaze, speech and dialogue state, and/or do not consider real-time production of reciprocal multimodal acts (cf. Frölich & Wachsmuth 1997, Hoffman et al. 1997, Rigoll et al. 1997, Horpraset et al. 1996, Sparrell & Koons 1994, Wahlster 1991). By recognizing two classes of manual gesture in unconstrained dialogue, Gandalf demonstrates the generality of the Ymir architecture for integrating a wide variety of multimodal events in real-time by contextually driven processing. Future extensions to Ymir of the remaining classes of gestures — pantomimic, self-

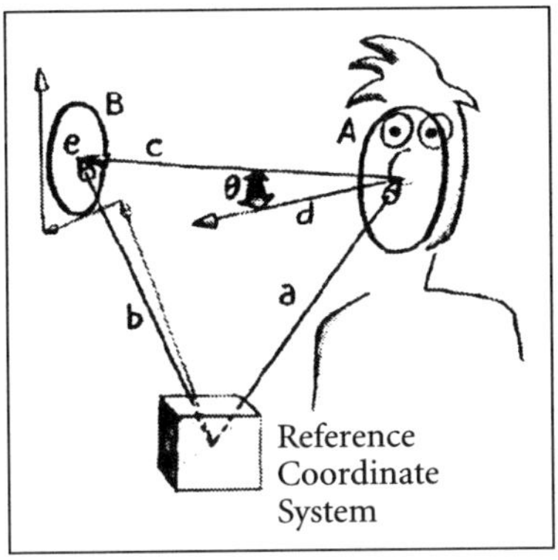

Figure 6. Geometry defining the "facing" function. Center of Face Plane A is defined by vector a; d is plane A's normal. Center of Plane B is defined by vector b. By comparing the angle between vectors d and c to a threshold, θ, one can determine whether the person on the right is facing plane B, which could e.g. represent the agent's face. This formulation was designed to correspond to our intuitive notion of "facing".

adjustors, metaphoric, emblematic and beat (McNeill 1992, Effron 1941) — involve the addition of modules, rules and interpretation mechanisms, but not new architectural constructs.

In contrast to automatic sign-language recognition (cf. Hermann & Grobel 1997) — where processing ends with deducing the correct meaning of well-formed gestures — free-form, co-temporal, co-spatial dialogue additionally means producing real-time gesture and other behavior interactively. The gesture recognition method used in the Gandalf prototype derives from Sparrell and Koons' work on co-verbal gesture (1994), modified to fit the larger psychosocial context addressed in Ymir, mainly by linking the interpretation mechanisms to the bottom-up, top-down processing scheme. Hand posture is classified into different shape categories by Unimodal Perceptors; hand placement is categorized as in and out of gesture space, and the hands' distance from the trunk is also tracked. In sign language, placement of hands has been given a-priori meaning (Heinz & Grobel 1997) — natural gesture is more complex, and most cannot be interpreted without reference to context and cross-modal indexing (McNeill 1992, Goodwin 1981). Multimodal Integrators combine this data with data from the perceived dialogue state (e.g. "does the user have the turn?"), speech activity (e.g. "is the user speaking?"), shape of the hand and its placement relative to the user's body, to produce a perception of a communicative gesture.

When processing data bottom-up, with no evidence from other modes or context, gesture space is a very good first approximation to isolating communicative gesture. Self-adjusters (e.g. scratching, adjusting clothing), which seldom have a communicative function, are mostly excluded by lifting the gesture space 10 cm from the body of the user (plane B in Figure 5). Should they happen outside gesture space the gesture could still be caught based on context and the user's speech acts. (However, its processing might not be as fast since the analysis would rely on slower top-down methods.) Gesture space thus serves several roles in the Ymir architecture. (1) It is a strong real-time indicator of the presence of *intentional, communicative* gesturing, which mainly happens in the space right in front of the speaker's body (Rimé & Schiaratura 1991). (2) It is useful for estimating if people are looking at their hands, often an indication of iconic gestures. (3) It is useful in data stream segmentation, when there is uncertainly about where (in time) a gesture occurred, and (4) gesture space has turned out to be useful for directing the agent's attention, for example to look at the speaker's face or to gestural referents at the right moments in time. McNeill's research (1992) has indicated that the type of gesture and its place of articulation may be correlated. If this turns out to be the case, a finer division of gesture space would be useful for determining the function of manual gestures (but not their presence).

Iconic and deictic gestures

Among the features used to recognize deictic gesture are *hand posture* (index finger extended, other fingers mostly bent), *position of hand relative to the gesturer's body* ("in gesture space") as well as *vocalization in a given temporal proximity of the hand-arm motion.*[5] As mentioned, all perception events are time-stamped: Data about the direction of the index finger (and/or arm) at the time of the pointing is used to compute the direction the user pointed in, to produce a referent object, often after the fact. To be able to glance in the direction of the user's pointing *while* the user is pointing, Gandalf can sample the user's gaze direction, which is continuously computed. This often proves satisfactory for producing correct glancing. Of course, a precursor to actually looking in the direction pointed is that we know that the hand/arm movement represents a communicative gesture, and that the type of the gesture is in fact deictic (the only communicative gestures whose single function is to direct spatial attention). This information comes from Multimodal Integrators looking at a holistic picture of the user's actions: body posture, gaze, prosody, hand posture, etc., which are provided by processes mainly in the Reactive Layer and Process Control Layer (see Figure 3).

In addition to co-verbal deictic gestures, Gandalf recognizes iconic gesture (e.g. "Tilt it like this [wrist motion indicating direction]"). Iconic gestures have less strict a morphology[6] than deictic ones, and are harder to detect in real-time (at the actual time of occurrence). Like deictic recognition, iconic recognition relies heavily on Multimodal Integrator classification between *communicative* versus *non-communicative* gestures. Without this high-level distinction reliability of iconic recognition falls significantly.

In summary, four main features characterize the vision work described above: (1) The vision mechanisms support interpretation of behavior during completely natural, spontaneous dialogue; (2) The vision system support contextualized, high-level percepts, combining knowledge-based (top-down) and data-driven (bottom-up) processing; (3) Vision mechanisms are embedded in a real-time architecture, constrained by a requirement to perform dialogue behavior in a natural manner, based on data from natural human interaction (c.f. Goodwin 1981, Duncan 1989, Yngve 1970); and (4) The vision mechanisms are integrated with other perception (prosody and speech content) in a unified way. Together these characteristics set this work apart from a majority of other computer vision research.

Hearing

Gandalf hears *speech* sounds, recognized via two mechanisms: A *prosody analyzer* and an off-the-shelf *speech recognizer*. Words are teased out of the speech stream through continuous-speech, grammar-based, methods. Instead of waiting for a significant pause at the end of an utterance, as is frequently done in commercial speech recognizers, the prototype demonstrated the superior method of triggering speech recognition based on multimodal data and turn-state. To implement this in Ymir a Decider is constructed that looks at the output of selected Multimodal Integrators and initiates, given the right conditions, recognition to be done on the audio collected since *last turn*. The same goes for interpretation: Once words have been received in the Content Layer interpretation is initiated by Deciders that monitor the state of the speech recognizer and the turn-taking system. The delay time for the recognition of an average sentence (form the end of the utterance) is around two seconds. In a speech-only system this would be a significant problem, since turn-taking in human telephone dialogue expects faster responses to *speech content* (~500–1000 ms), and immediate responses to *turn-taking cues* (~0–250 ms) (Goodwin 1981). This is different for face-to-face dialogue, where other modes come into play. In spite of this "mental limitation" in processing speech content, Gandalf's turn-taking is socially acceptable (frequently within 300 msec — and with appropriate repair of failures) because of data that the real-time prosody analyzer and body tracking provide, which allows it more intelligent management of dialogue behavior during turn transitions via relevant gaze, eyebrows and head movements.

Real-time prosody analysis

Methods have been suggested for automatic analysis of prosody (Todd & Brown 1994, Pierrehumbert & Hirschberg 1990), but few have focused on real-time analysis (Nöth et al. 1997). As mentioned in the introduction, we view the human perceptual system as highly opportunistic and flexible: Any cue can be used to aid interpretation and creation of meaning structures.

The analyzer developed here detects the following boolean, time-stamped events in real-time: (1) *Speech on,*[7] (2) *Intonation going up*, (3) *Intonation going down*, (4) *Intonation flat.* The intonation analysis is performed using a windowing technique, where a window is 300 ms. A new window starts where the last one ended. The slope of the intonational contour is estimated for each window and checked against a threshold. If over the threshold and different from last window, a time-stamped status report is posted on a blackboard about intonational direction. This is used for increasing the reliability of end-of-utterance detection, and inferring the type of utterance (e.g. question or command). In a future version of the system interpretation mechanisms will use this for identifying where the emphasis lies in a sentence.

By running this prosody system on a dedicated machine, relatively robust, real-time performance is achieved (Figure 7). The reliability is high enough for an interactive system: roughly one utterance in ten is impossible to analyze in real-time — other modes help correct for occasional failures in this unimodal analysis.

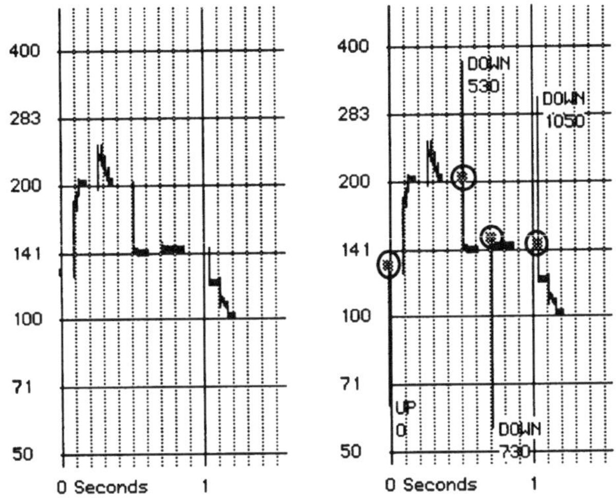

Figure 7. Example of intonation for the utterance "Take me to Jupiter" plotted to a logarithmic frequency scale (y-axis). On the right we see the result of the real-time intonation analysis. Segmentation of pitch is marked with vertical bars, giving timing (in ms) and direction. All features in this example took less than 10 ms to compute. Any delay in computing is estimated based on the raw data and then subtracted when time-stamping the event.

5. Conclusions & future work

The perception scheme modeled in Ymir results in fluid dialogue, as evidenced by interactions between novice users and Gandalf (performance results are reported in Thórisson (1999) and (1996)). Some of that success can be attributed to the data collection (dressing the user up in the agent's perceptual "organs"), which produces in high-speed, partially processed, and relatively noise-free data. But the bulk of it is undoubtedly due to the hierarchical perception-action structure of Ymir, which was modeled as a unified system and designed from the ground up to support real-time multimodal behavior. Ymir already provides the framework for perceiving facial gesture in context, and the full range of manual gesture. Including these is a matter of adding input devices such as cameras for face sensing, and a complementary lexico-geometric knowledge bases of face and gesture. The number of perception modules (26 in total) in Gandalf could easily be extended to support these for a significantly more capable agent, increasing robustness, number of manual gesture types recognized, facial gesture recognition, and more.

Although intended primarily for embodied, multimodal, task-oriented dialogue, Ymir is not restricted to perceptions of communication. The architecture's perceptual mechanisms seem for example nicely suited for characters inhabiting virtual worlds. Preliminary results indicate that skills such as navigation, story telling, walking, flying, etc. in virtual worlds can be implemented in the same framework (Bryson & Thórisson 2001).

Future work on these perception mechanisms focuses on more sophisticated attentional control and various methods for perceptual classification. Part of this work will involve strengthening the connection between perception and knowledge, thus improving the agent's responses and understanding of the dialogue. Integrating increasingly sophisticated knowledge representation into the architecture will be a significant part of future work.

Acknowledgments

I would like to thank the sponsors of this work: Thomson-CSF, the M.I.T. Media Laboratory, RANNÍS, TSG Magic and the HUMANOID Group. My thanks also to Pattie Maes, Richard A. Bolt, Justine Cassell and Steve Whittaker for inspiration and brilliant guidance; Joshua Bers, David Berger & Hannes Vilhjálmsson for programming, advice, and suggestions.

Notes

1. Now at Communicative Machines Inc., 131 E 23rd St., Suite 20, New York, NY 10010, U.S.A.

2. "Ymir" is pronounced *E*-mirr. The names Ymir and Gandalf are from the Icelandic Sagas.

3. Gandalf speaks using an off-the-shelf speech synthesizer and uses its built-in rules for generating intonation and prosody.

4. All perceptual solutions in the Gandalf implementation are independent of tracking technique — the relatively intrusive tracking methods used for Gandalf could be replaced with cameras. Pre-processing in the body model used here (Bers 1996) is based on the same knowledge-based techniques used in many computer vision systems (e.g. Wren et al. 1997).

5. This last feature is a useful heuristic for filtering out non-communicative gestures while the agent has the turn.

6. Morphology is the form of a gesture, i.e. the way its posture or motion *looks*, as opposed to function.

7. Although detecting a feature such as "speech on/off" may seem trivial, this is only true when using a dedicated microphone which is unlikely to pick up anything besides the dialogue participant's speech. Using signal processing with remote-mounted microphones makes this a significantly more difficult task. In any case, the perception is one that humans have to solve successfully in real-time during dialogue and thus a valid feature with which to provide a virtual humanoid.

References

Aloimonos, Y. (ed.). (1993). *Active Perception.* Hillsdale, NJ: Lawrence Earlbaum Associates, Inc.

Bers, J. A (1996). Body Model Server for Human Motion Capture and Representation. *Presence: Teleoperators and Virtual Environments*, 5(4), 381–392.

Blumberg, B. M. & Galyean, T. A. (1995). Multi-Level Direction of Autonomous Creatures for Real-Time Virtual Environments. Proceedings of SIGGRAPH '95 August, 47–54.

Bolt, R. A. (1980). "Put-That-There": Voice and Gesture at the Graphics Interface. *Computer Graphics*, 14(3), 262–70.

Brooks, R. & Stein, L. A. (1993). Building Brains for Bodies. M. I. T. Artifical Intelligence Laboratory memo No. 1439, August.

Bryson, J. & Thórisson, K. R. (2001). Dragons, Bats & Evil Knights: A Three-Layer Design Approach to Character-Based Creative Play. In D. Ballin (Ed.), *Virtual Reality, Special Issue on Intelligent Virtual Agents*, spring. Heidelberg: Springer-Verlag, (5), 57–71.

Clark, H. H. & Brennan, S. E. (1990). Grounding in Communication. In L. B. Resnick, J. Levine & S. D. Bahrend (eds.), *Perspectives on Socially Shared Cognition*, 127–149. American Psychological Association.

Cullingford, R. E. (1986). *Natural Language Processing: A Knowledge-Engineering Approach.* NJ: Rowman & Littlefield.

Dodhiawala, R. T. (1989). Blackboard Systems in Real-Time Problem Solving. In Jagannathan, V., Dodhiawala, R. & Baum, L. S. (Eds.), *Blackboard Architectures and Applications*, 181–191. Boston, MA: Academic Press, Inc.

Duncan, S. Jr. (1989). Some Signals and Rules for Taking Speaking Turns in Conversations. Journal of Personality and Social Psychology, 23(2), 283–292.

Effron, D. (1941/1972). *Gesture, Race and Culture.* The Hague: Mouton.

Essa, I. A., Darrell, T. & Pentland, A. (1994). Modeling and Interactive Animation of Facial Expression using Vision. M. I. T. Media Laboratory Perceptual Computing Section Technical Report No. 256.

Frölich, M. & Wachsmut, I. (1997). Gesture Recognition of the Upper Limbs — From Signal to Symbol. In I. Wachsmut & M. Frölich (Eds.), *Gesture and Sign Language in Human-Computer Interaction*, 173–184. Berlin: Springer.

Goodwin, C., (1981). *Conversational Organization: Interaction Between Speakers and Hearers.* New York, NY: Academic Press.

Horpraset, T., Haritaoglu, I., Harwood, D., Davis, L., Wren, C. & Pentland, A. (1996). Realt-Time 3D Motion Capture. *Proc. of the 2nd Workshop of Perceptual User Interfaces*, Nov. 4–6, San Francisco, U. S. A.

Grosz, B. J. & Sidner, C. L. (1986). Attention, Intentions, and the Strucutre of Discourse. *Computational Linguistics*, 12(3), 175–204.

Hienz, H. & Grobel, K. (1997). Automatic Estimation of Body Regions from Video Images. In I. Wachsmut & M. Frölich (Eds.), *Gesture and Sign Language in Human-Computer Interaction*, 135–145. Berlin: Springer.

Hoffman, F. G., Heyer, P., Hommel, G. (1997). Velocity Profile Based Recognition of Dynamic Gesture with Discrete Hidden Markov Models. In I. Wachsmut & M. Frölich (Eds.), *Gesture and Sign Language in Human-Computer Interaction*, 81–95. Berlin: Springer.

Kleinke, C. (1986). Gaze and Eye Contact: A Research Review. *Psychological Bulletin*, 100(1), 78–100.

Koons, D. B. & Thórisson, K. R. (1993). Estimating Direction of Gaze in Multi-Modal Context. Presented at *3CYBERCONF — The Third International Conference on Cyberspace*, Austin TX, May 13–14.

Litman, D. J. (1996). Cue Phrase Classification Using Machine Learning. *Journal of Artificial Intelligence Research*, 5, 53–94.

Maes, P. (1990). Designing Autonomous Agents: Theory and Practice from Biology to Engineering and Back. In P. Maes (Ed.), *Designing Autonomous Agents*, 1–2. Cambridge, MA: MIT Press.

McNeill, D. (1992). *Hand and Mind: What Gestures Reveal about Thought.* Chicago, IL: University of Chicago Press.

Nöth, E., A. Batliner, A. Kiessling, R. Kompe & H. Niemann (1997). Suprasegmental modelling. *Informal Proceedings of NATO ASI on Computational Models of Speech Pattern Processing*, St. Helier, Jersey Channel Islands.

Pierrehumbert, J. & Hirschberg, J. (1990). The Meaning of Intonational Contours in the Interpretation of Discourse. In P. R. Cohen, J. Morgan & M. E. Pollack (Eds.), *Intentions in Communication.* Cambridge: MIT Press.

Pols, L. C. W. (1997). Flexible, Robust, and Efficient Human Speech Recognition. Technical Report, Institute of Phonetic Sciences, University of Amsterdam Proceedings 21, 1–10.

Rigoll, G., Kosmala, A. & Eickeler, S. (1997). High Performance Real-Time Gesture Recognition Using Hidden Markov Models. In I. Wachsmut & M. Frölich (Eds.), *Gesture and Sign Language in Human-Computer Interaction*, 69–80. Berlin: Springer.

Rimé, B. & Schiaratura, L. (1991). Gesture and Speech. In R. S. Feldman & B. Rimé. *Fundamentals of Nonverbal Behavior*, 239–281. New York: Press Syndicate of the University of Cambridge.

Sacks, H., Schegloff, E. A. & Jefferson, G. A. (1974). A Simplest Systematics for the Organization of Turn-Taking in Conversation. *Language*, 50, 696–735.

Sparrell, C. J. & Koons, D. B. (1994). Capturing and Interpreting Coverbal Depictive Gestures. *AAAI 1994 Spring Symposium Series*, Stanford, USA, March 21–23, 8–12.

Thórisson, K. R. (2002). Natural Turn-Taling Needs No Manual: Computational Theory and Model, From Perception to Action. In B. Granström (Ed.), *Multimodality in Language and Speech Systems*. Heidelberg: Springer-Verlag, 173–207.

Thórisson, K. R. (1999). A Mind Model for Multimodal Communicative Creatures and Humanoids. *International Journal of Applied Artificial Intelligence*, 13 (4–5), 449–486.

Thórisson, K. R. (1998). Real-time Decision Making in Face-to-Face Communication. *The Second ACM Conference on Autonomous Agents*, Minneapolis, MN, 16–23.

Thórisson, K. R. (1997). Layered Modular Action Control for Communicative Humanoids. *Proceedings of Computer Graphics Europe*, June 5–7, Genieva, 134–143.

Thórisson, K. R. (1996). Communicative Humanoids: A Computational Model of Psychosocial Dialogue Skills. Ph.D. Thesis, Massachusetts Institute of Technology.

Thórisson, K. R. (1995). Computational Characteristics of Multimodal Dialogue. *AAAI Fall Symposium Series on Embodied Language and Action*, November 10–12, Massachusetts Institute of Technology, Cambridge, 102–108.

Todd, N. P. M. & Brown, G. J. (1994). A Computational Model of Prosody Perception. *Proceedings of the International Conference on Spoke Language Processing (ICLSP-94)*, Yokohama, Japan, Sept. 18–22, 127–30.

Wahlster, W. (1991). User and Discourse Models for Multimodal Communication. In J. W. Sullivan & S. W. Tyler (eds.), *Intelligent User Interfaces*, 45–67. New York, New York: ACM Press, Addison-Wesley Publishing Company.

Waltz, D. (1999). The Importance of Importance. *AI Magazine*, AAAI-98 Presidential Address, fall, 19–35.

Wilson, S. W. (1991). The Animat Path to AI. In J-A. Meyer & S. W. Wilson (eds.), *From Animals to Animats*. Cambridge, MA: MIT Press.

Wren, C. Sparacino, F., Azarbayejani, A. J., Darrell, T. J., Starner, T. E., Kotani, A., Chao, C. M., Hlavac, M., Russell, K. B., Pentland, A. P. (1997). Perceptive Spaces for Performance & Entertainment: Untethered Interaction using Computer Vision & Audition. *Applied Artificial Intelligence*, June, 11 (4), 267–284.

Yngve, V. H. (1970). On Getting a Word in Edgewise. *Papers from the Sixth Regional Meeting*, Chicago Linguistics Society, 567–78.

Communicative rhythm in gesture and speech

Ipke Wachsmuth
Faculty of Technology, University of Bielefeld, Germany

1. Introduction

Gesture and speech are the corner stones in natural human communication. Not surprisingly, they are each paid considerable attention in human-machine communication. It is apparent that advanced multimedia applications could greatly benefit from multimodal user interfaces integrating gesture and speech. Nevertheless, their realization faces obstacles for which research solutions to date have barely been proposed. The multimodal utterings of a user have to be registered via separate channels, as concurrent speech and gesture percepts. These channels have different time delays, that is, information from signal preprocessing is distributed in time. In order to process gesture and speech in their semantic connection, their temporal correspondence must first be reconstructed.

Observations in diverse research areas suggest that human communicational behavior is significantly rhythmic[1] in nature, for instance, in the way how spoken syllables and words are grouped together in time (speech rhythm) or how they are accompanied by body movements, i.e. gestures.[2] In theoretic and practical approaches attempting to mimic natural communication patterns in human-computer interaction, rhythmic organization has so far played a non-existent role. This paper takes a stance that rhythmic patterns[3] provide a useful mechanism in the establishment of intra-individual and inter-individual coordination of multimodal utterances. Based on a notion of timed agent systems, an operational model is proposed which is stimulated by findings from empirical research and which was explored in multimodal perception and integration of concurrent modalities, in particular, speech and hand gestures.

In the next section, we discuss representative findings from empirical research that substantiate the function and role of rhythm as it pertains to human communication. We then argue, in Section 3, that the idea of rhythmic organization should be a good starting point to deal with some problems of multimodal interfaces for accepting open input. The original contribution of the article lies in conceptualizing an agent-based model, described in Part 4, that accounts for some of the empirical findings and makes them available for technical solutions. A multimodal input agency is described which builds on rhythmic patterns and which served as a framework for conceptualizing a human-computer interface. Results and further prospects are discussed in Part 5. In the age of information society, rhythms might also be a more general paradigm for human machine communication, and we conclude with a brief vision of this aspect.

2. Rhythm in human-human communication

Various findings from psychological and phonetics research have revealed forms of rhythmic synchronization in human communicational behavior, with respect to both the production and the perception of utterances. Like the coordination of rhythmic limb movement (for a review, cf. Schöner & Kelso 1988), speech production and gesturing requires the coordination of a huge number of disparate biological components. When a person speaks, her arms, fingers, and head move in a structured temporal organization (self-synchrony), which was found to be synchronized across multiple levels (Condon 1986). The so-called gesture stroke is often marked by a sudden stop which is closely coupled to spoken words. Particularly for stress-timed languages,[4] when spoken fluently, temporal regularities are observed between stressed syllables and accompanying gesture strokes. They are more clear for pointing gestures/deictics (McNeill 1992), whereas gestural beats and verbal stress are not synchronized in a strict rhythmic sense (McClave 1994). Furthermore, it was found that the rhythm in a speaker's utterances is readily picked up by the hearer (interactional synchrony), in that the body of a listener, within short latency following sound onset, entrains to the articulatory structure of a speaker's speech (Condon 1986); there may even be interpersonal gestural rhythm (McClave 1994).

Under constrained conditions, Cummins and Port (1998) found a metrical 'foot' to be a salient unit in the production of speech for native English speakers. Quasi-rhythmical timing phenomena in unconstrained speech production (text reading, mostly Swedish) are reported by Fant and Kruckenberg (1996): An average of interstress intervals[5] of the order of 500 ms (milliseconds) appears to function as a basic metrical reference quantum for the timing of speaking pause duration, and quantal rhythmic sub-units of the metrical foot are suggested by average durations of stressed syllables, unstressed syllables and phoneme segments of the order of 250 ms, 125 ms and 62.5 ms. The tempo and coherence of rhythmic patterns is speaker-specific; and average segment durations within a phrase are influenced by the density of content words and thus are not entirely "on foot". Similarly, Brøndsted and Madsen (1997) have found intra-speaker variabilities in speech rates of English and Danish speakers due to time equalization of stress groups and utterances.

As for perception, Martin (1972; 1979) observed that rhythmic and segmental aspects of speech are not perceived independently in that segmentation is guided by rhythmic expectancy. Temporal phenomena were identified by Pöppel (1997) on two significant time scales. Indication was found for a high-frequency processing system that generates discrete time quanta of 30 ms duration, and a low-frequency processing system that sets up functional states of ~3s. Evidence for the high-frequency processing systems comes, in part, from studies on temporal order thresholds: Independent of sensory modality, distinct events require a minimum of 30 ms to be perceived as sucessive. The low-frequency mechanism binds successive events of up to 3s into perceptual units. Support for such a binding operation comes from studies on the temporal reproduction of stimuli with different duration; temporal integration for intervals up to 2–3s has also been observed with movement control and with the temporal segmentation of spontaneous speech. This integration is viewed to be automatic and presemantic in that the temporal limit is not determined by what is being processed.

Explanations found by the above-mentioned researchers agree in the observation that communicative rhythm may be seen as a coordinative strategy which enhances the effectiveness of speaker-listener entrainment. By expectable periodicities, rhythm seems to provide anticipations which help listeners perform segmentation of the acoustic signal and synchronize parts of speech with accompanying gesture. That is, the listener is apparently able to impose a temporal, 'time window'-like structure in the perception of utterances which aids in the grouping and integration of the information transmitted. A specific universal integration mechanism is suggested by the (Pöppel 1997) studies: Intervals of up to 3s can be mentally preserved, or grasped as a unit. This is particularly true for cross-connections among the different sensory modalities, and this temporal integration is viewed as a general principle of the neuro-cognitive machinery.

3. Rhythm in human-machine communication

As was argued above, there is evidence that communication among humans is strikingly rhythmic in nature. When this is true, then this observation should also be relevant in human-machine communication. For instance, Martin (1979) has suggested that computational models of speech perception by humans should incorporate a *rhythmic expectancy component* which, starting from utterance onset, extrapolates ahead within the constraints supplied by the current information. In human-machine communication such approaches to mimic biological communication patterns have yet to be attempted.

At the same time the call for multimodal user interfaces, like interfaces that combine the input modalities of speech and gesture in a computer application, requires a more explicit understanding of how these modalities are perceived and integrated. Multimodal input facilities are crucial for a more natural and effective human-computer interaction where information of one modality can serve to disambiguate information conveyed by another modality (Maybury 1995). Building multimodal input systems requires, on the one hand, the processing of single modalities and, on the other hand, the integration of multiple modalities (Coutaz et al. 1995). To enable a technical system to coordinate and integrate perceived speech and gestures in their natural flow, two problems have to be solved (Srihari 1995):

The segmentation problem: Given that the system is to process open input, how is the right chunk of information determined that the system takes in for processing at a time? How are consecutive chunks linked together?

The correspondence problem: Given that the system is to integrate information from multiple modalities, how does it determine cross-references, i.e., which information from one modality complements information from another modality?

To date, research solutions have barely been proposed how to reconstruct a user's multimodal utterings, which are registered on separate channels and distributed in time, in their natural temporal connection. Early attempts to realize a multimodal input system are the PUT-THAT-THERE system (Bolt 1980) and CUBRICON (Neal & Shapiro 1991). These systems are restricted to analyze speech and gestural input sequentially, and they do not allow gestural input in a natural form but, rather, as static pointing direction. More recent systems, e.g. (Koons et al. 1993; Bos et al. 1994; Nigay & Coutaz 1995), allow the parallel processing of two or more modalities. Nevertheless these approaches do not support what is called open input, i.e. instructing a system without defining where an instruction starts or ends, as well as the resolution of redundancies or inconsistencies between pieces of information of different modalities.

The observations in the previous section suggest that the analysis of communicative rhythm could be used to improve technical mediator systems between humans and machines. By exploiting segmentation cues, such as gesture stroke and stress beat in speech, the communicative rhythm could be reproduced, and possibly anticipated on, by the system. It could help to impose time windows for signal segmentation and determine correspondence of temporally distributed speech and gesture percepts which precede semantic analysis of multimodal information.

4. A multimodal interface based on timed agents

In a first technical approach we have employed the idea of communicative rhythm to determine how spoken words and hand pointing gestures belong together. For a preview, the multimodal input stream is segmented in time windows of equal duration, starting from utterance onset in one modality. Input data from multiple modalities registered within one time cycle are considered as belonging to the same instruction segment, and cross-references are resolved by establishing correspondence between gesture percepts and linguistic units registered within a time cycle. As this will not always work, time-cycle-overspanning integration needs also be considered. These ideas are in the first place motivated by the above-mentioned findings on temporal perception in humans (Pöppel 1997) and earlier ideas about rhythmic expectancy in speech perception (Martin 1979).

Materials and methods

The setting of our work is communicating with virtual environments, i.e., computer-graphics-based three-dimensional scenes which can be changed interactively by user interventions. The study reported here was carried out in the VIENA project (Wachsmuth & Cao 1995) where the prototypical application example is the design of a virtual office environment. The VIENA system can process instructions from a user to execute alterations of the scene by means of an agent-based interface. Instructions can be transmitted by spoken natural language and by pointing gestures which are issued via a simple Nintendo data glove. In this study we have used a Dragon Dictate Version 1.2b speech recognizer which processes (speaker-dependent) isolated words. An instruction is spoken as a sequence of words:

put | <gesture> this | computer | on | <gesture> that | table

where the sound onsets of consecutive words follow each other by approx. 600 ms. Pointing gestures are issued, at about the time of the spoken "this" or "that", by glove-pointing at one of the displayed objects. A glimpse of the environment that was used in this study can be obtained from Figure 1.

As the principal method to register and process information perceived from different sensory channels, we use a processing model that realizes distributed functionalities by the interplay of multiple software agents. The single agent is an autonomous computational process that communicates and cooperates with other agents based on a variant of the contract-net protocol (Wooldridge & Jennings 1995). A system of such agents, termed "agency", realizes a decentral processing of information. The core of the VIENA agency (cf. Figure 2) consists of a number of agents that take part in mediating a user's instruction to change the scene in color and spatial layout. Typically, the functionality of each single agent is achieved in a sense-compute-act cycle, i.e., *sense* input message data, *compute* function, *act* by sending resulting messages to other agents, or to effectors like the graphics system.

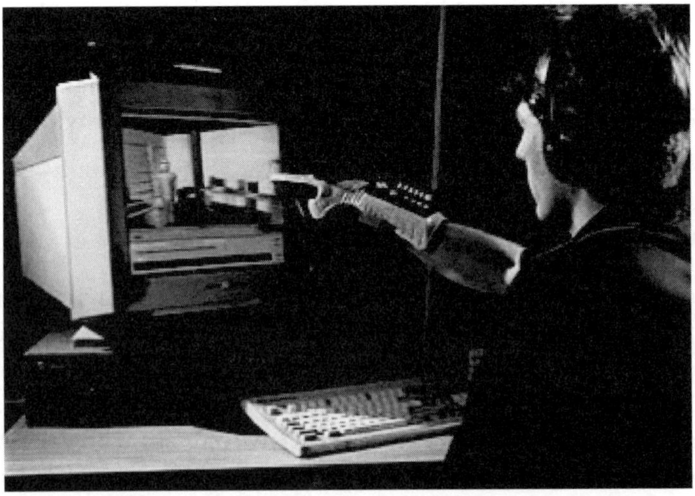

Figure 1. Instructing the VIENA system by combined speech and gesture input

The basic model of agent performance is event-driven, that is, there are no temporal constraints as to when a cycle is completed. However, in the context of integrating modalities from different sensors, temporal processing patterns become also relevant and especially so when taking into account a close coupling of speech and gesture input. Led by this observation, we have extended the basic agent model to be *timed*. To this end, we have provided for a temporal buffer for sensed information and, besides event-driven control, temporal constraints by way of time-cycle-driven patterns of processing, supporting a low-frequency "rhythmic" segmentation procedure.

In our first approach, time cycles spanning a sense-buffer-compute-act sequence executed by the single agents have a fixed duration which can be varied for experiments. The multimodal input agency described below is comprised by a number of agents dedicated to (1) sensory and linguistic input analysis and (2) the coordination and processing of multimodal input information.

Multimodal input agency

To address the aspects of open input and correspondence in multimodal instructions, we have developed a multimodal input agency, as shown in the right part of Figure 2. It is comprised by a set of timed listener agents which record, analyze, and elaborate input information from different sensory channels, and a coordinator mechanism, also realized as a timed agent system, which integrates analyzed sensory information. This information is then passed on to the application system (mediating agency) shown in the left part of Figure 2.

The input agency consists of a set of modality-specific input listeners, a parser for linguistic analysis, and a coordinator. Three listener agents, i.e., a speech listener, a type listener, and a gesture listener, track and analyze sensor data from the microphone, the keyboard, and the data glove, respectively. Assisted by the parser, the coordinator analyzes and integrates the inputs received from the listeners and generates an internal task description that is posted to mediator agents. The mediating agency determines the according changes in the virtual environment and updates the scene visualization. Multimodal instructions are issued by speaking to the microphone and using the glove for pointing. Typewritten input can be used in unimodal (verbal) instructions.

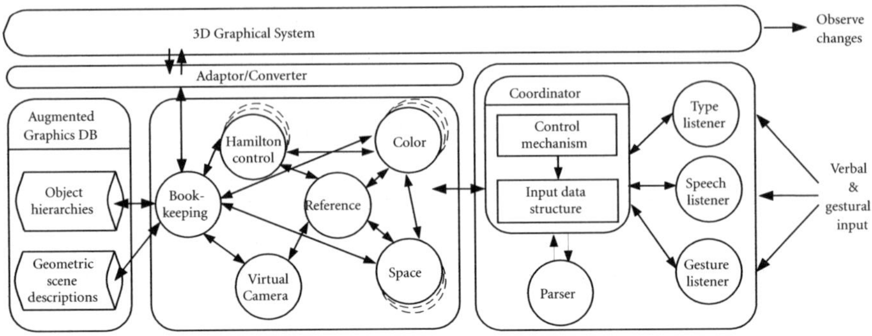

Figure 2. VIENA agent interface with mediators (left) and multimodal input agency (right)

The input agency performs a time- and event-driven routine to integrate multiple (speech and gesture) modalities. Whereas input agents are "listening" for input events in short polling cycles of 100 ms, the coordinator agent processes information in fixed time cycles of a longer periodicity of 2 seconds. The actual values were found by experiments with the VIENA system which have shown that time cycles with durations of 100 ms and 2 seconds, resp., work best for the single-word recognition system and glove-based gesture recognizer used in the study. The 100 ms rhythm was determined by the fact that the glove sends a maximum of 10 data packets per second; thus a higher-frequency polling would cause unnecessary communication overhead.

The 2s integration rhythm was determined in experiments probing the overall computational cost of the VIENA system, as measured from the onset of a speech instruction to the output of a new scene visualization while varying the length of the integration cycle time by 1-second increments. In these experiments we used instructions of different lengths, i.e. a 4-word, a 7-word, and a 10-word instruction. The sound onsets of consecutive words were computer-controlled to follow each other by 600 ms, independent of whether one-, two-, or four-syllable words were spoken in. That is, speech input for the 4, 7, 10-word sentences took a bit more than 1800, 3600, and 5400 ms, respectively. The following, unimodal, spoken instructions were used ("saturn" and "andromeda" are names that refer to the two computers shown on the screen in Figure 1):

move | the | chair | left
put | the | palmtree | between | saturn | and | andromeda
put | the | palmtree | between | the | back | desk | and | the | bowl

The integration process realized in the input agency is a combination of time and event-driven computations. In the following sections we explain in more detail how the segmentation and the correspondence problem (cf. Section 3) are treated in the VIENA multimodal input agency. In full detail the method is described in (Lenzmann 1998).

Open input segmentation: The tri-state rhythm model

The basic approach to segment the multimodal input stream is to register input events from the different modalities in time cycles imposed by the coordinator agent, resulting in a tri-state rhythm model which is illustrated in Figure 3. As input data within one time cycle is considered as belonging to the same instruction segment, the coordinator agent, accordingly, buffers information received from the speech and gesture listeners, to integrate them when a cycle is completed (cf. next sub-section).

The first time cycle (z1) starts at signal onset when the user inputs a (verbal or gestural) instruction, resulting in a first input event (e1 at time te1). This causes the coordinator to reach a state "swing" which continues as long as signals are received on one of the listener channels, modeling a rhythmic expectancy. The coordinator subsides swinging when no further input event occurs within a full cycle. The "subside" state changes to "wait" once that k, e.g. 2, event-free cycles are recognized or, when triggered by a new event, returns to "swing". The "wait" state is of indefinite time; it will change to the "swing" state again upon receiving a new input event.

The time- and event-driven integration method is interwoven with the segmentation process. It consists of a cyclical four-step process comprised by functions *sense, buffer, compute,* and *act.* Whereas *sense* and *buffer* are contin-

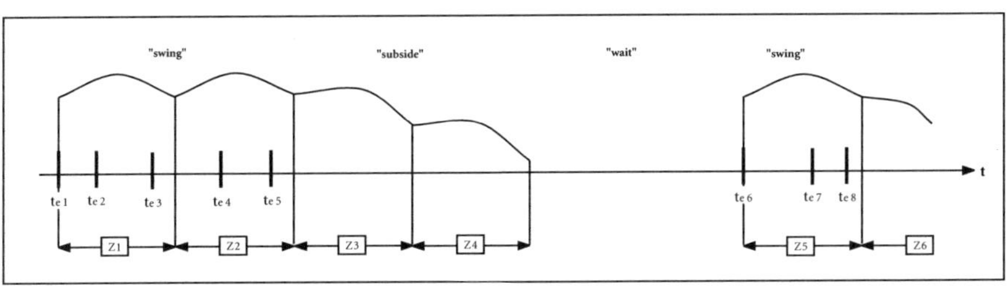

Figure 3. Tri-state rhythm model (swing – subside – wait); each cycle in state "swing" or "subside" timed equally

ued until the current time cycle is completed, *compute* and *act* are executed at the end of each time cycle. The function *sense* allows that input events sent by the listeners are received as messages, whereas the function *buffer* extracts relevant message information and collects them in an input data structure which is organized in time cycles. The coordinator agent performs these two steps as long as the current time cycle has not elapsed. At the end of a time cycle, the function *compute* interprets the multimodal information stored in the input data structure. Afterwards, the function *act* determines appropriate agents in the mediator agency and posts the corresponding tasks to them.

Correspondence in multimodal integration

The interpretation function *compute* resolves cross-references between verbal and gestural information in the input data structure and produces an overall task description that corresponds to the multimodal input of the user. Two cases are distinguished: (1) in the *time-cycle-internal interpretation*, information of just the most recent time cycle is used; (2) in the *time-cycle-overspanning interpretation*, data of the last *n* time cycles is used. Having determined what kind of interpretation has to be performed, the coordinator analyzes the speech and gesture modality separately and merges information of the different modalities in a multi-step evaluation procedure that considers both temporal and linguistic features to compute the most appropriate cross-references. Then it disambiguates all kinds of references with the help of specific agents in the mediator agency, and checks whether or not the resulting instruction is complete with respect to domain-dependent requirements. If incomplete, the coordinator waits for information that expectedly would occur within the next time cycles or, when cycling has subsided, it presents the user with his/her incomplete instruction for editing.

The actual integration in the *compute* phase is done by establishing correspondence between gesture percepts and so-called gesture places within integration intervals. *Gesture places* are time-stamped information slots, determined in spoken-language analysis, which formalize expectations about events that provide missing object or direction specifications from the gesture channel. Potential gesture places are specifications of reference objects or locations derived from speech input. The valuation of gesture places is calculated by the heuristics "the more ambiguous a reference described in the verbal instruction, the higher the valuation of a gesture place." If there are two gesture places for only one gesture percept, resolution of correspondence between cross-modal events is led by their closeness in time and by comparing ambiguity values associated with speech sections; e.g., "the chair" is less ambiguous (with respect to reference) than the deictical "there" in the sentence "put the chair there." An example where closeness in time is relevant is the instruction "put this computer on that table" if only one gesture percept is available (presupposing that one indexical is clear from previous context). In this case closeness in time would be indicative in that one of the pairs "<gesture> this" or "<gesture> that" would have higher weight. Further examples for possible combinations of speech and gesture inputs to disambiguate objects and locations are following:

put | <gesture> this | computer | on | the | blue | table
move | <gesture> that | to | the | left
make | <gesture> this | chair | green
put | <gesture> this | thing | <gesture> there
put | the | bowl | between | <gesture> this | and | <gesture> that | computer

Segmentation of multimodal input streams is thus realized in a way that open input is possible where the start and end of instructions need not be defined. Augmented by a multi-step fusion mechanism, redundancies and inconsistencies in the input stream can be handled comfortably to establish correspondence in multimodal integration.

5. Discussion and further prospects

This exploratory study was carried out in the context of research toward advanced human-computer interfaces and with the rationale to establish more natural forms of multimodal human machine communication. In detail we have described a method that is based on processing patterns which coordinate different input modalities in rhythmic time cycles. Based on the novel notion of timed agents realizing rhythmic mechanisms in temporal perception, we were able to

- develop a theoretical model of temporal integration of multiple input modalities
- implement the model in a prototype application and show that it is operational
- gain further insights into advantages of the 'right' rhythm by exploring the running model in experiments

In our first experiments we have used data-glove pointing and a simple word-by-word speech recognizer, allowing only very crude speech rhythm. Nevertheless, the very fact that the production as well as the technical perception of multimodal user utterings was rhythmically constrained in time was decisive for the comparably simple solution of multimodal integration. Realizing rhythmic expectancy, the tri-state segmentation model sustains equal temporal constraints beyond the current portion of signal transmitted and aids in the processing of a steady input stream. Even when our method is still far from mimicking communicative rhythm more succintly, we feel that some progress was made with respect to open input segmentation and the correspondence problem. There is reason to believe that these ideas carry further even when more obstacles have to be overcome.

The realization of a more elaborated system prototype, reaching from recognition of complex gestures over (continuous) speech-and-gesture integration to linkage with a target application of virtual prototyping, is now the goal of the SGIM project (Speech and Gesture Interfaces for Multimedia) in Bielefeld. We have taken steps to refine our basic approach to the demands of a more natural multimodal interaction. The illustrations in Figure 4, taken from the SGIM interaction scenario, convey that work is underway to realize more fluent speaking and gesturing in multimodal input. Segmentation cues are available from speech as well as gestural rhythm; we were able to make use of some of them in first instances. Work is underway to further build on these ideas (Sowa et al. 1999). We have also begun to research the issue of natural timing of generative gesture by making an articulated figure able to produce it in real time (Kopp & Wachsmuth 1999).

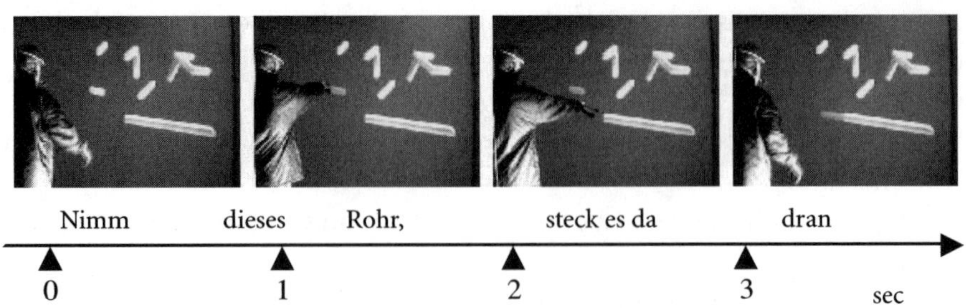

Figure 4. Natural speech and gesture input in a virtual construction scenario ("Take this pipe, mount it there-to")

An issue for future work is how the system could be enabled to entrain to the communicative rhythm exhibited by the individual user. We have successfully completed first experiments which support the idea that adaptive oscillators (McAuley 1994) could provide a method to adjust the so far equal-sized integration time windows in reasonably short latency, i.e., within about 1–2s. This adjustment might allow to mimic a stretching or shrinking of segmentation time windows (like musical ritardando or accelerando, resp.) by responding to the tempo of user utterances while preserving the hierarchical temporal structure of integration intervals. Of further interest in our research will be the .5s beat that seems to mark a grid on which accented elements (e.g., stressed syllables) are likely to occur (Kien & Kemp 1994). We hope to get insights as to how a low frequency segmentation mechanism, as used in the VIENA study, goes together with rhythm patterns on a finer-grained time scale.

Finally, I would like to take the chance to express my vision of an idea that I feel could be beneficial for future information society, namely, "rhythmic" systems. Whereas computer scientists and engineers have been mainly concerned with making throughput cycles of interactive applications faster, little thought was given to the question if speed is the only or most important issue. Given a choice of awaiting a system response as fast as possible, but at indeterminate time, or at *anticipatory* time, many users might prefer the second over the first option. Thus it seems worthy to conceive systems that are 'rhythmic' in the sense that they produce their response to a user's query in expectable time, so the user is not as much 'soaked' in waiting for a system output. Needless to say, such a conception would require a still more profound understanding of the communicative rhythm that is natural and comfortable to a human. It does not seem totally off hand to pursue technical solutions achieving steady throughput cycles which neither stress patience nor impose uncomfortable haste on users, by meeting rhythmic expectancy as experienced natural by humans.

Acknowledgment

This article was previously published under the same title in: Annelies Braffort et al. (Eds.) (1999), Gesture-Based Communication in Human-Computer Interaction, Lecture Notes in Artificial Intelligence, Vol. 1739, Berlin: Springer-Verlag, and is reprinted here by kind permission of Springer-Verlag.

This work profits greatly from contributions of the members of the AI Group at the University of Bielefeld. In particular, Section 4 builds on the dissertation by Britta

Lenzmann. Her assistance, as that of my research assistants and doctoral students Timo Sowa, Martin Fröhlich, Marc Latoschik, and Ulrich Nerlich are gratefully acknowledged. The VIENA project was in part supported by the Ministry of Science and Research of the Federal State North-Rhine-Westphalia under grant no. IVA3–107 007 93.

Notes

1. Rhythm: Following (Martin 1972) we define "rhythm" to mean relative timing between adjacent and nonadjacent elements in a behavior sequence, i.e., the locus of each element along the time line is determined relative to the locus of all other elements in the sequence.

2. Gesture: For the purpose of this paper it is sufficient to understand "gestures" as body movements which convey information that is in some way meaningful to a recipient.

3. Rhythmic patterns are event sequences in which some elements are marked from others (accented); the accents recur with some regularity, regardless of tempo (fast, slow) or tempo changes (accelerate, retard) within the pattern. Since rhythmic patterns have a time trajectory that can be tracked without continuous monitoring, perception of initial elements in a pattern allows later elements to be anticipated in real time; cf. (Martin 1972; 1979).

4. Stress-timed language: In general phonetics, it is assumed that "stress-timed" languages like English, German, and Danish tend to have a relatively constant duration of stress groups, independent of the actual number of phones or syllables involved in these groups. Thus, the time duration between the capitalized syllables in e.g. (a) "the BUS to CORK" and (b) "the BUSes to New YORK" may be expected to be approximately the same when spoken by the same speaker under the same external conditions; cf. (Broendsted & Madsen 1997).

5. Interstress interval: the time measured from the onset of the vowel in a stressed syllable to the onset of a vowel in the next stressed syllable, excluding those interrupted by a syntactic boundary.

References

Bolt, Richard A. (1980). "Put-That-There": Voice and gesture at the graphics interface. *Computer Graphics, 14*(3), 262–270.

Bos, Edwin, Carla Huls, & Wim Claasen (1994). EDWARD: Full integration of language and action in a multimodal user interface. *Int. Journal Human-Computer Studies, 40,* 473–495.

Broendsted, Tom & Jens Printz Madsen (1997). Analysis of speaking rate variations in stress-timed languages. *Proceedings of the 5th European Conference on Speech Communication and Technology (EuroSpeech)*, Rhodes, 481–484.

Condon, William S. (1986). Communication: Rhythm and structure. In J. Evans & M. Clynes (Eds.): *Rhythm in Psychological, Linguistic and Musical Processes* (55–77). Springfield, Ill.: Thomas.

Coutaz, Joëlle, Laurence Nigay, & Daniel Salber (1995). Multimodality from the user and systems perspectives. In *Proceedings of the ERCIM-95 Workshop on Multimedia Multimodal User Interfaces.*

Cummins, Fred & Robert F. Port (1998). Rhythmic constraints on stress timing in English. *Journal of Phonetics, 26,* 145–171.

Fant, Gunnar & Anita Kruckenberg (1996). On the quantal nature of speech timing. *Proc. ICSLP 1996,* 2044–2047.

Kien, Jenny & Anita Kemp (1994). Is speech temporally segmented? Comparison with temporal segmentation in behavior. *Brain and Language, 46,* 662–682.

Koons, David B., Carlton J. Sparrell, & Kristinn R. Thórisson (1993). Integrating simultaneous input from speech, gaze, and hand gestures. In M. T. Maybury (Ed.): *Intelligent Multimedia Interfaces* (257–276). Menlo Park: AAAI Press/The MIT Press.

Kopp, Stefan & Ipke Wachsmuth (1999). Natural timing in coverbal gesture of an articulated figure. Working notes, Workshop "Communicative Agents" at Autonomous Agents 1999, Seattle.

Lenzmann, Britta (1998). *Benutzeradaptive und multimodale Interface-Agenten.* Dissertationen der Künstlichen Intelligenz, Bd. 184. Sankt Augustin: Infix.

Martin, James G. (1972). Rhythmic (hierarchical) versus serial structure in speech and other behavior. *Psychological Review, 79*(6), 487–509.

Martin, James G. (1979). Rhythmic and segmental perception. *J. Acoust. Soc. Am., 65*(5), 1286–1297.

Maybury, Mark T. (1995). Research in multimedia and multimodal parsing and generation. *Artificial Intelligence Review, 9*(2–3), 103–127.

McAuley, Devin (1994). Time as phase: A dynamical model of time perception. In *Proceedings of the Sixteenth Annual Meeting of the Cognitive Science Society* (607–612). Hillsdale NJ: Lawrence Erlbaum Associates.

McClave, Evelyn (1994). Gestural beats: The rhythm hypothesis. *Journal of Psycholinguistic Research, 23*(1), 45–66.

McNeill, David (1992). *Hand and Mind: What Gestures Reveal About Thought.* Chicago: University of Chicago Press.

Neal, Jeanette G. & Stuart C. Shapiro (1991). Intelligent multi-media interface technology. In J. W. Sullivan and S. W. Tyler (Eds.), *Intelligent User Interfaces* (11–43). New York: ACM Press.

Nigay, Laurence & Joëlle Coutaz (1995). A generic platform for addressing the multimodal challence. In *Proceedings of the Conference on Human Factors in Computing Systems (CHI-95),* 98–105. Reading: Addison-Wesley.

Pöppel, Ernst (1997). A hierarchical model of temporal perception. *Trends in Cognitive Science, 1*(2), 56–61.

Schöner, Gregor & J. A. Scott Kelso (1988). Dynamic pattern generation in behavioral and neural systems. *Science, 239,* 1513–1520.

Sowa, Timo, Martin Fröhlich, & Marc E. Latoschik (1999). Temporal symbolic integration applied to a multimodal system using gestures and speech. In A. Braffort et al. (Eds.), Gesture-Based Communication in Human-Computer Interaction: Proceedings GW'99 (291–302). Berlin: Springer-Verlag (LNAI 1739).

Srihari, Rohini K. (1995). Computational models for integrating linguistic and visual information: a survey. *Artificial Intelligence Review, 8,* 349–369.

Wachsmuth, Ipke & Yong Cao (1995). Interactive graphics design with situated agents. In W. Straßer & F. Wahl (Eds.), *Graphics and Robotics* (73–85). Berlin, Heidelberg & New York: Springer-Verlag.

Wooldridge, Michael & Nick R. Jennings (1995). Intelligent agents: Theory and practice. *Knowledge Engineering Review, 10*(2), 115–152.

Signals and meanings of gaze in animated faces

Isabella Poggi and Catherine Pelachaud
Università Roma Tre / Università di Roma "La Sapienza", Italy

1. Introduction

The creation of conversational agents capable of expressive and communicative behaviors requires to define the relationship between the agent's communicative intentions and how these intentions are expressed in a coordinated verbal and nonverbal message. Suppose an agent S (a Sender) has the goal of communicating something to an interlocutor A (Addressee) in a particular situation and context; s/he has to decide what to say, which words to employ, which intonation, gestures and facial expressions to display in the various phases of the message. We are currently working on the automatic generation of verbal and nonverbal messages in order to animate a 3D agent. Our plan is to define nonverbal communicative acts in the same type of structure as is used for verbal communicative acts. Several problems need to be solved: how natural language generation systems may be extended to include the generation of nonverbal communicative acts; how planning operators should be refined to include them; and finally how verbal and nonverbal communicative acts may be synchronized. In this work, we restrict ourselves to only one aspect of the visual display of communicative acts, leaving aside body posture, hand gestures and so on. We focus on gaze behavior and propose a meaning-to-face approach, aimed at simulating automatic generation of face expressions driven by semantic data. The dynamic aspects of the generation of meanings in the flowing of discourse, which we do not deal in this paper, are addressed in other works (Poggi et al. 2000).

2. Gaze communicative acts

In the approach we adopt to build animated faces that communicate by gaze and facial expression, we categorise gaze communicative behavior by providing a cognitive representation of its semantic functions. Like any communicative signal, gaze necessarily includes two aspects, a 'signal' and a 'meaning'. The signal encompasses the set of physical features and the dynamic behavior of eyes in gaze, that is, their muscular actions and their physiological state; the meaning is the set of beliefs that gaze communicates. In order to analyze gaze from the signal and meaning side, we gathered a number of video recordings of TV talk shows and films, in order to find out which are the relevant aspects of gaze from the signal point of view and which are the meanings gaze can convey from the semantic point of view.

3. The signal side of gaze

Our hypothesis is that each single gaze can be analyzed in terms of a small set of physical parameters like eye direction, humidity, eyebrow movements and the like, each of which may be attributed a small set of values: the combination of those values (one value for each parameter) provides a precise description of

Table 1. List of gaze parameters

1. eyebrows: right / left eyebrow	
inner part:	up / central / down
medial part:	up / central / down
outer part:	up / central / down
2. eyelids: right / left eyelid	
upper:	default / raised / lowered
	default / tense / corrugated
	blinking / winking / closed
lower:	default / raised / lowered
	default / tense / corrugated
3. wrinkles	
	vertical / horizontal / curved / oblique
	central / lateral / all along forehead / between brows
	crow's feet / bulging (lower lid) / bagging (lower lid)
4. eyes: right / left eye	
humidity:	dry / wet / tears
reddening:	default / reddened
pupil dilation:	default / dilated / narrow
direction of head:	forward / up / down / left / right / backward
eye movements:	forward / up / down / left / right

any gaze under analysis. In other words, we have tried to do what Stokoe (Stokoe 1978) did for hand signs in Sign Languages: to find out the formational parameters of gaze. Using videotaped data, we have singled out the parameters (muscular actions and physiological states of the eye region) in terms of which we analyzed 300 items of gaze (Table 1).

3.1 Gaze parameters and their relevance

The anatomical portion of the face we take into account includes the following parts: eyebrows, upper eyelids, eyes, lower eyelids, and wrinkles. Within each part, different subparts, aspects or actions are considered relevant, or just their presence / absence. Why are these parameters relevant? Eyebrows are typically engaged in the expression of emotions like fear, anger, surprise, worrying (Ekman 1979), but also in greetings (Eibl-Eibesfeldt 1974) and in topic-comment marking and emphasis. Eyelids are important because they determine the openness of eyes, thus marking the withdrawing from interaction in cut-off, underlining excitement in flirting and so forth. As for eyes, humidity is relevant both in joy or enthusiasm (bright eyes) and in sorrow (tears); reddening may be a cue to crying (and then sadness) or to rage (bloodshot eyes). Pupil dilation is a cue to sexual excitement or other cases of arousal. In the eyes' spatial behavior, we must take into account the reciprocal relationships among eyes, head and trunk, and their relationship to where the interlocutor is.

3.2 From gaze parameters to Action Units

Various systems (Thórisson 1997; Lundeberg and Beskow 1999; Cassell et al. 2000) simulate face-to-face conversation with a user. Such systems combine several modules for the perception and generation of audio and visual signals. Conversational spoken dialogue modules (i.e., speech recognition and natural language understanding) are integrated with the analysis and recognition of nonverbal signals such as facial expressions, eye and hand movements. This audio and visual collected information is used to emulate turn-taking protocols (Thórisson 1997; Lundeberg and Beskow 1999; Cassell et al. 1994; Cassell et al. 1999) and to indicate objects of interest in the conversation (Johnson et al. 2000). These systems produce context-sensitive facial expressions, gaze and pointing gestures. In most of the mentioned agents, face simulation is triggered by verbal or intonational input (Pelachaud et al. 1996); the visual signal is therefore directly connected with an audio output corresponding to a specific linguistic act. The challenge of the system we designed is to generate a complex message that coordinates auditory and visual signals both stemming from cognitive/semantic information. Some values of the parameters above can be realistically used to simulate an animated face because they correspond to specific Action Units (AUs) of Ekman's FACS (Ekman and Friesen 1978). Each AU describes one or more actions of one or more specific muscles; and by simulating these AUs through computer graphics techniques it is possible to build (as was shown in Poggi and Pelachaud 1998) animated faces that exhibit communicative facial behavior. Table 2 shows how Ekman's Action Units correspond to values in the above parameters.

4. The meanings of gaze

Beside looking for the relevant aspects of the signal of gaze, we also tried to find which are the meanings that gaze can convey. We used a top-down approach: we first wondered which are, in principle, the meanings we may wish to communicate in visual interaction, we extracted a typology of meanings, and then tried to find in our data whether and which types of these meanings can be conveyed by gaze. Two broad types of meanings can be distinguished (Poggi 2002): Information on the World and Information on the Sender's Mind. The first class includes all the places, times, objects and events (either concrete or abstract) to which we refer in our verbal or nonverbal discourse; the second one includes the Sender's mental states that give rise to, or anyway have something to do with ongoing interaction: namely, the Sender's beliefs, goals and emotions. Our hypothesis is that different gaze categories can convey these different kinds of information. To formalise these different meaning types, we use a formalism (Poggi et al. 2000) where *x* is a variable, a constant or a function, *a* denotes, in particular, a domain 'action' and *b* is an atom denoting a domain 'fact'. 'S' stands for Sender and 'A' for addressee. In each communicative act S has the goal that A gets some beliefs. This is represented in our formalism by:

Goal S Bel A

4.1 Information on the World

The first kind of Information on the World are events and their spatial and temporal location; within events, we may refer to properties of concrete and

Table 2. Correspondence FACS - gaze parameters

Eyebrows: right / left eyebrow	
AU1	inner and central part of eyebrow UP
AU2	outer part of eyebrow UP
AU4	inner part / inner and central parts / inner, central and outer parts of eyebrow DOWN
AU1 + AU2	inner, central and outer parts of eyebrow UP
AU1 + AU4	inner and central parts of eyebrow UP and CENTRAL
AU1 + AU2 + AU4	inner, central and outer parts of eyebrow UP and CENTRAL
Eyelids: left / right eyelids	
AU5	upper eyelid RAISED
AU41	upper eyelid LOWERED
AU42	upper eyelid (very) LOWERED
AU43	upper eyelid CLOSED
AU6	upper eyelid (LOWERED and CORRUGATED) + lower eyelid (RAISED and CORRUGATED)
AU7	upper eyelid (LOWERED and TENSE) + lower eyelid (RAISED and TENSE)
AU44	upper eyelid LOWERED + lower eyelid ((very) RAISED and (very) TENSE)
AU45	BLINK
AU46	WINK
Eye opening	
AU5	wider
AU6, AU7	narrow
AU41, AU42, AU44	
AU4 + AU5	inner and central parts of eyebrows LOWERED and CENTRAL + upper eyelid RAISED
AU5 + AU7	upper eyelid RAISED + lower eyelid (RAISED and TENSE)
Head (direction of head)	
AU51	LEFT
AU52	RIGHT
AU53	UP
AU54	DOWN
AU55	TILT LEFT
AU56	TILT RIGHT
AU57	FORWARD
AU58	BACKWARD
Eye (eye movements)	
AU61	LEFT
AU62	RIGHT
AU63	UP
AU64	DOWN
AU65	wall-eye
AU66	cross-eye

Table 2. Continued

Wrinkles	
AU1	VERTICAL / OBLIQUE between brows
AU2	HORIZONTAL lateral part of forehead
AU4, AU1 + AU4	VERTICAL between brows
AU4 + AU5	
AU1 + AU4	CURVED central part of forehead
AU1 + AU2 + AU4	+ OBLIQUE between brows
AU1 + AU2	HORIZONTAL all along forehead
AU7, AU5 + AU7, AU44	BULGE lower lid
AU6, AU6 + AU43	CROW'S FEET

abstract entities (objects, persons, animals, discourses...) and to relations among them. Gaze can bear some meanings of this kind. For instance:

Deictic eyes

Eyes can make reference to specific places or to entities located in them: in other words, by using a deictic gaze we can point at specific things or persons in a spatial context. This kind of gaze might be paraphrased as follows: "I am referring to something in that place", where 'something' might be a single entity, like a person or an object, as well as a whole event, and then it can be represented as:

Goal S Bel A Intend S (Look-At S *x*)
Goal S Bel A Intend S (Refer-To S *x*)

Adjectival eyes

Eyes may also have an "adjectival" function, in that, as adjectives in verbal languages, they may mention properties of things. In fact eyes can mention a small number of physical properties of things. By squeezing eyes, we may refer to very small objects, and by opening eyes wide, to very large things, in both a concrete and a metaphorical sense: for instance, we may refer to a small box or a big house but also to a subtle concept or a great man. Adjectival eyes are formalised as:

Goal S Bel A (Consider S (P *x*))

with P denoting a 'property' of *x*. If, for instance, P = Small, then the previous formula means that "S wants A to know that S is considering *x*'s property of being small".

Table 3. Gaze behavior corresponding to word and gaze mind markers for the category **Belief**

	Vocal Mind Marker	Gaze Mind Marker
Certainty eyes	I suppose, perhaps	eyebrows up
	of course, no	eyebrows central and down
Metacognitive eyes	I'm thinking	eyes up
	I'm trying	eyes down
	to remember	sideways

In general, then the information about the world that can be conveyed by gaze is quite general and limited as opposed to the information on the Sender's mind which we are going to see now. In this sense it is true in fact that eye is the mirror of soul.

4.2 Information on the Sender's Mind:

During communication, the Sender may communicate, through words, gestures, gaze or posture, information about his/her beliefs, goals, and emotions, that is, Information on his or her Mind. The signals (in whatever modality) devoted to communicating this kind of information may be called Mind Markers (Poggi 2002). The gaze categories used as Mind Markers are the following:

4.2.1 *Beliefs*

Three types of Information on the Sender's beliefs can be conveyed by gaze: degree of certainty and metacognitive information (Table 3).

Certainty eyes

While communicating a Sender can mark if the information conveyed is certain, only likely or very unlikely, by simply using eyes: when we are not sure of what we are saying, we may raise our eyebrows without opening eyes wide; when we are sure of something, we exhibit a serious face, with a low intensity frown. In our formalism, uncertainty is represented by the mental atom 'Maybe'. For computational simplicity, at the moment we consider only three degrees of certainty: Bel, Maybe, Bel $\neg$. So, "I am not sure", which is communicated by raising eyebrows, may be represented as:

Goal S Bel A Bel S (Maybe *b*)

Metacognitive eyes - the gaze of thought
Eyes can be used to inform about the source (perception, memory or inference) of the information we are talking about. Usually, by looking up we inform that we are thinking (more specifically, maybe, we are trying to draw inferences), while by looking down sideways we inform that we are trying to remember:

Goal S Bel A Mind S (Is-Thinking-About S *x*)
Goal S Bel A Mind S (Is-Trying-To-Remember S *x*)

4.2.2 *Goals*
We may distinguish: a) information about the goal of a single communicative act (the performative of a sentence); b) information about a whole hierarchy of goals, namely the planning of a sentence (sentence goals), or c) of a mono-logic discourse (meta-discursive goals), or d) of the overall arrangement of conversation (meta-conversational goals), in particular the regulation of turn-taking and back-channelling. Let us see which of these types of information are related to specific gaze actions.

Table 4. Performative of imploring

S's request is for S's goal	S keeps head right
S claims being in power of A	S bends head aside
S is potentially sad	S raises inner brows

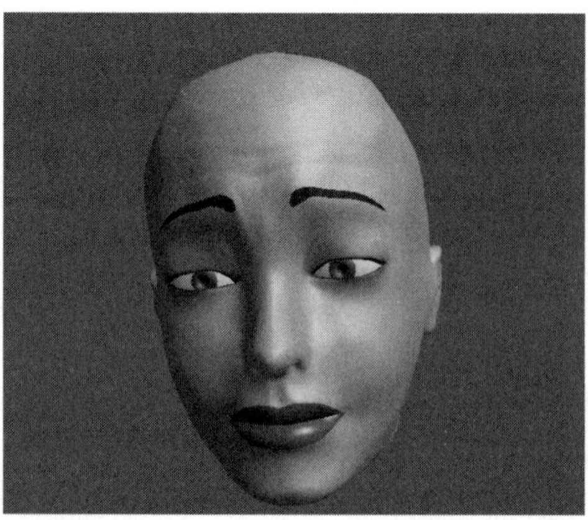

Figure 1. The imploring expression

Performative eyes

As we mentioned in a previous work (Poggi and Pelachaud 1998), gaze may have a performative function. For instance, in the face that makes a performative of imploration explicit, the inner parts of eyebrows are up and drawn together like in sadness. A peremptory order is marked by a frown, like in anger. This is because in both ordering and imploring I ask you some action useful for my goal, but in ordering I have power over you, and if you do not perform the requested action I will be angry at you; in imploring you have power over me, I am dependent on you, so if you do not do that action I will be sad. Table 4 shows the correspondence between cognitive units and gaze signals for implore. Figure 1 is an example of our 3D agent imploring.

Topic-comment eyes

In a sentence, the topic is the information S takes for granted as being shared with the interlocutor, while the comment is the information S considers to be new and relevant contribution to the ongoing discourse, and therefore the part S specially wants A to pay attention to. We typically stress the comment part by raising eyebrows, while clearly and ostentatiously directing our gaze to our interlocutor. During the topic part instead we gaze less at the interlocutor. The comment gaze category is formalised as:

$$\text{Goal S Bel A Bel S Intend S (Pay-Attention A } x\ p)$$

"S wants A to pay attention to *x* being the comment (the new information) of S's current sentence *p*".

Meta-discursive eyes

By gaze we can meta-communicate about the plan of our discourse, about its rhetorical structure: for example, when I want to add more precise information, my slightly narrow eyes tell: "I specify, I state more precisely...". Another example occurs when the word 'but' is accompanied by an eyebrow raising which has the meaning to warn of a contrast between beliefs, just as adversative conjunctions do. The relation between two beliefs may be represented as:

$$\text{Goal S Bel A Intend S Bel A (RS } b_i\ b_j)$$

with RS being a rhetorical structure. For example RS could be a relation of contrast between the two beliefs b_i and b_j or a relation stating the precision brought by b_i over b_j.

Table 5. Gaze behavior corresponding to word and gaze mind markers for the category **Goal**

	Vocal Mind Marker	Gaze Mind Marker
Performative eyes	I suggest	head aside eyebrows up
	I implore	head aside inner eyebrows up and central
Topic-comment eyes	pitch accent	eyebrows up eyes toward A
Meta-discursive eye	more precisely	narrow eyes
Meta-conversational eye: turn allocation	speak now	eyes toward A

Meta-conversational eyes

Gazing at a conversationalist is a way to pass speaking turn, while asking for a speaking turn is better done by wide opening eyes, like in breathing to start speaking:

> Taking turn: Goal S Bel A Intend S (Speak S)
> Passing turn: Goal S Bel A Intend S (Speak A)

4.2.3 *Affective eyes*

Gaze can show both 'social emotions', ones we can feel towards another person (like love, admiration, scorn, anger) and 'individual emotions', eventually triggered by natural events but not directed towards anyone in particular (fear, terror, joy, sadness, surprise, excitement, worrying, dismay). The general representation of the affective gaze is the following:

> Goal S Bel A (Feel-Emotion S *x*)

S wants A to know that S is feeling some Emotion *x*, where *x* will be specified in turn with its formal representation.

5. Conclusion

In order to produce virtual agents that communicate multimodally, we have focused on the communicative functions of gaze. Gaze may have different functions in a conversation, it may communicate various kinds of information, and it does through very different physiological states and muscular actions. To simulate the signal side of gaze we presented a way to analyze it based on a parametric analysis of real gaze items, and we proposed which of Ekman's Action Units may correspond to specific gaze states or behaviors. On the other hand, to simulate the meaning side of gaze we singled out some categories of meanings that can be conveyed by gaze: two broad classes have been distinguished, Information on the World and Information on the Sender's mind. We also put forward a formalism to represent the meanings of different gaze communicative acts. Of course, simulating gaze in animated faces requires taking into account the problem of timing and synchronization with other signals in the multimodal message. This is typically very important, say, in simulating topic-comment marking and turn-taking behavior. More generally, what triggers the operating of a specific Action Unit, or combination of them? This has to do with the dynamic flow of meanings that is generated online in the mind underlying the face, and that governs the planning of discourse in multimodal interaction and the synchronization of the different signals with each other.

Acknowledgment

We are indebted to Nicoletta Pezzato who carefully analyzed the videotaped gaze occurrences.

References

Cassell, J., Bickmore, J., Billinghurst, M., Campbell, L., Change, K., Vilhjálmsson, H., and Yan, H. (1999). Embodiment in conversational interfaces: Rea. In *CHI'99*, 520–527. Pittsburgh, PA.

Cassell, J., Pelachaud, C., Badler, N., Steedman, M., Achorn, B., Becket, T., Douville, B., Prevost, S., and Stone, M. (1994). Animated conversation: Rule-based generation of facial expression, gesture and spoken intonation for multiple conversational agents. In *Computer Graphics Proceedings, Annual Conference Series*, 413–420. ACM SIGGRAPH.

Cassell, J., Sullivan, J., Prevost, S., and Churchill, E. (eds.) (2000). *Embodied Conversational Characters*. MIT Press, Cambridge, MA.

Eibl-Eibesfeldt, I. (1974). Similarities and differences between cultures in expressive movements. In Weitz, S. (ed.), *Nonverbal Communication*. Oxford University Press, Oxford.

Ekman, P. (1979). About brows: Emotional and conversational signals. In von Cranach, M., Foppa, K., Lepenies, W., and Ploog, D. (eds.), *Human ethology: Claims and limits of a new discipline: contributions to the Colloquium*. Cambridge University Press, Cambridge, England; New York.

Ekman, P. and Friesen, W. (1978). *Facial Action Coding System*. Consulting Psychologists Press, Inc., Palo Alto, CA.

Johnson, W., Rickel, J., and Lester, J. (2000). Animated pedagogical agents: Face-to-face interaction in interactive learning environments. *International Journal of Artificial Intelligence in Education*, 11: 47–78.

Lundeberg, M. and Beskow, J. (1999). Developing a 3D-agent for the August dialogue system. In *Proceedings of ESCA, AVSP'99 workshop*, Santa Cruz, USA.

Pelachaud, C., Badler, N., and Steedman, M. (1996). Generating facial expressions for speech. *Cognitive Science*, 20(1):1–46.

Poggi, I. (2002). Mind markers. In Rector, M. Poggi, I. and Trigo, N. (eds.), *Gestures, Meaning and Use*. Universidad Fernando Pessoa Press, Porto.

Poggi, I. and Pelachaud, C. (1998). Performative faces. *Speech Communication*, 26:5–21.

Poggi, I., Pelachaud, C., and de Rosis, F. (2000). Eye communication in a conversational 3D synthetic agent. *Special Issue on Behavior Planning for Life-Like Characters and Avators of AI Communications*, 13(3): 169–181.

Stokoe, W. (1978). *Sign language structure: An outline of the communicative sysystems of the American deaf*. Linstock Press, Silver Spring.

Thórisson, K. (1997). Layered modular action control for communicative humanoids. In *Computer Animation '97*. Geneva, Switzerland. IEEE Computer Society Press.

Speech, vision and aphasic communication

Elisabeth Ahlsén
Göteborg University, Sweden

1. Aim

The aim of this study is to demonstrate the influence of activity factors, among them especially the degree of verbal-vocal focus versus nonverbal, visual focus, and their consequences for the "constitution" of a person as having a more or less severe communication handicap.

2. Background

Communication in context

There is by now a well established tradition of studying communication in context. Many influences have led to approaches of this type, some of the most important ones being Wittgenstein's concept of language games (Wittgenstein 1952), Austin's original speech act theory (Austin 1962), and Grice's conversational principles and maxims (Grice 1975), all of which consider language in terms of the actions that it performs in context. Other important influences have come from Goffman (1974), Garfinkel (1967) and the ethnomethodological approach, including Conversation Analysis (Sacks, Schegloff and Jefferson 1974, Goodwin and Heritage 1990).

The role of nonverbal and nonvocal communication in context and the relation to degree of communication handicap

In face-to-face interaction, the verbal-vocal part is performed and perceived as only part of the total communicative behavior, which also contains nonverbal and nonvocal parts. Peirce's concepts of iconic, indexical or symbolic communication are very useful in this context (Peirce 1940), since iconic and indexical communication is more important in nonverbal and nonvocal than in verbal-vocal communication. The degree of interrelation between vocal-verbal and nonvocal-nonverbal communication is a topic under discussion. Close association, i.e., integration, is advocated by McNeill (1992). Studies of linguistic feedback, turntaking and other phenomena in face-to-face interaction show that large parts of the regulation of communication interaction, the communication of feelings and attitudes and also of factual communication (e.g. emblems and illustrators) are handled by non-vocal and non-verbal channels (Allwood, Nivre & Ahlsén 1990, 1992; Sacks, Schegloff & Jefferson 1974). Turning to studies of aphasia and the special relevance of context and of the nonverbal-nonvocal aspects of communication, we can consider the World Health Organization definitions of impairment, disability and handicap. *Disability* is the aspect of a disorder that is related to reduced ability of an individual to meet the needs of daily living and *handicap* the disadvantage in society that results from either impairment or disability (Wood, 1980). With this perspective, we can pose the question whether a person with aphasia is constituted as having more or less of a handicap in a particular setting and what factors are crucial in determining this. Thus, by applying a functionalist, activity based communication analysis (Allwood 1976, 1984, 1995) and the WHO definition of handicap, this is an attempt to demonstrate from a case study how the degree of communication handicap is constituted relative to determining factors of the activity at hand.

Aphasia, communication in context and nonverbal-nonvocal communication

From about 1980, researchers have pointed to the use of compensatory strategies by aphasics in interaction (Prinz 1980, Holland 1982, Green 1984, Ahlsén 1985, 1991, Glosser et al. 1986, Penn 1987, Smith 1987, Feyereisen et al. 1988, Le May et al. 1988, Hermann et al. 1989, Klippi 1990, Hadar 1992, Laakso 1992, Milroy and Perkins 1992, and Goodwin 1995). Studies by Larkins and Webster 1981, Feyereisen 1983, Ahlsén 1885, Smith 1987, Le May et al. 1988, Hermann et al. 1989 and Hadar 1991 all point to the fact that nonverbal-nonvocal communication is one of the possible compensatory strategies and that it is actually used more by persons with aphasia in interaction, than by participants in interactions only involving non-aphasic persons. Available studies of communication in context involving participants with aphasia have generally focused on describing contexts where mainly verbal-vocal communication would be the most natural among persons without aphasia. When non-verbal and non-vocal communication is introduced it is as a strategy used by the participants to overcome verbal-vocal problems caused by the aphasia. In the present study, the focus is also on a situation which naturally contains a great deal of nonverbal-nonvocal action and interaction with visual support and a here-and-now focus. Since we know less about communication in this type of activity, it is of interest to get a picture of the role of verbal-vocal communication in this type of context and how this affects the role of the person with aphasia.

3. Method

The main subject was a 69 year old man, OO, with aphasia of the acoustic-mnestic and semantic type, according to clinical diagnosis by a speech and language pathologist. His speech was clearly "fluent" and his main problem appeared to be word finding. Two videorecordings of interactions involving OO and other persons were analyzed. Recording A (with more verbal focus) was a conversation in OO's living room, involving OO, his wife and a third person, who was a researcher and guest, also responsible for videorecording the interaction. The interaction is two hours long. OO is in view all the time, his wife is in view most of the time, and the guest is not in view at all. All three participants were audiorecorded. Recording B (with more visual focus) was made in the occupational therapy (OT) kitchen, during a one hour joint effort making waffles. The participants are OO, an occupational therapist and two other male patients, both younger and having more problems of communication and mobility than OO. Sequences which were considered typical of the communicative interaction were extracted from both recordings and transcribed using a combination of conversation analytic procedure and MSO (modified standard orthography for Swedish spoken language) (Nivre 1999). Nonverbal-nonvocal communication and other actions relevant for the communication were also described. The sequences were analyzed with respect to turntaking, linguistic feedback (backchanneling) and typical sequences, including repair sequences. The analyzed phenomena were then related to the main background factors influencing the two activities at hand and specifically to OO's role and communication.

4. Results

(1) The living room conversation.
(For reasons of space, examples will only be given in English translation.)
(O = man with aphasia, A = O's wife, B = guest)
(: = lengthening, [ ] = overlap, / = self-interruption, (…) = inaudible word)

```
A: on monday we will go to x-berg because then we have a
   child that will be thirteen
B: yes you told me so
C: yes not me but
A: oh yes you will come
O: noo [I'm not coming]
A: [ha ha ha]
O: [I have other things] to do
A: [you could come]
A: yes of course you have other things to do you can do what
   you want for me
O: ye:s [sometimes]
A: [if] it's good weather you can go
B: yes sure
A: yes:
O: yes you can
A: and in august/ and then in july my daughter's husband
   then he will be forty
B: which one of them
A: e out here in x-berg yes
B: I'm asking [(…)]
A: [I only have one] [daugther's husband]
B: [yes right]
O: [yes] how much does he cost
A: and what
O: how much does he cost
A: forty he he will be
O: forty yes:
A: forty years
O: a
A: and then in august them bittan in x-berg will be
   thirtyfive and otto will be seventy
O: yes that I have forgotten
A: and little eva will be two [years]
O: [yes]
A. so we have three in august [yes]
O: [yes] [that should be enough]
A: [we have] yes little eva
```

```
   "gummalumsan"
C: little neva
A: but we are planning to go away when otto has his birthday
   you see
B: you were going to do [that]
A: [yes] we were planning to go away then yes because it is
   no use having lots of things
B: then maybe you get that when you come home anyway
A: [no but I think that]
C: [yes: yes that will be] the same
A: no but
C: yes that's just it [you know] if you've done something
   then you are anyway [back then you are] still there
A: [no]
A: [noo noo that that] we will not be like that [at all
   because] I think that I think that you can spend as well
   on yourself
C: [noo]
B: m
C: [yes but what]
A: [as to spend] on all kinds of people
```

In this three person interaction, B who is the guest/observer tries to keep in the background, thus having only 8 contributions, whereas O's wife (A) has 22 and O has 17. The basic pattern of interaction is that A is telling B about family events, B gives feedback and O also mainly gives feedback. 13 out of his 17 utterances are pure second pair parts giving feedback. His feedback is varied and shows that he is following the conversation well. Once he asks A how old a relative will be on his birthday, producing the verb substitution *how much does he cost.* A asks *what,* O repeats and then gets a correct answer *he will be 40.* A second initiative is when he tries to explain why they are going away for his own 70th birthday, but A interrupts him and argues against him and he has to give up. The conversation and turn exchange is quite fast with many overlaps. We can see that O's utterances are overlapped more than A's and B's utterances, 59% of O's utterances are overlapped, compared to 48% of A's and 38% of B's. There are no pauses and O and A compete for the turn, making turnkeeping while trying to find the right words hard or impossible for O. He is, thus, given quite a passive role, although he strives to participate and be active. The topic of conversation, future events involving person data and place names, also makes it problematic to bring up new information for O with his word finding problems.

(2) Aphasic (O) in OT kitchen:

```
OT: yes a liter measure (.) six deciliters of water you
can
                                                      1
    measure up in this
B:  water
    2
OT: do you see is there a tap
B:  tap
O:  for example one goes here (.) there goes one
                              3        4
B:  where
O:  there we have one
B:  a tap
O:  how big will you have then
B:  little
O:  little water
B:  how big will YOU have then
     5
OT: six deciliters
O:  six deciliters (.) yes (.) let's see then
                                        6
B:  here
    7
O:  sure yes I am not bad at that I am not bad at that
```

Actions:

1. OT takes down measuring utensil and gives to B
2. O starts to move up from behind the OT to B
3. points to the faucet
4. points to the faucet
5. B turns to the OT
6. O turns on the faucet
7. OT helps B to hold the measure

Here the OT gives B a more specified instruction about measuring up six deciliters of water. O starts to move around from behind the OT to a position next to B. B does not really react, so after a short pause she tries to direct him to the faucet in front of him. B answers *faucet*, but still does not act. O now points to the faucet and states that it is a faucet. B says *what,* O repeats his message and pointing. B again repeats *faucet.* O moves on to ask how much water B should pour in. O's utterance involves a semantic substitution, he actually asks *how big* instead of *how much.* B answers *little,* O repeats and B turns to the OT, repeating B's question to her. The OT specifies and O confirms with *six deciliters yes* and starts pouring the water in B's place with the phrase *let's see then*, indicating a joint effort. B joins in assisting with the measuring utensil, saying *here*, and O, in a very satisfied tone of voice, mumbles *sure I am not bad at that I am not bad at that.* O takes the role of helper or assistant to the OT, possibly in order to speed things up, prompting B to act, and "showing off" as someone knowledgeable in the art of making waffles.

(3) Aphasic (O) in OT kitchen:

```
OT: with otto's help you can pour six deciliters of water
    in that
B:  yes eh
    1
O:  not too little
B:  too little no
O:  you must have much bigger
B:  much
O:  you must have you must have I don't remember what it
    was ten fifteen twenty
B:  yes so much then it's right
O:  yes like that I think I am not sure
B:  a
O:  I am not sure at all you must ask about it
OT: so can you put it there
O:  I thought it was a little too little maybe but it
B:  do you think so
OT: come and measure then
O:  yes be calm I will go and see
                              2
```

Actions:
1. points
2. gesture: palm towards B

The OT has accepted O as her assistant to help B and suggests a new attempt to pour six deciliters of water. B answers rather vaguely adding a hesitation sound, but starts to pour water. O stands by B's side and admonishes him not to pour too little water and then tries to specify, producing the semantic word substitutions *ten fifteen twenty* and expressing uncertainty. At the same time he shows by pointing. B gives feedback and asks for O's approval. O says that he thinks it's right but is not sure. B gives feedback to the first part of O's utterance with yes, O repeats that he is not sure (possibly because he did not get *no* as feedback from B) and adds that B has to ask. When the OT breaks in, O asks her, B gives hesitating feedback, the OT tells them to come and measure and O is the one who goes, telling B to be calm. O once again takes on the helper role which is now also given to him explicitly by the OT. He directs B (not paying too much attention to B's answers). He tries to get B to check the amount of water, but when B hesitates he takes over himself.

(4) Aphasic (O) in OT kitchen
(B and D are sitting at the table. O walks up to them):

```
O: have you seen this before
   1
B: no
O: this here there
        2    3
B: yes
   4
O: you have
B: but not
O: you have was it something to see that no
```

Actions:
1. opens waffle iron and turns it towards B
2. points into the open waffle iron
3. points into the open waffle iron
4. leans forward

Here O walks over to the table where B is sitting. He turns the waffle iron towards B and opens it, asking if B has seen this before, B answers *no*, O persists and clarifies by pointing into the open waffle iron and adding *this here there.* B then answers *yes* and O confirms *you have.* B adds *but not*, possibly intending to go on, but O ends the sequence by jokingly adding *you have was it something to see that*, answers *no* himself and shuts the waffle iron. This seems to be just a "joke" section, where O has some time on his hands and starts a little interaction with B, possibly just aiming at activating B in some talk. Also here, O does not really wait for B (who is rather slow in his answers) to develop his thoughts, but rounds off the conversation himself.

In general, we can see that O is impatient, he does not want to be inactive himself and he tries to activate the others. He likes to start up short conversation sequences where he is in control. He keeps the initiative and produces mainly first-pair part utterances, sometimes even adding second-pair parts himself. The conditions in this activity are the following. There is often silence. The other patients are less verbally and generally active than O. O is in fairly good control of the activity. O is given an intermediate assistant role by the OT, after his own initiative in this direction. Short here-and-now focused interaction sequences are natural and O can start them up without the risk of getting stuck because of his word finding problems, since the nonverbal activity with objects in reach is in focus and makes it possible to disambiguate utterances nonverbally. The others accept O's role, there is no competition for the turn and no pressure to produce anything specific verbally.

5. Discussion

Comparison of the two activities — O's disability and the constitution of his communication handicap

O's disability lies mainly in his inability to find the words he wants to use to express his intentions. The focus on the *nonverbal actions*, the lack of pressure on his speech, and his proficiency in the nonverbal activity of making waffles make it possible for him to contribute as a fairly proficient participant in the OT kitchen activity. The interaction-by-talk only of the living room conversation, on the other hand, makes O's disability a crucial obstacle for full participation, since he can hardly contribute any new information. The *here and now focus* of the OT kitchen makes reference easy, by deixis and nonverbal means, and it makes semantic substitutions and vague references possible to disambiguate from the immediate context. Deictic and non-verbal reference work and there is visual support also for verbal reference. The topics of the living room conversation builds on producing names of persons, places, dates and months, which O's word finding problems make impossible. Deictic, nonverbal and vague reference does not work very well and there is no visual support for reference. To a certain extent, however, vague reference and semantic substitution can be used by O. The *silent periods and lack of competition for the turn* make it easy for O to say something, to take verbal initiatives and to keep the turn and the verbal initiative as much as he wants to. The short verbal exchange sequences typical of this activity also make O's interaction skills fairly efficient, although the verbal content of his utterances is sometimes a little off target. In the living room interaction, on the other hand, there is constant competition for the turn and no pausing is possible. O can, therefore, not keep his turn while searching for words. His contributions are reduced to feedback and it is very hard for him to take initiatives. Given the differences in conditions of the two analyzed activities and the nature of O's communication disability, we can see that the degree of handicap constituted in the two activities also differs considerably. As a consequence of the converging factors above, all mostly more favorable to the OT kitchen interaction, O's disability is perceived as less of a handicap in this situation. This, of course, also affects factors like the degree of tension caused by verbal demands and O's self confidence.

The analysis once again points to the importance of studying communication in context, and in different contexts, in order to get a reasonable picture of a language and communication handicap. It also stresses the importance of considering variations in factors determining a specific conversation type and conversation occurrence, as well as doing a detailed interaction analysis.

Acknowledgments

This work was supported by the Swedish Council for Social Research, project 91–0061 C, 'Activity Based Communication Analysis of Aphasia', Department of Linguistics, Göteborg University. The data on OO was collected by Bengt Rundström, in the DSF project E86/172 'Aphasia in Daily Life' at the Department of Communication Studies, Linköping University.

References

Ahlsén, E. (1985). *Discourse Patterns in Aphasia. Gothenburg Monographs in Linguistics,* 5. Göteborg University, Department of Linguistics.

Ahlsén, E. (1991). Body communication as compensation for speech in a Wernicke's aphasic — a longitudinal study. *Journal of Communication Disorders,* 24, 1–12.

Allwood, J. (1976). *Linguistic Communication as Action and Cooperation. Gothenburg Monographs in Linguistics,* 2, Göteborg University, Department of Linguistics.

Allwood, J. (1984). On relevance in spoken interaction. In S. Bäckman and G. Kjellmer (Eds.) *Papers on Language and Literature, Acta Universitatis Gothoburgiensis* (18–35). Göteborg: Göteborg University.

Allwood, J. (1995). An activity based approach to pragmatics. *Gothenburg Papers in Theoretical Linguistics,* 76. Göteborg University, Department of Linguistics.

Allwood, J., J. Nivre & E. Ahlsén (1990). Speech management — On the non-written life of speech, *Nordic Journal of Linguistics,* 13, 3–48.

Allwood, J., J. Nivre & E. Ahlsén, (1992). On the semantics and pragmatics of linguistic feedback, *Journal of Semantics*, 9 (1), 1–26.

Austin, J. L. (1962). *How to do Things with Words.* Oxford: Clarendon Press.

Feyereisen. P. (1983). Manual activity during speaking in aphasic subjects. *International Journal of Psychology,* 18, 545–556.

Feyereisen, P., M. Barter, M. Goosens, & N. Clerebaut (1988). Gestures and speech in referential communication by aphasic subjects: channel use and efficiency. *Aphasiology,* 2, 21–32.

Garfinkel, H. (1967). *Studies in Ethnomethodology.* New Jersey: Prentice-Hall.

Glosser, G, M. Wiener & E. Kaplan, (1986). Communicative gestures in aphasia. *Brain and Language,* 27, 345–359.

Goffman, E. (1974). *Frame Analysis.* New York: Free Press.

Goodwin, C. (1995). Co-constructing meaning in conversations with an aphasic man. *Research on Language and Social Interaction,* 28, 233–260.

Goodwin, C. & J. Heritage, (1990). Conversational Analysis. *Annual Reveiw of Anthropology,* 19, 273–307.

Green. G. (1984). Communication in aphasia therapy: some of the procedures and issues involved. *British Journal of Disorders of Communication,* 19, 35–46.

Grice, H. P. (1975). Logic and conversation. In P. Cole & J. L. Morgan (Eds.) *Syntax and Semantics, 33: Speech Acts.* New York: Seminar Press, 41–58.

Hadar , U. (1991). Speech-related body movement in aphasia: period analysis of upper arms and head movement. *Brain and Language,* 42, 339–366.

Hermann, M., U. Koch, H. Johannsen-Horbach & C-W. Wallesh (1989). Communicative skills in chronic and severe nonfluent aphasia. *Brain and Language,* 37, 339–352.

Holland, A. (1982). Observing functional communication of aphasic adults. *Journal of Speech and Hearing Disorders,* 47, 50–56.

Klippi, A. (1990). Afasiapotilaiden kommunikatiivisten intentioiden välittyminen ryhmäkeskusteluissa (The transmission of communicative intentions in aphasic group discussions) Unpublished licentiate thesis of Logopedics. University of Helsinki, Department of Phonetics.

Laakso, M. (1992). Interactional features of aphasia therapy conversation. In R. Aulanko & M. Lehtihalmes (Eds.) *Studies in Logopedics and Phonetics,* 3. Publications of the Department of Phonetics. University of Helsinki, Series B: Phonetics, Logopedics and Speech Communication 4.

Larkins, P. & E. Webster (1981). The use of gestures in dyads consisting of an aphasic and a nonaphasic adult. In R. Brookshire (Ed.) *Clinical Aphasiology Conference Proceedings* (120–126). Minneapolis: BRK.

McNeill, D. (1992). *Hand and Mind. What Gestures Reveal about Thought.* Chicago: The University of Chicago Press.

Nivre, J. (1999). Modified Standard Orthography, V6. Göteborg University, Department of Linguistics.

Penn, C. (1987). Compensation and language recovery in the chronic aphasic patient. *Aphasiology,* 1, 235–245.

Peirce, C. S. (1940). *The Philosophy of Peirce: Selected Writings,* edited by J. Büchler. London.

Prinz, P. (1980). A note on requesting strategies in adult aphasics. *Journal of Communication Disorders,* 13, 65–73.

Milroy, L. & L. Perkins (1992). Repair strategies in aphasic discourse: towards a collaborative model. *Clinical Linguistics and Phonetics,* 6, 27–40.

Sacks, H., E. A. Schegloff & G. Jefferson (1974). A simplest systematics for the organization of turntaking for conversation. *Language,* 50: 696–735.

Smith, L. (1987). Fluency and severity of aphasia and non-verbal competency. *Aphasiology,* 1, 291–295.

Wittgenstein, L. (1953). *Philosophical Investigations.* Oxford: Blackwell.

Wood, P. (1980). Appreciating the consequences of disease: The WHO classification of impairments, disabilities, and handicaps. *The WHO Chronicle,* 34, 376–380.

Synaesthesia and knowing

John G. Gammack
School of Management, Griffith University, Australia

1. Introduction – a sense of synaesthesia

Recent years have seen a resurgence of interest in the phenomenon of synaesthesia, where sensory modalities are confounded, arousing experiences such as hearing colours or tasting shapes. Explanations typically emphasise the mediating neurophysiological correlates, while descriptive phenomenologies and other studies identify evidence suggesting relevant genetic or psychodevelopmental factors. Its role in metaphorical thinking, language imagery, and performance or other art is also well represented in the literature. The experience however, is often associated with a noetic quality, and its relation to the subjective nature of human knowing is of particular interest here. One common form, the integration of colour imagery with language or musical notes, is a particular type of synaesthesia found to be of relevance in this regard. This position paper outlines briefly some salient details of synaesthesia and its interpretations, and points to an explanation suggested by an esoteric understanding of mental phenomena, with specific linkages to the nature of human knowing, aiming to indicate a possible distinctive direction for further investigation.

Synaesthesia has been reported as a phenomenon in the lives of numerous individuals known for their creative works, and also many less famous cases. Characteristic quotes illustrate the experience:

> When I see equations, I see the letters in colors — I don't know why. As I'm talking I see vague pictures of Bessel functions from Jahnke and Emde's book, with light tan j's, slightly violet-bluish n's and dark brown x's flying around. And I wonder what the hell it must look like to the students.
>
> (Feynman 1988, p59)

> the days of the week have colours … Monday's a pale yellow, and Tuesday's navy. Everyone's name has a colour.
>
> (Maher, quoted in Dow 1999: 18)

Scientific luminaries and ordinary people (Maher is a systems analyst), along with many creative artists, writers and composers, have all been identified as synaesthetic. Scriabin for example had a correspondence between notes and colours, which his symphony *Prometheus, the Poem of fire* aimed to demonstrate through a keyboard that controlled a coloured light display. Rimsky Korsakov was also a synaesthete, but his correspondences differed. For example the key of C major, which was red to Scriabin, was white to Rimsky Korsakov (Rossotti 1983). Other examples are to be found in the literature, and indicate the personal nature of specific synaesthetic associations. Van Campen (1997) has written widely on the relations between synaesthesia and art, and in particular on the distinction between Scriabin's and Rimsky Korsakov's synaesthesias. Scriabin's is considered genuine, and based noetically in his emotional experience, whilst Rimsky Korsakov's may rather arise associationistically through empirical experience if not actual artifice. This proposition can be contested, as discussed later, but it epitomises an established distinction between authentic and pseudo synaesthetic experiences.

Estimates concerning synaesthesia's prevalence, have varied from 10 in a million to 1 in 25 000 (Cytowic 1993). It depends however, on how and what is counted: current estimates suggest that almost half of all people worldwide equate higher pitch (increased tonal frequency) with increased (visual) brightness and higher altitude. It appears to be more frequent in females, left handers and runs in families. Memory in synaesthetes is especially good, (Luria's (1968) S. is a prime example) and mathematical and spatial skills sometimes suffer, although as Dow (1999) observes, counterexamples show the stereotypes don't always hold. Synaesthetes are also more prone to experiences that challenge theories of consciousness, such as déjà vu, clairvoyance, precognitive dreams and the sensing of a presence (Cytowic 1993). One intriguing possibility however, consistent with the demographic data, is that synaesthesia is a normal brain function that everyone has, but which only reaches consciousness in a handful (Cytowic 1993, p166). Maurer (1993) has suggested that neonates typically lose the ability around 4 months old. Psychodevelopment typically increases linguistic differentiation, and trades direct apprehensions for socialised categories. This is a necessary ontological evolution, but may substitute the holism of immediate impression for a complex filtering and differentiation. In attempting to integrate the complex combinations of information carried in particular senses, we would suggest that abstract conception, particularly in creative fields, make use of this ability in an integrative manner, approaching the truth of things through multimodal triangulations. This may be conscious or involuntary, but the different states of consciousness implied are held to be symptomatic of individual's advanced perceptual access to noetic conditions. We hold that individual human beings differ in their capacity to apprehend knowledge at any given time, although not ultimately. We also believe that evolution is a complex process with spiritual and temporal dimensions not yet understood by science, and that the faculties of the mind implicated in the phenomena of consciousness require a science sensitive to their existence. Such traditions of inquiry exist, and Wilber (1995) provides a thorough consideration in this context.

Suggestions that colours empirically associated with alphabetical letters (as may be the case for many pseudo-synaesthetes) are merely learned pairs due to the accidents of childhood posters or particular sets of wooden blocks, are insufficient. They do not explain (for example) the young Nabokov's assertion that the colours on his toy blocks were all wrong. His mother, also a synaesthete, understood, and had similar associations herself. Other experienced cross modal associations likewise do not appear to be learned in such a sense. A contribution from nurture to nature however does account for a percentage of the evidence. Such learned associations are considered secondary to original, authentic forms of synaesthesia. Empirical knowledge, arising from sensory perceptions and cultural conceptions is exposed and discussed by Rudhyar (1977), as being one mode of knowing, but by no means the most basic. This points to a deeper origin in the mind governing specific correspondences, and one for which concepts of basic physical and spiritual energies provide an explanatory framework. Further acceptance of these concepts implicates a willingness also to embark on interior and interpretative modes of enquiry, with which traditional science has generally been uncomfortable. Without making further argument here, it is a subtext of this paper that contemporary science requires to be extended to provide satisfying explanations and understandings of noetic phenomena.

2. Vibration, harmony and synaesthesia

Although esoteric traditions have established theories on correspondences between sound and colour harmonies, it may be relevant to investigate this subject as an area for "objective" scientific inquiry. Intellectuals of the calibre of Pythagoras, Goethe, Aristotle and Newton have worked in this area, all variously concerned with the shared meaning underlying qualia and their common spiritual bond (Braun 1997: 6–8). In noting this, Braun provides an explanation of correspondence in terms of Hermetic law, one of whose principles is that "everything vibrates" and that there is a sympathetic connection between vibrations at higher and lower levels. Contemporary physics itself is bringing notions of consciousness into its theories, and the properties of light and electromagnetic energy are well established by impeccable science. Energies vibrating at frequencies manifest somehow, are understood by particular senses, and measurable by specific apparatus. Findings in this regard have been mapped reliably using the concepts of the day and of the field, and linked to beliefs, theories or "knowledges" accepted by particular communities. Movements such as Theosophy provide a literature in this regard. Scriabin himself was a Theosophist, and his *Prometheus* was intended as far more than some gimmicky multimedia experience. "(His) juxtaposition of chordal harmonies and light changes symbolised the act of creation and the evolution of human consciousness ... certain musical tones and intervals were used to depict the descent of spirit into matter and other actions of the Creative Principle" (Braun 1997, pp7–8). The deliberate manipulation of accepted correspondences may however, have been theoretically driven, rather than naturally occurring. Did Scriabin have some sort of "perfect pitch" whose cognition was naturally synaesthetic on a basis that agreed with Theosophical and Hermetic theory, and possibly objectively describable knowledge itself? Or was he devoid of authentic synaesthetic experience, and merely manipulating esoteric information? Rimsky Korsakov, like several other composers, was aware of fashionable norms, and these apparently were distinct from any synaesthetic correspondences he may have had. We return to this point later.

Visual keyboards did not originate with Scriabin however, and Braun traces some attempts to develop such. A particularly sophisticated one, the Luxatone, was developed and publicly demonstrated by Dr H Spencer Lewis in 1933, (anon 1997: 10–13), and its design was fully informed by explicit theory and extensive action research concerning the relationship between colour and music. A. Wallace Rimington (1912) tabulated the mathematical correspondences between vibrations per second, approximate colour and musical note, and this equates with the formulation of Isaac Newton, in which the spectrum ROYGBIV essentially corresponds to quantisation of increasing vibrational frequency. Ultraviolet, whilst detectable, is invisible to human eyes, though not to bees, and similarly infrared in other species. Different sensing associates with different frequencies and implies different experiences. An implication of this (cf. Wittgenstein's observation that if a lion could speak we could not understand) is that immediate experience, sensory or otherwise is one thing, and its reduction into perceptual or linguistic categories engender the potential for misunderstandings. The representational forms available, and the ability of the recipient to accept or recognise, restrict communication. Longer term implications of this research concern design of truly sensitive interfaces, and responsive virtual environments (Mc Kevitt and Gammack 1996; Zeltzer and Addison 1997: 61–64).

Attributes distinguishing knowledge from information include certainty, timelessness and universality, and knowledge cannot be confined to any particular form of symbolic reduction. In the context of immediate, unreduced personal experience however, a sense of certainty may be found. In this context synaesthesia is considered to be a perceptual correlate of a personal way of knowing, accessing deep faculties of the mind involved in coming to know what may be known. This in no way implies that synaesthetes have special knowledge, or a royal road to truth, only that they may experience consciously some epiphenomena of a sense making process in the human mind.

Our physical experience may be understood as patterns of energy and vibration, interpreted though senses available within a conscious mind. The ideational categories are doubtless partly personal, and partly shared in some degree. Certain experiences are best understood at a transpersonal level, whilst others, (e.g. direct nerve stimulation) are simply reducible to physicalistic investigation.

A Musico-poetic interlude

For some time Nachmanovitch (1990–99) has researched and developed synaesthetic software, informed by the Pythagorean tradition, which allows musical signals (tones and nuances of pressure) to be visualised non-randomly in geometric patterns. The interactivity between player and display has a three way synaesthetic quality of touch, light and sound. The Western Australian composer and artist Ilya Nikkolai (1997) has also studied what it is about images, movement, colour and shapes which appeals to people and holds their attention, and has advanced that certain configurations of these elements are "hard wired" in the brain. When visual elements conform to these human requirements, and in their correct combination with music, blissful relaxation is claimed to result. His work *liquid music* creates synaesthetic experience equivalents, putting abstract visual images to music, and has latterly been inspired by an attempt to recreate a near-death experience that he had. He notes a focus and certainty to his work since that time which was not there before. Near death experience and its relation to knowing and consciousness is also considered lucidly, and with advanced scientific awareness by the biologist Darryl Reanney (1994).

Similarly Halpern (1978) has researched and demonstrated the relations among colour, musical tone and stress levels, measuring physiological correlates of music designed to have a positive emotional affect. Kirlian photography was used to detect colour changes in the field of electrical discharges from their fingertips before and after the music, under controlled conditions. An observable increase in the colour rose, and decrease in red was shown in 95% of subjects, compared to 25% in the control group. The colours are associated with relative stress levels. Other sonic artists work in these multimedia art forms, for example JC Allison (Allison, n.d.) has researched and/or demonstrated multimedia correspondences for over 30 years, and his web site details some interesting observations here. Such artists are presumably interested in creating synthetic artistic effects according to criteria proper to their art, rather than being synaesthetic or investigative. Was Flann O'Brien however merely being lyrical when he described the rare gift of reading the colour of the winds, and the sub-winds:

> ....of indescribable delicacy, a reddish-yellow half-way between silver and purple, a greyish-green which was related equally to black and brown.
>
> (O'Brien 1967, p32)

and suggesting later (O'Brien 1967, p35) that:

> (the policemen) must be operating on a very rare colour, something that ordinary eyes could not see at all.

Perhaps O'Brien was evoking a sensitivity to realities operating on other frequencies, meaningfully interpretable by the gifted, and ignored by or lost to, the mundane comprehensions of the dense. If that should be the case, perhaps what we call our normal sensory existence is a reduction from a vastly greater possibility. Blind sight phenomena are considered significant in confirming the ability of many to discriminate colours through other senses such as touch. Furthermore, this ability can be learned by the sighted. A controlled study has shown that colours have signature textures: "yellow is slippery, red is sticky, and violet has a braking effect on the fingers". This was established using 80 sighted people detecting the colour of papers in insulated trays (Novomeisky 1965, described in Watson 1970), and further in Ostrander and Schroeder (1970).

"Naming is treacherous/ for names divide/truths into less truths,/enclosing them in a coffin of counters" (Graves 1965). In a psychodevelopmental progression in which linguistic distinctions are increasingly drawn, it is little wonder that neonates lose their synaesthetic ability as their perceptual systems modularise, and they socialise to the world of named categories and appearances. This extends Maurer's (1993) hypothesis, is consistent with Cytowic's theories, and is scientifically considered by Baron Cohen (1996). Such questions extend scientific disciplines, and touch on the nature of knowledge, consciousness, perception and reality, exercising Nobel laureates and others in such fields as neuroscience, physics and the philosophy of science, as their original writings attest.

3. An epistemological position

The working philosophy or epistemology embraced in this paper, and by many established scientists such as Eccles, Wigner, Reanney and others considering these questions, is *dualistic* in the sense akin to that understood across the occult and mystical traditions. This does not exclude an epistemological position based on monistic idealism (e.g. that of Goswami (1995)), but allows some pragmatic distinctions to be made to expedite theory and understanding. Without subscription to any particular formulation (although cohesive and comprehensive theories and thought systems are to be found), two general tenets may be advanced. Firstly, discerning a conceptual opposition between spirit and matter, and secondly accepting that higher and lower levels of being can be referenced in human experience, allows an approach to the study of phenomena not bounded by disciplinary paradigms. Such a stance allows productive conceptions to be formulated. Explanations in which the physical brain is considered only a part of the mind, acting as a filter and sensor of levels of mental experience (but not co-extensive with the full self or mind), can be investigated and accommodated. Accepting such an epistemology permits coherent investigation of the noetic phenomena of concern, beyond a purely materialist focus. Tart (1978) elaborates a similar point in presenting emergent interactionism as an approach to understanding related phenomena of consciousness.

This primacy of mind, and the mechanisms of neural transmission are elucidated in the writing of Eccles (Eccles 1965; Popper and Eccles 1977) and to be sure there are identifiable specific physiological events associated with thoughts and experiences which no-one questions. Specific experiences may be triggered by direct stimulation of nerves, as is well known, but inasmuch as the physical body itself is subject to laws of vibrational frequencies, resonating in harmony or otherwise with thoughts in consciousness, direct relations may be mapped among energies in various forms.

Red light's vibratory rate is 4.6×10^{14} Hz, blue's is 7.5×10^{14} Hz, and the harmonic affinities of degenerate light at lower levels produce colours, sounds, and forms of increasingly stabilised duration (Gimbel 1980). Emotional states, although linguistic nuances associated with refinement of qualia may be discerned, essentially have a positive or negative affective quality (Fridja 1988: 349–358), but, like colours, can be distinguished into some "basic" or archetypal groupings, and the numerous sophisticated shadings of same may be conventionally named, or culturally understood. These span a range from anger, whose expression registers at 4.8 "vibrations per second" (i.e. around the frequency of 4.6×10^{14} Hz), to reverence, at 9.8 vps (Macdonnell 1994). Colours directly correspond to these psychological states, and induce specific emotional effects, as is understood in the considerable applied psychological literature addressing interior design, colour therapies and advertising.

A reliable association between shapes in product packaging and taste perceptions has been found in the marketing literature, and is known as sensation transference. Cheskin for example (detailed in Hine 1995), compared identical products in packages with circle or triangle designs. Hundreds of interviews established the finding that over 80% believed boxes with a circle design contained a higher quality product, and furthermore, this general belief remained after tasting. Further descriptions, including specific associations between shapes and colours are given in Macartney (1999). In general, at the red end of the spectrum are attributed warm, active, and nerve exciting qualities compared to the cool, calming and passive qualities of blue, violet and green (see Miner 1998).

Such qualititative perceptions seem to be shared by many, and are found consistent with occult correspondence theories extant across cultures and ages. The colour perceptions available to higher species, and more highly evolved cultures are described by Berlin and Kay (1969), who note the fixed and deep developmental processes both ontogenetically and phylogenetically described in relation to synaesthesia by Gammack and Begg (1997). The original hypotheses proposed by Berlin and Kay (1969) were that (1) universal constraints exist on the patterns of colour naming across languages and (2) there are also universal constraints on the temporal development of systems of basic colour terms. Their original methodology was criticised, but subsequent studies have largely validated their substantive claims in this area (Kay and Berlin 1997). The controversy is thoroughly considered by Saunders and Van Brakel (1997), and several peer reviewers. Such arguments can be taken to imply hard biological constraints, which is not the only interpretation, especially given our knowledge of the active perceptions and cultural factors involved in naming. Without implying reductive materialistic conclusions, such studies can suggest an objectively ordered unfolding of consciousness and enhanced perceptions underlying personalised phenomena, and ultimately govern the dynamics of synaesthesia. Our related work in colour is intended to give an empirical handle on recondite phenomena of consciousness (Gammack and Denby 1999; Denby and Gammack 1999).

4. Knowing and abstraction

A secondary, but presently significant, meaning of synaesthesia (found in older versions of the Oxford English Dictionary) is: *a stage in the development of sympathy*. This brings us to the issue of knowledge itself.

In agreement with Cytowic, we submit that synaesthesia reflects a deep sense making, if not noetic process in every human mind. Forms are secondary to thoughts, which are naturally more abstract than the modalities associated with specific manifestations or expressions. The forms produced by thought may reflect an involuntary consequence of such processing, in contrast to which conscious attempts to fuse sensory experiences are considered as essentially contrivances. Returning to the distinction raised earlier between Scriabin and Rimsky Korsakov, in which it was alleged that Scriabin's was genuine, whereas Rimsky Korsakov's was acquired, van Campen's (1997) analysis of this is interesting, illuminating a well-established distinction between true (deep) synaesthesia, from that with a basis in empirical perceptual association. Could it be that Scriabin's associations were theoretically driven by his theosophist beliefs, whereas those of Rimsky Korsakov reflected a personal and authentic mode of creativity? Apparently not, as Scriabin's associations were involuntary, and the literature seems consistent on this point. And if genuine, it may suggest that there *are* objective constraints on the forms of universal thought that can be mapped, aligned in realised individuals, and taking precedence over empirically derived correspondences. This of course is only one hypothesis at this stage.

In separating deep conceptions from their characteristically modal expression, Kandinsky has eluded simple categorisation due to the abstract nature of his expression, which found form both in music and in art. From musical parents, and a musician himself in boyhood, these may be seen as formal outlets for his creative impulses, later to find expression in his pioneering development of abstract art forms. Pushing the boundaries of form and the potential of a specific modality can be seen as a quest to do justice to the wholeness of a conception in its abstract, pre-formal origin. In the study of human memory, the deeper the involvement in which an experience is encoded, the better it can be recalled. If evolution tends towards the complex, approximations of increasingly greater abstraction and comprehension will asymptote towards pure forms and archetypes of original conception. The typically excellent memory of synaesthetes, and its relationship to creativity and feeling-of-knowing is a promising area of especially relevant investigation within cognitive science.

Although we wish to go beyond a purely nosological interpretation, the clinical diagnosis of synaesthetic perception is detailed by Cytowic (1989) as having various salient features including: involuntary, but elicited; projected outside the body; durable associations over a lifetime; memorable sensations; and emotional and noetic. This latter is particularly interesting, as "synaesthetic experience is accompanied by a sense of certitude … and seem not just a state of perception, but of knowledge". Savant syndrome, where prodigious feats of art, music, calculation or memory are displayed also suggests affined access to knowledge sources, communal memories, or optimal cognitive processing. The typical assurance of such activity is consonant with a deep origin within individual minds.

The Kantian distinction between noumenal and phenomenal truth here is also found helpful, although it is not the intention of this paper to persuade or convince through academic philosophical argument. For that, the work by the philosopher Campbell (1931) is particularly helpful, in considering the range of philosophical arguments around deterministic conceptions of knowledge and in elaborating the case for a supra-rational absolute comprehending free will. Contemporary philosophy on these themes in relation to consciousness is also to be found in the archive maintained by Chalmers (n.d.). In the noumenal understanding, truth is to be found only in that thought which has become identical with reality: correspondence and coherence are complete, and this unnameable knowledge lies beyond the grasp of the finite intellect. The degeneration of this original knowledge forms phenomenal, perceptual systems, mediated, finite, chosen, and named into accepted linguistic correspondences. The higher the abstraction level at which these forms occur, the less linguistically encultured is the knowledge, and the more it is related to deeper physical and physiological structures which mediate the evolution of human consciousness. Aristotle's common sensibles have been adduced by Cytowic (1993, p87) already in hypothesising synaesthesia as occurring at the highest level of abstract processing in the brain. Campbell's philosophical analysis leads him to hold the propositions that will energy is made known ONLY through direct experience, and that there is no good reason for supposing that the native *capacity* for energising ultimately varies between persons. Although developmental choices may distinguish persons subsequently, this view is consistent with Maurer's hypothesis, and allows a conception reconciling original creativity with the differentially actual cognitive work done to bring it forth.

Cytowic (1993, p78) draws explicit parallel between the qualities of synaesthesia and those of ecstasy as described by William James (1902). These qualities comprise ineffability, passivity, noetic quality and transience. They are "states of insight into depths of truth unplumbed by the discursive intellect" and carry a lasting sense of authority. These qualities of involuntary and direct experience, coupled with an enduring certitude characterise various mystical states of consciousness, and these are interesting inasmuch as they lend a noetic basis for deciding matters of mere perception and argument.

Evolving beyond disciplinary limits, the scientific search for knowledge continues, and contributions from e.g. language studies, neuro- and developmental psychology, the cognitive sciences generally, and phenomenological enquiries all have their place. An integration or synthesis of their deep insights may yet unify the sciences. The science journalist Horgan (1996) produced a "wonderful, provocative" book on "the end of science", in which he interviewed numerous contemporary luminaries in major scientific fields to give a realistic picture of the prospects of each. No-one can doubt his credentials to do so, nor that his assessments are other than fair to the viewpoints current in those fields, although the argument that science was finished was and is, predictably, disputed. His epilogue to the book however reports a mystical experience that he underwent, and still considers to be the most important event of his life. This personal experience leads to conclusions which are perhaps best considered elsewhere, but which concern the ambivalence in human knowledge between seeking truth, and recoiling when it is at hand. Maslow's description of this human phenomenon is "the need to know and the fear of knowing", and this taboo on progressing an understanding beyond the limits of scientific conception are ably discussed by Harman and Rhinegold (1984).

Science at the end of the 20th century has manifestly struggled with abstruse phenomena of consciousness, and Cytowic's understandable emphasis on the primacy of emotion has pointed to a redress of the imbalance of an overly rationalistic tradition (Dann 1998). Yet a true science can make use of the gains of this tradition, fusing with the awareness of those who know in other, romantic, ways. Noetic Science approaches provide such a comprehension, encompassing the diverse ways of knowing. As Harman (Harman and Rhinegold 1984) describes it: "Noetic Sciences is the systematic study of these all inclusive ways of knowing, which form the basis of how we see ourselves, each other and our world." The most significant studies predicted for the millennium concern the studies of human consciousness, and humanity is surely now becoming able to dissociate nascent understandings, and enduring insights from new age charlatanism and poor scholarship. Wrestling with phenomena such as synaesthesia through various investigative techniques promises us some access to the reality we may finally know.

Acknowledgments

The author is grateful to three anonymous reviewers for helpful suggestions that have improved this paper. Internet sources have been cited (where available) for the convenience of readers.

References

Allison J. C. (1997). website http://www.livingston.net/allison/docs/page1.htm (accessed Dec 20th 1999).

Anon (1997). The relationship of color to sound. *Rosicrucian Digest* 75, (1) 10–13.

Baron Cohen Simon (1996). Is there a normal phase of synaesthesia in development? PSYCHE, 2(27), http://psyche.cs.monash.edu.au/v2/psyche-2–27-baron_cohen. html (accessed Dec 20th 1999).

Berlin, Brent and Paul Kay (1969) *Basic color terms.* Berkeley : UCP.

Braun, Melanie (1997). The spectrum of music: the color organ. *Rosicrucian Digest* 75, (1) 6–8.

Campbell, Charles A (1931). *Scepticism and construction.* London: Macmillan.

Chalmers, David (n.d). Online papers on Consciousness archive http://www.u.arizona.edu/~chalmers/online.html (Accessed Dec. 20th 1999).

Cytowic, Richard E. (1989). *Synesthesia: a union of the senses.* New York: Springer-Verlag.

Cytowic, Richard E. (1993). *The man who tasted shapes.* London: Abacus.

Dann, Kevin T. (1998). *Bright colors falsely seen: synaesthesia and the search for transcendental knowledge.* Yale University Press. Excerpt at: http://www.uvm.edu/~kdann/excerpt.htm (accessed Dec 20th 1999).

Denby, Ema and John Gammack (1999). The naming of colours: investigating a psychological curiosity using AI Proc 6th International Conference on Neural Information Processing (ICONIP), T. Gedeon, P. Wong, S. Halgamuge, N. Kasabov, D. Nauck and K. Fukushima Perth (Eds.), November, pp. 964–973.

Dow, Steven (1999). Colour coded. *The Australian Magazine* Feb 6–7 18–21.

Eccles John C. (1965). *The Brain and the person.* The Boyer Lectures, Sydney: Australian Broadcasting Commission.

Feynman, Richard P. (1988). *What do you care what other people think*? London: Unwin paperbacks p.59.

Fridja, Nico H. (1988). "The laws of emotion", *American Psychologist*, 43, (5), 349–358.

Gammack, John and Carolyn E. Begg (1997). *Evolution, emergence and synaesthesia.* In: Philosophical Aspects of Information Systems (Eds.) R. L. Winder, S. K. Probert and I. A. Beeson. London : Taylor & Francis. 205–214.

Gammack, John and Ema Denby (1999). The true hue of grue: investigating a psychological curiosity. *Dialogues in Psychology: A Journal of Theory and Metatheory*, 9.0 July. Electronic Journal archived at: http://hubcap.clemson.edu/psych/Dialogues/9.0.html also in S. Ó Nualláin and R. Campbell (Eds.), Proceedings of MIND-4, Dublin City University, August, pp. 11–25.

Gimbel, Theo (1980). *Healing through colour.* Saffron Walden: CW Daniel.

Goswami, Amit (1995). 'Monistic idealism may provide better ontology to cognitive science: a reply to Dyer', *Journal of Mind and Behavior*, 16, 13 5–150.

Graves, Robert (1965). The unnamed spell, *Collected poems.* London : Cassell.

Halpern, Steven (1978). *Tuning the human instrument.* Spectrum Research Institute, Belmont CA.

Harman ,Willis and Howard Rheingold (1984). *Higher creativity.* Los Angeles: Tarcher.

Hine, Thomas (1995). *The total package.* New York: Little, Brown, and Company.

Horgan John (1996). *The end of science.* London : Abacus.

Johnston, D. Barton (1974). Synesthesia, Polychromatism, and Nabokov in CR Proffer (Ed) A book of things about Vladimir Nabokov, Ann Arbor : Ardis.

Kay, Paul and Brent Berlin (1997). Science ≠ imperialism: there are nontrivial constraints on color naming. *Behavioral and Brain Sciences* 20:2 196–201.

Klein, A. B. (1937). *Coloured light: an art medium.* London: The Technical Press.

Luria, Alexander R. (1968). *The mind of a mnemonist.* New York, Basic Books.

Macartney, Jennifer (1999). Website http://township.net/color/html/market.html (accessed Dec 20th 1999).

Macdonnell, Wendy (1994). Colour and sound. *Golden Age* 21 49–51 also at http://www.newage.com.au/library/colour2.html (accessed Dec 20th 1999).

Maslow, Abraham H. (1968). Toward a psychology of being (2[e]) Cincinnati: Van Nostrand.
Maurer, Daphne (1993). *Neonatal synesthesia: implications for the processing of speech and faces.* In B. de Boysson-Bardies, S. de Schonen, , P. Jusczyk , P. McNeilage, & J. Morton, (Eds) Developmental Neurocognition: Speech and face processing in the first year of life. Dordrecht: Kluwer Academic Publishers.
Mc Kevitt, Paul and John Gammack (1996). The sensitive interface. *Artificial Intelligence Review,* 10 (3–4), 275–298.
Miner, John E (1998). *The complete color reference manual* Kombu International http://www.kombu.com/Colbook (accessed Dec 20th 1999).
Nachmanovitch, Stephen (1990–99). Visual Music Tone Painter ™ http://www. freeplay.com/vismus.htm (accessed Dec 20th 1999).
Nikkolai, Ilya (1997). *Liquid music* http://www.iinet.net.au/~satori/lmusic.htm (accessed Dec 20th 1999).
Novomeisky, A. (1965). The nature of the dermo-optic response. *International Journal of Parapsychology,* 7 (4).
O'Brien, Flann (1967). *The third policeman.* London: MacGibbon and Kee.
Ostrander Sheila & Lynn Schroeder (1970). *Psychic discoveries behind the iron curtain.* Prentice Hall.
Popper Karl and John C. Eccles (1977). *The self and its brain.* Berlin: Springer Verlag.
Reanney, Darryl (1994). *Music of the mind.* Melbourne: Hill of Content.
Rimington, A. Wallace (1912). *Colour-music, the art of mobile colour.* London: Hutchinson & Co.
Rossotti, Hazel (1983). *Colour.* Harmondsworth: Penguin.
Rudhyar, Dane (1977). *Culture, crisis and creativity.* Wheaton IL: Quest Books.
Saunders, Barbara A. C. and van Brakel, Jap (1997). Are there nontrivial constraints on colour categorisation? *Behavioral and Brain Sciences* 20:2 196–201.
Tart, Charles T. (1978). Transpersonal realities or neurophysiological illusions: toward an empirically testable dualism Paper presented at the 1978 Meeting of the American Psychological Association in Toronto, online at URL http://www.csp.org/experience/docs/tart-trans_real.html (accessed Dec 20th 1999).
van Campen, Crétien (1997). Synesthesia and artistic experimentation *PSYCHE,* 3(6), November http://psyche.cs.monash.edu.au/v3/psyche-3-06-vancampen.html (accessed Dec 20th 1999).
Watson, Lyall (1973). *Supernature.* Garden City, N. Y.: Anchor Press.
Wilber, Ken (1995). *Sex, ecology, spirituality.* Boston: Shambhala.
Zeltzer, David & Addison Rita K. (1997). Responsive virtual environments. *Communications of the ACM,* 40 (8) 61–64.

What synaesthesia is (and is not)

Sean A. Day
National Central University, Taiwan

Synaesthesia is the general name for a related set (a "complex") of various cognitive states having in common that stimuli to one sense, such as smell, are involuntarily simultaneously perceived as if by one or more other senses, such as sight or/and hearing. For example, I myself have a type of synaesthesia: The sounds of musical instruments will sometimes make me see certain colors, about a yard in front of me, each color specific and consistent with the particular instrument playing. A piano, for example, produces a sky-blue cloud in front of me, and a tenor saxophone produces an image of electric purple neon lights. One highly documented case of synaesthesia involved Michael O. Watson, who felt at or within his right hand different flavors — the flavor of spearmint, for example, felt like smooth glass columns (see Cytowic 1989, 1993).

Synaesthesia is additive; that is, it adds to the initial (primary) sensory perception, rather than replacing one perceptual mode for another. With my colored musical instruments, I both hear and "see" the sounds; the visual images do not replace the auditory sensations. Both sensory perceptions may thus become affected and altered in the ways they function and integrate with other senses. Synaesthesia is generally "one-way"; that is, for example, for a given synaesthete, tastes may produce synaesthetic sounds, but sounds will not produce synaesthetic tastes. However, there have been a few rare cases of synaesthetes who have had "bi-directional" synaesthesia, in which, for example, music induces (synaesthetic) colors and seeing colors induces (synaesthetic) sounds — the correspondences, however, are not the same in both directions! Furthermore, these bi-directional synaesthetes can get trapped in "loops", where, for example, a sound produces a synaesthetic color, which produces a synaesthetic sound, which produces a synaesthetic color, which . . . and so on, until the process is drastically broken by some new, major sensory stimulation.

Actually, synaesthesia may be divided into two general, somewhat overlapping types. The first, which I will call here "synaesthesia proper", is as described above, in which stimuli to a sensory input will also trigger sensations in one or more other sensory modes. The second form of synaesthesia, which I will call "cognitive" or "category synaesthesia", involves synaesthetic additions to culture-bound cognitive categorizational systems. In simpler words, with this kind of synaesthesia, certain sets of things which our individual cultures teach us to put together and categorize in some specific way — such as letters, numbers, or people's names — also get some kind of sensory addition, such as a smell, color or flavor. The most common forms of cognitive synaesthesia involve such things as colored written letter characters (graphemes), numbers, time units, and musical notes or keys. For example, the synaesthete might see, about a foot or two before her (the majority of synaesthetes are female), different colors for different spoken vowel and consonant sounds, or perceive numbers and letters, whether conceptualized or before her in print, as colored. A friend of mine, Deborah, always perceives the letter "a" as pink, "b" as blue, and "c" as green, no matter what color of ink they are printed with. The distinction between "synaesthesia proper" and "cognitive" synaesthesia is, I believe, a fundamental one towards discerning the rather distinct differences in neural pathways and cognitive processes involved in various types of synaesthesia. Synaesthesia proper is, in many ways, almost basic direct sensory response to stimulus; cognitive/categorizational synaesthesia is far more complex, involving learned categories whose items are assigned specific meanings.

Synaesthesia has definite neurological components and is apparently partially heritable and autosomal dominant, with one (trigger?) component perhaps passed down genetically on X-chromosomes (Bailey and Johnson 1997; Cytowic 1989, 1993; Frith and Paulesu 1997; Baron-Cohen and Harrison 1997). The percentage of the general human population which has synaesthesia varies with the type involved; estimates run from 1 in 500 for basic types of cognitive synaesthesia (colored letters or musical pitches), to 1 in 3,000 for more common forms of synaesthesia proper (colored musical sounds or colored taste sensations), to 1 in 50,000 or more for people with rare (such as one synaesthete I know of who synaesthetically tastes things she touches) or multiple forms of synaesthesia proper. Perhaps more than half of all humans have a basic form of synaesthesia in which they consider "higher" sounds to be "brighter" and "lower" sounds to be "darker" (Melara 1989a, b; see also Marks 1982).

Many writers have proposed that synaesthesia is perhaps an atavistic throwback to our primitive ancestors. They then turn to evoke various forms of Romanticism. Others (such as Scriabin) have proposed that synaesthesia is perhaps the next stage in the evolution of humans, an "advancement" of some type. Both concepts, of course, show little knowledge of genetics and how evolution works. Evolution cannot go backwards, thus atavism is impossible. Likewise, evolution is not teleological — we can't predict where we are going. Instead, current research indicates that most forms of synaesthesia result from neoteny, the increase retention of juvenile traits phylogenetically into adulthood. This process is commonly appears in domesticatory processes, and humans are the example par execellence of domestication. More specifically, in the synaesthete, certain genetic triggers either fail to go off, or are disrupted by other genetic triggers, resulting in certain specific sections of the brain not receiving messages to mature on towards more adult form. Those parts of the brain "stay young", and synaesthesia results (see Maurer 1997; see also Gould 1977, 1980). Although loci in the brain for synaesthesia have not yet been pinpointed, it appears that the hippocampus (see Cytowic 1989, 1993; Paulesu et. al 1995; Baron-Cohen and Harrison 1997) and the extrastriate visula cortex (area 19) (see Zatorre et al. 1994) play prime roles in many types. Current research is underway with MEG technologies to better map various synaesthesiae.

Debates concerning whether physiological, neuronal synaesthesia and poetic synaesthetic word-play are related or disjunct phenomena have a long and convoluted history. A prime element in these debates, an element still rampant today, is whether synaesthesia is inherited or learned; nature or nurture; hard-wired or soft-ware.

It might seem an odd thing to start a history of a neurological condition with a look at ancient mathematicians and astronomers, but some of them offered important initial cornerstones to later theories on synaesthesia. Around the year 550 B.C., to begin with, the Pythagorans offered mathematical equations for the musical scales, showing that musical notes could be seen as relationships between numbers. The "higher" end-note of an octave could be deemed the mathematical doubling of the frequency of the lower of the two notes; for example the frequency of 400 (2 X 200) is an octave higher than 200, which itself is an octave higher than 100. Thus, the interval of an octave is rooted in the ratio 2:1. A frequency of about 262 is middle "C" on a piano; thus 524 and 1,048 are also about "C"s. The ratio of a musical "fifth" is 3:2; if 262 is a "C", 393 would be the "G" above it, or the "so" above the initial "do". A "fourth" has the ratio of 4:3; for "C" ("do") as 262, the "F" ("fa") above it would have a frequency of about 349.33. A "whole tone", or "whole step" has a ratio of 9:8; if we go an octave higher, with "C" ("do") having a frequency of about 524, the next note in the Major scale, "D" ("re") would have a frequency of about 589.5. So, here we have a straightforward linking of numbers and mathematics with musical notes.

Almost 200 years later, around 370 B.C. or so, Plato (n.d. (370 B. C.)) wrote *Timaeus*, in which the soul of the world is described as having these same musical ratios. A cosmology was emerging in which the planets' radii (the planets' order actually varied, depending upon the author) were set with a ratio sequence of 1:2:3:4:8:9. Later, ratios would emerge with the following ratio sequence: Moon = 1; Venus = 2; Earth = 3; Mars = 4; Jupiter = 14; Saturn = 25. This sequence approximated the Greek diatonic musical scale's ratios, thus the planets were tied to music, and a concept of "the music of the spheres" was initiated.

Shortly after Plato, around 330 B.C., Aristotle (1976 (c. 330 B.C.)) wrote to maintain that the harmony of colors were like the harmony of sounds. This set the stage for a later equating of specific light and sound frequencies, as Aristotle's works were translated and incorporated into European sciences.

In another 400 years, around about 151 A.D., Ptolemy (1952 (151 A.D.)) wrote his *Almagest*, in which he also attempted to show ratio relationships between the distances of the planets. The ratios changed over time, as observers made better measurements and checked their accuracy. Thus, over a thousand years later, in 1543, Nicolaus Copernicus (1952 (1543)) proposed the following, which is mathematically somewhat different than what had gone before: if Earth = 1, then the radii of the other planets have distances of 1/3rd for the Moon, 3/4th for Venus, 1.5 for Mars, 5 for Jupiter, and 9 for Saturn.

In 1619, Johannes Kepler's *Harmonices mundi* ("Harmonies of the World") (1952 (1619)) was published. Here, each planet was not only given an individual basic note but was also actually given a sequence of musical notes based upon its movements — not enough for a full "melody", really, but at least enough for a "motif".

In 1704, Sir Isaac Newton's treatise *Optics* (1952 (1704)) was first published, which dealt, among other things, with the parallel between colors of the spectrum and notes of the musical scale. In a sense, this was a revival of Aristotle's theories of the resemblances between light and sound; but Newton's efforts were far more elaborate and mathematical. Newton mathematically but quite arbitrarily divided the visible light spectrum into seven colors. He then noted that the mathematical relationships of these seven colors was similar to those of the musical scale, with the following concordances:

red	=	tonic
orange	=	minor third
yellow	=	fourth
green	=	fifth

blue	=	major sixth
indigo	=	seventh
violet	=	eighth (octave)

Although Newton himself basically only held these concordances as an analogy, and later discarded notions that there was any true connection between colors and the musical scale, by around 1742, the French Jesuit monk Louis-Bertrand Castel, the well-known mathematician and physicist, was a firm advocate of there being direct solid relationships between the seven colors and the seven units of the scale, as per Newton's *Optics.* Castel proposed the construction of a *clavichord oculaire*, a light-organ, as a new musical instrument which would simultaneously produce both sound and the "correct" associated color for each note (see Galeyev 1988; Dann 1998). This theme was returned to in 1790, when Erasmus Darwin (Charles Darwin's grandfather) wrote about the parallel between colors and musical notes.

If we consider five senses — Hearing, Smell, Taste, Touch, and Vision — this gives us a possibility for 20 ((5 X 5) — 5) different combinations of primary stimulus to ("secondary") synaesthetic perception. If we add a sixth sense — say, temperature sensation — this would increase the number of combinations to 30. Considering these six senses, the following tabulates which types of synaesthesia are more frequent, less so, or yet unseen among 365 reported cases I have so far come across. Note that some of these cases are people with multiple synaesthesiae.

Col. Graphemes	=	244/365	=	66.8%
Colored Time Units	=	70/365	=	19.2%
Col. Mus. Sounds	=	53/365	=	14.5%
Col. Gen. Sounds	=	44/365	=	12.1%
Col. Mus. Notes	=	38/365	=	10.4%
Colored Phonemes	=	35/365	=	9.6%
Colored Tastes	=	23/365	=	6.3%
Colored Odors	=	21/365	=	5.8%
Colored Personalities	=	16/365	=	4.4%
Colored Pain	=	16/365	=	4.4%
Colored Temp.	=	8/365	=	2.2%
Colored Touch	=	7/365	=	1.9%
Smell → syn. Sound	=	1/365	=	0.3%
Smell → syn. Touch	=	4/365	=	1.1%
Sound → syn. Smell	=	4/365	=	1.1%

Sound → syn. Taste	=	10/365	=	2.7%
Sound → syn. Temp.	=	2/365	=	0.5%
Sound → syn. Touch	=	10/365	=	2.7%
Taste → syn. Hearing	=	1/365	=	0.3%
Taste → syn. Temp.	=	1/365	=	0.3%
Taste → syn. Touch	=	3/365	=	0.8%
Touch → syn. Hearing	=	2/365	=	0.5%
Touch → syn. Smell	=	1/365	=	0.3%
Touch → syn. Taste	=	2/365	=	0.5%
Vision → syn. Hearing	=	4/365	=	1.1%
Vision → syn. Smell	=	4/365	=	1.1%
Vision → syn. Taste	=	7/365	=	1.9%
Vision → syn. Temp.	=	2/365	=	0.5%
Vision → syn. Touch	=	2/365	=	0.5%

Other Possible Combinations I Have Not Yet Found:

Smell → syn. Taste	"tasting odors"
Smell → syn. Temp.	"hot & cold odors"
Taste → syn. Smell	"smelling flavors"
Temp. → syn. Smell	"smelling temperature flux"
Temp. → syn. Taste	"tasting temperature flux"
Temp. → syn. Touch	"feeling temperature flux"
Touch → syn. Temp.	"hot & cold touches"

As both a synaesthete and a researcher of synaesthesia, let me address some frequently asked questions regarding synaesthesia, music, language, vision, and creativity and art in general.

First, music. Was Scriabin a synaesthete? Probably not. Scriabin appears to have used a simple, basic mathematical sequence to determine his colored musical key correspondences (see Dann 1998; Baker 1986; de Schloezer 1987 (1923); and of course, Scriabin 1995 (1908 & 1911)). It would be highly unusual that naturally occurring synaesthesia for colored musical keys should follow such a basic algorithm so perfectly and completely.

Are there any true synaesthete composers out there who used their synaesthesia as an aid to writing? Yes. Lots of them, including Amy Beach, Olivier Messiaen, and Michael Torke.

In general, does synaesthesia connected to music help the musician or composer? Usually not. Usually, it is just "there", neither helping much nor hindering much. It might aid in distinguishing certain pitches, timbres, or such, but does not often does not supply an overwhelming assistance.

What about truly synaesthete authors? There are lots of them, too. Vladimir Nabokov is probably most famous (see Nabokov 1966), but there were and are others. Most others use their synaesthesia far less than Nabokov, if they even use it at all.

Regarding colored music or colored letters, it is quite distinctly not the case that all synaesthetes all see the same color for the same letter, musical pitch, instrument, or what-not. There are no total "universals". Does this mean we should totally discount the concept of colored music, or other types of synaesthetic art-forms? Absolutely not, for, although there are no "universals", there are some major tendencies and trends:

Regarding music, an increase in frequency (pitch) can generally be synaesthetically equated with an increase in surface brightness and illumination. An increase in volume (decibels) can usually be equated with an increase in color saturation. If what is seen are discrete objects, an increase in volume can generally be equated with bringing the object closer to the viewer in the third dimension, while perhaps also expanding its range in the first and second dimensions. An increase in pitch will usually correspond to an increase in height (Marks 1978, 1982; Melara 1989a, b; Wheeler 1920; Argelander 1927).

Regarding language, we need to focus mainly on vowel phonemes. Worldwide, there is a generally tendency for the vowels [i] and [I] to be associated with the color white, the vowel [e] with light yellow or off-white, the vowel [a] with red, the vowel [o] with black, and the vowel [u] with very dark shades of various colors. [i], [I], and [e] are also generally equated with high, small, beautiful, bright and shiny things, [a], [o], and [u] with low, big, ugly, dull, things (Hagman 1977; Hinton et. al 1994; Shostak 1981; Traill 1985, 1994).

Regarding written language, lets look at colored graphemes first. The Roman letter "A" tends most often correspond to the color red, "E" to yellow, "I" to black and white combinations, "O" to white, and "U" to dark shades of various colors. "S" and "Y" have a high frequency of corresponding with yellow (Day 2001).

Are there reports of synaesthetic colored graphemes for other writing systems? Yes; I have obtained reports of such in Cyrillic, Greek, Turkish, Arabic, and Chinese, as well as the various diacritical elaborations upon the Roman alphabet.

Could someone learn to have synaesthesia, developing it as a skill? Several experimental attempts have been made to do this over the past century. They have all uniformly failed quite miserably (see Kelly 1934; Howells 1944). True synaesthesia is a perceptual trait of true synaesthetes. Non-synaesthetes might be able to understand and relate to synaesthesia quite well, but they will not thereby become synaesthetes.

Can various drugs induce synaesthesia? Is drug-induced synaesthesia in any way similar to natural synaesthesia? Yes, certain drugs, such as LSD, opium, or amyl nitrate, can induce synaesthesia (see Pollard, Uhr, and Stern 1965; Cytowic 1989, 1993; Lewis and Elvin-Lewis 1977; also Simpson and McKellar 1955). Of course, beyond the fact that they are currently illegal, I wouldn't recommend them anyway, as they have far too much potential to cause damage, outweighing any possible benefit. The type of synaesthesia produced is short-term, more akin to hallucination (real synaesthesia is distinctly not anything like hallucinations), and does not have most of the perceptual qualities of true synaesthesia.

To conclude, regarding synaesthetic art-forms, I see at least three possible ways we could go: (1) We could just eschew the whole issue altogether, and not attempt anything of any such type; (2) We could go for a conception of synaesthesia based on (non-synaesthetes') general concepts of what synaesthesia could or might be like; or (3) We could try to make our arts as true to real synaesthesia as possible. I feel that option #1 would rob us of huge realms of potentially great art; it doesn't seem to me to be a "real" option for a naturally inquisitive human. Option #2 is what has most frequently been done over the past century and a half. However, such a course might well miss "connecting" with an audience by not taking advantage of naturally synaesthetic associations that the majority of us make. Option #3 is not very practical, as true synaesthesia is so highly individualistic and so frequently against the grain of general public likes and dislikes that the artworks produced simply "wouldn't fly". Furthermore, if we were to go wholly for true synaesthesia, whose synaesthesia would we choose as our model, and why would that model be superior to others?

Thus, I push for option #4: Artists would most likely benefit by becoming more familiar with true synaesthesia, rather than making up uninformed fantasies about what synaesthesia might possibly be like. Then, artists could use their informed knowledge as a springboard to be creative and inventive. I feel that art works best when there are very definite, distinct, clear boundaries and constraints — and when those constraints and boundaries are then tweaked and toyed with. The best synaesthestic art will be art on the edge — not within or outside — of true synaesthesia.

References

Argelander, Annelies (1927). *Das Farbenhoeren und der synaesthetische Faktor der Wahrnemung.* Jena: Verlag von Gustav Fischer.

Aristotle (c. 330 B.C./1976). *De anima.* With translation, introduction, and notes by Robert Drew Hicks. New York: Arno.

Bailey, Mark E. S., and Keith J. Johnson (1997). "Synaesthesia: Is a Genetic Analysis Feasible?" In S. Baron-Cohen and J. Harrison (Eds.), *Synaesthesia* (182–207). Cambridge, Massachusetts: Blackwell.

Baker, James M. (1986). *The Music of Alexander Scriabin.* New Haven and London: Yale UP.

Baron-Cohen, Simon, and John E. Harrison (Eds.) (1997). *Synaesthesia: Classic and Contemporary Readings.* Cambridge, Massachusetts: Blackwell Publishers.

Coperniçus, Nicolaus (1543/1952). On the Revolutions of the Heavenly Spheres. Translated by Charles Glenn Wallis. In Hutchins (Ed.), *Great Books of the Western World,* Volume 16, (497–838). London: Encyclopaedia Britannica, Inc.

Cytowic, Richard E. (1993). *The Man Who Tasted Shapes.* New York: Putnam.

Cytowic, Richard E. (1989). *Synaesthesia: a Union of the Senses.* New York: Springer-Verlag.

Dann, Kevin T. (1998). Bright Colors Falsely Seen: Synaesthesia and the Search for Transcendental Knowledge. New Haven and London: Yale UP.

Day, Sean A. (2001). "Trends in Synesthetically Colored Graphemes and Phonemes".
http://www.ncu.edu.tw/~daysa/Colored-Letters.htm

de Schloezer, Boris (1923/1987). *Scriabin: Artist and Mystic.* Translated by Nicolas Slonimsky; with introductory essays by Marina Scriabine. Berkeley: U of California P.

Frith, C. D., and E. Paulesu (1997). The physiological basis of synaesthesia. In S. Baron-Cohen and J. Harrison (Eds.), *Synaesthesia* (123–147). Oxford, England: Blackwell.

Galeyev, Bulat M. (1988). The Fire of Prometheus: Music-Kinetic Art Experiments in the USSR. *Leonardo, 21,* 383–396.

Gould, Stephen Jay (1977). *Ontogeny and Phylogeny.* Cambridge, Massachusetts: The Belknap Press of Harvard UP.

Gould, Stephen Jay (1980). *The Panda's Thumb: More Reflections in Natural History.* New York: Norton.

Hagman, Roy S. (1977). *Nama Hottentot Grammar.* Bloomington: Indiana University Press.

Hinton, Leanne, Johanna Nichols, and John O. Ohala (Eds.) (1994). *Sound Symbolisms.* Cambridge: UP.

Howells, T. H. (1944). The Experimental Development of Color-Tone Synesthesia. *Journal of Experimental Psychology, 34,* 87–103.

Kelly, E. Lowell (1934). An Experimental Attempt to produce Artificial Chromaesthesia by the Technique of the Conditioned Response. *Journal of Experimental Psychology, 17,* 315–341.

Kepler, Johannes (1619/1952). Harmonices mundi. In Hutchins, (Ed.); *Ptolemy, Copernicus, Kepler* [Volume 16 of Great Books of the Western World]. London: Encyclopaedia Britannica, Inc.

Lewis, Walter H., and Memory P. F. Elvin-Lewis (1977). *Medical Botany; Plants Affecting Man's Health.* New York: Wiley.

Marks, Lawrence E. (1982). Bright Sneezes and Dark Coughs, Loud Sunlight and Soft Moonlight. *Journal of Experimental Psychology: Human Perception and Performance, 8*, 177–193.

Marks, Lawrence E. (1978). *The Unity of the Senses.* New York and London: Academic P.

Maurer, Daphne (1997). Neonatal synaesthesia: implications for the processing of speech and faces. In S. Baron-Cohen and J. Harrison (Eds.), Synaesthesia, (224–242). Oxford, England: Blackwell.

Melara, Robert D. (1989a). Dimensional Interaction Between Color and Pitch. *Journal of Experimental Psychology: Human Perception and Performance, 15.1*, 69–79.

Melara, Robert D. (1989b). Similarity Relations Among Synesthetic Stimuli and Their Attributes. *Journal of Experimental Psychology: Human Perception and Performance, 15.2*, 212–231.

Nabokov, Vladimir (1966). *Speak, Memory: An Autobiography Revisited.* New York: Putnam.

Newton, Sir Isaac (1704/1952). Optics. In Hutchins (Ed.), *Great Books of the Western World*; Volume 34, (373–544). London: Encyclopaedia Britannica, Inc.

Paulesu, E., J. Harrison, S. Baron-Cohen, J. D. G. Watson, L. Goldstein, J. Heather, R. S. J. Frackowiak, and C. D. Frith (1995). The Physiology of Coloured Hearing: A PET Activation Study of Colour-Word Synaesthesia. *Brain, 118*, 661–676.

Plato (c. 370 B.C./n.d.). *The works of Plato.* Translated by B. Jowett. New York: Tudor Publishing Company.

Pollard, John C., Leonard Uhr, and Elizabeth Stern (1965). *Drugs and Phantasy: The Effects of LSD, Psilocybin, and Sernyl on College Students.* Boston: Little, Brown.

Ptolemy (151 A.D./1952). The Almagest. Translated by R. Catesby Taliaferro. In Hutchins (Ed.), *Great Books of the Western World*, Volume 16; (vii-478). London: Encyclopaedia Britannica, Inc.

Scriabin, Alexander (1908 & 1911/1995). *Poem of Ecstasy; and Prometheus: Poem of Fire.* In full score. Mineola, New York: Dover.

Shostak, Marjorie (1981). *Nisa: The Life and Words of a !Kung Woman.* New York: Vintage Books.

Simpson, Lorna, and Peter McKellar (1955). Types of Synaesthesia. *Journal of Mental Science, 101*, 141–147.

Traill, Anthony (1994). *A !Xoo Dictionary.* Koeln: Ruediger Koeppe Verlag.

Traill, Anthony (1985). *Phonetics and Phonological Studies of !Xoo Bushman.* Hamburg: Helmut Buske Verlag.

Wheeler, Raymond Holder (1920). *The Synaesthesia of a Blind Subject.* Eugene, Oregon: University of Oregon Press.

Zatorre, Robert J., Alan C. Evans, and Ernst Meyer (1994). Neural Mechanisms Underlying Melodic Perception and Memory for Pitch. *Journal of Neuroscience, 14*, 1908–1919.

Synaesthesia is not a psychic anomaly, but a form of non-verbal thinking

Bulat M. Galeyev
Institute "Prometei", Kazan, Russia

Art researchers often run into poetic revelations of such kind as "dawn-blue sound of the flute" (the Russian poet K. Balmont) or "thin, cutting whistle, like the dazzlingly white thread, is winding round the throat" (the Russian writer M. Gorky). Then we have Scriabin, who confessed that, for him, C-major is of red colour; Kandinsky, as well as Balmont, "tinctured" the timbres of musical instruments. While encountering these facts, the researchers "never noticed" that they dealt with metaphors, though unusual ones, connected with intersensory transfer. Trying to understand these so-called synaesthesiae, they drew various explanations: the physical analogy between light and sound ("both are wave phenomena"); anatomic anomalies ("maybe the nerve fibres have gotten entangled"); atavism ("the relapse of the pristine syncretism"); psychopathology — although useful in some senses ("sound never can be regarded as a cutting or shining thing"); psychodelic dreams ("using drugs leads to hallucinations and sounds may actually become visible"); and the miraculous, esoteric features of the psychic ("it is open only to selected persons who have accepted the mystery knowledge"). In any case, synesthesia and, in particular, "colour hearing" was regarded as a deviation from the norm — either a positive or negative one. This is the source of the common prejudices which are revealed in encyclopaedic and even academic publications: "Synaesthesia is a sensory system anomaly; such artists as Rimbaud, Baudelair, Balmont, Block, Scriabin, Rimsky-Korsakov, Kandinsky, and Messiaen suffered from this (disease). In the 20th century, endeavors have become very popular to develop abstract painting and a new sort of art, "colour music", on the basis of synaesthesia (in its concrete form of "colour hearing") ...". Such prejudices are very stable both in Russian and Western science.

Actually, synaesthesia (at least in the case of the above-mentioned artists) is no more than intersensory association, often a multi-level and systemic one; this is the manifestation of metaphoric thinking, which, as it is known, is based upon the association mechanism. Even the "colour hearing" concept itself appears to be a metaphor! But whereas the metaphor "girl-lily" is the comparison of the "visual to visual" type, the comparison of the girl with "Elegy" by Massenet is of a different, namely synaesthetic, type. Metaphors, as it has been established long ago, descend from "associations by resemblance". In the case of synaesthesia, this association is settled by the resemblance of phenomena of different modes. It looks like "sense mixing" or, more precisely, intersensory transfer. The resemblance may be either in the content (meaning, emotional impression — see the above cited metaphor by Balmont) or in the form (structure, Gestalt — see Gorky's metaphor). Intersensory transfer, synaesthetic comparison, as like any comparison "by resemblance", is an operation of thinking! But in this case, the thinking proceeds, so to say, within the frame of the sensible-emotional sphere. That is, it relates to the area of non-verbal, sensible-imaginative thinking, the non-verbal thinking being more complicated in this case than, for example, simply visual or musical thinking, because it realizes the connections in the whole multi-modal sensory system. This act of synaesthetic thinking often takes place with the participation of the subconsciousness (due to the coupling of protopathic components of the senses related to different modes). In the light of consciousness, only the final result is seen, often being fixed in the word (like "dawn-blue sound of the flute"), which imparts the element of mystery in synaesthesia, thus causing the above-mentioned prejudices of "educated knowledge".

Now, after such an assaulting preamble, let us refer to the history of science, where, as you know, it appears that the concept of "general sense", close to that of "synaesthesia", had been under consideration and discussion long ago. But again with no definite result. In terms of mysteriousness, the problem under our review is also close to those dating from the 17th–19th centuries which mention the out-of-aesthetic and especially natural-philosophic juxtapositions of sound and colour as natural phenomena. In Newton's times, these analogies had eventually taken the form of the naive and preposterous idea of "music of colour", or "music for eyes", which was based on absurd attempts to translate from sound to colour. But it is these scholastic ideas that had caused attention to be paid to the now purely "human" (that is, psychic) correlations between aural phenomena and colour. And so, the exotic term "colour hearing" came into being (during the end of the 19th century). As already noted above, "colour hearing" is a particular manifestation of the more common human faculty named "synaesthesia", being studied here by us.

And it is note-worthy that "colour hearing" also was first analyzed by philosophers and theorists of art rather than by psychologists.

Today, there are some remnants of all this nomenclative discordance, one can trace them even in the works of the scientists who seem to find the right interpretation of the phenomenon itself. Thus, in order for researchers to "find a common language", I would like to give a warning about the quite variant understandings of the limits of the concept of "synaesthesia" being studied by us. For example, for some researchers it involves only the phenomenon called "colour hearing"; for others, only that which was formerly believed to be "general sense". Some others confine themselves to positions of gestalt-psychology. I should like to offer a common explanation of synaesthesia wherein there will be room both for "general sense" and for "colour hearing", and moreover for other manifestations of this phenomenon. (The major senses are seeing and hearing; therefore it is convenient for us to base our explanation upon interconjunctions between those ones).

So, determining consciousness, being also determines the initial level of it — polysensory perception, with all its particular morphological and functional qualities. In this regard, the functions determine, as usual, structure, and thereby the system of sensational reflection is always a reflection of reality. Speaking more simply, organs of senses are kinds of windows of consciousness. And they have already been investigated in detail as topics of study for Physiology and Psychology. But why are they just what they are, and their number five? With this question, philosophers, rather than psychologists, seem to vex their minds. Beside that, philosophers keep hard at work deliberating the question, and debating about the potential existence of a certain "general sense" which either unites the others or operates its common characteristics. It was called "*Koinon aistherion*" by Aristotle, while others cogitated over "*Sensorium commune*", and "*Gemeinsinn*" (Kant, Herder, Engels, etc.). But this question could not have any rational solution, on account of the scholasticism of the old times — up to nowadays, when this epistemological problem has gotten its psychological, natural background.

Probably, a help in solving this problem is suggested by our theory of synaesthesia, which studies the system interactions in the sphere of sensational reflection (Galeyev 1987). For its compressed and capacious exposition, we use a graphic method, and, in this case, one based on the well-known thesis: method is an analogue of subject (see Figure 1). The expedient which underlies the method is "splitting" some essential faculties of human nature which are under our consideration; that conforms to the thesis: dividing of the single, and cognition of its contradictory aspects, are a core of dialectics. Without pretensions of universality and completeness, the suggested diagram illustrates an object of our interest — one section alone of a holistic system. This section is a plane and, accordingly, the figure is a two-dimensional system of axes, representing demonstrably the well-known principle of binary opposition.

So, let us place bisensory "homo-perceptor" (H-P) in the middle of this system. The dichotomy "sight — hearing", which is our primary interest, is marked by the horizontal, while the verical marks out the dichotomy "form — contents", reflecting the dialectics of subjective and objective aspects of sensational reflection, which provides for the forming of mental images in our consciousness. Here the "subjective" is a modality of mental image, while the "objective" is a structure of mental image. Components put presciented and limbed from "H-P " to every side are: (1) audial perception; (2) visual perception; (3) the modality of hearing; (4) the modality of sight; (5) the structure of visual perception; and (6) the structure of audial perception. Naturally, we are operating with the supposition that all these components belong and are consistent with an action of the brain whose position can conventionally be presented as the central cell embodied in "H-P". As a matter of fact, the present schematic abstraction is not quite conventional; it represents an integral act of sensational reflection which is really differentiated by science into sensation and perception (more accurately, there is a differentiation of the characters of reflection, those "primary" and "secondary" qualities, by John Locke) (1690/1961).

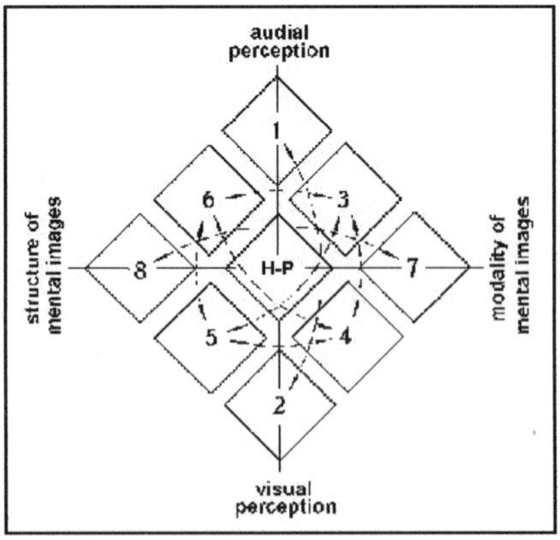

Figure 1. System of multisensorial perception

As is well-known, any system conserves its integrity by some cemented conjunctions between its elements. There are conjunctions of the "association" type (in this case, they are intersensorial), as we have already noted above, that are called "synaesthesia". In the figure, they are designated by dotted lines. (And, of course, there exist other conjunctions, including the anomalous ones which result in a deformed activity of the perceptual system, for example, the uncontrollable and real "co-sensations" shown in LSD research or in sensory isolation, but that is not of interest for art psychology and aesthetics.)

Actually, synaesthesiae arise between components 1 and 2, but the multitude of synaesthesiae includes those in which either primary or secondary qualities in some conjunction can be accented. For example, such poetic tropes as "red call of trumpet" or musical analogies "colour — timbre", "colouring — harmony" (that is what was once called "colour hearing") are relevant to the conjunctions 3–4. And, for example, such synaesthetic universals as "melody — graphics", "music — architecture" or "music — ornament" are relevant to the conjunctions 5–6. Of course, cross-conjunctions of 4–6 or 3–5 types are possible, too.

In our opinion, in cell 7 belong the so-called "intermodal qualitats" — these are some common qualities of every sensation which characterize its tonus (intensity, activity, saturation). In any event, behind the "intermodal qualitats" stand some characteristics of quality and intensity of the sensations of various modalities taken outside their structural formalization, mediated by unity of their common affective tone. It is well-known that the words "bright — dark", "hot — cold", "acute — blunt", "heavy — light", and "hard — soft" are used for emotions (feelings, moods) themselves, over time, and also for sounds (colours, smells, tastes). "Intermodal qualitats" underlie the most universal synaesthesiae. It is regarding these synaesthesiae that such researchers as E. Hornbostel (1925) and L. Marks (1978) make an emphasis.

To all appearances, in cell 8 must belong characters similar to "intermodal qualitats" which unify structural characteristics of perception. In point of fact, gestalt-psychologists based their ideas upon these characters when they stated the possible existence of certain amodal "synthetical shapes". It would seem their belief was substantiated by their prominent experiments with "tekete" and "maluma" though, of course there can not be any exact complete structural similarity of phenomena of different modalities (see Figure 2). However, the "qualitats" of 8 can be united by the above-mentioned characters "acute — blunt", "soft — hard" etc., which makes the "intermodal qualitats" of 7 and 8 close together.

What in these figures is "maluma" or "tekete"? (Let us change the question: Where is "March" and where is "Waltz" drawn here? Where is "Sword Dance" by Khachaturian and where is "Elegy" by Massnet? I think that everybody will answer these question identically. In our opinion, it is an aggregate of these system "intermodal qualitats" 7 and 8 that constitutes an essential of the mysterious "Sensorium commune". And if anybody does not agree with this conclusion, as the saying goes, "propose your own". This conclusion falls, at least, within the submissions of Aristotle, who attributes to "koinon aistherion", explained in his work De Anima, just what we have in cell 8 (although outside of this context, unity of the senses by the characteristics of cell 7 is also specified by Aristotle). He was of the opinion that each of our senses has its own object.

As for the general attributes, he believed in the existence of a "general sense". And the most principal thing, according to him, is that there cannot "be a special organ for the perception of common objects". We circumstantially perceive with every sense "movement, rest, number, shape, size" (Aristotle). And there is no contradiction between the above conclusion and another standard-bearer of common sense, F. Engels. In Dialectics of Nature, he arrives at the conclusion that intersensual associations are necessarily formed on the basis of an experience of collaboration of organs of senses — hereupon it is not necessary for human beings "to have one `general sense' instead of five specialized senses" or to have the ability for seeing or hearing smells (to all appearance, both of the suggestions are equally nonsensical for him) (Marx and Engels 1961).

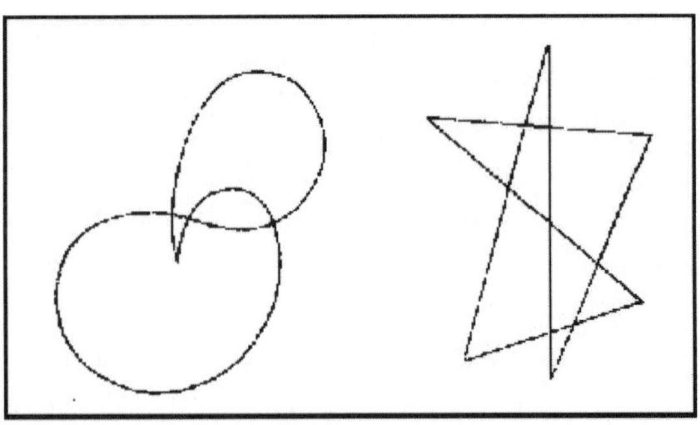

Figure 2.

There are no odd pages in the history of culture and on its new pages the content of ancient ones comes before us in new appearance. In our opinion, such is the destiny of the concept "general sense", closely related with that of "synaesthesia", which was actively studied recently, and also with that of "colour hearing" as the most exotic and subjective form of it. Correspondingly, the explication of conception of "music of colour" ("music for the eyes") is represented differently today. But, anyway, that is the topic for another discourse (Galeyev 1995).

Translated by N. Bondartzova and V. Skorokhodov
Edited by Sean A. Day

References

Aristotle. (1991). Cit. from the article: O. Neumaier: Unity and Multiplicity of the Senses. In Roscher, W., Allesch, Ch. G. and Krakauer, P.M. (Eds.), *Polyaisthesis* [collection of articles] (42). Verband der wissenschaftlichen Gesellschaften Österreichs, Wien.

Galeyev, Bulat M. (1987). *Man, Art, Technology (the problem of synaesthesia in the arts).* Kazan: KGU Press. (In Russian). Galeyev, Bulat M. (1993). The problem of synaesthesia in the arts. *Languages of Design, 1,* 201–203. Galeyev, Bulat M. (1993). Synaesthesia and musical space. *Leonardo, 26,* 76–78.

Galeyev, Bulat M. (1995). On the true sources of light-music. *Languages of Design, 3,* 33–34.

Galeyev, Bulat M. (2001). Open Letter on Synesthesia. *Leonardo, 34, 362–263.*

Galeyev, Bulat M., Vanechkina, Irene L. (2001). Was Scriabin a Synesthete? *Leonardo, 34, 357–361.* See also the synesthetic section of our web-site: (http://prometheus.kai.ru).

Hornbostel, E. (1925). Die Einheit der Sinne. *Melos, 4,* 290–297.

Locke, John. (1690/1961). *An Essay Concerning Human Understanding.* New York: Dutton.

Marks, Lawrence. (1978). *The Unity of Senses: Interrelations of Modalities.* New York: Academic Press.

Marx, Karl, Engels, F. (1961). *Works, 2nd Edition,* vol. 20 (548). Moscow: Iospolitizdat Politizdat.

Part II
Language & music

Seán Ó Nualláin
Nous Research, Dublin, Ireland

The inspiration for the call for this workshop came largely from Chapter 7 of my *The Search for Mind* (Ablex, 1995; Intellect, 2002). It was obvious to me as I wrote "Search" that syntactic features like recursivity, ambiguity, and so on were common to language and music. What was much less obvious was how the intuitions of those of us who feel that music "speaks" to us in some profound way can be corroborated. Listening to music, we feel that we, the composer and interpreter(s) are all in contact with some objective reality. Both of the first two papers in this section attempt to construct a framework in which such intuitions can be justified. In his thoughtful paper, Griffith makes much reference to Lakoffian notions of schema and metaphor. However, as we shall see, he eventually falls victim to the classic Lakoffian problem of psychologism, i.e. the reduction of knowing to purely psychological functions, without the necessary reference to external reality. Lakoff's precursor Piaget was much warier of this problem.

Both language and music, Griffith argues, are dependent for their noetic qualities on a single perceptuo-cognitive system devoted to the organisation of causation. This has the problem of reducing language, as well as music, to a psychologistic semantics. Similarly, Callaghan and McDonald's attempt to seek solace in semiotics to explain the noetics of music, though ultimately a surer path, fails to provide one with a route from symbol to object. Both these papers could have benefited greatly from consideration of the example of mathematics. As it probes the space of the rational, mathematics often throws up hopeful monsters that unexpectedly turn out to have reference. For example, Riemann geometry languished for decades as a forgotten formalist game until Einstein used it to describe the reality of space-time. Can it be the case that music is referential in this way, or even better that its emotional dimension allows us apprehend realities with mind and heart simultaneously (to speak metaphorically)?

The next two papers deal with computational processing of word and note. Karma finds that dyslexia is based on a structuring problem common to language and music. Tillmann and Bigand investigate how local and global contexts interact with consonance/dissonance judgements. Sabah discusses how his Caramel system finds a role for consciousness in providing a capacity to reflect on symbol-production. We then return to that interaction of symbol-crunching and emotion which is music's unique emphasis. Very astutely, Nemirovsky and Davenport note that emotions are potentially informational, and that this information could be used to guide a traveller. Their Guideshoes project first assesses the attractiveness of musical phrases before using them to direct a traveller towards and away from particular direction choices. Finally, some fascinating but preliminary research ends this section. Rather bravely, Poggi attempts to find some reason behind conductors' changes of expression; Bonardi and Rousseaux attempt the ages-old dream of finding pictorial equivalents for music as it is played; and Antonini outlines a system that, if fully implemented, would completely integrate language, vision, and music.

Finally, to a few project notes. My paper deals, inter alia, with the political conditions that hampered the full harmonic development of Irish music. Its current remarkable popularity will inevitably result in a "Celtic" jazz form; I discuss the harmonic structures, such as they are, that currently exist. Treharne focusses on rhythm and its role in language development. It is possible that rhythm, an intersection of affect, embodiment, and cognition, will have a central role in future theories of child development (as exemplified by Bill Rowe's work in progress). Treharne concludes that children who can best imitate rhythms similarly show most facility in using rhythmic cues for meaning. Finally, Romano starts his work in the hope that language will reveal something like the role of the fifth in musical argument. His preliminary work indicates that rising-falling and tension-resolution patterns manifest some semantic completeness cues. Whether this is a manifestation of a common semiotic structure, or a metaphorical transfer from singing to speaking, is a question he leaves open.

Music and language

Metaphor and causation

Niall Griffith
University of Limerick, Ireland

1. Introduction

Our developing understanding of the similarities and dissimilarities between the structure and constituents of music and language has been productive and enlightening. For example, it has lead to the application of grammar-based approaches to music comprehension and composition. This paper discusses the idea that it is the functional as well as the structural similarities between the two that are important: in particular the idea that their similarity arises because they are articulations of a single perceptual/cognitive system that is concerned with the understanding of causation.

The relationship between language and music can be posed in several kinds of question. One kind proposes analysis of how shared structural principles might have arisen from overlapping cognitive subsystems. For example "What is the developmental relationship between linguistic prosody and music?"; or "Do music and Language share a common linear organisation based on temporal (i.e. rhythmic/metric) units?". These questions imply that if the answer is affirmative, that "sharing" implies similar, or homologous organisational processes within linguistic and musical perception and conception. But while music and language are often viewed as similar, they are seldom viewed as equal (Pinker 1996). The assumed dependence of music on language is stated generally in questions such as "What is the evidence for the evolution of music from Language?". To be fair this question is often reversed or stated in terms of a common ancestor from which both music and language developed. More generally we find the pre-eminence of language assumed in questions such as, "Can we speak meaningfully about a semantics of music?". Semantics can obviously be discussed in language and so the question implies that music is somehow lesser in its capacity to "mean" *something,* because it cannot discuss itself — without of course entertaining the disadvantages, e.g. infinite regress, that may arise from self-description. Semantics are assumed to be quintessentially a property of language, although the cognitive implications of linguistic categories for perception is not as simple (Lakoff 1987) as it was conceived to be fifty years ago. More generally, (perhaps more objectively?) now we have questions such as, "What common cognitive processes underlie our competence in these disparate modes of thought?"; or "What cognitive capacities underlie Music and Language?", or "What functions are shared between Language and Music".

Popper's (1972) classification of the functional levels of language is a useful point at which to start discussing music and language in the context of human cognition and communication. Popper defined four functional levels:

1. **Expressive** A being reveals or hides its internal states
2. **Signalling** A being signals to others to elicit some general response
3. **Descriptive** A being describes states of the world with more and less truth
4. **Argumentative** A being rationally constructs arguments about the nature of the world

Human language is considered to encompass all four, but which levels can be ascribed to animals, in particular great apes is contentious. If we consider music; while most people would agree that it involves expression and signalling (levels 1 and 2) there would be less agreement about its capacity to describe and argue (levels 3 and 4). If we accept levels 3 and 4, then by Popper's analysis we are saying that music is a language just like spoken or written language. If we reject it, then we accept that music is a language metaphorically but not actually. If music is unable to carry description and argument, why is this so?

One of the functions of language (serving Popper's levels 3 & 4) seems to be that it articulates the integration of our perceptual modalities. It is not sensed but understood. Yet, it is mediated both by sounds and images, and thus is both heard and seen. Language is meta-modal. Its development in the human case has involved cross modal integration. This possibility may have arisen for one of two reasons. (a) Irrespective of the nature of the input being processed by the nervous system, it is physiologically constrained and therefore patterns of activity are similar, even though the actual stimuli are different (e.g. light and sound). Because they are similar, they can be treated together. (This notion of Common Sense or Common Faculty goes back to Aristotle). (b) The nervous activity of the different senses is so distinct, that specific processes are needed to mediate their activity into a common representational form that can be processed (conceived) in similar ways (Fodor 1983). Whatever occurs, effects such as the *McGurk Effect* (McGurk & MacDonald 1976) show that perception in one sense can be affected by perception in another.

2. Musical grammars

In psychological, cognitive and computational modelling of music the application of linguistic structure, i.e. syntax, has been widespread since the 1970s, (Roads 1979; Steedman 1984; Sundberg & Lindblom 1993; Winograd 1969), to name but a few. There is a broad acceptance of the usefulness of a "linguistic" metaphor for music. Both involve structured sequences of information. Both seem susceptible to being organised and understood in a hierarchical manner. A grammar allows a single "concept" or piece to be unfolded in time via a sequence of actions that specify what will happen next — or conversely, what should happen next if we are using a grammar to validate a sequence.

However, while we may be able to describe a piece of music with a grammar, this is not the same as saying that the music is caused by a process that is described by the grammar. Rather a grammar is just shorthand for the organisation of productions, without anything significant to say about how those productions are created. For example, grammars can be used to describe improvisations in Indian Tabla playing (Kippen & Bel 1992). But, there is no causal implication in this grammar of the generation of patterns of motor activity, or of the relationship between such patterns and social conventions that determine the grammar. The grammar describes conventional use, not origin. This distinction is also implicit in the idea of a transformational grammar (Chomsky 1957) which links deep and surface structure. This distinguishes form from function, and also distinguishes using language and grammars to comprehend and describe music, from music itself.

Another difficulty with a purely syntactic and linguistic approach is that music is regarded as ineffable. It is possible to find correspondences between levels of organisation — notes and phonemes, words and phrases (Bernstein 1974; Patel & Peretz 1997). However, there is no direct attachment of meaning to music and while it is possible to analyse consistencies and regularities in auditory and musical structure (Bregman 1990; Narmour 1990; Lerdahl & Jackendoff 1983) it is almost impossible to gain agreement about the consistent semantic and emotional attachment of musical structure. This is in marked contrast to language where meaning is intrinsic to and coeval with the arbitrary symbols it employs. If you start from the assumption that musical and linguistic mechanisms/processes/structures are similar, then this state of affairs seems to imply that music is somehow lacking. Sometimes this *music as secondary cognitive ability* is stated in an extreme way (Pinker 1997). However, it is also possible to see music's ineffability as revealing a limitation in language. If we invert the relationship and ask if music can describe language, the answer is a partial yes. Music can represent both the singing and speaking voice. Prosody is essentially musical. Written words in a foreign language are meaningless symbols. Yet if they are spoken, the inflections in the voice allow us to approximate their meaning. Sometimes this recovery is complete enough for us to approximate a translation of the intention of the unknown utterance. Thus, there are several aspects of music and language that suggest the conclusion that music is secondary is wrong or at least incomplete and that the relationship is more complex.

3. The ineffability of music

The ineffability of music has been discussed by Raffman (1992) in an analysis focussed on the Generative Theory of Tonal Music (GTTM), (Lerdahl & Jackendoff 1983). GTTM outlines a set of four, hierarchical reductions spanning metrical, and tonal structure. These are taken to form the understanding an acculturated listener has of western tonal music. It has been questioned (Deliege 1987) as to whether GTTM is a psychological theory, able to account for, say the structure of Serialism, or a specifically western music theoretic analysis. However, let us accept that it is a particular instantiation of musical organisation that is universally hierarchical, i.e. that there is a set of hierarchical process at work in all music. The hierarchies may be different in Indian or Japanese Music, but they are all hierarchical. These hierarchical/reductive processes can be viewed as input processes that are responsible for encoding perceptual material in a form that can be processed formally (Fodor 1983). The focus of Raffman's discussion is how GTTM is consistent with the fact that music cannot be fully described by language. The equivalence of language and music is, she argues, to be found in both domains being structured according to syntactic principles, that constitute a listeners understanding of a piece. The acquisition of this structure is a matter of acculturation or experience, and this is highly variable, both between individuals and over time for one individual. However, the syntactic structure is conceived to sequentially organise perceptually constant atomic elements or components, such as pitches, that arise from categorical processes. The difference between music and language is that in music this process of categorisation leads to a loss of perceptual detail — i.e. *nuance*. Raffman's argument is (in a nutshell) that what we cannot categorise we cannot remember and what we cannot remember, we cannot articulate in language. Hence, there are large amounts of musical experience that we basically forget and cannot talk about. A corollary is that music can still be categorised hierarchically so we expect to be able to extract all meaning in a way analogous to language, but this is frustrated because musical pitches have no intrinsic meaning.

Raffman's view appears at first sight to be a convincing — certainly plausible — argument. However, there seem to be three problems with it. Firstly, there is the assumption that categorisation and syntactic conformance are coeval with meaning in language. That all we are concerned with in language is categorisation, and once this is achieved, we understand the utterance. However, this is not the case. For example, if I say to someone "I am going to pour cold water over you". This may mean what it says, it may be a threat or a joke. The differentiation of these alternatives arises from the situation and the speaker's tone of voice. The meaning of a sentence is not reducible to the extraction of constituents/categories that are arranged in some syntactically correct fashion. Our interpretation is based upon the context and nuances of the utterance, and this is held in what are categorically unimportant aspects of the utterance, i.e. the pronunciation of the words. How are these nuances different from those involved in hearing a musical passage? Secondly, there is a more general question of whether or not nuances are remembered? If the argument: we cannot remember nuances because we cannot categorise them, is true; how can musicians learn a performance and also how can one musician teach another musician an interpretation? Thirdly, the basis of comparison that Raffman uses; that musicians cannot exactly reproduce a performance, is arguably as applicable to a verbal tradition, e.g. an actor speaking lines. A verbal performance, like a musical performance interprets the written word. There is of course more to memory than schematising and reducing experience to categories and the passivity of sensory perception. There is also the memorisation of motor skills and their relationship to perceptual changes. For movement, co-ordination and continuity are pre-eminent.

Raffman's analysis leaves the impression that there is a substantive, yet elusive set of correspondences between language and music, including: an hierarchical organisation of constituents, recursion, self-reference — including metaphor and analogy, ambiguity, and systematic organisation. This is because her (and Lerdahl & Jackendoff's) analysis is of an abstraction that ignores music as an activity that is not only mediated by social convention but is realised by motor activity. It also ignores another crucial aspect of music which is it's metaphoric content, which although strictly ineffable is as concrete and communicative as anything within linguistic utterance.

4. Metaphor and music

Metaphor is traditionally something we achieve with words. However, the transfer of structure and meaning between domains or modalities that lies at the heart of metaphor is not restricted to language (Lakoff & Johnson 1984). The notion of mapping from a known domain to an unknown domain seems to be a powerful and widely used human cognitive strategy. However, metaphoric transfer and extension (Lakoff 1987) does raise questions. The first is that in conceptual metaphors the mapping from known to unknown is on the basis of similarity between the domains (Lakoff & Johnston 1984), i.e. there is some actual substantive similarity between the domains that allows the metaphor to make sense. In this case, linguistic metaphor could be construed as an aspect of categorisation, a convenience that saves on words by using concrete terms for abstractions. For example, we recognise that breaking a stick and breaking a promise share the notion of the destruction of integrity. The question is, how? In what way do we apprehend the breaking of a stick to be similar to the breaking of a promise? In information processing terms what are the shared perceptual properties that can be transferred or compared between domains? Lakoff and Johnston (1984) argue that the transfer of metaphor is because the domains are similar. But what makes breaking one's promise better than killing, drowning, throwing away, burning or sinking one's promise? Perhaps a promise was originally a physical object and breaking it was akin to tearing up a contract? We can only judge the metaphor consciously through some notion of why the metaphor may be appropriate or not. There is the possibility of good and bad metaphors and the possibility of different people conceiving different properties to be important (Lakoff & Turner 1989). Also some metaphors are so deeply embedded in our thoughts that we seldom, if ever, realise that we are using them. These *everyday* metaphors (Lakoff & Johnston 1984) are often associated with verbs and prepositions that carry spatial orientation and change, e.g. rising, falling, being down or up, on time, coming along, etc — some are disguised by etymological history, e.g. sinister being the Latin for left-handed. The transfer of the qualities in language applies to actions and objects and the process, (in as much as we know it directly) and is from a known physical event or object to which the term is literally applicable to something else that is either emotional, abstract or both, e.g. his shattered dreams.

The core of metaphor is transfer and arguably, it is equally applicable to music. In fact it is arguable that music is understood entirely through metaphor (Scruton 1983; Cook 1990; Friberg & Sundberg 1999; Zbikowski 1998). The notions that we have of pitch, for example, as being high or low is arguably founded in *image schemata* that organise aspects of fundamental bodily experience (Lakoff & Johnston 1984). However, we need to be careful about accepting linguistic metaphors for music. It is possible to describe music in metaphorical terms. People in western musical cultures generally think in terms of pitch rising and falling. But there are other possibilities (Zbikowski 1998). Given that there may be varying metaphorical schema linking music and language in one culture and another, does this affect the meaning of the music that is heard? Did the ancient Greeks hear music differently and did what they heard mean something different, because they spoke of pitch as *sharp* and *heavy* rather than high or low. Or perhaps this was because their music was structured in a particular way and was played with a set of instruments with physical affordances and characteristics? Irrespective of the fact that we cannot enter ancient Greek experience, we can say that if we argue that the nature of metaphor determines meaning, then we are saying that the meaning of music to a culture is also inextricably bound to its language. It is difficult to escape this if metaphor is conceived as a cognitive mechanism through which we comprehend and communicate qualities that are otherwise inaccessible to us. On the other hand, if we say that the linguistic metaphors of music do not affect musical meaning, we are saying that music is truly ineffable and any linguistic articulation of its structure may be appealing but irrelevant. This seems to be a problem because it appears to set aside some aspects of meaning that we know we derive from our apprehension of music. There is no doubt that we hear pitches as higher because we call them higher. The metaphor wouldn't work otherwise. However, although music can be described through metaphor, these metaphors of structure are not its meaning, just a result of the fact that music is also a phenomena that we need to describe linguistically. The fact that we hear a pitch as higher is unimportant because we are really concerned with other aspects of its semantics that are carried by highness and lowness. These characteristics are corollaries of the physical signal rather than arising from linguistic description. As in language, the sound or form of a phrase or word is the carrier of the meaning. We are not concerned with that form, but the meaning it conveys to us. So also in music we don't hear the sound, so much as understand its meaning. Yet, we cannot convey that meaning in words. What is it exactly that music means? How does this relate to Popper's descriptive and argumentative linguistic functions?

5. Metaphor and causation in language and music

The idea that music is a means of metaphorical extension (Scruton 1983) seems incomplete as it does not define why this metaphoric aspect is important or how it is achieved. Perhaps we need to shift our focus away from the structural similarities (Patel and Peretz 1997) between language and music, and concentrate on the common cognitive functions that they presuppose. A theory that links the two — that assumes their homology — needs to identify how they are functionally related. The fact that music is continuous and non-symbolic while language is categorical and arbitrarily symbolic obscures their functional similarity. It is their essential similarity in purpose, via different means, that I will now try to argue.

A complementary theory to the metaphorical theory is what may be called a Causal Theory of Music and Language. A causal theory of language and music runs something like this. Hearing, like other perceptions, is dynamic not static. We and other species need to know what is happening over time and what is of significance to us. We are interested in causation. How much a species understands about causation depends on how sophisticated its memory is — how much components of reality can be separated, identified and related to others over time. So one of the things that a central nervous system needs to be able to achieve in order to act and plan non-reactively, is to make a distinction in its perceptual fields, between things and what happens to those things, i.e. between objects and actions. This distinction is found at a very high level in the linguistic function of nouns and verbs, but it is not necessarily clear-cut. Separating objects and actions may be seen to have two major cognitive corollaries — perceptual invariance and process. It is not clear which species possess the ability to differentiate their perceptual fields into objects and actions. There is likely to be a spectrum of complexity. However, while reactive behaviour may be based upon holistic, ecological perceptual fields it is difficult to conceive of how complex (wilful/intentional) behaviour can arise, without representation and memory capable of distinguishing constituents and the processes that operate upon them. In as much as intentional behaviour is an advantage, we can argue that complex memory and perceptual differentiation serve that advantage. At the level of conscious human mentality, this is tied in with the distinction of the 1st and 3rd person perspectives: the notion of sensation that is self-centred and perception that is concerned with the relationship between a circumambient reality and the self.

As memory develops in sophistication, behavioural repertoire may also be expected to develop (Sherry & Schacter 1987). There is also a fundamental relationship between actions and iconic meaning (Goldin-Meadow 1991). This is very evident in the communication of non-human primates in which the relationship between signs and actions is very close (Savage-Rumbaugh 1994). Externalised signs or symbolic actions can be understood as condensations of causal understanding. While it is possible to use arbitrary gestures to compose a natural language such as American Sign Language, it is also possible to use iconic actions as direct carriers of metaphoric correspondence. Savage-Rumbaugh (1994) records an instance where a circular motion of her hand prompted a chimpanzee to repeat a somersault. The iconic equivalence here is striking (in two ways: mimicry and analogy — here both directly referenced via actions) and it is consistent with a evolutionary progression of gesture and language. However, what such iconic actions can carry is limited in one way because they are not arbitrary. Imagine if we wanted to communicate gradations of meaning (analogous perhaps to the qualification of a noun by an adjective) through a system of continuously changing gestures. It would be difficult because of the lack of calibrating reference points. At what point would *hot stone* become *warm stone*. The other strategy is to compose structures of arbitrary signs in which qualification is a result of the structure of constituents rather than continuous variation of sign. This is a trade off which seems to be worthwhile given the perceptual load we are subject to and the granularity of the categories that are significant for us. But it does involve an emphasis, which is that the actual metaphorical correspondences disappear. Or rather, they are objectified in associations, we have them labelled and collected as abstractions of regularities in the causal aspects of our experience.

This is where music comes in. Music, while involving categorical perception — we hear pitches and phrases — does not attach meaning to the arbitrary signs that it identifies. While language breaks down, analyses and labels and separates itself from the flow — moulding experience with *the pale cast of thought*, music maintains the link between action and metaphor in its process. It adopts a complementary strategy to language — allowing the use of sound to represent change and causation by using it in direct physical metaphors that maintain their origin in action and change. This is cognitively possible because music originates in (but is not limited by) physical activity. Causal correspondences are also understood via controlled motor actions similar to the manipulation involved in tool making and other human activity (Friberg & Sundberg 1999). This relationship is fundamental in music making — vocalisation and manipulation makes sounds that are metaphors of physical change. It is this metaphorical representation that gives music its emotional power — and apparent emotional origin. It plays with causal expectations, not to create feelings — this is the hook that keeps us listening — but to keep us in sync with the flow of cause and effect in the world. Arguably, music communicates the direct, causal links between motor schemes and perceptual schemas.

The presence in language — and absence from music — of arbitrary symbols allow it to carry its precise semantics. However, this linguistic understanding is incomplete because of the arbitrary and discrete nature of its constituents (i.e. words). The apparent completeness or coherence of linguistic meaning is a corollary (illusion?) of the mechanism that apprehends the arbitrary sign. In this view, rather than being an evolutionary luxury that provides little more than pleasure (a widely held conventional view c.f. Pinker (1998)): music allows us to engage in a variety of *continuous* "virtual" or "imaginary" causalities. These mirror and facilitate the exploration and manipulation of possible and actual worlds in sound. Language is excluded from these as the result of its abstraction into arbitrary signs. Non-symbolic sound can represent change in natural events via constructed perceptual analogy in a way that the words (e.g. up/down) are incapable. Abstract or virtual manipulation of direct cause and effect in music is complementary to rather than secondary to Language.

Perhaps it is time to return to Popper's analysis of language. In linguistic terms music is not descriptive and propositional. A propositional system assumes a stable syntax, and an axiomatic basis. But whereas language describes causes and relations, music experiments with causation, temporal and qualitative relations. It manipulates expectations in the abstract, as unattached sound, not symbolically attached and constrained; yet highly structured and ordered. It is literally in its own element — sound. Virtually anything can go, as long as outrageous acts are resolved to a recognisable, consistent, i.e. repetitious or transformational structure.

In music, syntax seems to be concerned with a different kind of internal consistency than that found in language. It reconciles variation and order, change and continuity. It is manifested as invariant structures such as scales and chords, metric and rhythmic patterns. There is a basic relationship between pattern, structure, transformation and abstraction. However, these cannot be defined by comparisons between objects over their properties — and hence attachment — alone. Musical associations are not intrinsic to concatenations of sound. In language, we are not allowed to arbitrarily change the meaning of sentences by changing the spelling of words. But in music, a chord progression's function is defined by its context (position in a scale), and not simply by the intervals between the successive chord roots (its spelling). Also, a chord's function can be qualified in all sorts of ways by the addition and omission of notes (i.e. by changing its spelling). The role of context in the definition of the meaning of a musical event is almost diametrically opposed to the identification and function of constituents in language. In music, pattern recognition arises as much from the transitions between states, as from the states themselves. Continuity and change is a function of the relations between constituents within a temporal structure. In language, time is simply what passes while we read or hear a sentence. Viewed in these terms an invariant structure such as a musical scale becomes a specification for the change (causes and effects) that can occur. It is a context sensitive description. In this sense it is syntactic, but not at the level of utterance or sentence, which is the level at which syntax operates in language.

To explore this kind of view we need culturally non-specific models of musical descriptors and parameters. Narmour's (1990) Implication-Realisation model of melodic structure is one such causal model. The way that sound can be organised to manifest change is limited by its productive technology, and our memory and processing capacity. The selection and use of parameters to maintain coherence arises through conventions such as scales. But the articulation of these descriptors is little understood in Western Music let alone universally. Theories such as GTTM and analyses such as Raffman's, concentrate on aspects of the musical listener, performer or composer through models developed relative to Western music theory, that all tend to mark up and highlight the distinction between music and language. This is largely because they concentrate on how we perceive and memorise sound. But musical and linguistic cognition is not simply a matter of different organisations of auditory perception and memory, but is, I would argue, concerned with the overall integration of perceptual and motor schemas. Thus, our understanding music also involves a model of how it is produced by physical action (manipulation of an instrument, voice, dance). These productive actions are similar to other real actions, and thus music performance has the capacity to experiment directly with the relationship between perceived change (causal structure) and actions (motor schemas) and this kind of experimentation is arguably at the centre of wilful creativity.

References

Bernstein, Leonard (1976). *The Unanswered Question.* Cambridge: Harvard University Press.

Bregman, Albert (1990). *Auditory Scene Analysis.* Cambridge: MIT Press.

Chomsky, Noam (1957) *Syntactic Structures,* The Hague: Mouton.

Cook, Nicholas (1990). *Music Imagination and Culture.* Oxford: Clarendon Press

Deliege, Irène (1987). Grouping Conditions in Listening to Music: An Approach to Lerdahl and Jackendoff's Grouping Preference Rules. *Music Perception, 4,* 325–360.

Eccles, John (1989). *Evolution of the Brain: Creation of the Self.* London: Routledge.

Fodor, Jerry (1983). *Modularity of Mind: A Monograph on Faculty Psychology.* Cambridge: MIT Press.

Friberg, Anders & Johan Sundberg (1999). Does music performance allude to locomotion? A model of final *ritardandi* derived from measurements of stopping runners, *Journal of the Acoustical Society of America, 105,* 1469–1484.

Goldin-Meadow, Susan (1991). When does gesture become language? In K. R. Gibson, & T. Ingold, (Eds.) *Tools, Language and Cognition in Human Evolution.* Cambridge: CUP.

Greenfield, Patricia (1991). Language, Tools, And Brain — The Ontogeny and Phylogeny of Hierarchically Organized Sequential Behavior, *Behavioural and Brain Science, 14,* 531–550.

Ivry, Richard & Lynn C. Robertson (1998). *The two sides of Perception,* Cambridge: MIT Press.

Kippen, Jim & Bel, Bernard (1992). Modelling music with grammars: formal language representation in the Bol Processor. In A. Marsden & A. Pople., (Eds.), *Computer Representations and Models in Music* (207–238). London: Academic Press.

Lakoff, George (1987). *Women Fire and Dangerous Things: What categories reveal about the mind.* Chicago: University of Chicago Press.

Lakoff, George & Mark Johnson (1980). *Metaphors we live by.* Chicago: University of Chicago Press.

Lerdahl, Fred & Ray Jackendoff (1983). *A Generative Theory of Tonal Music.* Cambridge: MIT Press.

McGurk, Harry & John MacDonald (1976). Hearing lips and seeing voices. *Nature, 264,* 746–748.

Narmour, Eugene (1990). *The Analysis and Cognition of Basic Melodic Structures.* Chicago: University of Chicago Press

Patel, Aniruddh & Isabelle Peretz (1997). Is music autonomous from language? A neurospychological appraisal. In I. Deliege & J. Sloboda (Eds.) *Perception and Cognition of Music.* Psychology Press.

Pinker, Steven (1997). *How The Mind Works.* London: Penguin Books.

Popper, Karl (1972). *Objective Knowledge. An Evolutionary Approach.* Oxford: Clarendon Press.

Raffman, Diana (1993). *Language Music and Mind.* Cambridge: MIT Press.

Roads, Curtis (1979). Grammars as Representations of Music. *Computer Music Journal,* **3**, 48–55.

Savage-Rumbaugh, Sue & Roger Lewin (1994). *Kanzi: The Ape at the Brink of the Human Mind.* New York: John Wiley & Sons.

Scruton, Roger (1983). Understanding Music. *Ratio, 25,* 97–120.

Sherry, David & Daniel Schacter (1987). The Evolution of Multiple Memory Systems. *Psychological Review, 94,* 439–454.

Steedman, Mark (1984). A Generative Grammar for Jazz Chord Sequences. *Music Perception, 2,* 52–77.

Sundberg, Johan. & B Lindblom (1976). Generative theories in language and music descriptions. *Cognition, 4,* 98–122.

Rosenthal, David (1989). A Model of the Process of Listening to Simple Rhythms, *Music Perception, 6,* 315–328.

Wilkins, Wendy & Jennie Wakefield (1995). Brain Evolution and Neurolinguistic Preconditions. *Behavioural and Brain Science, 18,* 161–182.

Winograd, Terry (1969). Linguistics and the Computer Analysis of Tonal Harmony. *Journal of Music Theory, 12,* 2–49.

Zbikowski, Lawrence (1998). Metaphor and Music Theory: Reflections from Cognitive Science. *Music Theory Online, 4.*

Expression, content and meaning in language and music

An integrated semiotic analysis

Jean Callaghan and Edward McDonald
University of Western Sydney, Australia/National University of Singapore

1. Expression

Language and music as organised sound

Language and music are both examples of semiotic systems, i.e. systems where a set of contents is related to a set of expressions, in both cases the medium of expression being the human voice. Table 1 summarises the ways in which sound is utilised in the two systems.

Table 1. Utilisation of sound in language and music

System		**Language**	**Music**
Sound	pitch	intonation	tonality
	duration	rhythm	metre
resource	articulation	phonemics	—

The major difference between the two systems is that language, but not music, utilises a set of cross-cutting articulatory features such as voicing, closure, nasalisation etc., to define a set of basic sound units or phonemes which can be used to create different morphemes or basic units of wording: what the linguist Martinet referred to as the "double articulation of language" (Martinet 1964: 22–23). This is a profound difference since the double articulation of language is what enables it to express content, and it might therefore seem as if music was unable to express content in the same way. We will return to this question in a later section.

Language and music as physiological processes

In recent years, the likelihood of physical and mental links between music and language has been reinforced by investigation into foetal and neonatal development. It seems that the origins of both music and language lie in the connection between the neural development of the foetus and its sound environment in the womb (Abrams & Gerhardt 1997; Storr 1992). After birth, the affective expression of crooning, cooing and babbling develops into speech and song (Storr 1992), with the distinction between the two often unclear (Welch 1994).

As Tomatis (1991: 44) says: "One sings with one's ear." He might well also have said "One speaks with one's ear." The ear provides an important link between music and language. The process of hearing, perceiving and remembering sound forms a loop with the production of sound. In speaking and singing, the sounds being produced by the vocal mechanism are constantly being fed through this loop, dictating what is produced by the vocal apparatus. Even when the physical sound is not there, we are able mentally to hear the music we see notated or are about to improvise, just as we are able mentally to hear the sentence we read silently or the words we are about to say. Gordon has termed this inner hearing "audiation" and made the point that "audiation is to music what thought is to speech" (1993: 13). Audiation, then, is a process involving physical hearing, perception, cognition and cultural conditioning.

2. Content

As soon as we begin to investigate the content of linguistic and musical expressions — in other words, to determine what these organised sounds relate to outside themselves — we may view them as cultural systems, as cognition, or as semiotic systems.

Language and music as cultural systems

Language is necessary for the transmission of the detailed knowledge that constitutes the cultural component of human behaviour. Every human society, however materially or technologically simple its culture, possesses a complex language system, and in the same way, there is no human culture which lacks music.

Many writers have remarked on the universal tendency of music to heighten experience or to cause bodily and emotional arousal (McAllester 1971; Wachsmann 1971; Walker 1990; Storr 1992). Others have speculated about universals based in perception and cognition (Harwood 1976; Serafine 1988; Aiello 1994; Patel & Peretz 1997) or in panchronic emotional signals in music (Fónagy & Magdics 1963); or such formal universals as the tendency to some kind of tonal centre, the tendency to "move" in a certain "direction" and the tendency to patterning and to establish a beginning and an end (McAllester 1971; Aiello 1994).

As soon as we begin to consider which vocal sounds are used, by which aggregation of human beings, in which particular human environment, language sets people of one group apart from those of another: it is a form of cultural variation. This is not just a matter of objective observation, but also a matter of psychological reality for members of the language community. In the grammatical and lexical/semantic aspects of a language system, there exist correlations with traits of the culture of the group which speaks it, either as the culture exists at any given moment, or as it has existed earlier. The vocabulary of the language correlates with the elements of the physical and social environment which are significant in the culture.

Music is also a form of cultural variation. Unlike language, music does not catalogue the things, events and processes in the human environment. Different musical traditions, do, however cut up the field of perception into meaningful elements, just as language does. The way in which this is done varies from culture to culture and over time, affecting which sounds are chosen as musical elements and how they are combined in structures. As with language, these differences in musical style contribute to the ways in which one group sees itself as different from another.

Human beings have the unique capacity for creating and responding to symbols. The realities of the physical world become cultural realities through the symbol system of language. It has even been suggested that language, far from being simply a technique of communication, is itself a way of directing the perceptions of its speakers and dictating habitual modes of analysing experiences into significant categories (Sapir 1949, Whorf 1956). In this sense language operates as a system of cultural symbols. As with language, music has often been regarded as a system of cultural symbols, a system in which the forms of the natural or human world are invested with analogical signification. Such analogical signification may be reduced to certain basic elements, certain archetypes, which may then be structured in a system to produce an extremely complex symbolic, even mystical meaning (Walker 1990). It is significant in this context that Lévi-Strauss (1963) used music as a key to unravelling the complex meanings of myth. As a system of cultural symbols, music is inseparable from its cultural context, the values, attitudes and beliefs — the *Weltanschauung* — of the people who create it. The musical work imposes its particular form of relevance on the listener, but relies on the listener supplying the cultural content which gives meaning to the form. Music-making is also, like speech, symbolic *behaviour*, possessing in all cultures a significance far beyond the actual production of sound, including the strengthening of social relationships, association with ritual, and specific social functions, such as an accompaniment to dance, drama and work. Music is often associated with myth, religion and magic in rituals, and a performance event may have a ritual of its own.

Language and music as cognition

An understanding of cognition in both language and music lies in the nature of these modes of communication and how they are learnt. Both language and music rely on the oral-aural channel and early learning can proceed without relation to physical objects. Neurobiological research suggests that children's learning of both modes is achieved by the establishment of mental representations which are reflected by cortical activation patterns (Deacon 1997; Gruhn 1997).

An adequate model of language cognition should account for linguistic universals and culturally diverse languages, spoken and written language, and linguistic production and linguistic reception. Given the similarities identified between language and music, one would expect models of music cognition to meet these same criteria. This, however, is rarely the case. Many focus more on perception than cognition, many are grounded in understandings of music based on the written tradition of Western art music which are then not generalisable to other musical traditions, and many address musical reception while neglecting musical production. Fiske (1992) has identified three types of theories of music cognition: psychoacoustic theories that explain musical behaviour in respect of the mechanisms involved in auditory perceptual activity; pattern structure theories concerned with musical thinking in relation to the perceptual identification of features or components related to the recognition and recall of musical patterns; and those that assume the presence of language-like grammatical protocols underlying mental construction of musical patterns.

This last type seems better to answer the case, subsuming the theories of the other two types. We assume that music cognition refers to the mental processes that take place following psychoacoustic processing, i.e. to musical thinking. The theories of Heller and Campbell, of Lehrdahl and Jackendoff, of Serafine, and of Fiske are worth consideration. In a series of publications (Heller & Campbell 1976; Campbell & Heller 1980, Campbell & Heller 1981; Heller & Campbell 1982), Heller and Campbell put forward the view that music cognition is pattern construction and pattern management, having both universal and style-specific components, with musical understanding being the product of music acculturation. They see music processing as similar to language processing. They (and many other writers on music cognition) assume that the musical process is a tripartite one involving composer, performer and listener. This raises problems in relation to the many musical traditions in which composer and performer are one; few theories of music cognition account for improvised music-making and oral traditions.

Lerdahl and Jackendoff (Lerdahl & Jackendoff 1983; Jackendoff 1987) agree with Heller and Campbell and with Serafine that music is heard as organised patterns and that processing these patterns depends on knowledge of a particular music system. The Lerdahl and Jackendoff theory derives from Noam Chomsky's school of generative linguistics (Chomsky 1965, 1975). Jackendoff (1993) postulates a universal mental grammar comprising an innate and a learned component. However, while in relation to language the theory accounts for generation and reception, in relation to music it is difficult to see how the theory accounts for generation outside the written tradition of Western tonal music.

Serafine proposes a bipartite model. She is unusual in insisting that "the critical interaction is not that between composer and listener, or performer and listener, or composer and performer, but rather that between one of those actors and a piece of music" (1988: 6). Her central claim is that "music is a form of thought and that it develops over the life span much as other forms of thought develop, principally those such as language, mathematical reasoning, and ideas about the physical world" (Serafine 1988: 5). Serafine's theory better accounts for cultural diversity and for musical performance (i.e. musical creation, including composition, improvised performance, and interpretation of another's composition).

Fiske identifies in the theories of Heller and Campbell, Lerdahl and Jackendoff, and Serafine two components (the first, the innate — processing — component; and the second the learned component, comprising a description of the perceived tonal-rhythmic patterns resulting from exercising the rules of the first component). He proposes a third component which he identifies as a generic decision-making mechanism, "a description of the activity that leads to realizing those musical structures and interstructural relationships" (1992: 371).

Language and music as semiotic systems

We have shown above that language and music exhibit significant and certainly not accidental commonalities in their material substance (the organisation of sound), physiological bases, cultural significance, and cognitive processing. It is of course possible to compare the two systems on these terms alone, but this would ignore the fact that both language and music are essentially semiotic systems. A semiotic system sets up a dialectical relationship between a content system and an expression system, the content being correlated with expression through certain rules (Eco 1976). While Saussure's theory of semiotics (1916/1960) was based in language and Barthes' early work assumed that "there is no meaning which is not designated [i.e. expressed through signs], and the world of signifieds is none other than that of language" (1967: 16), semiotics has developed as a field concerned with the nature of communication codes generally, and the nature, form and function of signs. Signs may be images, gestures, sounds, or objects, and their signification ("meaning") need not be denotational. Semiotics has proved a useful way to describe and analyse music (Ruwet 1967, 1972; Nattiez 1973, 1990) and may form a basis for comparing the language and music of a culture (Callaghan 1986).

Whereas from a cultural or cognitive perspective, language and music are investigated for their links with some form of organisation outside themselves, a semiotic approach allows us not only to understand their internal organisation as systems, but also how this organisation enables them to be linked to their cultural context and their cognitive/neurological bases. We will do this by investigating the nature of meaning as expressed by the two systems.

3. Meaning

From a semiotic point of view, the question in relation to the two semiotic systems of language and music is whether the similar expression substance of language and music embodies comparable types of meaning. In order to deal with this question, we will need a broader conception of "meaning" than the traditional one, where meaning is largely equated with "content," i.e. the relationship of expression to the external world. A useful approach for this purpose has been developed in the school of linguistics known as systemic functional linguistics (e.g. Halliday 1978, 1985), whose major contribution to the understanding of meaning in language can be summarised in the concept of metafunction. Metafunction refers to the different general functional types of meaning according to which linguistic patterns may be interpreted: ideational, construing a model of the world; interpersonal, enacting social relationships; and textual, creating relevance to context (Halliday 1994). Such a notion has obvious relevance outside language, and more recently has been applied to other semiotic systems such as visual image and displayed art (Kress & van Leeuwen 1996; O'Toole 1994) and music (van Leeuwen 1999).

Halliday goes on to draw a correlation between these different types of meaning and the associated types of structure by which they are expressed (Halliday 1979). Ideational meanings tend to be expressed by segmental, or part-whole structures, which enable us to distinguish discrete elements of experience and show relationships between them; in Halliday's analysis this consists of the process, or type of action or behaviour, the participants involved in this process, and the associated circumstances or features of the setting. Interpersonal meanings tend to be expressed by prosodic structures, associated with the act of meaning as a whole, whereby certain meanings apply within particular boundaries but cannot necessarily be assigned to one or just one element: for example, the characterisation of a sentence as a whole as a question or a statement; or meanings such as those of positive or negative polarity which are often scattered throughout the sentence (cf the old music hall song "we *don't* know *no-one* who *don't* want *no* nine-inch nails"). Textual meanings tend to be expressed by cumulative or wave-like structures, where for example the prominence of different items of information tends to build up from the beginning to the end of the sentence ("I'm telling you you have to go to *bed*!"), or else to be set apart as a separate "peak" at the beginning ("*That one*, he's a real loser").

Similar types of structure can also be identified in music, as we will show below, but cannot necessarily be as directly related to the same types of meaning as in language. To put these issues in context, and see how such a multifunctional model of a linguistic semiotic system might be applied to music, we will analyse Erik Satie's piano piece, *La Pêche* (*Fishing*).

Musical texture

La Pêche/Fishing is an example of an artistic creation that combines all three modalities — verbal, visual and musical — in the one work. It is one piece in the collection *Sports et divertissements* (*Sports and diversions*) (Satie 1914), commissioned to "illustrate" a set of pictures by the fashionable French artist Charles Martin depicting various sports and pastimes. In composing these pieces, Satie also supplied a short verbal text for each musical piece, supplementing and elucidating the music. The meaning of this piece of music would thus seem to be completely determined by its associations with the original picture and the verbal text (see appendix for the original published version of the picture and the accompanying music and verbal text): we are told repeatedly by the original picture, by the title at the top of the musical score, by the little "narrative" of the music itself — albeit a counterpoint rather than a simple reflection of the visual image — where words and music seem to fit each other perfectly. The water murmurs; a fish arrives, another, two others; they ask a question, answer it, and acknowledge the answer; they all go back home; and the water goes on murmuring.

However, this still begs the question of whether this meaning is inherent in the music itself, or whether the music is simply mimicking — certainly with

Table 2. Systems in music

System	Gloss	Associated Type of Structure
METRE	the semioticisation of durations as a regular alternation of strong and weak *beats*	cumulative: recurring peaks and troughs of prominence (strong and weak beats), layers of rhythmic structure built up over this basic alternation
TONALITY	the semioticisation of pitches as movement away from and back to a *tonic* pitch	prosodic: tonic key established by relation to its associated intervals, moved away from, then returned to
COUNTERPOINT	the interplay between different melodic (combined pitch and rhythmic) lines or voices, traditionally understood in terms of a. the texture, whether *monophony* (single line), *polyphony* (multiple lines), or *homophony* (melody + accompaniment) b. relationships of *consonance* and *dissonance* between pitches	segmental: voices established as identifiable entities, then modified, rearranged, combined in various ways

great economy and wit — the content of the picture and the words. To resolve this question, we need to look at the music as text, i.e. as a coherent entity, and analyse how its texture is built up through the interaction of a number of musical systems and their associated structures. The ones we will examine here are metre, tonality and counterpoint. These systems are glossed in Table 2, their associated structures briefly summarised, and in the following discussion their contribution to the texture is described.

Metre

Figure 1 represents diagrammatically the metrical organisation of this piece (in a somewhat shortened form to save space). It can be seen from this analysis that the music has a regular cumulative structure, with a strong beat (marked by the vertical barline) recurring every six of the basic beats, and that it has a very balanced overall organisation, with different rhythmic patterns marking the changing sections of the piece.

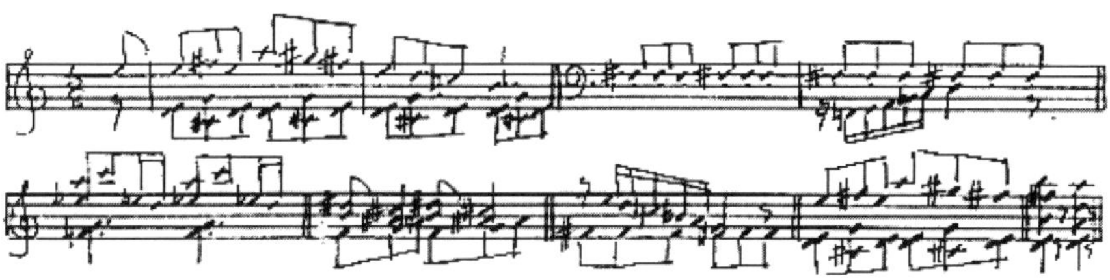

Figure 1. Metrical organisation

Tonality

Figure 2 represents diagrammatically the tonal organisation of this piece. It can be seen from this analysis that the piece as a whole has a regular prosodic structure, starting and finishing in the key of D major, with the bass line tracing a D major chord through the progression of the piece, apart from the middle section (representing the question) which goes into the distantly related key of F major. These changes of key work together with the rhythmic patterns identified above, so that each section of the piece tends to be both tonally and rhythmically distinct.

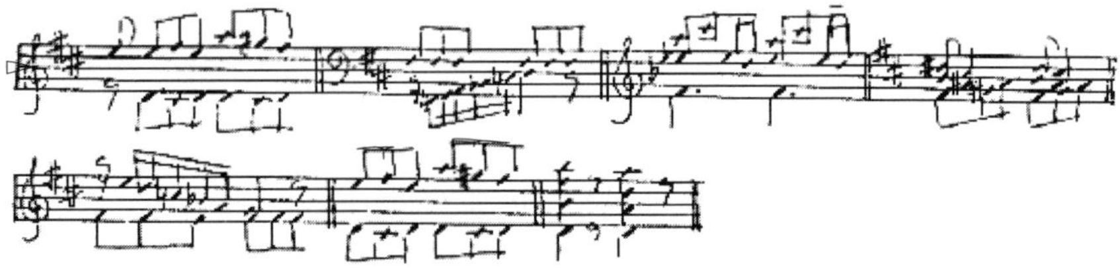

Figure 2. Tonal organisation

Counterpoint

Figure 3 represents diagrammatically the contrapuntal organisation of this piece (again shortened). It can be seen from this analysis that the piece has a segmental structure, whereby particular sections or melodic figures may be identified with stages of the narrative or its processes, participants and circumstances. The texture of *La Peche/Fishing* is basically homophonic, i.e. melody plus accompaniment, divided between a harmonic bass in the left hand (for the most part representing the continual flow of the stream) and a melodic treble in the right hand. The only overtly polyphonic sections, i.e. with separate distinct melodic lines, are those representing the arrival and departure of the fish, where each fish is given its own separate musical line. In terms of the relationships of consonance and dissonance, Satie uses these cleverly to highlight the key points of the action, particularly in the question and answer sections. The question is represented by a chord based on F, noted above as a rather distant tonality for the key of D major. For the answer, this chord is then transformed into a B major chord which at first clashes with the F in the bass (a note not in the key of B major), the latter then "resolving" to F# (the fifth or dominant of B major) . What we have played out in the relationships of consonance and dissonance is a symbolic representation of the tension raised by the question and then resolved by the answer.

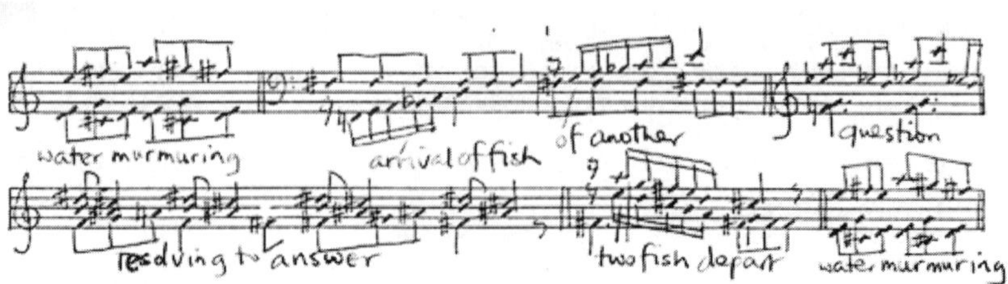

Figure 3. Contrapuntal organisation

Meaning in music

The three systems examined above jointly establish the overall coherence of the piece. As we have noted above, the types of structures associated with these systems are cumulative, prosodic, and segmental respectively, but whether we can then say that they are expressing textual, interpersonal, and ideational meanings is less clear. It could in fact be argued that these different patterns are basically self-contained, without the need for any other associations. If we then want to apply meanings to these patterns, as we obviously are easily able to do in the case of this piece, this is a distinct second step: there is nothing in the various textural features that *requires* them to express these particular meanings. This would then suggest that the music itself is basically meaningless, a conclusion which seems counterintuitive, to say the least! To resolve this conundrum if would be useful to go back to the concept of metafunction introduced above and examine it in more detail.

In the analysis of language, the concept of metafunction goes together with that of stratification which distinguishes different strata, or levels of abstraction in a semiotic system: typically for language, sound (phonology), wording (lexicogrammar), and meaning (semantics). Given that we are characterising music as a semiotic system, we must by definition recognise at least two strata, content and expression, though the term "content" has such strong ideational associations that we might replace this by a less loaded pair of terms such as meaning and form. If we have then at least two strata, meaning and form, the next question is whether music shows the sort of "double articulation" we find in language, where form is organised first into significant units of wording, which are themselves organised into distinctive units of sound (Martinet 1964: 22–23). In other words, is there a distinction in music comparable to that between lexicogrammar and phonology in language?

If we examine the sorts of patterns of form we saw above in the analysis of *La Pêche/Fishing*, there does not seem to be any significant difference between what we might call by analogy a stratum of sound and a stratum of wording. The sorts of differences that *do* exist are analogous to those between phones and phonemes in language, i.e. the basic vocal "noise" and how it is utilised distinctively in a particular language, contrasting the basic acoustic facts of duration and pitch with their semioticisation as metre and tonality, or the heard patterns of the rhythm and pitch of a piece of music with its underlying metre and key.

We might therefore put forward the following two-stratum model for music. A lower stratum of phonotactics, covering at least the systems of pitch and rhythmic organisation and linear texture, i.e. tonality, metre, and counterpoint. Others of course could be added according to the purpose of the analysis: thus, for performers and listeners the system of prominence is also very important, i.e., the means by which various aspects of the texture are highlighted or backgrounded; we could also include systems like timbre/sound quality (including such factors as vocal styles and instrumentation), spatiality (the adaptation of music to the performance space), and so on. If we characterise this stratum metafunctionally, we must acknowledge it as in essence textual, or perhaps better textural, i.e. not as a mechanism for making ideational and interpersonal meanings relevant to their context, but rather as consisting of independent text-forming resources in its own right.

The second stratum would be that of interpretation, corresponding to the level of semantics in language. The use of this term emphasises that, unlike in the case of language, there is no direct link between patterns of musical form and patterns of musical meaning analogous to that between patterns of wording and meaning in language; instead particular interpretations are opened up once the musical text is formed. These interpretations can be either interpersonal or ideational, or perhaps again, since these terms carry associations from language, we might rename them interactional and figurative.

4. Features of an integrated semiotic approach

To show the ways in which this model can handle both language and music, we sum up its main features as follows:

- The description draws on a basic distinction between the system or semiotic potential and the text or instantiation of that potential.
- The description is polysystemic, i.e. we need to recognise a number of distinct systems whose contribution to the text can be analysed separately.
- The description is comprehensive, i.e. it attempts to be totally accountable to the text as a whole in a way that shows how all its significant features contribute to the coherence of the whole.
- The description is stratified, i.e. it identifies patterns at different levels of abstraction: sound, wording and meaning in language; sound and meaning in music.
- The description is distributed metafunctionally according to the three types of ideational, interpersonal and textual meaning.

Tables 3 and 4 show how these two systems differ in the relations between the different strata and types of metafunctional meaning (terms in small caps refer to specific systems at each strata — the main textural ones were discussed above for interactional and figurative systems, see van Leeuwen 1999; for language, see Halliday 1994).

Table 3. The semiotic system of language (Halliday 1994)

Stratum / metafunction	Semantics	Lexicogrammar	Phonology
ideational	IDEATION	TRANSITIVITY	PHONEMICS
interpersonal	SPEECH FUNCTION	MOOD	TONE
textual	CONJUNCTION	THEME, INFORMATION	TONICITY

Table 4. The semiotic system of music

Stratum / metafunction	Interpretation	Phonotactics
textural		METRE, TONALITY, COUNTERPOINT
interactional	PERSPECTIVE, INTERACTION	
figurative	FIGURATION, NARRATIVITY	

Regarding language and music as subsets of the larger set of semiotic systems allows us to examine their similarities and differences in a way that is not biased towards one or the other. A semiotic approach, as outlined above, must focus on both content, the meanings expressed by the two systems, and expression, the substance which embodies those meanings and how it is organised as form. From the point of view of form, language and music share obvious similarities in that both are essentially organised sound, and utilise the basic acoustic facts of duration and pitch, semioticised as rhythm and intonation in language, and as metre and tonality in music. A consideration of form also leads us to the observation that language and music share common physiological and cognitive bases in the human body/mind. From the point of view of meaning, language and music exhibit a crucial difference in regard to the role of ideational meaning, central in language, (and in other visual semiotics like art — see van Leeuwen 1999), but essentially peripheral in music, for which textural meaning, i.e. the text-forming devices that create a musical unity, is central, with textural patterns then open to figurative (ideational) or interactional (interpersonal) interpretations.

References

Abrams, Robert M. & Kenneth K. Gerhardt (1997). Some aspects of the foetal sound environment. In I. Deliege & J. Sloboda (Eds), *Perception and cognition of music* (83–101). Hove, UK: Psychology Press.

Aiello, Rita (1994). Music and language: Parallels and contrasts. In Rita Aiello (Ed.) with John A. Sloboda, *Musical perceptions*. New York and Oxford: Oxford University Press.

Barthes, Roland (1967). *Elements of semiology* (Annette Lavers & Colin Smith, Trans.). London: Jonathan Cape.

Callaghan, Jean (1986). *Did Elgar speak English? Language and national music style: Comparative semiotic analysis.* Paper delivered at National Conference, Musicological Society of Australia, Melbourne.

Campbell, Warren & Jack Heller (1980). An orientation for considering models of musical behavior. In D. Hodges (Ed.), *Handbook of music psychology* (29–36). Lawrence: National Association for Music Therapy.

Campbell, Warren & Jack Heller (1981). Psychomusicology and psycholinguistics: Parallel paths or separate ways? *Psychomusicology*, *1*(2), 3–14.

Chomsky, Noam (1965). *Aspects of the theory of language.* Cambridge, MA: MIT Press.

Chomsky, Noam (1975). *Reflections on language.* New York: Pantheon.

Deacon, Terence (1997). *The symbolic species. The co-evolution of language and the brain.* New York and London: Norton.

Eco, Umberto (1976). *A theory of semiotics.* Bloomington IN: Indiana University Press.

Fiske, Harold (1992). Structure of cognition and music decision-making. In Richard Colwell (Ed.), *Handbook of research on music teaching and learning* (360–376). New York: Schirmer Books.

Fónagy, Ivan & Klara Magdics (1963). Emotional patterns in intonation and music, *Zietschrift für Phonetik, Sprachwissenschaft und Kommunikationsforschung, 16*: 193–326.

Gordon, Edwin (1993). *Learning sequences in music. Skill, content, and patterns.* Chicago: GIA Publications.

Gruhn, Wilfried (1997). Music learning — neurobiological foundations and educational implications. *Research studies in music education, 9,* 36–47.

Halliday, M. A. K. (1978). *Language as social semiotic.* London: Edward Arnold.

Halliday, M. A. K. (1979). Modes of meaning and modes of expression: Types of grammatical structure, and their determination by different semantic functions. In D. J. Allerton, E. Carney & D. Holcroft (Eds) *Function and context in linguistic analysis* (57–79). Cambridge: Cambridge University Press.

Halliday, M. A. K. (1994). *An introduction to functional grammar* (2nd ed.). London: Edward Arnold.

Harwood, Dane L. (1976). Universals in music: A perspective from cognitive psychology, *Ethnomusicology, 20*(3): 521–533.

Heller, Jack & Warren Campbell (1976). Models of language and intellect in music research. In A. Motycka (Ed.), *Music education for tomorrow's society* (149–180). Jamestown: GAMT Music Press.

Heller, Jack & Warren Campbell (1982). Music communication and cognition. *Bulletin of the Council for Research in Music Education, 72*: 1–15.

Jackendoff, Ray (1987). *Consciousness and the computational mind.* Cambridge, MA: MIT Press/Bradford.
Jackendoff, Ray (1993). *Patterns in the mind. Language and human nature.* New York: Harvester/Wheatsheaf.
Kress, Gunther & Theo van Leeuwen (1990). *Reading images.* Geelong: Deakin University Press.
Kress, Gunther & Theo van Leeuwen (1996). *Reading images: The grammar of visual design.* London: Routledge.
Lerdahl, Fred & Ray Jackendoff (1983). *A generative theory of tonal music.* Cambridge MA: MIT Press.
Lévi-Strauss, Claude (1963). *Structural anthropology* (Claire Jacobson & Brooke Grundfest Schoepf, Trans.). New York: Basic Books.
Lévi-Strauss, Claude (1970). *The raw and the cooked: Introduction to a science of mythology* (John and Doreen Weightman, Trans.). London: Jonathan Cape.
McAllester, D.P. (1971). Some thoughts on "universals" in world music, *Ethnomusicology, 15*: 379-380.
Martinet, Andre (1964). *Elements of general linguistics* (E. Palmer, Trans.). London: Faber & Faber.
Nattiez, Jean-Jacques (1973). Linguistics: A new approach for musical analysis?, *International Review of the Aesthetics and Sociology of Music, 4*(1): 51–68.
Nattiez, Jean-Jacques (1990). *Music and discourse. Towards a semiology of music.* Princeton, NJ: Princeton University Press.
O'Toole, Michael (1994). *The language of displayed art.* London: Leicester University Press.
Patel, Aniruddh & Isabelle Peretz (1997). Is music autonomous from language? A neuropsychological appraisal. In Irène Deliège & John Sloboda (Eds), *Perception and cognition of music* (191–215). Hove, UK: Psychology Press.
Ruwet, Nicolas (1967). Musicology and linguistics, *International Social Science Journal, 19*(1): 79–87.
Ruwet, Nicolas (1972). *Langage, musique, poesie.* Paris: Le Seuil.
Sapir, Edward (1949. *Selected Writings.* Berkeley: University of California Press.
Satie, Erik (1914/1921). *Sports et divertissements.* Facsimile ed. New York: Dover.
de Saussure, Ferdinand (1960). *Course in general linguistics* (Wade Baskin, Trans.). London: Peter Owen. (Original work published 1916)
Serafine, Mary Louise (1988). *Music as cognition. The development of thought in sound.* New York: Columbia University Press.
Storr, Anthony (1992). *Music and the mind.* London: Harper Collins.
Tomatis, Alfred A. (1991). *The conscious ear. My life of transformation through listening* (S. Lushington, Trans., B. M. Thompson, Ed.). New York: Station Hill Press.
van Leeuwen, Theo. 1999. *Speech, music, sound.* London: Macmillan.
Wachsmann, Klaus P (1971). Universal perspectives in music, *Ethnomusicology, 15*(3): 381–384.
Walker, Robert (1990). *Musical beliefs. Psychoacoustic, mythical, and educational perspectives.* New York: Teachers College Press.
Welch, Graham F. (1994). The assessment of singing, *Psychology of Music, 22:* 3–19.
Whorf, Benjamin Lee (1956). *Language, thought and reality: Selected writings of Benjamin Lee Whorf.* Cambridge, MA: The Massachusetts Institute of Techonology Press.

Appendix 1: Original picture

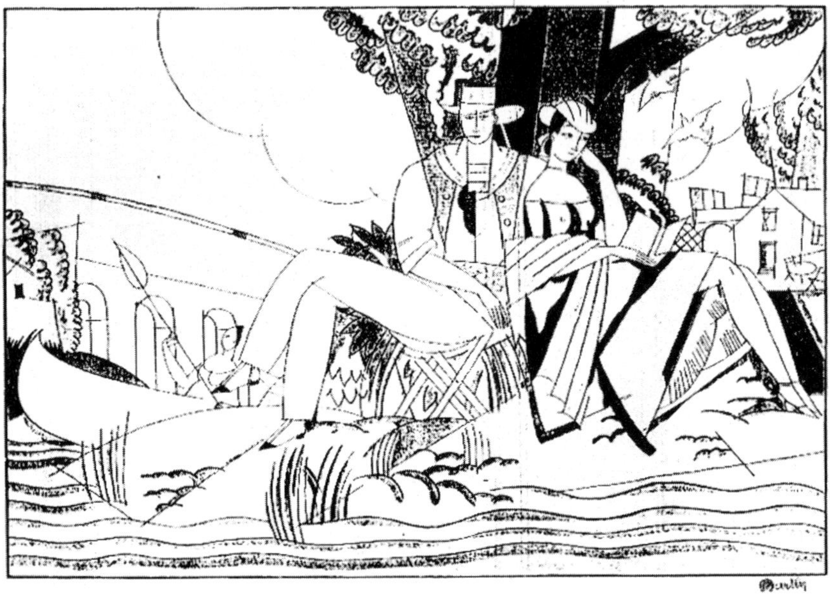

Appendix 2: Music and verbal text

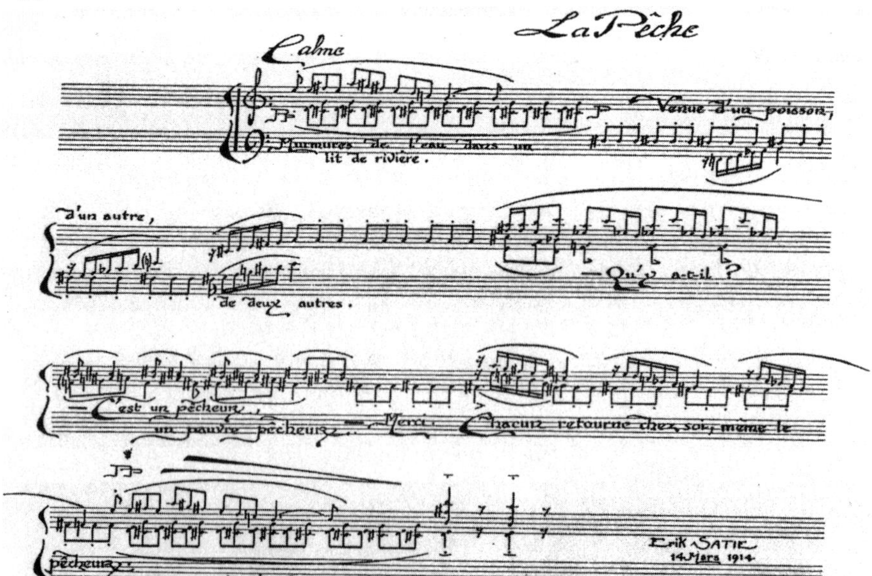

Auditory structuring in explaining dyslexia

Kai Karma
Sibelius Academy, Helsinki, Finland

1. Introduction

Musical aptitude

No generally accepted definition of musical aptitude exists; there is room for many different views as long as they obey the principles of scientific concept formation. Two rough extremes can be seen in the proposed constructs of musical aptitude and, consequently, tests devised to measure it. One tradition can be seen as sensory oriented and the other as musically oriented. The best known example of the first tradition is Seashore and his Measures of Musical Talents, especially those parts of the test where small differences in pitch, length, duration and timbre are to be discerned in tone pairs (Seashore 1919).

The "musical" tradition can be exemplified by Wing and his Measures of Musical Intelligence (Wing 1960), as well as Gordon's earlier work and the Musical Aptitude Profile (Gordon 1965). In these tests, the items consist of real music or music-like material and even esthetic judgement is required from the subjects.

These extremes have properties which risk or diminish their value as measures and definitions of musical aptitude. The sensory type of thinking and measuring tends to forget the relations between individual tones and the meanings carried by these relations. This is why this tradition is often called "atomistic". The "musical" tradition very easily leads to thinking and measures which are culture-dependent and subjective.

In order to avoid these risks, this writer wants to define musical aptitude as an auditory structuring ability. A general ability to relate tones with each other is assumed; this ability is seen as clearly different from sensory acuity, i.e. the ability to hear small differences in the different parameters of sound. Auditory structuring ability would be similar to spatial ability in that both consist of perceiving patterns or relationships; the role of single elements is just to form these structures by having certain relationships to each other. The difference between auditory structuring and spatial ability is that in the former the relationships are mainly temporal and auditory, while in the latter they are mainly static and visual. (Karma 1984)

In the same way that spatial ability may form the basis for more experience-related abilities like the mechanical-technical ability, auditory structuring ability is seen as the generally human, unspecific basis for abilities which are affected by culture and training. In the western musical culture, for instance, auditory structuring ability would develop into the senses of tonality, rhythm, harmony etc. In other cultures, different abilities would develop onto the same general basis. Defining musical aptitude this way makes it independent of music styles or cultures and gives it explaining power also outside music by making it a potential explainer of perceiving any patterned auditory information, in this case spoken language.

This writer has developed a musical aptitude test according to these guidelines. All the items in the test consist of two patterns: first a longer one in which a short basic pattern is played three times without any indications where one basic pattern ends and another begins. After a pause a comparison pattern is heard; this may be the same as the basic pattern repeated in the first part, or a structural variation of it where the number or the order of the tones is changed. The subjects are instructed to divide the first pattern into three similar parts in their minds and then compare this subgroup with the comparison pattern. Answer alternatives are thus "same" and "different". (Karma 1983, 2000)

The basic patterns are not music but simple sequences like low-high-high or long-short-short-long etc. By repeating them a hierarchic structure is formed. The subject does not know in advance how many tones there are in the patterns; dividing the series correctly into subgroups is one important cognitive operation in the test. Although the test seems to be mainly one-dimensional, there seems to be some interesting factors in it. The most important ones are breaking strong gestalts, forming expectations and changing expectations (Karma 1985).

Rather much information has accumulated which shows that the test is a satisfactorily valid measure of auditory structuring which, in turn, can be seen as musical aptitude. For instance, musically selected groups invariably get higher scores in the test, correlations with earlier music training are low. High and low scoring groups selected according to results in the test had significantly different event-related brain potentials (Tervaniemi et al. 1997). The potentials of the high scoring group were earlier and stronger than those of the lower scoring group for four-tone sound patterns. There was no similar difference when the task consisted of hearing the absolute differences in tone pairs; this supports the validity of the test as a structuring test. This writer's feeling that auditory structuring is spontaneous and unconscious was also supported by this study: the event related potentials were very similar also in an ignore condition where a book was read and the sounds were ignored as much as possible.

If musical aptitude is defined as an auditory (temporal) patterning ability, an interesting problem arises: which is the defining property of music and musical aptitude, sound or temporal organisation? This writer has tested the hypothesis that temporal organisation is the key property in musical perception, i.e. that the same property can be measured without sound stimuli. A silent, blinking variant of the auditory structuring test had a rather high correlation with the auditory version; normally hearing and congenitally deaf persons seemed to use very similar processes when taking this test (Karma 1994).

Dyslexia as an auditory problem

Dyslexia or a specific reading and writing impairment is a somewhat vague construct but it is mainly defined by clear difficulties in reading and writing which cannot be explained by external factors like a different mother tongue or low general intelligence. Traditionally, there have been two main directions from where the causes of dyslexia have been sought: the visual/spatial and the auditory/temporal. Although evidently both types of syndrome exist, explanations based on auditory/temporal deficiences are more common today. Even some problems which superficially look visual can be explained as problems in associating visual stimuli with an unclear auditory memory store (Duane 1983, Bigsby 1985). According to some research results, this combining of the auditory and the visual may be difficult for dyslexics even if these areas separately seemed to be normal (Hicks 1981, Payne & Holzman 1983). There are research results according to which the auditory problem in dyslexia is slowness of processing the auditory stimuli (Merzenich et al. 1996, Tallal et al. 1996, Hari & Kiesilä 1996). This is obviously an important part of the explanation but we are here interested in the role structuring has when the stimuli are presented rather slowly.

Key constructs in dyslexia research today are phonological awareness and phonemic awareness. Alhough these constructs are often used interchangeably, it seems that making a difference between them describes the phenomena better. Phonological awareness would then be a general feeling and ability to hear the phoneme patterns in speech while phonemic awareness can be defined as knowledge of the elements of spoken words phoneme by phoneme. Phonological awareness can be measured by comparing words by their general similarity or rhyming, while phonemic awareness is reflected in counting the phonemes of words or telling which sounds they are made of. The important difference of these two is that phonological awareness is a basic, natural property which predicts reading and writing, while phonemic awareness is a consequence of learning to read and write (Goswami & Bryant 1990). Because the topic of this article is predicting problems in reading and writing, phonological awareness is the construct of interest here.

If phonological awareness is an ability to hear the phoneme structures in speech, could it be a result of applying the general auditory structuring ability to speech sounds? Could auditory structuring be a useful construct also in explaining the auditory processes in perceiving speech, not only in explaining the culture-dependent abilities in music? Could deficient musical aptitude be an important explainer of dyslexia? Can dyslexia be better predicted if auditory/visual matching is added to auditory structuring?

2. Method and problems

Measures

Two measures are used in the present study. Auditory structuring ability is operationalised with the 1993 version of the test described above. The ability to combine the (temporal) auditory and the (static) visual signals is measured with a computerised test programmed by this writer. The program works as follows. First, the program draws a linear pattern onto the screen. The pattern is a graphic equivalent of a monophonic stream of sounds, for example long-short-short-long-long. After a couple of seconds the synthesiser of the computer plays the pattern as tones. The testee's task is to "read" the visual pattern as it is played and to hit the space bar simultaneously with the last sound. If the testee has followed the pattern correctly the task is very easy. If, however, following the visual pattern has not been successful, it is very difficult to hit at the correct moment. The program saves information about hits and misses as well as about the exact moment when the space bar was hit.

A central point in the test is that it is completely non-verbal. It attempts to diagnose and train such cognitive operations which are necessary conditions for learning to read and write successfully, not reading and writing themselves. Earlier studies show that the test or a corresponding game may help in reading and writing problems as well as diagnose such problems even before beginning to read and write (Karma 1989).

Because the computer test measures the exact times the responses are given for each item, each subject has a distribution of times and thus a mean and a standard deviation for these times. Four measures are thus available: total score in the auditory structuring test (number of correct responses, max. 40), total score in the auditory/visual matching computer test (number of correct responses, max. 44), hit time mean and hit time standard deviation. The total scores are the most important but the other two offer interesting extra information.

Research problems

The questions presented above were condensed into the following research problems:

1. How do the dyslexics differ from the controls on the variables measured?
2. Can dyslexia be better predicted if auditory/visual matching is added to auditory structuring?

Subjects

The subject group consisted of 121 persons, 66 dyslexics and 55 controls. In the dyslexic group the age varied from 8 to 56 years. Sex distribution in this group was 45 males and 21 females which is rather typical in the population. The control group was formed by seeking persons who would match the dyslexic group as to age, sex and education, but it was very difficult to find volunteers who would form a matching group in all these respects simultaneously. The biggest compromise had to be made as to the gender of the controls: the control group consists of 41 females and 14 males.

Because the majority of the subjects were adults, the dyslexic group had a long history of reading and writing problems and could rather safely be diagnosed as dyslexic. The classification for the younger subjects was based on class teachers' and special reading teachers' statements which again are based on tests as well as observation in teaching situations. Although it is thus rather sure that the subjects in the experimental group are dyslexics and those in the control group are not, more accurate information about the type of dyslexia was not available.

3. Results

The reliabilities (alpha coefficient) were .75 (auditory structuring) and .92 (computer test, hit/miss) and .90 (computer test, hit time). The measures can thus be considered sufficiently free of chance factors to be used in a study like this.

Group differences

To answer the first problem, group means (dyslexic/control) and the significances of their differences are collected into Table 1.

Table 1. Group means and statistics about their differences on the four variables measured in the study.

Variable	Group	N	Mean	Std.dev.	t	sig.
Auditory	dyslexic	51	26.65	4.78	3.87	.000
structuring	control	44	30.50	4.89		
Aud/vis.	dyslexic	65	38.35	6.63	5.25	.000
hit/miss	control	54	43.15	1.12		
Hit time mean	dyslexic	64	119.67	127.67	2.99	.003
msec.	control	54	61.61	68.91		
Hit time	dyslexic	64	206.39	114.30	5.63	.000
std.dev. msec.	control	54	105.56	71.06		

The group differences are highly significant on all the four variables. Controls are better in auditory structuring and auditory/visual matching. The hit times are computed from the correct moment forwards, i.e. positive values indicate that the space bar has been hit after the beginning of the last sound of the pattern. Both groups are a bit late. Although the difference between groups is small it shows that dyslexics tend to hit later than controls. The difference is clearer in the standard deviations: the typical deviation of a dyslexic subject (mean of hit time standard deviations) is almost twice as large as that of the controls. This shows that the dyslexics are much more uncertain in their responses. Even the responses of one person tend to spread rather much in time.

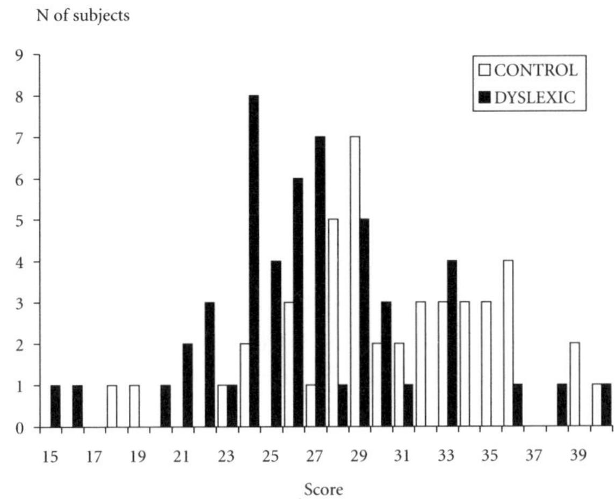

Figure 1. Total scores in the auditory structuring test

The nature of the differences on the two main variables, auditory structuring and auditory/visual matching can be further specified by graphic presentation of the data.

The distributions of both groups in the auditory structuring test are roughly normal (Figure 1). There is a clear difference between the means although overlapping is relatively large. No ceiling or floor effect can be seen.

The distribution in the scores of the auditory/visual matching test has some properties worth closer observation (Figure 2). First, there is a clear ceiling effect: about half of the controls have passed all the items (total score

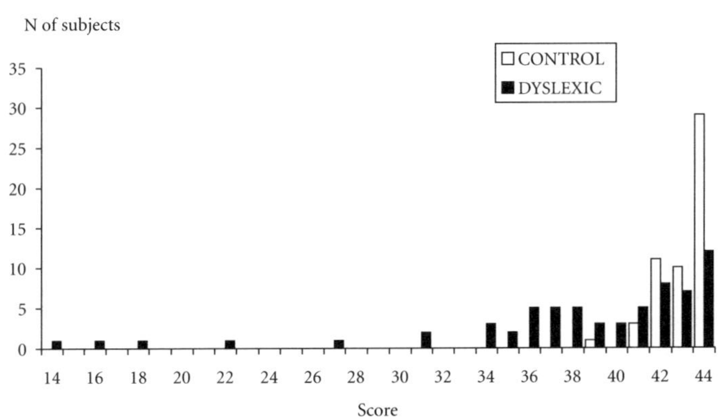

Figure 2. Total scores in the auditory/visual matching test

44). The difficulty level for the test has deliberately been chosen so that the test is very easy for persons with no impairments in this area. Without this ceiling effect, the difference between dyslexics and controls would be even bigger.

Second, there is overlap only at the higher end of the distribution. A score under about 40 points is a very sure indication of dyslexia.

Third, the dyslexics' distribution is rather clearly bimodal. This is not usual in empirical data and can be interpreted so that there are subgroups in the data. The lower end of the distribution seems to consist of subjects who have temporal or auditory/visual impairments; dyslexics at the upper end probably have some other kind(s) of problem unknown at this stage of this research.

Auditory structuring and auditory/visual matching as explainers

The answer for the second problem was sought by using stepwise multiple regression analysis where the presence of dyslexia is predicted from the two main explainers (Table 2). Auditory structuring test is alone in the first step, auditory/visual matching was added to the second. Also analyses with hit mean and standard deviation were tried. Their correlations with the total score of the matching test were so high, however, that they did not add much to the explanation. These analyses are not used here. The change from step 1 to step 2 was significant which indicates that predicting dyslexia improves when auditory/visual matching is added to auditory structuring alone.

4. Discussion

As in any research, the results depend on the validities of the measuring instruments used. The musical aptitude test can be considered a relatively pure measure of auditory structuring but the auditory/visual matching test may be more multidimensional. At least some kind of auditory and visual structuring

Table 2. Stepwise multiple regression. Dependent Variable: Presence of Dyslexia (0,1). Independent Variable(s), Step 1: Auditory Structuring, Step 2: Auditory Structuring + Auditory/Visual Matching.

Step	R	R sqr	R sqr change	F change	Sig.F change
1. Aud.	.373	.139			
2. Aud.+aud/vis.	.467	.218	.079	9.07	.003

is needed to be able to match these structures with each other; it is difficult to imagine a pure measure of matching.

Both auditory structuring and auditory/visual matching seem to be valuable predictors of dyslexia. Auditory/visual matching improves the prediction when compared with auditory structuring alone.

Because the matching test seems to find a subtype of dyslexia it may have potential not yet unveiled by this study. Among other things, further research will try to find out how those dyslexic groups which have good and bad scores in the matching test differ from each other. Both behavioral measures and event related brain potentials will be used in this research.

References

Bigsby, Pamela (1983). The nature of reversible letter confusions in dyslexic and normal readers: misperception or mislabeling? *British journal of psychology*, 55, 264–272.

Duane, Drake D. (1983). Neurobiological correlates of reading disorders. *Journal of educational research*, 77(1), 5–15.

Gordon, Edwin E. (1965). *Musical aptitude profile.* Boston: Houghton Mifflin.

Goswami, Usha & Peter Bryant (1990). *Phonological skills and learning to read.* Hove: Lawrence Erlbaum.

Hari, Riitta & Päivi Kiesilä (1996). Deficit of temporal auditory processing in dyslexic adults. *Neuroscience letters*, 205, 138–140.

Hicks, Carolyn (1981). Reversal errors in reading and their relationship to inter- and intramodality functioning. *Educational psychology*, 1(1), 67–77.

Karma, Kai (1983). Selecting students to music instruction. *Council for research in music education bulletin* no 75, 23–32.

Karma, Kai (1984). Musical aptitude as the ability to structure acoustic material. *International journal of music education*, no 3/84.

Karma, Kai (1985). Components of auditive structuring — towards a theory of musical aptitude. *Council for research in music education bulletin* no 82, 1–13.

Karma, Kai (1989). Auditive structuring as a basis for reading and writing. In H. Breuer & K. Ruoho, (Eds.), Pädagogisch-psychologische Prophylaxe bei 4–8 jährigen Kindern. *Jyväskylä studies in education, psychology and social research*, 76–84.

Karma, Kai (1994). Auditory and visual temporal stucturing: How important is sound to musical thinking? *Psychology of music*, 22(1), 20–30.

Karma, Kai (2000). Karma Music Test, research version. Glen Ellyn, IL: The Ball Foundation.

Merzenich, Michael M., William M. Jenkins, Paul Johnston, Christoph Schreiner, Steven L. Miller & Paula Tallal (1996). Temporal processing deficits of language-learning impaired children ameliorated by training. *Science*, 271, 77–81.

Payne, Martin C. & Thomas Holzman (1983). Auditory short-term memory and digit span: Normal versus poor readers. *Journal of educational psychology*, 765, 424–430.

Seashore, Carl E. (1919). *Manual of instructions and interpretations of Measures of Musical Talent.* Chicago: C. H. Stoelting.

Tallal, Paula, Steven L. Miller, Gail Bedi, Gary Byma, Xiaoqin Wang, Srikantan S. Nagarajan, Christoph Screiner, William M. Jenkins & Michael M. Merzenich (1996). Language comprehension in language-learning impaired children improved with acoustically modified speech. *Science*, 271, 81–84.

Tervaniemi, Mari, Titta Ilvonen, Kai Karma, Kimmo Alho & Risto Näätänen (1997). The musical brain: brain waves reveal the neurophysiological basis of musicality in human subjects. *Neuroscience letters*, 226, 1–4.

Wing, Herbert (1960). *Manual for standardised tests of musical intelligence.* Sheffield: Greenup & Thompson.

A comparative review of priming effects in language and music

Barbara Tillmann and Emmanuel Bigand
Université de Bourgogne, LEAD-CNRS, Dijon, France

1. Introduction

Language and music are both two instances of rich and well organised structures processed by the human brain. In both domains, discrete elements are ordered in hierarchical patterns according to certain principles of combination. Experienced listeners in a given linguistic or musical culture show implicit knowledge of structural patterns and organisational principles in a number of ways. This knowledge permits for example to develop expectancies as a function of the previous context and influences the processing of further incoming events (i.e. linguistic or musical). Both semantic and harmonic priming research illustrates that the identification of a target event is facilitated by the prior presentation of a related prime context. In psycholinguistic studies, the semantic priming paradigm has been used in numerous research to study the effect of contexts on word processing: for one word contexts (e.g., Meyer & Schvaneveldt 1971) and for longer contexts such as sentences or paragraphs (e.g., Stanovich & West 1979). In music research, a harmonic priming paradigm has been developed more recently for the analyses of single-chord contexts (Bharucha & Stoeckig 1986, 1987; Tekman & Bharucha 1992) and of long-chord contexts (Bigand & Pineau 1997; Bigand, Madurell, Tillmann & Pineau 1999, Tillmann, Bigand & Pineau 1998; Tillmann & Bigand 2001) on chord processing.

The present paper reviews a set of semantic and harmonic priming experiments. The harmonic priming studies are presented in parallel to semantic priming studies that had been based on a similar rationale. They are regrouped in four subsections as a function of the used context and its manipulation in the experimental designs: a) local context (one word, one chord), b) global context (sentences, sequences), c) combined local and global contexts and d) normal vs. scrambled global contexts. Overall results showed that the processing of both a word and a chord is facilitated by a locally related context and by a globally related context. However, results in language and music are diverging concerning the combined influence of local and global contexts together and concerning the presentation order of events in the global context (normal versus scrambled order). In contrast to semantic global relatedness effects, an integrative stage of processing seems not to be indispensable to account for global relatedness effects in harmonic priming. In the last section, results and theoretical frameworks are discussed.

2. Local context effects

In psycholinguistic studies, it has been well established that the processing of a target word *(nurse)* is faster and more accurate when it follows a prime word which is semantically related (*doctor*) than a prime word which is semantically unrelated *(bread)* (Meyer & Schvaneveldt 1971).

In music research, Bharucha and colleagues adapted the priming paradigm to music (Bharucha & Stoeckig 1986, 1987; Tekman & Bharucha 1992). Participants heard a prime chord followed by a target chord. The prime and target were either closely related (belong to the same key) or distantly related harmonically. For example, if the prime chord was C major, Bb major would be a related target and F# major an unrelated target. On half of the trials, the target chord was slightly mistuned, and participants were asked to make a speeded intonation judgement, i.e., to decide as quickly as possible whether the target chord was in tune. The priming effect was shown by (1) a bias to judge targets to be in tune when they were related to the prime, and (2) shorter response times for in-tune targets when they were related to the prime, and for out-of-tune target when they were unrelated to it. Thus, a single chord can generate expectancies for related chords to follow, resulting in greater perceived consonance and faster processing for expected chords.

3. Global context effects

In language and music processing, it is an important issue to understand how priming effects occur in more ecologically valid situations involving larger contexts than one word or chord. Semantic priming effects have been extended to longer contexts such as sentences or discourses. The processing of a target word was facilitated if that word formed a congruent ending for the sentence context than when it formed an incongruent completion (e.g., the cowboy fired the *pistol* vs. the interpreter knew the *pistol*) (Fischler & Bloom 1980; Stanovich & West 1979).

Recent studies extended harmonic priming effects to large contexts. Bigand and Pineau (1997) manipulated the global context of eight-chord sequences. Just as in the sentence priming experiments presented above, the expectations for the last chord (the target) were varied by changing the harmonic context created by the first six chords. The last two chords were held constant. In the expected condition, the last chord was a harmonically stable tonic chord, part of an authentic cadence (V–I). In the unexpected condition, the last chord took the form of a less stable fourth harmonic degree following an authentic cadence (I–IV). Participants were faster and more accurate in their intonation judgement of the last chord when it was expected. These results suggest that harmonic priming involves higher level harmonic structures and does not occur only from chord to chord.

Global harmonic priming was extended to wider harmonic contexts (Bigand et al. 1999). The global context was manipulated in 14 chord sequences at three levels, while holding constant the chord prior to the target (local context). The function of the target chord was changed by transposition. In the highly expected condition, the whole sequence is played in the same key, and the target chord is part of an authentic cadence (V–I) that closes the overall structure. In the unexpected condition, the sequence is played in the dominant key and the target chord is the fourth harmonic degree following an authentic cadence (I–IV). These two conditions replicated those of Bigand and Pineau (1997) with longer chord sequences. In the middle expected condition, the first half is harmonically identical to the first half of the highly expected condition and the second half to that of the unexpected condition. Although the chords of the second half are strictly identical, the target chord in the middle expected condition is no longer the fourth harmonic degree following an authentic cadence. In this context it may be analysed as part of the authentic cadence (V–I) that returns to the main key. The results provide evidence that musical expectations derive from various levels of hierarchical structure. Strongest facilitation was observed for highly expected targets, as the target chord was expected at both high and intermediate levels. Facilitation was reduced when it was expected at the higher level only (i.e. middle expected condition). The weakest priming effect was observed when the target chord was not strongly expected at both high and intermediate levels.

4. Global and local context effects

In psycholinguistics, Hess, Foss and Caroll (1995) manipulated both global and local contexts prior to the target word. The relationship between the target and the general topic of the discourse ("global context") was crossed with the relationship between the critical word and the sentence prior to it ("local context"). For example the target word *poem* was considered as related to both local and global contexts when it occurs in a sentence like "the English major wrote the *poem*", and when the overall topic of the discourse, in which the sentence occurs, is about an English major who fall in love. It was no more related to the global context when the sentence occurs in a story about a computer science major being in the hurry to finish writing a program.[1] The main outcome of Hess et al.'s (1995) experiments was that the facilitation of a target word depended on whether the global context was related to the target, regardless of the local context. According to the authors, this result provides evidence that "the locus of context effects is primarily outside of the lexicon, in processes that determine semantic relationships among incoming words" (Hess, et al. 1995: 63).

In music research, Tillmann, Bigand & Pineau (1998) performed crude changes in harmonic relationships and varied the target's relatedness at both global and local levels in harmonic sequences. For example, in a C major key, the target chord was globally and locally related (GRLR) when it was a tonic chord (C) and was preceded by a dominant chord (G). It was globally related but locally unrelated (GRLU) when the preceding dominant chord was played one semitone higher (G#). In this case, the target and the preceding chord do not belong to the same key. The target was globally unrelated but locally related (GULR) when only the first six chords of the sequences were transposed one semitone above (i.e., in the C# major key). Here the key of the first six chords is weakly related to the keys of the target chord and its preceding chord (i.e., C and G major keys). Finally, the target chord was both globally and locally unrelated (GULU) when the first seven chords were transposed one semitone above (in the C# major key). The performance of participants demonstrated a strong effect of both global and local contexts. Target chords were processed more accurately and quickly when they were locally or globally related to the previous context. Facilitation decreased for targets that were only locally or only globally related, and was the lowest for locally and globally unrelated targets. Furthermore, the effect of global context tended to be more pronounced at a fast tempo.

5. Global context effect in normal and scrambled contexts

The global relatedness effect in long contexts was further studied by comparing target words in sentences to target words in lists or scrambled sentences. A change in the temporal order of words in a sentence strongly decreased the strength of the related priming effect (Masson 1986; O'Seaghdha 1989; Simpson, Peterson, Casteel & Brugges 1989). In Simpson et al. (1989), sentences were presented visually either in a normal form (The auto accident drew a large crowd of *people*) or in scrambled form (Accident of large the drew auto crowd a *people*). Normal sentences showed facilitation for related targets and inhibition for unrelated targets, but there was no effect of relatedness for scrambled stimuli. The findings highlight the role of syntactic connectedness and suggest that contextual facilitation depends on the ease of integration of new words with the current text-level representation.

In music, a recent study focused on the influence of structural coherence on global harmonic relatedness effects (Tillmann & Bigand 2001). Chord sequences with either a related or an unrelated target were presented in a normal version and in a scrambled version. Two strengths of scrambling were defined: permuting chords two by two and four by four. Scrambling the order of chords violates several harmonic transitions usual in Western music and decreases the coherence of the sequences. Nonmusicians and musicians were sensitive to these structural manipulations: Scrambled sequences were judged as less coherent than normal sequences. Recognition memory was affected by the scrambled sequences which seemed to favour a bias to reject an excerpt as having occurred in the unstructured sequence. The principal aim of the study was to investigate if scrambling the temporal order of chords influences the facilitated processing of a related target chord in contrast to an unrelated target chord. The harmonic priming data pointed out that the processing of the related target chord was facilitated in both the normal and scrambled sequences, even when a stronger scrambling was used and when subjects had to attend attentively to the sequences due to a secondary recognition task. Scrambling chords in a sequence left nearly unaffected the facilitation due to global relatedness. Participants thus perceived changes in the structural organisation of the normal and scrambled sequences, but this change had no reliable impact on the priming effects. The fact that a sequence is more or less conform to a coherent overall structure, may be of perceptual importance, but seems to tap into other cognitive processes that those underlying the processing of a chord.

6. Discussion: Spreading activation versus integration?

Semantic and harmonic priming data pointed out that a preceding context influences the processing of further incoming events. Both semantic and harmonic priming effects had been extended from a single event to larger contexts (i.e., sentence, chord sequence). In psycholinguistic, two potential sources of priming were distinguished for sentences and discourses. One source is located inside the mental lexicon (i.e., intralexical priming): priming rests on a fast and automatic activation that spreads via the long-term connections between semantically related items (Forster 1979; Duffy, Henderson & Morris 1989; Neely 1991). The sentence context is assumed to contain at least a single word that is semantically associated to the target word. Activation spreading from this context word activates the semantically related target and facilitates its processing. Spreading activation may also result from combination of words that do not prime individually. A second source of priming arises from the processes that integrate local structures within a coherent whole (Sharkey & Sharkey 1987; Hess et al. 1995). Facilitation occurs for target words that are easily integrated into the ongoing discourse representation (discourse priming).

The discourse-based model was strongly supported by the finding that priming effects do occur across intervening material, even when it is semantically unrelated to the prime (Foss 1982, Foss & Ross 1983; Hess, et al. 1995). According to Hess et al. (1995), an intralexical spreading activation model predicts that the processing of the target word would be facilitated when it is semantically related to the local context, regardless of the global context. On the opposite, a strong version of a discourse-based model would predict a greater facilitation for the target word when semantically related to the global topic of the discourse regardless of the local context. Results of their study were interpreted as evidence for a priming source other than activation inside a mental lexicon. The spreading activation account was further challenged by studies that compared target words in normal and scrambled sentences. A change in the temporal order of words in a sentence strongly decreased the strength of the related priming effect (Masson 1986; O'Seaghdha 1989; Simpson et al. 1989). If context effects arise from activation spreading among words, such a manipulation of the prime's structure should not affect the processing of the target word. The results demonstrated that "the intralexical spreading activation by itself is a rather poor candidate to account for sentence context effects" (Simpson et al. 1989: 95). Processes that integrate local structures within a coherent whole thus represents a second source of semantic priming in sentences and discourse.

In a similar way, the effect of global harmonic context in music may potentially be understood in the light of two theoretical frameworks. Effects of global context might result from activation spreading through a schematic knowledge set (as in Bharucha's (1987) model) or from the ease with which subjects integrate musical events into the overall structure of the piece. The former model focuses on *tonal hierarchies* (i.e., a nontemporal schema of Western tonal hierarchies stored in long term memory), the latter account focuses on an *event hierarchy* (i.e., a hierarchy of specific pitch-time events inferred from the ongoing temporal sequence of musical events). An event hierarchy implies the activation of a tonal hierarchy *plus* the integration of the events in their specific temporal context (see Lerdahl & Jackendoff 1983 for an extensive account).

In music, the harmonic priming effects of single chords and of chord sequences can be explained in the frame of a musical spreading activation model that represents the knowledge of Western harmony in a pattern of connections (Bharucha 1987). According to Bharucha (1987, 1994), this knowledge may be conceived of as a network of interconnected units. Once learning has occurred (Bharucha 1994; Tillmann, Bharucha & Bigand 2000), these units are organised in three layers corresponding to tones, chords, and keys. When a chord is played, activation reverberates in the network until equilibrium is reached. The activation pattern of the chord units reflects Western tonal hierarchy and takes into account the key-memberships of a chord. In other words, a chord activates the units of related chords more strongly than the units of unrelated chords. When a chord sequence is played, activation due to each chord is accumulated and weighted according to recency. The accumulation of activation patterns over time determines the tonal hierarchy that underlies the incoming sequence. Highly activated events represent important events in the tonal hierarchy and the processing of these events is facilitated.

For all presented harmonic priming experiments, neural net simulations were performed according to Bharucha's (1987) model. The activation pattern of chord units simulates harmonic expectations of human subjects after a single chord context (Bharucha & Stoeckig 1987) and also in long sequence contexts accounting for the facilitation of the processing of related chords (Bigand et al. 1999). The simple accumulation of tonal hierarchy patterns takes into account the priming effects observed for local and global contexts. The influence of tempo also suggests that tonal hierarchy patterns are added and weighted by decay (Tillmann et al. 1998). The musical spreading activation model simulates an effect of global relatedness for expected and unexpected sequences independently of the temporal order of chords (Tillmann & Bigand 2001). Results of the harmonic priming study described above suggest that the harmonic relatedness effect is based on automatic activation processes of tonal knowledge. The relatedness effect depends on the tonal hierarchy, but not on the temporal order of chords in a sequence. Consequently, it seems to be quite robust against the structural manipulations due to scrambling. In contrast to semantic priming effects that vanished in scrambled sentences, changing the temporal order of chords in a sequence did not eliminate the relatedness effects in harmonic priming.

The outcome of the simulations generally fit well with human performance suggesting that priming effects in music result from activation spreading via a schematic knowledge of Western harmony. In contrast to language, an integrative stage of processing seems not indispensable to account for global context effects in harmonic priming.

Future research in the field of music has to determine whether a spreading activation model can satisfactorily account for the context effects on chord processing or if other theoretical frameworks are required. The present findings suggest that Bharucha's connectionist model (1987) provides a possible explanatory framework. During chord sequences, activation consecutive to the context are accumulated in a buffer and this added activation determines the processing of the target. In other words, harmonic priming effects seem to be the result of activation spreading via a stable cognitive structure that links related chords.

Notes

1. If the story was about a computer science major who falls in love, the target word "poem" was said globally related, but locally unrelated when it occurs in the sentence: "the computer science major wrote the *poem*".

References

Bharucha, J. J. (1987). Music cognition and perceptual facilitation: A connectionist framework. *Music Perception, 5*, 1–30.

Bharucha, J. J. (1994). Tonality and expectation. In R. Aiello & J. Sloboda (Eds.), *Musical perceptions* (213–239). Oxford: University Press.

Bharucha, J. J., & Stoeckig, K. (1986). Reaction time and musical expectancy: Priming of chords. *Journal of Experimental Psychology: Human Perception & Performance, 12*, 403–410.

Bharucha, J. J. & Stoeckig, K. (1987). Priming of chords: Spreading activation or overlapping frequency spectra? *Perception & Psychophysics, 41*, 519–24.

Bigand, E., & Pineau, M. (1997). Global context effects on musical expectancy. *Perception & Psychophysics, 59*, 1098–1107.

Bigand, E., Madurell, F., Tillmann, B., & Pineau, M. (1999). Effect of global structure and temporal organization on chord processing. *Journal of Experimental Psychology: Human Perception and Performance, 25*, 184–197.

Duffy, S. A., Henderson, J. M., & Morris, R. K. (1989). Semantic facilitation of lexical access during sentence processing. *Journal of Experimental Psychology: Learning, Memory, and Cognition, 15*, 791–801.

Fischler, I. & Bloom, P. A. (1980). Rapid processing of the meaning of sentences. *Memory & Cognition, 8*, 216–225.

Forster, K. I. (1979). Levels of processing and the structure of the language processor. In W. E. Cooper & E. Walker (Eds.), *Sentence processing: Psycholinguistic studies presented to Merril Garrett* (27–85). Hillsdale, NJ: Erlbaum.

Foss, D. J. & Ross, J . R. (1983). Great expectations: Context effects during sentence processing. In G. B. Flores d'Arcais & R. J. Jarvella (Eds.), *The process of language understanding.* (169–191). Chister: Wiley.

Foss, D. J. (1982). A discourse on semantic priming. *Cognitive Psychology, 14*, 590–607.

Hess, D. J., Foss, D. J., & Carroll, P. (1995). Effects of global and local context on lexical processing during language comprehension. *Journal of Experimental Psychology: General. 124*, 62–92.

Lerdahl, F. & Jackendoff, R. (1983). *A generative theory of tonal music.* Cambridge Mass: MIT Press.

Masson, M. E. (1986). Comprehension of rapidly presented sentences: The mind is quicker than the eye. *Journal of Memory and Language, 25*, 588–604.

Meyer, D. E., & Schvaneveldt, R. W. (1971). Facilitation in recognizing pairs of word: Evidence of a dependence between retrieval operations. *Journal of Experimental Psychology, 90*, 227–234.

Neely, J. H. (1991) Semantic priming effects in visual word recognition: A selective review of current findings and theories. In D. Besner & Humphreys, G. (Eds.). *Basic processes in reading: Visual word recognition* (264–336), Hillsdale, NJ: Lawrence Erlbaum.

O'Seaghdha, P. G. (1989). The dependence of lexical relatedness effects on syntactic connectedness. *Journal of Exp. Psychology: Learning, Memory and Cognition, 15*, 73–87.

Sharkey, N. E., & Sharkey, A. J. (1987). What is the point of integration? The loci of knowledge-based facilitation in sentence processing. *Journal of Memory and Language, 26*, 255–276.

Simpson, G. B., Peterson, R. R., Casteel, M. A., & Brugges, C. (1989). Lexical and sentence context effects in word recognition. *Journal of Experimental Psychology: Learning, Memory and Cognition, 15*, 88–97.

Stanovich, K. E., & West, R. F. (1979). Mechanisms of sentence context effects in reading: Automatic activation and conscious attention, *Memory and Cognition, 7*, 77–85.

Tekman, H. G., & Bharucha, J. J. (1992). Time course of chord priming. *Perception & Psychophysics, 51*, 33–39.

Tillmann, B., Bharucha, J. J., & Bigand, E. (2000). Implicit learning of music: A Self-Organizing Approach. *Psychological Review, 107*, 885–913.

Tillmann, B. & Bigand, E. (2001). Global relatedness effect in normal and scrambled musical sequences. *Journal of Experimental Psychology: Human Perception and Performance, 27*, 1185–1196.

Tillmann, B., Bigand, E., & Pineau, M. (1998). Effects of global and local contexts on harmonic expectancy. *Music Perception, 16*, 99–118.

The respective roles of conscious- and subconscious processes for interpreting language and music

Gérard Sabah
LIMSI-CNRS, Orsay, France

1. Consciousness and natural language understanding

CARAMEL (Sabah 1990a, 1990b, Sabah and Briffault 1993) is the acronym of "Compréhension Automatique de Récits, Apprentissage et Modélisation des Échanges Langagiers", which translates into English as "Automatic Story Understanding, Learning and Dialogue Management". CARAMEL is a generic natural language understanding system, that was initially designed in order to be applicable to various kinds of applications (e.g., man-machine dialogue, story understanding, abstracting). In order to be modular while avoiding artificial ambiguities CARAMEL relies on a multi-expert systems (inadequacy of the control mechanisms in classical systems to allow for an explicit and dynamic control) and reflectivity (the capacity to represent its own behaviour and to reason dynamically about its representations).

However, the system was not integrated into a general model of reasoning and intelligence. Bearing this in mind, I have reached the conclusion that even if explicit control of all the processes is cumbersome, it is necessary, yet it does not account for automatic reflex processes, which are also an essential aspect of natural language understanding (be it for reasons of computational efficiency or for reasons of cognition). This is why I suggested to add a blackboard extension (the *Sketchboard*) allowing for different kinds of relations between the different processes and in particular to allow for feedback loops between the different processes that do not know each other.

In order for these two types of processes (controlled and subliminal) to collaborate, consciousness clearly has a central role to play. The new version CARAMEL (general cognitive model) is based on the assumption that language is a necessary condition for intelligence. Attention and learning are two factors which are also considered within the model, currently under development (we use Smalltalk 80 for the implementation).

By taking all these factors into account, CARAMEL now means (in French): Conscience, Automatismes, Réflexivité et Apprentissage pour un Modèle de l'Esprit et du Langage (in English: Consciousness, Automatic processes, Reflectivity and Learning for a Model of Mind and Language). This new model is described in more details in (Sabah 1995, 1997a, 1997b). It is based on ideas coming from various sources: Baars (1988) and his global workspace and the competition between unconscious processes to take control of it; Harth (1993) and his model of feedback between unconscious processes; Edelman (1989, 1992) and his definition of semantics as correlations between concepts, sensory input and symbols, the role of language for symbol manipulations and his TSGN theory.

With a given point of view, "to speak" is equivalent to "to make conscious", and from this, language gives us extraordinary possibilities to extend our memory: our short term memory, first, with the inner speech, our long term memory afterwards, thanks to communication with other people, and lastly with written language and books... Therefore, language is the greatest means of storing knowledge and plays an essential role within any conscious episode that makes past, present or future events explicit. This leads Edelman to a remark that undermines the main role of consciousness for natural language understanding: « *The main reason why computers are unable to tackle the problem of semantics becomes clear: the implementation cannot be correct since it does not lead to consciousness* » (Edelman 1992).

2. An architecture for natural language understanding

The need for two kinds of processes

Understanding is not only based on logical criteria, it is also the emerging result of non rational processes that cannot be described in an algorithmic way. When we think, we may either say something about the underlying mental processes (a kind of introspection called "conscious processes"), or are able to say something only about the produced results ("unconscious") (Baars 1988).

Even if non controlled, unconscious cognitive processes are supposed to be exhaustive and independent of the cognitive load (Newell 1990), this need not be true at every level. As they come closer to consciousness, they have to limit themselves, since they have to compete for space in working memory. We propose here a simple explanation for this transition between subliminal perception and conscious perception.

In order to control the rules necessary for analysis, and in order to avoid the problem of combinatorial explosion, classical rational approaches use metaknowledge (Pitrat 1990). However, if it is difficult to anticipate all possible conflicts only by using logical reasoning, it is even more difficult to solve them solely by these means. For example, during syntactic parsing, the best interpretations usually follow the *minimal attachment* principle (*don't postulate, in the syntactic tree, a potentially useless node*) and the *differed closing* principle (*if grammatically possible, attach the new element to the current phrase*). A big problem with such general principles is that they do not allow us to easily detect exceptions (corpus based studies allow us to set up general rules but do not handle specific cases). This is why these regularities cannot be used as formal parsing rules. However, they may be explained as an emerging consequence of the competition between interpretative processes: usually, the interpretations that follow *minimal attachment* and *differed closing* are the most simple ones to build, and as a consequence, the first ones to be consciously perceived.

While there is no doubt that rational thought is an important part of understanding, it should intervene only *after* the spontaneous perception of meaning (this distinction allows us to distinguish between "true" ambiguities, due to the communicative situation — these are the ones that should be solved by a dynamic, rational planning — and "artificial" ambiguities that remain unknown without a particular exhaustive linguistic analysis).

Our hypothesis is that data in working memory is transferred to short-term memory (i.e., become conscious) when a given threshold of persistence is reached, depending upon their accessibility and their life cycle. This transfer is probably what we mean when we say "I understand" (*feeling of understanding*). This process generally concerns only one interpretation at a time. Such an interpretation is perceived globally as an already built entity which may then become the basic element of the process of simulating rational thought.

As psycholinguistic experiments using the technique of semantic priming have shown (e.g., (Meyer and Schvaneveldt 1971)), knowledge structures are characterised by variable and dynamic accessibilities. This property has to be taken into account in an ergonomic model of understanding. Indeed, the cost of each elementary operation of interpretation is closely linked to the time necessary to access knowledge stored in the memory. Therefore, interpretations which are coherent with the most accessible knowledge are the most likely to become the best ones: being built more rapidly, the cognitive machinery in charge of building them can devote more attention to them. Thus, the system "prefers" the interpretations that match optimally the activated knowledge, i.e., the most relevant one, given some state of context.

Due to the fact that the attention of a process may be distributed among several interpretations, the analysis is performed in parallel. However, this skill is not very flexible, since the computed entities are stored in a limited-buffer. The cognitive system should use this memory in the most efficient way, that is by an automatic, non-conscious process of optimisation: attention is focused on the most relevant interpretations.

This allows us to take advantage of the dynamic properties of the memory: Frequently accessed knowledge becomes more and more accessible, which makes the relevant interpretations more and more likely, which in turn makes the relevant knowledge more and more accessible, and so on (recursive *positive feedback*). The newly available space is used for more useful tasks, and the associated interpretations slow down or disappear. Then, an explicit evaluation of relevance is no longer necessary, since it is implicitly performed with regard to the state of knowledge evolution: dynamic accessibility of knowledge and parallel analysis are sufficient to explain the emergence of most relevant interpretations. The interpretations are not compared anymore on the basis of formal, structural properties but through their competition to occupy memory.

Individually, each possible interpretation is computed in a bottom-up (data-driven), sequential way. Nevertheless, context implies that the whole system converges towards one or several resulting interpretation(s). Indeed, the interpretations are developed at different speeds, depending upon the plausibility of the chosen solution, i.e., lastly depending upon the accessibility of the knowledge they are based on. The state of the cognitive context acts as a set of hypotheses that favour the most relevant interpretations. This predictive mechanism differs dramatically from classical top-down analysis.

Thus, while trying to make explicit the subliminal processes underlying our language ability, we want to define a more realistic model of understanding (which may substantially differ from a linguistic analysis!). Here, we do not want to account for an explicit, formal reasoning process, but for spontaneous, non controlled inferences that allow information to go from the subliminal, perceptive level to the conscious level.

Consciousness: A bridge between controlled and unconscious processes

The previous considerations result in a "revised model of CARAMEL", which can be used not only for understanding and generating natural language, but also as a general model for intelligent behaviour, since, as we will argue in the conclusion, understanding language is a prerequisite and fundamental for intelligence in general.

In Figure 1 below, consciousness is modelled as a controlled process able to trigger various sub-processes. Its data are either permanent (linked to the self) or results coming from the Sketchboard (candidates to become conscious). The various sub-processes are in charge of managing and evaluating the permanent goals, evaluating the relevance of the candidates from the Sketchboard, maintaining the self representation and so on.

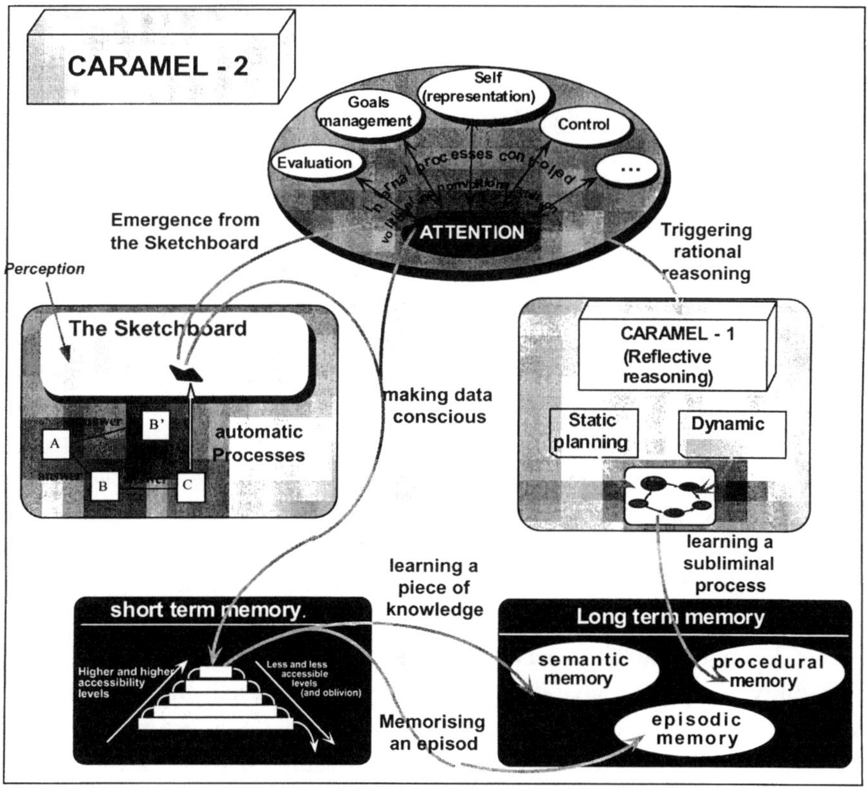

Figure 1. Consciousness as a bridge between subliminal and controlled processes.

When a piece of data is about to become conscious (see below), it is written in the short term memory which acts as a blackboard for consciousness. Control of consciousness decides whether a piece of data or a specific problem deserve to be consciously processed or not; it also evaluates conscious processes, which, when encountered on several occasions, give rise to unconscious processes (compilation). In this respect our short term memory is very similar to Baars' global conscious workspace (Baars 1988), which unconscious processes are competing for in order to take control of. This global blackboard is managed through a stack mechanism: any conscious event that becomes redundant may be replaced by a more informative subsequent event.

An important role of the interaction between the Sketchboard and the controlled processes through consciousness is to unify disparate results into a coherent whole. Therefore, it has a constructive function that neither unconscious processes, nor controlled processes, are able to perform on their own.

Here are some criteria used to decide whether a piece of data should be made conscious or not. As mentioned above, different sequences of unconscious processes may act in parallel within the Sketchboard, and these sequences are analogous to Baars' competing contexts. Therefore, consciousness may be viewed as a process that permanently reads the Sketchboard, taking care of updating the short term memory. Only stable results (*deserving* it) are written into this blackboard.

The notion of "deserving" relates to three other notions: the *feeling of understanding*, the *feeling of ambiguity*, and the *feeling of contradiction*.

The *feeling of understanding* leads to some results becoming conscious. This kind of intuition is represented through some sort of stability within the Sketchboard. This stability is recognised when no significant shift appears after several iterations. When such a situation is detected, the final result is transmitted to the short-term memory, with the goal of integrating this new piece of information within the currently active knowledge, in order to produce locally coherent data.

Another important reason for a result to become conscious is the *feeling of ambiguity*. Cases where several solutions are relevant correspond to situations where data in the Sketchboard waver between several configurations (a "lasting instability"). This will give rise, not to a conscious result, but to a problem which is to be consciously solved: when no intuitive decision is suitable, the choice will be left to a controlled process. Therefore, partial results obtained from the Sketchboard are written into the higher control level blackboard, with the goal of resolving the ambiguity.

Finally, there is the *feeling of contradiction.* Such a situation is detected when a stable result in the Sketchboard is in contradiction with a conscious goal. In the same way as above, these results are transmitted to the conscious level in order for the problem to be solved consciously.

These criteria imply that only the results obtained through conscious perceptions are made available to other sources of knowledge, even though unconscious perceptions may influence further processing. This is explained in our model by the fact that fleeting results in the Sketchboard may imply some reordering of the goals of consciousness, even if those are not made conscious thereafter.

3. Common aspects of language, vision and music

Neurobiological evidence and computational aspects

First, it should be noted that there is no homunculus scrutinising the state of the brain: the brain analyses itself, creates and examines again its own productions in a « truly *creative loop* » (Harth 1993). This is particularly obvious for the process of vision, where the existence of top-down paths has been demonstrated at the neurobiological level many years ago (Ramón y Cajal 1933), yet it is still a topic of interest (Kosslyn 1980, Kosslyn and Kœnig 1992). It has also been shown that these paths actively participate in the vision process by injecting *new information* (not present in the initial message) coming from the higher levels: the initial message is modified on the basis of this auto-referential process (bootstrap). Furthermore, Restak (1979) has convincingly argued that these auto-referential loops govern the whole nervous system.

This mechanism is basically unstable (possibly explaining creativity). This means that cerebral zones are not seen as relays where data are stored, but as zones where the cortex produces sketches, modifies them and reinterprets them. This flexibility is a necessary characteristic to allow for adapting to an ever modifying environment, as argued by Edelman who suggests a Darwinist interpretation of the evolution of the brain (Edelman 1989, 1992) . (Harth 1993) takes the same kind of approach and shows how various kinds of feedback allow to account for normal vision processes as well as for optical illusions.

A priori, blackboards (initially presented in Hearsay II (Erman, et al. 1980) and extended later versions (Hayes-Roth 1985, Nii 1986)) seem interesting as a way of modelling this kind of process. They allow for an efficient, dynamic ordering of the processes to be triggered. However, this opportunistic behaviour does not allow higher modules (e.g., semantics, pragmatics) to feedback information to lower levels (e.g., perception): even with a sophisticated system such as BB1 (Hayes-Roth 1985), processes taking place late have no influence on the results of earlier ones. Feedback from higher levels in blackboards is limited to choosing among several possible solutions: inferences from higher levels allow to select the most relevant process in a given context, but they cannot directly interfere with the behaviour of a process. This kind of feedback does not model the situation where a given process is capable of adapting its own behaviour in order to produce an improved result, better adapted to higher level knowledge.

This problem is linked to the notion of *meaning*: built objects have meaning only from an external point of view, not for the program itself, and therefore they cannot be the basis of semantic control. Furthermore, the fact that the more recent GUARDIAN (Hayes-Roth, et al. 1992) claims to be based on a rational use of knowledge does not seem to me to be a significant response to the problem raised here. Within the Sketchboard, higher levels of knowledge can provide feedback to lower levels so that the latter can adjust their behaviour in order to be as coherent as possible with the results of the former.

Another blackboard characteristic implies that all data is handled the same way. In other words, as soon as a process has discovered data that may act as an input, it is triggered. Since the global solution is not yet available, no control — no matter how sophisticated — will be able to evaluate the relative importance of partial results with regard to the final solution. The Sketchboard contains a mechanism for reactive feedback loops, generalised across all the modules that interact when solving a problem. As higher and higher level modules are triggered, the initial sketches become more and more precise, taking into account all the knowledge the system has.

Music and vision

Signal, sign, clue

Information theory is well aware of the differences between signal and code. For language, a faithful *signal* and a decoding symmetrical to the coding, allow to recognise not only the meaning of what is said, but also several aspects of the voice, features of the environment, etc. For example if someone has a throaty voice, we conclude that the speaker has caught a cold: we say that this feature of the voice is the *sign* of the cold. In fact, a sign is a couple composed of a signifier and a signified, where the signifier is bound to something different than to itself, with no causal relationship. In order to be precise, we should say that a throaty voice is a *clue*:, yet we tend to add to the signal all our knowledge concerning natural laws controlling human voice. In sum, this allows us to conclude that language cannot be only a code.

The complex cognitive behaviour necessary for understanding language is also necessary for the different kinds of perception in general and pattern recognition in particular, that is: vision and the recognition of object, audition and the recognition of sounds and timbers, touch and the recognition of sensations, all these processes imply a constructivist activity of consciousness as well as unconscious processes in order to "interpret, hence understand" the function and the semantic role of these signals.

The case of music is much more ambiguous: due to its numerical aspects (e.g., simple relations between intervals, logarithmic scale between values) and due to the simplicity of the coding (digital or analogical) we may have the feeling that analysing the signal is tantamount to understanding music. There seem to be causal relationships between music and the signal coding it, but as many experiments have shown, there too, there are great differences between the physical and the perceptive system.

Some experiments

It has been shown that some ordinary sounds (e.g., a deep piano sound) can be deprived of their fundamental characteristic and still be musically located correctly at the degree corresponding to the stuck key. The spectrum is often believed to characterise timbers of instruments, yet this need not be the case : a medium piano sound deprived of one or two seconds of its initial part is perceived as the sound of a flute. Physical times (measured in seconds) and musical durations (as they are perceived) do not correspond to each other ; sometimes measures are twice or three times greater or lower than musical judgements.

The second experiment, leads to the conclusion that we do not hear a fundamental sound, completed with harmonical timbers, but the fact that this sound is fundamental is concluded on the basis of its harmonics.

Therefore, in music too, every level has to be analysed in context: the meaning at a given level gives clues to interpret the functions of the elements of the next higher level. Jakobson's point of view concerning linguistics holds also for music (and for perception in general): "*any sign comprises constituent signs and appears as combined with other signs. This means that any linguistic unit is used as a context for simpler units, and finds its own context among more complex units*".

These three experiments, among many others, show that the interpretation of a musical signal is not only the result of an acoustical sequence hitting the ear, but also the result of our conscious activity (cf. Husserl's intentionality).

An example

Let us examine roughly the various cognitive tasks a musician has to carry out (I am not talking here of beginner sight-reading but of executing an already known score).

The first step is to read the score. The visual perception of the sequence of notes, chords and so on, triggers automatic processes that interpret the score: within the Sketchboard, subliminal processes analyse the visual input; higher and higher levels of knowledge come into play in order to produce an interpretation coherent with the previous musical knowledge of the interpreter. This process is very similar to reading and generates — internally — the same feeling as if the sounds were heard: as soon as these "representations" are stable in the Sketchboard, they become conscious and the performer "hears" what he intends to play (I mean here that he has the same feeling as if the sounds were actually perceived). This is stored in short-term memory and becomes the active plan to be completed. Consciousness has to decide now how to achieve the plan: either by using automatic processes, or with a much more resource consumptive, controlled planning process.

In this context it may be worth pointing out the difference between an expert and a beginner: the expert is able to trigger automatic processes allowing him to realise actually what he wants to hear, while the beginner (as well as the good player that plays a difficult score at sight…) has to trigger reflective processes, calculating the effect of each move at a time. This is clearly too time consuming in order to play well, yet is the natural way of learning a score: repeating several times the sequence of moves that allow the achievement of a specific effect (goal) will after a while allow to generate automatically the processes having the same effect; these processes are stored in long term memory and will be triggered later (when analogous goals are encountered).

Then, the produced sounds are analysed in the same way (in the Sketchboard, automatic processes will decode not only the actual notes, but various aspects of the interpretation). As soon as they are stable enough (again, that means that the built representation makes sense for the interpreter), these data are transmitted to the short-term memory and compared with what was expected (also stored in the short-term memory, since they have previously been made conscious).

4. Conclusion

The Caramel architecture is based both on conscious- (controlled) and unconscious- (subliminal) processes. The former — based on some extensions of reflective systems to the domain of DAI — allow for a flexible and efficient implementation of intelligent systems. In our implementation, control is explicit at various levels, thus making possible the use of strategic knowledge at varying degrees of generality. The latter concern a new data structure, the *Sketchboard*, an extension of Blackboards, allowing different modules to collaborate while solving a problem. This model allows feedback from higher levels to lower one, without requiring any explicit control.

While these ideas have been implemented independently (using Smalltalk), some aspects concerning the global architecture (consciousness as a bridge between these two models) remain to be implemented and tested through reasonably-sized experiments before a number of parameters of the model may be efficiently chosen.

However, the architecture actually accounts for these possibilities and the example about music presented above shows that many of the basic processes necessary for understanding language, interpreting visual scenes, and interpreting and producing music are the same. What is missing here (and this will be the basis of future research) is the capability to adapt, consciously and dynamically, automatic processes that are active when actually playing the score. This needs the extension of the conscious reasoning processes so that a closer intrication with unconscious processes could be achieved: when a controller must reach a given goal, it can act in a similar way as consciousness by first trying to find an unconscious process that may reach the goal (before trying to reach its goal with complex planning processes). An open question here is to decide whether such a situation implies that processes need to be triggered in the Sketchboard as presented above, or if the Sketchboard itself is distributed as well (with several Sketchboards respectively linked to various conscious controllers). Such an implementation would produce an entanglement of conscious and unconscious processes closer to what we can suspect about what happens in our brains…

References

Baars, Bernard (1988). *A cognitive theory of consciousness.* Cambridge University Press, Cambridge.

Edelman, Gerald (1989). *The remembered present: a biological theory of consciousness.* Basic Books, New York.

Edelman, Gerald (1992). *Biologie de la conscience.* Editions Odile Jacob, Paris.

Erman, L. D., F. Hayes-Roth, Victor Lesser and D. Raj Reddy (1980) The HERSAY-II speech understanding system : integrating knowledge to resolve uncertainty. *Computing surveys, 12*, 2, p. 213–253.

Harth, Erich (1993). *The creative loop; how the brain makes a mind.* Addison-Wesley, New York.

Hayes-Roth, Barbara (1985). A blackboard architecture for control. *Artificial Intelligence, 26*, p 252–321.

Hayes-Roth Barbara, R. Washington, D. Ash, R. Hewett, A. Collinot, A. Vina and A. Seiver (1992). Guardian: A prototype intelligent agent for intensive-care monitoring. *AI in Medicine, 4*, p. 165–185.

Kosslyn, Stephen (1980). *Image and mind.* Harvard University Press, Harvard, MA.

Kosslyn, Stephen and Olivier Kœnig (1992). *Wet Mind, The New Cognitive Neuroscience.* The Free Press, New York.

Meyer, D. E. and R. W. Schvaneveldt (1971). Facilitation in recognizing pairs of words: evidence of a dependence between retrieval operations. *Journal of Experimental Psychology*, 90, p. 227-234.

Newell, Allen (1990). *Unified Theories of Cognition.* Harvard University Press, Cambridge, Massachusetts.

Nii, Penny (1986). Blackboard Systems: the Blackboard Model of Problem Solving and the evolution of Blackboard Architectures. *The AI magazine, August*, p. 82–106.

Pitrat, Jacques (1990). *Métaconnaissance, futur de l'intelligence artificielle.* Hermès, Paris.

Ramón, y Cajal Santiago (1933). Neuronismo o reticularismo ? La prueba objectivas de la unitad anatomica de la celulad nervioses. *Archos. neurobiologicas, 13*, p. 217–291.

Restak, Richard (1979). *The Brain: the last frontier.* Doubleday, Garden City, New York.

Sabah, Gérard (1990a). CARAMEL : a flexible model for interaction between the cognitive processes underlying natural language understanding. Proceedings Coling, Helsinki.

Sabah, Gérard (1990b). CARAMEL : un système multi-experts pour le traitement automatique des langues. *Modèles linguistiques, 12*, Fasc 1, p. 95–118.

Sabah, Gérard and Xavier Briffault (1993). Caramel : a Step towards Reflexion in Natural

Language Understanding systems, Proceedings IEEE International Conference on Tools with Artificial Intelligence. Boston, p. 258–265.

Sabah, Gérard (1995). Natural Language Understanding and Consciousness, Proceedings AISB — workshop on "Reaching for Mind". Sheffield.

Sabah, Gérard (1997a). Consciousness: a Requirement for Understanding Natural Language, *Two sciences of mind.* John Benjamins, Amsterdam, p. 361–392.

Sabah, Gérard (1997b). The Sketchboard: A Dynamic Interpretative Memory and its Use for Spoken Language Understanding, Proceedings Eurospeech'97, Rhodes, Volume 2/5, p. 617–620.

Aesthetic forms of expression as information delivery units

Paul Nemirovsky and Glorianna Davenport
Interactive Cinema Group, MIT Media Laboratory, USA

1. Introduction

In this paper we explore the hypothesis that aesthetic forms of expression — such as music, painting, video — can be used for direct information delivery. In contrast to text or verbal narrative techniques, which require a conscious act of transcoding, these aesthetic forms stimulate a more direct, emotional response. If shown viable, such a hypothesis could open new channels for the delivery of various types of information, providing us with a background information channel in situations of information overload, leaving our foreground concentrated on the more thought-demanding tasks.

To develop a system based on the notion of using aesthetic forms of expression for direct information delivery, we need to develop its core elements. In this paper we define a core element called "emon", a small discrete unit of aesthetic expression, which generates an expected emotional response affecting human behavior. The study is currently restricted to the domain of music, with candidate emons being 1–15 seconds long loops of audio that are currently assumed to be the only audio source perceived by the user. The emons are characterized as units of an independently describable value, without the necessity of connection / abstraction to / from other pattern units — i.e. if a specific emon is played we will be able to relate to its qualities without accessing our knowledge about other emons. In the first half of this paper we discuss the guidelines for emons' creation, describe the categorizations process, and report the results of emons' testing performed by a group of fourteen users.

Given the hypothesis that certain musical patterns (emons) can be used to provide cues that affect behavior, we need a system that can provide a further validity to the usefulness of that approach. In the "Implementation" chapter we report the ongoing development of the GuideShoes wearable system, which assists a user in navigating an open space such as streets, by sequencing musical emons as navigational cues. It is then followed by a discussion of the navigation tools written for this project and future research directions.

2. Imagine…

…You are in Tokyo, facing the travelers' everyday problem of getting from point A to point B. It's an even harder problem in a city that doesn't have street names, with your ability to speak Japanese equal to your ability to compose a symphony. This time the situation is different — rather than panicking, you put your GuideShoes and a headset on, and tell it where you'd like to go. Upon your request, GuideShoes pack connects to the web, and finds out your current and desired locations. As you start walking down the street, your headset starts playing music. There are no signs or language to assist you — but you are language-independent. Musical patterns (emons) provide you with information regarding the correctness of your direction — they evolve in ways that you find natural and in correspondence with the emotional states of "right", "wrong", and the gray area in between. The patterns may indicate the duration of your journey and proximity to the destination. You no longer need to remember the map or think about how to get where you are going. The only thing that is required is your ability to hear. Have you entered an unfriendly neighborhood? GuideShoes will tell you. The GuideShoes try to do it by considering your musical preferences, merging the invisible and inadvertent emons into a meaningful tangible interface utilizing background information channels.

Finding your direction is only one example of a frustrating and time-consuming task that can be addressed using emons. People who can't or won't use printed or spoken instructions — small children, the visually impaired, users occupied with other, more urgent tasks — can be helped in new efficient ways instead of being left alone to deal with situations that require a significant amount of cognitive and perceptual skills.

3. Hypotheses

Defining the relationship between pattern and meaning has been the objective for a few generations of musicologists, cognitive scientists, and other researchers concerned with the interpretation of things played, drawn, and otherwise acted. Most theories are based on sequential systems of interpretation of artistic mediums — an artistic expression is first perceived, then recognized cognitively, and then referenced or given meaning beyond its initial domain. Theorists are doubtful regarding the ability of music to deliver meaning as it lacks the precise semantics present in verbal language. According to this widespread view, music cannot convey meaning as every listener may derive very different "meanings" from the same musical piece. Even among the heteronomists — the theorists that agree on the possibility that artistic expressions are valuable beyond their aesthetic appeal — only a few believe in the possibility that artistic mediums can be used as self-contained information containers using their emotional capacity. If proven possible, it could lead us to a design of new informational meta-mediums with fewer cognitive steps required during the recognition process of an incoming information stream.

Similar to the studies conducted by Konrad Lorenz et al. that proved the possibility of information imprinting on animal behavior, nowadays an extensive research is being conducted on how imprinting a specific combination of emotions on information can enhance that information's appeal for humans (Losee 1998). By studying the existing mappings of aesthetic forms onto behavior models of the brain as well as imprinting our own, we can possibly achieve higher efficiency of information and make a better use of users' emotional abilities. To use these mappings we need to know what the individual components of an emotion are. The whole — an aesthetic expression — should be dissected into affective (i.e. emotionally charged) units.

The GuideShoes project, described in the second half of this paper, represents our work on incorporating such units into a wearable device, which will provide users with information regarding their travel. The system provides users with emotional cues by employing a system of aesthetic information fragments, called *emons.*

The emon approach is based on the following hypotheses:

1. Aesthetic forms can be used as direct information delivery mediums.

   We hypothesize that human perception abilities are underused and can be further utilized with the emon approach. This paper focuses on the musical segment of that approach and the use of musical patterns as the building blocks. Musical emons are appropriate because of music's ability to communicate emotion in an immediate and efficient way. Music is also convenient because its high level of abstraction allows us to test the principles of emons' construction and find whether certain candidate emons get a consistent response/ratings in a series of tests. Candidate emons that demonstrated a consistent rating should then be considered the true emons and employed in the emon-based systems. System users who listen to the emons would then be able to use their musical and emotional judgment to recognize the emons' meaning.

2. Aesthetic information can be isolated into small autonomous elements (emons).

   According to the traditional approach, aesthetic expression consists of a continuous stream of elements. We hypothesize that by dividing the stream into discrete emo-informational elements it will be possible to open a new channel of information delivery, and achieve a more efficient perception process without increasing the learning curve.

   To provide an initial testing for this hypothesis we have created a library of candidate emons, and developed an evaluation application to check the efficiency and the consistency of emons' ratings (i.e. how high different emons scored, and how stable these scores are). A statistical tool to allow easy visualization/estimation of the testing results has also been developed. A further testing of this hypothesis is provided using the GuideShoes; a passive I/O device for a real-time delivery of emo-informative content (emons). The GuideShoes' aim is to help the wearer to navigate through an open space (such as streets), making navigation personalized and less cumbersome by maximizing information input, by incorporating emotional disposition and reaction, and by combining artistic and informative communication.

3. Emons can be recombined to produce predictable emotional/informative responses.

   The exploration of this hypothesis — defining the laws of "emons' combinatorics" — is a part of future emon research beyond the scope of this paper. It would be naïve to regard emotion as a mere sequence of positive/negative states; and indeed, this work does not have that goal. We do hypothesize however that the emotional power provoked by aesthetic means can be utilized in order to achieve a more efficient means of information delivery — granted the laws of emons' combinatorics have been defined. An initial examination of this hypothesis is provided using the GuideShoes system. We have also designed a front end to the emons' database, providing a further functional framework for the research of combination-related functions. More projects are in work to provide the necessary validity for that hypothesis.

4. Prior research

The emon approach is based on a number of concepts proposed by scholars in various fields. Here is an overview of a few of the ideas that inspired the theoretical approach and the practical application of emons. The ideas addressed in this chapter are relevant to emons' action, meaning, properties' definition, and composition process.

Marvin Minsky (1985) in his "Society of Mind" proposes a theory of how the brain learns/memorizes a concept. To explain that process, he introduces the concept of *paranomes*: "The idea is that, typically, what people call a "concept' is represented in the brain in several different ways. However, these will usually be cross-connected so that the rest of the mind can switch easily from one representation to another. The trick is that although each representation-method has its own type of data-structure, many of the "terminals" of their frames (or whatever else they might use) are activated by the same "pronome" signals". In this context emons can be viewed as triggers for different types of pronomes, affecting emotionally-charged concepts.

William Buxton (1995) in his "New Taxonomy of Telematics" proposes a two-dimensional model of human-computer interaction (HCI). In his model, the interaction happens on *either* background or foreground levels, so that any medium populates one of the two cells. He is aware of the power of the background information channels and proposes "...a means of sharing the periphery, the background social ecology, by means of appropriate technological prostheses". However, his model lacks flexibility to address the notion of switching between the foreground and background cells within the action frame of the same object. It is interesting to see whether the emons' approach could address the need of tangible objects to be easily transferable between those states. It would make them more adequate for use in a real world situation, where switches of our attention continuously cause dynamic reassignment of attention weights in regard to the surrounding artifacts. These new tangible objects would address the frame of action in more intelligent and modal ways, bringing us closer to the creation of natural forms of computational objects.

HCI researchers frequently address the question of modality. Hiroshi Ishii (1997) relates to it as one of the topics of his research in tangible interfaces. He writes, "...subconsciously, people are constantly receiving various information from the "periphery" without attending to it explicitly. If anything unusual is noticed, it immediately comes to the center of their attention". Ishii's view of a tangible user interface design is to "employ physical objects, surfaces, and spaces as tangible embodiments of digital information. These include foreground interactions with graspable objects and augmented surfaces, exploiting the human senses of touch and kinesthesia" and also "background information displays which use "ambient media" — ambient light, sound, airflow, and water movement." He seeks to "communicate digitally-mediated senses of activity and presence at the periphery of human awareness". Inspired by these ideas, we explore the notion of musical emons as basic elements of a new tangible approach — processed in the background, in parallel with other media sources, and reconfigurable to reflect the current state of the user and of the environment.

A combination of audio and wearable computing is explored by Peter Meijer (1997) in his "Auditory Image Enhancement". His vOICe system "translates arbitrary video images from a camera into sounds. This means that you can see with your ears, whenever you want to". While achieving a solution for an interesting technical challenge, it seems that mapping of the visual domain onto the auditory domain would be much more effective and easy to perceive if an emotional component played a more significant role. Meijer's approach may work well in static situations, such as in an interpretation of still pictures. However, in dynamic open-space environments, such as streets, his solution for the cognitive problem of navigation seems inefficient as it overloads the users' perception channels with vast amounts of unfiltered information and is problematic for tasks involving items of varying importance or priority.

5. The anatomy of an audio emon

Music has an infinite number of properties to play with. In this chapter we give an overview of our decisions during the emons' design process and discuss the axes that can be populated. It has to be noted that while this paper addresses the music domain, we are researching how a similar deconstruction could possibly be performed with other forms of aesthetic expression, such as video, stills, and text.

Approach

In order to build an information delivery system based on aesthetic forms of expression, we have to define the elements of which this system consists, and create a personalizable mapping system. "Colors, sounds, odors, tastes, tactile experiences, all may be "heavy" or "light" or have "volume" and dozens of other psychological similarities" (Faber Birren (1992), defining a correspondence between color segments and emotional states). We start with an attempt to demonstrate a correspondence between certain musical solutions and emotional states. Music has a variety of interesting properties to play with — rhythm, timbre, texture, and so forth. As a complex medium, music offers us great degrees of freedom — its high degree of abstraction allows us to manipulate and adjust it in almost any imaginable way. It also presents us with the challenge of inventing a technique to reliably convey an emotional state using a unified method.

Definition

Discrete units of emotional expression, or *emons*, are aesthetic information containers, which are capable of evoking a predictable emotional response that can affect human behavior.

The emons are characterized as units of an independently describable value, without the necessity of connection / abstraction to / from other pattern units — i.e. if a specific emon is played we will be able to relate to its qualities without accessing our knowledge of other emons.

Design & evaluation

In order to design a valid set of emons for various life situations, we first chose an emotional model and defined criteria for emons' construction. Subsequently, we composed a set of candidate emons, defined the evaluation methods, wrote the evaluation software, and started to conduct a line of tests — first with a group of subjects determining the real emons among the candidate ones and then with a different group using the selected emons for real-time navigation. A brief overview of the process follows.

Affective categories

We chose to base the emon categorization on a partial implementation of the circumplex model of the emotions, developed by Robert Plutchik (1994). The model is structured in a relatively simple (and therefore applicable) way, while being adequate in its perspective on the possibilities of emotion synthesis from individual components. The implementation described in this paper is limited to the primary emotions (as outlined by Plutchik), namely: Acceptance, Anger, Anticipation, Disgust, Fear, Joy, Sorrow, and Surprise. This is an initial attempt at exploring a practical application of Plutchik's vision of a possibility of emotional combinatorics, which may prove helpful in dealing with discrete emotional elements such as musical emons.

Construction principles

In order to test the emon approach a library of musical emons has been created. We classified the emons' inter-relationships into the following categories to aid the composition process:

1. Major ↔ minor as positive ↔ negative. The binary notion of right/wrong is not meant to imply a binary relationship, but rather a tendency in the emotional reaction to a composed emon. In this form, the right/wrong scale can be applied to all the following pairs, however the actual assignment of the emotional extremes to the positive/negative domains of the emotional scale is up to the actual users.
2. Loud ↔ quiet as positive ↔ negative.
3. Continuously fast tempo ↔ slow tempo as positive ↔ negative.
4. Continuous sound with a difference in pitch. High ↔ low pitch as positive ↔ negative.
5. Separate sounds unified by rhythmic patterns; steady ↔ unsteady rhythmical pattern as positive ↔ negative.
6. Instrumental density; the amount of simultaneously heard instruments mapped to the positive ↔ negative scale.
7. Melodic density; the notes/time ratio mapped to the positive ↔ negative scale.
8. Rhythmic and melodic repetitiveness versus [pseudo]randomness; the repetitiveness ratio mapped to the positive ↔ negative scale.

In order to test the emon approach, a number of libraries of candidate musical emons have been created. The emons were created with no restrictions on their style or form; their design was based on our sense of composition as well as an attempt to utilize the components of composition techniques from various musical styles. The candidate emons were created with no specific emotional category in mind.

A total of 200 emons have been composed, each one being a 1–15 second long loop. After recording, the emons were saved as separate MIDI loops, ready to be streamed in real time upon request.

Technical issues

All the emons were composed using Korg Trinity V3, Roland SoundCanvas SC-88, and NordLead synthesizers, edited in Steinberg Cubase VST/24, recorded onto the hard disk using MOTU 2408 & DigitalAudio CardD+, and converted to WAV-formatted loops in Steinberg Wavelab. The testing/categorization tool (fig. 1), used to classify the emons into various emotional/action categories, was written in Lingo, with additional Visual C++ modules for database access (with the MS Access connectivity package), MIDI files playback, drawing capability, and visual effects. Multiple clients can be run simultaneously via the network, with the database located on a server, hence allowing for a parallel and more efficient testing process.

Tests / evaluation of results

The testing process is aimed at gathering data for future exploration of various ways of mapping emotion/music to physical spaces. More specifically, the emons found in the testing are to be used in the GuideShoes system (aimed at providing us with a navigational means, as well as enhancing our awareness of the surroundings).

The emon categorization test gathers the data by asking a group of subjects to respond to a number of questions at each stage of the test. The test starts with a demographic questionnaire, asking for subject's age, gender, favorite musical styles, level of musical literacy, up to four personal emotional characteristics, current mood, and the arousal level. The subject then proceeds to the main part of the test. The test is performed by listening to each of the candidate emons, which are presented to each subject in a different order, to avoid a possible bias. During the test the subject: classifies each of the emons as related to one of the emotional categories; sets the intensity of the relationship; rates the candidate emon's environmental scales (as defined in software shown in Figure 1). There is also an option of contributing "custom" emotional states. After the end of the experiment, the subjects are asked to provide their comments in a free form essay.

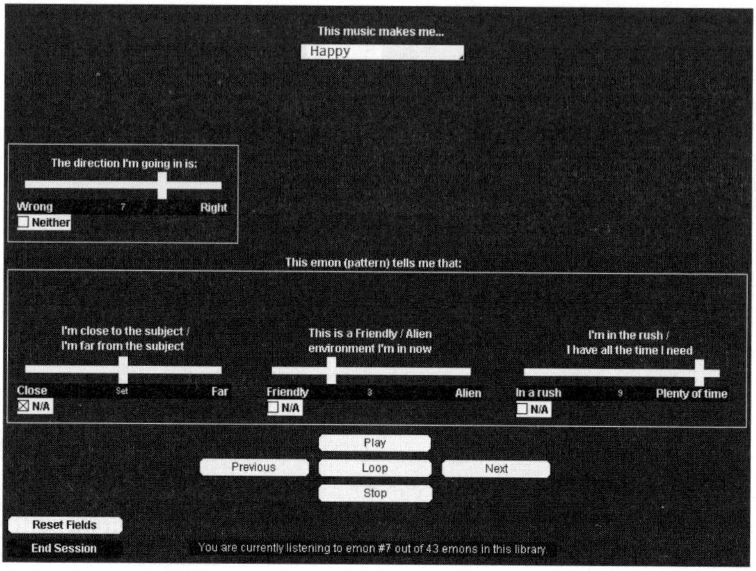

Figure 1. Audio emons' testing tool

6. Results of the emons testing

Granted the limitations of a small group testing, the overall results are surprisingly promising. Despite the fact that the emons were composed with *no* intent of addressing particular navigation-related qualities of the emons (their directional, proximity and other ratings), a surprisingly high number of candidate emons were rated as either "completely right" or "completely wrong" (values in [6.5000–7.0000] & [1.0000–1.5000] ranges respectively) on all the scales (direction, proximity, etc.) (Table 1).

Table 1. Full output of the testing procedure for 'all users' selection query

	%by Direction	by Time Rush	by Proximity	by Environment
Top/Bottom 15%	8/1	6/2	1/0	2/0
Top/Bottom 30%	36/11	20/22	20/4	26/9
Top/Bottom 45%	57/27	42/48	50/27	61/19
Neutral	21	15	27	25

The characteristics that seem to be most accurately conveyed by the emons are directionality and time-rush. The accuracy can be seen across the subject groups, with 8% of the emons rated in the highest ("most positive") range (top 15%) on the directionality axis and 6% on the time-rush axis (2% for proximity & 1% for environment factors). The highest value for the navigation axis (as rated by *all* subjects) was [7.00], and the lowest was [1.33]. While presenting a basis for an interesting hypothesis, these results should be tested with a far larger group of users. It does seem possible however to state that users seem to agree on certain musical fragments in relation to their direction- and time- related characteristics. As soon as the user group is narrowed demographically down from the "all" criteria, even more extreme similarities show up.

This paper represents a work in progress. While the current user base is small and the received results cannot be generalized beyond more than a limited group of users, a good basis can be seen from the initial tests for a future research regarding the use of emons as information cues affecting users' behavior. According to the initial tests, emons have the potential to become useful as information delivery units. As of now, ~10% of the candidate emons were defined by the subjects consistently as either "very positive" or "very negative", and that finding holds the premise of filling the first part of an emon grammar. More work is required to design additional libraries of emons and to understand the correspondence between compositional factors and users' ratings.

7. Implementation

The GuideShoes project was chosen as an initial platform for the test of the emons' approach. Our primary goal with the GuideShoes system is to test the emon-related hypotheses through musical emons-based information delivery, while hoping to design a new navigational tool. Navigational control was chosen as an example of a rather simple and expandable task that has opportunities for exploring both binary (right/wrong) and fuzzy (better/worse) relationships. Using the GuideShoes wearable interface is useful as it allows us to come up with multiple test scenarios to provide the validity for the emon approach (as outlined in the "Hypotheses" section).

Current scenario of interaction

A user comes to the base station, picks a destination point on the map, specifies a few optional profile details (such as age, gender, and favorite musical style), puts the GuideShoes pack on, and starts walking. Depending on the correctness of the direction, and compliance with the properties specified for the travel, the user hears different musical patterns that provide the necessary navigational cues to get to the destination, while presumably leaving the cognitive foreground open for more creative tasks.

System overview

The GuideShoes system consists of a wearable part — a leg-mounted pack equipped with a GPS, a wireless spread spectrum radio, a custom-built motherboard plus a pair of FM radio headphones — and a base station that acts as the central unit for path selection, data processing, and emons' retrieval/playback. The emons are produced by a MIDI synthesizer, or read from disk as audio files and then delivered to the user using an FM transmitter — at the place and time where they are needed. The placement of the wearable has been

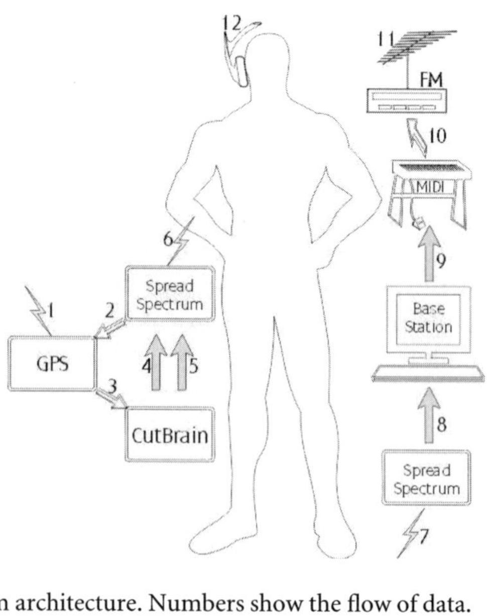

Figure 2. System architecture. Numbers show the flow of data.

chosen based on several factors: an unobtrusive location, an otherwise unused strong spot of the human body, and closeness to the body — thus allowing accurate readings for the attached sensors.

Structure Of GuideShoes

The client-server interaction schematic is shown in Figure 2. The client consists of a DGPS (Ashtech SK-8), custom-built CPU (CutBrain), spread spectrum radio (FreeWave OEM), and a pair of radio headphones. The base station runs a custom-built map UI with path selection features (MapTool, implemented in Tcl/Tk), and emons' retrieval engine (C++). It also controls the FreeWave base station, an SBX-2 differential beacon receiver, an additional SK-8 DGPS for detection of base station location, and a Veronica Kits FM transmitter used to deliver the audio to the GuideShoes user.

System operation

Every second, the base station sends differential corrections to the client's differential GPS, which sends the corrected user position back to the base station. The spread spectrum modules on both ends hold these and other data exchanges. The base station processes the corrected DGPS data and, based on the correctness of the movement, retrieves and sends one of the emons from its library back to the GuideShoes, where it is played through a wireless headset.

Navigational applications

GuideShoes is a navigational tool designed for a wide range of people that can be described as users with navigational difficulties, and users for whom the emons' approach presents a plausible alternative for the otherwise cumbersome task of "classical" navigation.

These groups of people include:

1. Children: The problem of children's safety (such as not getting lost while walking through a city) cannot be solved by GuideShoes; however the GuideShoes can attempt to make this problem more manageable. If a child has been exposed to the proper use of emons, the GuideShoes could provide him with a fun and helpful aid for getting to the place he needs to go and give parents the knowledge of his current location / alert them to potential direction problems.*

2. Orientation for the disabled (blind & psychological orientation impairment): The GuideShoes, if wisely implemented, may become an important navigational aid for people with severe vision problems. As the work of Peter Meijer (1997) aims to show, people can be conditioned to fairly complex patterns of movement expression using audio information. The melodic structure of the emons should make them easier to relate to for that community of users than to a purely algorithmically produced audio. Mapping emons to the validity of a walking direction (as well as potentially to the location of objects) could enhance their navigational abilities.
3. People with brain damage: According to experiments conducted by Martha Farah (1989), people with certain brain damage in the area of visual perception also had visual memory deficits "directly comparable to their perceptual deficits". Therefore, it will be interesting to test whether people with spatial disabilities (such as being unable to see relative locations of objects in a scene) can rely on GuideShoes as a complementary device to receive the same information through the alternative channel of music. **
4. Tourists: While not having the navigational difficulties similar to the three aforementioned groups, tourists have to find their way around cities without signs in their native languages. They would prefer to concentrate on the experience and not on the navigational task.
5. There is a substantial group of people who, while not facing the challenges mentioned above, prefer not to be overwhelmed with unnecessary information. Among these are the young people for whom the GuideShoes could represent an easy to adopt alternative, and people with well-developed auditory perception, that otherwise goes unused in their daily navigation process.

* As of today, the DGPS precision is limited to 2–5 meters.

** Testing with narrowly defined groups of population is beyond the scope of this study.

8. Continued development of the GuideShoes system

Technical

GuideShoes is a research project in progress. To further develop and demonstrate the emons' foundational principles, we plan to develop a larger library of emons for navigation-related purposes. That library, combined with a larger amount of test subjects, will allow us to further study the correlations between the emons' compositional parameters, their navigational ratings, provided by the test subjects, and the effect of such parameters on the GuideShoes' users.

We are also planning to increase the robustness of the GuideShoes system operation. We hope to achieve that by designin oes, securing the hardware elements in their positions, and developing an easier method for the battery charging process.

Conceptual

This paper describes the process of selecting musical emons to deliver navigational cues and describes the ongoing development of the GuideShoes system as the first artifact that utilizes the idea of emons. The question that drives the future development of the emon approach is: What other kinds of information can be delivered by emons and what kind of emons would these be? We have defined the four main related research directions as:

1. Merging between the emon approach and the recent psycho-physiological research.
2. Enhancing the emons domain by creating complete aesthetic musical-informational spaces with emons assigned to physical objects.
3. Developing additional applications based on the approach.
4. Expanding the emon approach to olfactory domains.

This research will hopefully lead us to the creation of an emon-enriched space, capable of monitoring and affecting the emotional state of its inhabitants and will evolve into a support system for educational and stress-relief purposes.

Acknowledgements

We would like to thank Dan Overholt, Dennis Kwon, Richard Tibbetts, Hristo Bojinov, and Raymond Luk for their help in creating the hardware and software components of the GuideShoes system.

References

Birren, Faber (1992). *Color Psychology and Color Therapy.* Citadel Press.

Buxton Bill (1995). *Integrating the Periphery and Context: A New Taxonomy of Telematics.* In proceedings of Graphics Interface '95.

Gardner, Howard (1983). *Frames of Mind: The Theory of Multiple Intelligences.*

Gray, Peter (1994). *Psychology.* Worth Publishers.

Ishii, Hiroshi., Ullmer, Brygg (1997). *Tangible Bits: Towards Seamless Interfaces between People, Bits and Atoms.* In proceedings of CHI '97, ACM Press.

Losee, Paul (1998). "The Creation of Memory and the Imprint Process", M+ research group, 1998.

Meijer, Peter (1997). *vOICe System.* http://ourworld.compuserve.com/homepages/Peter_Meijer/voice.htm

Meyer, Leonard (1956). *Emotion And Meaning In Music.* University of Chicago Press.

Minsky, Marvin (1985). *Society of Mind.* Simon & Schuster.

Picard, Rosalind (1997). *AVective Computing.* MIT Press.

Plutchik, Robert (1994). *The Psychology and Biology of Emotion.* Harper Collins.

The lexicon of the Conductor's face

Isabella Poggi
Università Roma Tre, Italy

1. Introduction

In the last decade, the multimodal aspects of communication have become an emerging field of research. Much work has been done on single systems of communication different from the verbal one — gestures, facial expression, gaze, body movements (see for example Kendon 1993; Ekman and Friesen 1978; Argyle and Cook 1976; Birdwhistell 1970) — and on the relationship among acoustic and visual modalities (Rimé and Schiaratura 1991; Mc Neill 1992). These studies provide information about how different modalities interact in accomplishing a common communicative task.

An interesting topic in this field is how communication in one modality can provide information as to what is to be done in another modality. A case of this is the orchestra Conductor's communication (Rudolf 1993). A Conductor has to communicate to players information about rhythm, timbre, loudness, expression in their playing, and does this by gesture, facial expression, gaze, body movement: here the visual modalities are used to provide information on how to perform in the acoustic modality. The Conductor's communicative behavior has mainly been studied on its gestural side. Boyes Braem and Braem (1999) provided a very interesting analysis of the Conductor's handshapes and their meanings. In this work I will analyze the communicative functions of the Conductor's gaze, head movements and facial expression, trying to show that these expressive signals are not idiosyncratic at all but very consistent and systematic indeed, to the extent that it is possible to write down a lexicon of them, a list of expressive items where each gaze or facial signal corresponds to a precise meaning.

To build such a lexicon two different approaches can be taken: if you adopt a bottom-up approach, you can record and analyze observational data, while trying to see whether, for instance, the same gaze or head signal always has the same meaning. With a top-down approach, on the other side, you wonder what are in principle the types of information that a Conductor may need to communicate to players in his conducting, and for each of them you figure out, on the basis of your communicative competence, and/or find out in observational data, what gaze, head and face signals the Conductor does or might perform to communicate that meaning. In this paper I start from both points of view: in Section 2. I try to figure out what are the meanings a Conductor may have to communicate, and what gaze, face and head signals are generally devoted to communicate them. In Sections 3. and 4. I present a procedure for the transcription and analysis of multimodal communication that is called "the musical score" of the vocal, gestural, facial, bodily communication; I adapt it (Sect. 5.) to the analysis of some fragments of Conductors' communicative behavior, to test whether the signals hypothesized in the first part are in fact used in real conducting; finally (Sect. 6) I outline a lexicon of the Conductor's face. I conclude (Sect.7) by discussing some general problems in the theory of communication regarding the mechanisms of polysemy and diachronic evolution of signals.

2. Signals and meanings in the Conductor's face

In this section I adopt the top-down approach described above. I do not start empirically from data but deductively from a general typology of possible meanings that can be conveyed in communication. By applying this deductive reasoning to the Conductor's communication, I wonder: what are the meanings a conductor needs to communicate to players during conducting? Can these meanings be conveyed only by gaze, head and face, without necessarily resorting, say, to gesture? By which face, head and gaze actions are they usually conveyed? And, are there meanings that cannot be conveyed by facial communication?

A Conductor has both to suggest players how they should play and to provide feed back about how they are playing in fact. The former thing is sometimes done in advance, before starting: by gesture and face, s/he may rehearse for the players a particular passage they will have to play, with some information on how to perform it; but more frequently this is done on-line while the players are playing, by communicating what they should do immediately next. The latter thing, too, providing feed back about how they are performing is done on-line, but its ultimate goal is, again, providing information about how to play on.

Within the first meaning, how players should play, the Conductor communicates **who** is to play, say, by *gazing at players*, and **when** to play or sing (information about openings) by *raising eyebrows* immediately before the start, then with a *head nod* at the very moment of starting. Then s/he may communicate **what sound** s/he wants from players: what melody, rhythm, speed, loudness and expression: s/he may ask for a "piano" by *raising eyebrows*, for a "forte" by a *frown*. Again, s/he may suggest **how** to produce the sound from a technical point of view, and finally provide a feed-back on current performance, say, approving sound with a *head nod* or disproving with a *head shake*. To each of the meanings listed, a specific signal corresponds, just like in a lexicon, i.e., a list of signal-meaning pairs, of the Conductor's facial repertoire.

Let us now adopt the bottom-up approach. I will present a procedure for the transcription and analysis of multimodal communication that is called "the musical score" of the vocal, gestural, facial, bodily communication. Adapting the score to the conductor's facial behavior will allow us to test whether the signals we hypothesized are in fact used in real conducting.

3. The "musical" score of communication

In audio-visual interaction we use multimodal communication: we communicate not merely through words but also through prosody, intonation, gesture, gaze, facial expression and body movement, and these different signals interact with each other in complex ways, with the overall meaning conveyed by the globality of them. But how are meanings distributed across modalities? Answering this question implies the use of some procedure that allows one to analyze all the meanings conveyed in multimodal communication and to distinguish the meaning individually borne by each communicative signal in each modality. Multimodal communication may be seen as a concert of many instruments playing together: following this musical metaphor, a procedure was elaborated to transcribe, analyze and classify chunks of multimodal communication, one similar to a musical score (Poggi & Magno Caldognetto 1997).

The "score" of multimodal communication is a procedure where signals in two or more modalities are transcribed, analyzed and classified. In a classical score, signals delivered in five different modalities are reported on parallel lines: verbal (the words and sentences uttered), prosodic (speech rythm, pauses, intensity, stress, intonation), gestural (hand and arm movements), facial (head and eye movements, gaze, smile and other facial expressions), bodily (trunk and leg movements, use of space, proxemics and so on). Each communicative item may be described in a discoursive way or through some notation system, and possibly classified according to some typology (say, a deictic gaze, an iconic gesture...); afterwards, its meaning can be expressed verbally, on the basis of the postulate that any communicative signal, qua communicative, by definition conveys some meaning, and any meaning can be glossed in a verbal language. Finally, it is assessed what the relationship is between that communicative signal and a parallel signal in another modality: whether it repeats the same meaning, adds information, provides information that is not provided in the other modality, contrasts the meaning conveyed in the other modality, or whether it bears no relation to the other concomitant signal.

4. Direct and indirect meaning: a two layers score

The score presented so far takes into account only the literal meanings of the signals in all modalities; which looks quite unsatisfactory, given the relevance of indirect meaning in communication. According to a model of communication in terms of goals and beliefs (Poggi & Magno Caldognetto 1997), a sentence is a Communicative Act, and its literal meaning can be reconstructed by processing the lexical meanings of its words and its syntactic form. The sentence literal goal is made up of a performative and a propositional content. The performative is the communicative intention with which the Sender performs one's Communicative Act, and it includes information on the kind of Action the Sender S requests from the Addressee A (whether to provide some information, like in the act of asking; to do some action, like in requesting; to believe some belief, like in informing) and on the relationship between S and A (a relation of power, like in an order, of benevolence, as in advice...). The propositional content is the content of the Act requested, of the information provided or asked.

Beyond its literal goal, though, any sentence may have one or more supergoals. A supergoal is a goal that is hierarchically superordinated to a goal, in that the goal is but a means to the supergoal. But while the goal of a sentence is to be understood merely through linguistic processing (lexical and syntactic rules), the sentence supergoal, even as it is a communicative supergoal, i.e., one that the Sender wants to be caught, is by definition not stated explicitely, it is a goal that the Sender wants the Addressee to catch by inference. Supergoals may be either idiomatic or creative. An idiomatic supergoal is a goal where the inferential path from literal to indirect meaning is crystallized (i.e., the same in any context) and condensed. A case of an idiomatic supergoal is the classical *Can you pass the salt?*, where the literal meaning ("I ask you if you are able to pass the salt") is bypassed, not event felt anymore, since the supergoal meaning ("I request you that you pass the salt") almost has a lexical status. To understand a creative supergoal, the Addressee may have to catch different goals in different contexts, through inferences generated on the basis of contextual knowledge. A case of a creative supergoal is when I ask a colleague of mine: *Are you going home?* If he knows my car is broken, he may infer the supergoal of asking for a lift. But if we work on the same computer, he will infer that my supergoal is to ask if I may use the computer. Now, not only a sentence, but also a gesture, a gaze, a posture can be Communicative Acts, hence they may have goals and idiomatic and creative supergoals. The gesture *hands up* has an idiomatic supergoal. Its literal meaning is: "I show you my hands empty, hiding no weapon", but in fact idiomatically it means: "I resign, I do not oppose you". Again, see a creative supergoal of a facial signal: by *directing gaze* to an interlocutor we ask for attention, but from this first meaning the interlocutor may infer different supergoals, depending on the context: I may ask your attention because I want to blame you, ask for complicity, or simply refer to something somehow linked to you.

Thus, since not only verbal but also nonverbal communication may undergo a second layer of interpretation (may have supergoals to infer), a two-layers score should be used to account for the second-layer interpretation of multimodal communication. In fact, a further development of the score procedure was put forth, where each signal in each modality goes through two layers of semantic analysis: both literal and indirect meaning are written down and classified as to their meaning and function. This new version of the score was applied to Totò, a famous Italian comic actor, and to political discourse (Poggi and Magno Caldognetto 1997).

5. The score of conducting a score

An adapted version of the two-layers score was applied to the analysis of the conductor's head, gaze and facial behavior. Two different conductors (Bruno Aprea and Massimo Freccia) were videorecorded, both conducting Beethoven's 9th Symphony, during a public concert and during a rehearsal. Some fragments of these videorecordings were analyzed through the score procedure.[1] For each item of gaze, mouth or head movement its literal and indirect meaning was assessed. The score of two fragments from Aprea's rehearsal is shown in Tables 1, 2 and 3.

Head movements and gaze are represented on parallel lines. On each line three aspects of the signal are described: direction, movement and, possibly, combination. More specifically, we write in what direction head and eyes look (up, down, right, left, forward, right-down, beyond the orchestra to the choir…); the type of movement performed (still, head tilt, head nod, frown…); and, sometimes, if the signal analyzed is combined with others, whether represented in the score or not (a specific gaze may combine with some head movement or with a gesture).

Each aspect of each signal is described and classified through three columns: in the first we write a description of the signal; in the second and third columns, respectively, we write a verbal formulation of the literal and of the indirect meaning of that aspect of the signal, and we classify the Communicative Act performed as an Information, Question or Request. On the fourth and last column to the right we write down what seems to be the overall meaning of the combination of signals analyzed.

Table 1.

		Signal	Literal Meaning	Indirect Meaning	Complete Communicative Act
Head	Direction	*Head upward*	I am in an alert position (I)	I ask you to be ready (R)	
	Movement	*Still*	I stand still before starting (I)	I'll start in a moment (I)	Choir, be ready to start
Gaze	Direction	*In front of himself, beyond the orchestra*	I am addressing you there (I)	I am addressing the choir (I)	(R)
	Movement	*Eyes around*	I am addressing each one of you (I)		

In the specific example of Table 1, head is upward and still: its first level meaning is: "I am in an alert position" (an Information), which means in its turn: "I ask you to be ready" (a Request). At the same time, gaze is directed forward, beyond the orchestra (then to the choir) and eyes look around like in gazing at each singer one by one. The meaning is then: "I am addressing the choir, and each of you singularly". The overall meaning conveyed by head and gaze is a complex Communicative Act made up by a vocative ("You choir") plus a Request ("Prepare to start").

Table 2.

		Signal	Literal Meaning	Indirect Meaning	Complete Communicative Act
Head	Direction	*Head forward*	I address you in front of me (I)	I address you wind instruments (I)	
	Movement	*Moving slowly right and left*	No, don't do that (R)	Play soft (R)	You wind instruments play soft and gently
Gaze	Direction				
	Movement	*Eyes shut*	I am concentrating (I)	Play gently (R)	(R)

In Table 2, head forward (="You wind instruments") slowly moves right and left, meaning "No" ("Don't do that"), which in this case is a Request to play softly. At the same time, eyes shut, meaning "I am concentrating", which in this context may be interpreted as "Play gently". The overall meaning is a vocative plus a double Request: "You, wind instruments, play soft and gently".

Table 3.

		Signal	Literal Meaning	Indirect Meaning	Complete Communicative Act
Head	Direction	*Head forward*	I address you in front of me (I)	I address you strings (I)	
	Movement	*Scanning time*	I am scanning time (I)	I ask you chords strong and scanned (R)	I ask you stressed and clearcut chords
	Combination	*Head + Hands + Body*	I show it with all my body (I)	It is important for you to do this (I) I strongly ask you this (R)	(R)

In Table 3, as it is represented by the line "combination", the movement of the head combines with the symultaneous movements of the hands and the whole body. The very fact that they all combine is not simply redundant: doing the same thing at the same time with different instruments is a metacommunication that means: "that I am scanning time (line 2, column 3), is something that I show with all my body (line 3, column 3)", which indirectly conveys the Information "this is a particularly important message" (line 3, column 4) and hence the Request "I strongly ask you to do this".

6. A lexicon of the Conductor's face

Table 4 represents a sample of the Conductor's facial lexicon, that is, a list of correspondences between facial signals and meanings, as they result from the combination of our top-down approach (Section 2) with the score analysis (Section 5).

In columns 1 and 2 we write the classes and subclasses of meanings the conductor has to convey; in col.3 a specific facial signal, in columns 4 and 5 respectively the "apparent" and the "real" meaning (where the "real" meaning is generally the indirect one, except when only the literal meaning holds).

In suggesting players how to play, the information about **who** is to play is usually communicated by a deictic use of head or gaze direction; when Aprea looks in front of himself beyond the orchestra, he is referring to the choir in a deictic way, that is through pointing at it. As for **when** to play (or sing), the conductor can provide information about openings before opening by *raising his eyebrows*, which means "I am in an alert position", so "be in alert position", then "be ready to open"; at the moment of opening, he *strongly nods*: "Open now!". He can also signal when it is not yet time to open, by *looking down* or by *closing his eyes.*

Another important information concerns **what sound** to produce: specifically, what **melody**, **rhythm**, **speed**, **loudness**. *Raising face up* or *dropping it down* may mean "I want a high tune" or "I want a low tune"; the kind and speed of *head movements* can inform analogically about the due rhythm and tempo. Different signals are devoted to inform about loudness. A *frown* or a *grimace*, by expressing determination, generally mean "Play aloud"; among the facial signals that ask of playing softly, the most frequent and idiomatized ones are to *move head left and right* as in saying "No", and to *raise eyebrows* like in saying "I'm alarmed". An alternative more idiosyncratic way (one seen in nonrecorded observation) is to show a disgusted or horryfied face (performed by *shutting eyes*, *frowning* and *opening the mouth*), that produces the inferences "What a distressing sound" and then asks for a softer one. In all of these cases, the meaning "Play more softly" is an indirect, generally idiomatized meaning.

Table 4. The Conductor's lexicon

TYPE OF MEANING		SIGNAL	APPARENT (LITERAL) MEANING	REAL (INDIRECT) MEANING
	Who is to play	*Look at the choir*		you choir
	When to play	*Raised eyebrows*	I am alerted (emotion)	prepare to start
		Look down	I am concentrating (mental state)	you concentrate, prepare to start
		Fast head nod		start now
		Look down	I am not alerted	do not start yet
	What sound to produce			
Suggest how to play	**Melody**	*Face up*		high tune
	Rhythm	*Staccato head movements*		Staccato
	Speed	*Fast head movements*		Svelto
	Loudness	*Frown*	I am determined (mental state)	play aloud
		Raised eyebrows	I am alarmed (emotion)	it is too loud, play more softly
		Left-right head movements	No! (not that loud)	Play more softly
	Expression	*Inner eyebrows raised*	I am sad	Play a sad sound
	How to produce the sound	*Wide open mouth*		Open your mouth wide
		Rounded mouth		Round your mouth
Provide feed back	**Praise**	*Head nod*	Ok	go on like this
		Closed eyes	I'm relaxed (emotion)	Good, go on like this
		Oblique head	I'm relaxed (emotion)	Good, go on like this
	Blame	*Closed eyes + Frown + Open mouth*	I'm disgusted (emotion)	Not like this

One more information typically provided by head, face and gaze is about **expression.** Here of course facial expression is the most apt way to exhibit the emotions that the Conductor feels or pretends to feel, and that he is calling for in players, so they can display them in their music. The Conductor, for instance, by *raising the inner parts of his eyebrows* shows sad, then meaning "play a sad sound".

This concerns the sound quality that is to be the output of the players' playing. But sometimes the Conductor also informs about **how** this output should be produced, by suggesting the techniques to use for producing the sound required. A choir conductor, for instance, can *open his mouth wide* to ask singers to open it wide. He can also *round his mouth* to mean "Sing with rounded mouth", with the indirect meaning "produce a softer and more delicate sound".

Let us come to the feed-back signals. A conductor may approve or disprove of the players' playing. As he *slowly nods* or *closes his eyes*, he is communicating "This is ok, go on like this". The same meaning may be indirectly conveyed when he *keeps his head oblique*, which is a relaxed position, thus meaning "I feel ok like this"; "You are playing well". A blame instead is communicated in the case above, when the conductor closes his eyes but at the same time frowns and opens his mouth, as in an expression of disgust. The indirect meaning conveyed by this negative feedback is often "Do not play this way".

7. Indirect meaning and the creativity of facial language

An aspect of the Conductor's communication that pops out thanks to the score is the issue of literal and indirect meaning. Often the conductor's head and gaze signals have a literal meaning but they mean something else in fact: they have an indirect meaning. For instance, by opening eyes wide when music is too loud, the Conductor means "I feel alarmed" as a literal meaning, but "Please, play softer" as an indirect meaning. The literal meanings are linked to the indirect meanings through inference chains of this kind:

I am stressing rhythm	→ stress rhythm	
I am pointing at you	→ I am addressing you	→ prepare to start
I am alerted	→ be alerted	→ prepare to start
I am alarmed	→ this sound is too loud	→ play softer
I am sad	→ feel sad	→ play a sad sound

Also in this case, as well as in verbal direct and indirect communicative acts, some of the indirect meanings are of the idiomatized type, in that the literal meaning can be interpreted only in one way, while other indirect meanings can change across contexts. We have an idiomatized indirect meaning when the conductor nods to the orchestra, which almost always means "I like how you are playing, go on like this". A scared or horryfied face, meaning "I am afraid" or "I am horryfied (by this loud sound)", at the indirect level idiomatically means "Play softly". But take the signal of eyes shut, which generally means: "I am concentrating": this might mean "Prepare to start", when music has not started yet; but it might also mean "Play lower" or "Play in a mystic or misterious way": different inferences, hence different indirect meanings, are triggered in different contexts.

Analyzing the Conductor's face communication through the two-layers score is also of help to solve some theoretical problems. Firt, the ambiguity of signals. A problem with the list in Section 2 was that some signals seemed to have more than one meaning: a head nod may mean "Start now" but also "Go on like this". Now, thanks to a score analysis that carefully distinguishes the components of gaze from head and face, and within each component different possible directions and movements, we can tell that signals seemingly identical are not in fact exactly the same: for example, the opening *head nod* (Table 4, line 4) is faster than the *head nod* that means "go on like this" (line 15). Thus, the presence of ambiguity is challenged already by the score analysis at its first level. But the discovery of an indirect level of meaning may account for both ambiguity and synonymy of facial signals: the same signal may have the same meaning at the literal level but two or more different meanings (mediated by different inferences) at the indirect level. This is the case for *eyes shut* which mean "I am concentrating" at the first level, and may mean either "prepare to start" or "play soft" at the second level. And also, two different signals may be synonyms at the indirect level: both *eyes shut*, that means "I am concentrating" and *wide open eyes*, that means "I am alerted" have as an indirect meaning "prepare to start". The existence of ambiguity and synonymy in the conductor's face communication, and the possibility to account for them, shows that this can be considered a lexicon in its own right, since the link between signals and meanings is as precise and systematic as in word and gesture lexicons.

One more reason why it is important to take indirect meanings into account is that they widen the range of meanings that can be conveyed in this communication system. In fact, how many meanings can the Conductor's face mean? There are, maybe, some kinds of meanings that a Conductor should communicate but that cannot be expressed by face, while they can, say, by gesture (Boyes Braem and Braem 1999). For instance, by combining gesture and face a Conductor may ask some players to play soft because the music theme is held by other instruments. Now, I think this could not be done by face only. Nonetheless, indirect meanings do widen the range of meanings that can potentially be conveyed by face only.

The creation of new signals in a communicative system is constrained by two things: the Agent's communicative needs (the meanings it needs to convey) and its resources (the perceivable objects, forms, movements it can produce). Now, a Conductor's communicative needs are to convey the meanings of Table 4, while the resources he is endowed with are his face, head and gaze, who can only do three kinds of communicative actions: a. point at some places by head or gaze; b. perform rhythmic movements by head; c. express states of mind (states of thought, like "I am concentrating", or emotions, like "I am sad"). By these mere resources, the only meanings a Conductor's face could convey literally would be: referring to players or instruments; showing rhythmic movements of his own; expressing his own mental states of emotions. But if we add a bunch of inference rules to these meanings that the Conductor can convey literally in a natural way, a fair amount of other meanings can be conveyed indirectly, whether idiomatized or not. Two of the inference rules that may account for the development of new meanings from the basic ones above are: (1) *pointing* (by pointing at players or singers, the Conductor often addresses them, and may even perform a request, like "Prepare to start"); and (2) *mirror* (by moving his head he may imitate the movements the players should perform on their instruments, and then ask them to perform those movements); where a *mirror* inference can also be applied recursively (by expressing an emotion he can ask them to feel the same emotion and to play in such a way to induce that emotion in other people).

These inference rules give rise to semiotic devices that are at work not only in the language of the Conductor's face, but in many, if not all, communication systems. Also in everyday interaction, pointing is a way to make reference to things or people, and then possibly to address them. But the device of mirroring looks particularly interesting in the evolution of signals, since a mirroring device is often used to induce in other people the same behavior as ours: a mother, while feeding her child, instinctively opens her mouth to have him open his mouth; smiling to a person is the best way to elicit her smile; as we want to emphasize the comment of our sentence, we raise our eyebrows, a signal of surprise which has the function of inducing the same surprise and consequent attention in our interlocutor (Poggi and Pelachaud 2000).[2] In this sense the face of the Conductor is a microworld where the same semiotic devices hold as in other communication systems.

The primary function of Language is to influence other people, that is, to cause them to do what we want; and this function is so compelling that language finds its way in fulfilling it not only in a straightforward manner, but also through indirect devices. Just because of the distance between what the Conductor has the goal of communicating and what our head and face naturally allow us to communicate, in the diacronic evolution of a shared code between a Conductor and an orchestra or a choir, some inferential links have been built and then idiomatized; these links allow people to understand, from a movement of the Conductor's face, a movement requested of the players, and from an emotion of the Conductor, a request for a particular sound, or an opening, or a particular expressive rendering.

Notes

1. I am indebted to Mara Mastropasqua who collected and carefully analyzed the videotaped fragments of orchestra conduction, while working on her thesis in Theory of Communication, at the Faculty of Education, University Roma Tre.

2. Might this have to do with Rizzolatti et al. (1997) *mirror neurons*, the monkeys' neurons that fire both while the monkey is producing a gesture and while it is seeing it?

References

Argyle, M., & M. Cook (1976). *Gaze and Mutual Gaze.* Cambridge: Cambridge University Press.

Birdwhistell, R. (1970). *Kinesics and Context: Essays on Body Motion Communication.* Philadelphia: University of Pennsylvania Press.

Boyes Braem, P., & Th. Braem (1999). A pilot study of the expressive gestures used by classical orchestra conductors. In K.Emmorey & H. Lane (eds.) *The Signs of Language Revisited: An Anthology in Honor of Ursula Bellugi and Edward Klima.* Mahwah: Lawrence Erlbaum Associates.

Ekman, P., & W. V. Friesen (1978). *Facial Action Coding System.* Palo Alto: Consulting Psychologists Press.

Kendon, A. (1993). Human Gesture. In T.Ingold & K.Gibson (eds.) *Tools, Language and Intelligence.* Cambridge: Cambridge University Press.

McNeill, D. (1992). *Hand and Mind.* Chicago: University of Chicago Press.

Poggi, I., & E. Magno Caldognetto (1997). *Mani che parlano. Gesti e psicologia della comunicazione.* Padova: Unipress.

Poggi, I., & C. Pelachaud (2000). Emotional Meaning and Expression in Performative faces. In A. Paiva (ed.) *Affective Interactions. Towards a New Generation of Computer Interfaces.* Berlin: Springer.

Rimé, B., & L. Schiaratura (1991). Gesture and Speech. In R.Feldman & B.Rimé (Eds.), *Fundamentals of Nonverbal Behavior.* New York: Cambridge University Press.

Rizzolatti, G., Fadiga, L., Fogassi, L., & Gallese, V. (1997). The space around us. *Science* 277 (11 July 1997): 190–191.

Rudolf, M. (1993). *The grammar of Conducting.* New York: Schirmer.

How do interactive virtual operas shift relationships between music, text and image?

A. Bonardi and F. Rousseaux
Université Paris VIII / Université de Reims, France

1. What are virtual operas ?

We define as a virtual interactive opera any opera implemented on a personal computer, enabling some interactivity with its audience. This new genre is not based on the simple transposition of existing operas in the framework of new computing technologies; it takes into account the shiftings of uses and meanings induced by multimedia computing, assuming they could arouse new writings and ways of creativity (Bonardi 1998b).

Interactivity is based on free choices among different paths. Only open forms that have specially been designed for listeners can enable it. This specification leads us to give up the classical narrative "aristotelician" mode. This implies two possibilities of formal and temporal articulation:

1. either consider the hypertext model and possibilities of automatic text generation (Balpe et al. 1996) to design an opera where hypermedia components strongly depend on text; this is the case in Jean-Pierre Balpe's *Barbe-Bleue* project,
2. or take into account the specificities of computer-aided writing to design a new kind of "musical action" as Luciano Berio (Berio & Eco 1994) defined it: "Between a musical action and an opera, there are substantial differences. Opera is based on a 'aristotelician-like' narrative mode, which tends to have priority on musical development. On the contrary, in a musical action, the musical process rules the story". We have chosen this very direction for our research and our *Virtualis* project. In this interactive opera, the listener wanders in an open space, being essentially guided by metaphors of music rather than combinations of narratives.

In our paper, we deal with relationships between music, text and image, comparing what they used to be in former classical operas and what they could become in this new genre.

2. Relationships between music, text and visual aspects in traditional operas

Many authors have noticed that opera has been oscillating for four centuries between music predominance and text predominance. However, if we consider individual works, we can state that each opera has its own balance between music and text, and moreover that it remains constant during the whole work (Bonardi 1997). It often has to do with the macroscopic form of operas, either based on musical constraints or on dramatic ones.

On the other hand, analysts like Michel Poizat (Poizat 1986) claim that the main dialectic in opera consists of tension between an homeostatic delight principle based on the intelligibility of language and a pleasure principle, as an asymptote of an exaltation drifting without any back force towards a sung shout. This does not contradict the former statement if we consider that the interaction between text and music in traditional operas as multiple, happening on various levels.

For instance, if we examine *The Magic Flute* by Mozart, we find that the general design of the work matches musical constraints, which is consistent with Mozart's position in his correspondence which claims that poetry should be the obedient daughter of music. In the precise case of *The Magic Flute*, let us notice that the predominance of music reinforces the philosophical aspects of the work since many philosophical symbols are encoded in the score more or less explicitly. Though singing only two arias, the Queen of the Night is a very interesting character since she actually embodies the conflict between delight and pleasure. In the second act, she encourages her daughter Pamina to murder Sarastro: this is musically emphasized by a progression at the beginning of the aria, accumulating an extreme tension. The surprise comes from the resolution of this tension, which does not lead to a climax, but to what Poizat calls the scansion of the singing exercise, with highly broken virtuosic passages. In fact, Mozart avoids the climax, which should be like a sung shout, but is not suitable at the classical age. Mozart goes further and nearly gives up words to the benefit of music in these virtuosic passages.

Concerning the importance of visual aspects in traditional operas, we could say that they are necessary but not sufficient. For instance, the audience often seems frustrated when an opera is played in a concert version. This means we need sets, costumes and lighting. But they just build a framework where music confronts text.

3. Opera and interactivity

Collective interaction

The first introduction of interactivity in opera happened in 1968, when *Votre Faust*, by Henri Pousseur and Michel Butor was created. In this "Fantaisie variable" written for five actors, four singers, twelve musicians and magnetic tape, some chances of interaction were given to the audience, so that the plot could be altered. One can really wonder whether selecting paths in an open work can be a collective action: can an opera be based on an interactive process driven by a kind of vote? Is it possible to import a political paradigm, the democratic vote, as a principle of artistic design?

Individual feedback

Contrary to this approach based on collective interaction giving average results, we claim that interactivity must also lead to individual feedback, that is, even though several people can take part together to the same process at the same time, each of them gets both collective and individual responses.

Using computers seems to be an interesting way to achieve this goal, in the framework of what we just named virtual interactive operas. Let us first notice that, with personal computers, the interaction necessarily happens through graphical elements. This means that visual aspects are predominant in these new operas, and therefore the main dialectic does not oppose music to text but images to another component, which can either be an hypertextual set or a musical set. As we said in the introduction of this paper, we are interested in the second kind of dialectic, between images and music.

If we want this interaction to happen in an open work, we have to give users possibilities of navigation among different music entities, that is creating a kind of "hypermusic" environment, which is quite different from an hypertextual one. Though music is a language based on a syntax (Boucourechliev 1993), it has no other meaning than itself. And yet, in the hypertextual environment, information nodes often contain textual pointers, able to designate or describe other information nodes in the user's context. These hypertextual links are obviously semantic. As a music entity is unable to designate by itself other entities, we need graphical metaphors to enable this navigation.

Text then takes a new role, which has less to do with narrative aspects than with sound and graphical ones. It means that we are closer to poetry than to theater. Indeed, words can be used in this context as sound resources or even as elements of the set.

4. Using graphical metaphors of music

The different roles of graphical metaphors

As we just said, the role of graphical metaphors is to enable users to navigate through music. Offhand they have three different roles of mediation between music and listeners:

1. the first role is to make explicit musical structures and processes handled by composers and analysts; metaphors are then used as translators.
2. the second approach is interested in the listener's point of view: in a given context, what does the listener perceive, which categories are relevant for him? That was Pachet's (Pachet & Delerue 1998) basic idea when developing their MIDI Spatializer named "Midispace" which enables users to move instruments on a stage, the program taking into account consistency constraints simulating the action of a sound engineer.
3. the third role consists in arousing a kind of convergence between music and graphism, without making it necessarily explicit. The listener does not then know how to designate the musical phenomenon he has perceived, but he is able to associate it with geometric or color configurations.

Let us first say that these three aspects are often mixed. For instance, some researches in the field of psychoacoustics have shown that such structural elements as the tempo and the mode of a piece have an important influence on the emotion aroused, sometimes more than the musician's interpretation (McAdams & Bigand 1994).

Using GUIDO music notation language

Being interested in metaphors of structural elements of music, we address the problem of music annotation. We implemented an extension of the GUIDO music notation language (Hoos et al. 1998). The main advantage of GUIDO is to enable the direct handling of aggregations, either temporal aggregations as phrases, or vertical aggregations as chords. Contrary to other descriptions (Mendes 1999), GUIDO does not separate elementary elements (for instance notes) from aggregations.

Let us consider for instance the very beginning of the *Diabelli Variations* for piano by Beethoven (opus 120, Figure 1).

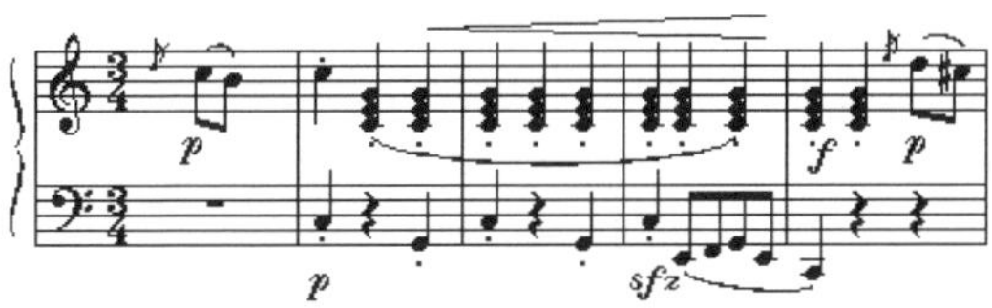

Figure 1. Beginning of the Diabelli Variations by Beethoven

Here are the basic rules to use GUIDO :

1. what is played sequentially is encoded with brackets : []
2. what is played simultaneously is encoded with braces {}
3. notes are encode using english notation (rests are represented by _)
4. durations are indicated by the corresponding ratios
5. octave and duration information are implicit : C1/4 D E indicates to play three quarters C, D, E in the same octave
6. there are tags (for instance \staff) that enable to indicate various levels of information.

   This extract by Beethoven should be encoded like this :
   {[\staff<1> \slur<D2/16 C B1/8> C2/4 \slur<{C1 E G} {C E G} etc…>]
   [\staff<2> _/4 C0 _ G-1 C0 _ G-1 C0 \slur <E-1/8 F G E C/4>]}

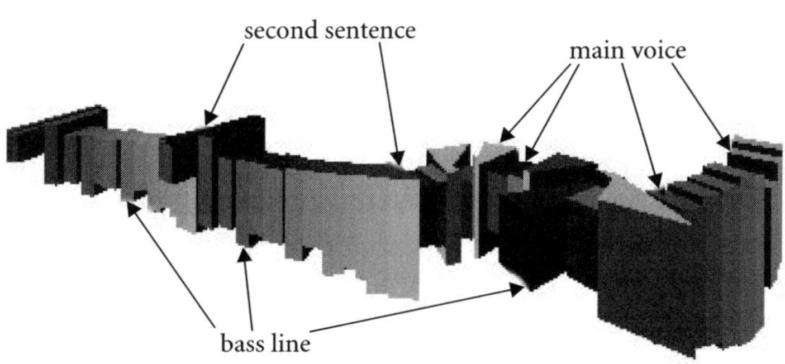

Figure 2. Tunnel built according to the beginning of Beethoven's piece

Two examples of graphical metaphors

We can build various graphical metaphors from GUIDO annotation files. First of all, we have thought of tunnels that would be a synthesis of many musical properties as shown in Figure 2 above.

In this case, we have the following mapping: the roof follows the main line, the floor follows the bass line, the bends and the colors correspond to the phrases, and the width to the vertical density.

We were also interested in visualizing polyphonies. Let us consider an extract of Mozart's *Piano Sonata K.282* (first part) (Figure 3).

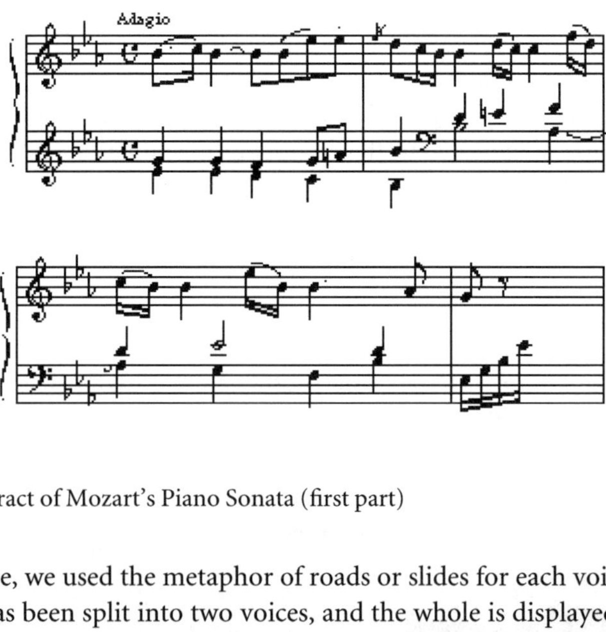

Figure 3. Extract of Mozart's Piano Sonata (first part)

For this piece, we used the metaphor of roads or slides for each voice. The left hand part has been split into two voices, and the whole is displayed as a three voice piece. In the following example, three different instruments (piano, guitar, cello) have been attributed to the three voices and appear on the ground of each slide (Figure 4).

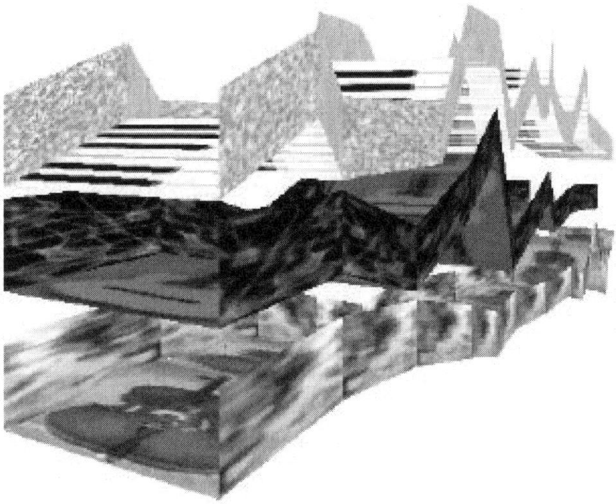

Figure 4. Vizualisation of Mozart's Piece

These representations can also be used efficiently in the case of vocal music, and especially opera. Following the same principles, we have generated corridors that match each singing part. In this case, they also support semantic links, as pictures of the characters and some lyrics are displayed on the walls and are clickable. This enables the creation of a kind of « hyper-vocal music ». The two examples given come from Mozart's Magic Flute, more precisely from Tamino's Aria at the beginning of the first act (Figures 5 and 6).

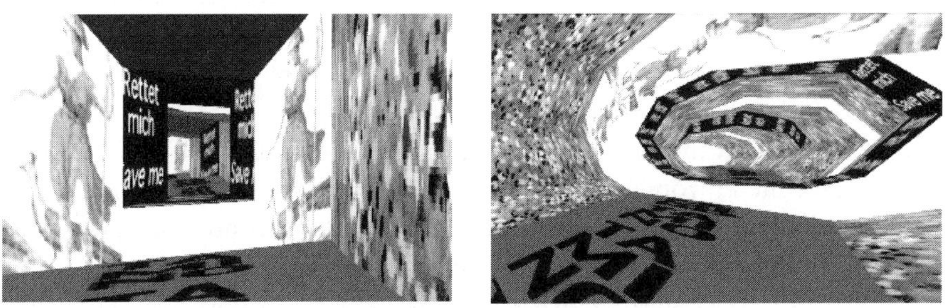

Figures 5, 6. Examples of vizualisation of Tamino's Aria in the first act

5. The ALMA environment

Handling music in computer-aided open forms requires a specific environment for creation. It first implies that music cannot be considered any longer as a resource stored in files, which is the common way it is processed in such multimedia authoring softwares as Director (Macromedia). Moreover, these authoring environments do not enable the composer to have a clear apprehension of then open form he wants to create since they were not designed for music purposes.

We have therefore started developing our own authoring system, named ALMA (as a tribute to Alma Mahler and also Gustav Mahler). This is a hierarchical object-oriented system where logical descriptions of music or stage indications (encoded thanks to an extension of the GUIDO language presented above) are separated from physical files to be played, either music files (audio or MIDI files) or graphics files (we can choose a metaphor for every piece, for the moment only tunnels or roads as shown above are available).

In this environment, text may have three different roles:

1. either used for textual descriptions of music or stage indications using extended Guido,
2. either used as a sound: for instance, \text("if music be the food of love") can be associated with different audio files from different speakers saying "if music be the food of love",
3. or become a graphical element, thanks to graphical metaphors.

The ALMA system includes different modules:

1. two annotation modules; the first one enables to add such descriptions as slurs or harmonic data to MIDI files; the second one is used to annotate audio files thanks to a corresponding MIDI file that was previously annotated with the first module.
2. a COMPOSER module to edit and put together entities and links. Entities can be edited through four windows: a first one to edit texts written with the description language (extended GUIDO); a second window for the score; a third to watch the result of the graphical metaphor chosen for this very entity; a last one to manage physical resources (sound files, 3D generation modules, ...). Let us notice that links can be either sequential (telling that one entity should be played after another), or based on a loop (so that an entity should be repeated several times) or conditional (with tests).
3. a PLAYER module that performs the interactive score prepared with the COMPOSER module.

6. Conclusion

In the context of new virtual operas, traditional dialectics and focuses are shifted by the predominance of images, and the new temporal dimension given by open forms. We are only beginning our exploration of new fields of interactive and multimedia musical composition, also experimenting new relationships between operas and their listeners.

References

Auffret, Gwendal, Jean Carrive, Olivier Chevet, Thomas Dechilly, Rémi Ronfard & Bruno Bachimont (1999). Audiovisual-based Hypermedia Authoring : using structured representations for efficient access to AV documents. Proceedings of the 10th ACM Hypertext'99 Conference, 169–178.

Balpe, Jean-Pierre, Alain Lelu, Frédéric Papy & Imad Saleh (1996). *Techniques avancées pour l'hypertexte.* Paris: Hermès.

Berio, Luciano & Umberto Eco (1994). *Eco in ascolto — Entretien avec Luciano Berio*, in *Musique: texte, les cahiers de l'Ircam — Recherche et Musique n°6.* Paris: Ircam.

Bonardi, Alain (1997). *Vers un opéra interactif.* Mémoire de DEA, formation doctorale "Musique et Musicologie du XX° siècle" EHESS/Paris IV Sorbonne.

Bonardi, Alain & Francis Rousseaux (1998). *Premiers pas vers un opéra interactif*, Proceedings of the « Journées d'Informatique Musicale 1998 » (JIM 98). LMA Publication n°148, Marseille, CNRS.

Bonardi, Alain & Francis Rousseaux (1998). *Towards New Lyrical Forms*, in the Papers from the 1998 AAAI Fall Symposium — Technical Report FS-98–03. Menlo Park (USA, California): AAAI.

Boucourechliev, André (1993). *Le langage musical.* Paris: Fayard.

Eco, Umberto (1962). *L'opera aperta.* Milan: Bompiani.

Elliott, Conal (1999). *Modeling Interactive 3D and Multimedia Animation with an Embedded Language*, forthcoming in the *IEEE Transactions on Software Engineering* 1999, can be browsed at the following URL: http://www.research.microsoft.com/~conal/papers/ds19.

Hoos, Holger, Keith Hamel, Kai Flade & Jurgen Killian (1998). *GUIDO Music Notation — Towards an Adequate Representation of Score Level Music*, Proceedings of the « Journées d'Informatique Musicale 1998 » (JIM 98), LMA Publication n°148. Marseille, CNRS.

Mc Adams, Steve & Emmanuel Bigand (1994). *Penser les sons. Psychologie cognitive de l'audition.* Paris: Presses Universitaires de France.

Mendes, David (1999). *Knowledge Representation Suitable for Music Analysis*, Proceedings of the « Journées d'Informatique Musicale 1999 » (JIM 99). Publication du CEMAMu, Issy-les-Moulineaux.

Pachet, François & Olivier Delerue (1998). *A constraint-based Temporal Music Spatializer.* 10th ACM Multimedia Conference Proceedings.
Poizat, Michel (1986). *L'opéra ou le cri de l'ange.* Paris: Editions A. M. Métailié.
Pousseur, Henri (1997). *Musiques croisées.* Paris: L'Harmattan.
Winkler, Tod (1998). *Composing Interactive Music, Techniques and Ideas Using Max.* Cambridge (Massachusetts, USA): The MIT Press.

Let's Improvise Together

A testbed for a formalism in language, vision and sounds integration

Riccardo Antonini
Consorzio Roma Ricerche, Università di Roma "Tor Vergata", Italy

In the Amusement project one of the goals is the integration between different aspects of the interaction at distance through Virtual Worlds. During the process of pursuing that goal we experienced the need of language, vision and music integration in a multi-user distributed virtual environment. Hence we implemented a game 'Let's-Improvise-Together' as testbed for our views on integration. In the following a discursive as well as a formal description of the game is illustrated, the formal description will be used to discuss our view on language, vision and music integration, and finally some conclusions are drawn.

1. Goals of the game

The researchers of the Amusement project,[1] creators of 'Let's-Improvise-Together', adhere to the idea that while there is a multitude of online games now available in cyberspace, it appears that relatively few are focused on providing a positive, friendly and productive experience for the user.

In the Amusement project we have designed and implemented a virtual environment oriented towards the experience of:

- the importance of cooperation,
- the importance of creativity, and
- the importance of emotion.

While online on Amuse (1998a) or Amuse2 (1998b) (Figure 1, 2, 3) the users practice their cooperation skills working together on the construction of their Virtual Multimedia Sculpture (Figure 1). The creativity of the users is also stimulated when they arrange the pre-defined objects, add animated textures

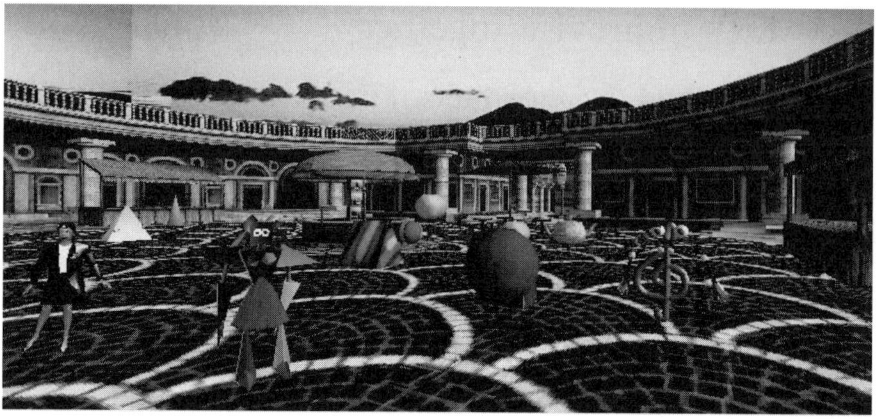

Figure 1. The virtual piazza

and sounds to them. The more creative among the users can design their own objects, textures, animations and sounds.

The *ability to cooperate* is a valuable skill, but we humans do not always do what is best for us, a fact evidenced by the large number of computer games which pander to the opposite end of the spectrum of human nature. Moreover the sensibility towards the cooperation/competition balance is growing, and, in fact, a world dedicated to peace education through cooperation has been open in the Active Worlds universe: Peace World (1999).

Moreover, while many games are tightly rule-based, on the other hand improvisation is one of the most proving fields of investigation on *creativity* as testified, for example, by the fact that it has been taken as "leitmotif" of the "Doors of Perception 5" Conference (1998), among others.

High *emotional impact.* To be clear: the emotional impact is on the players themselves, not on the avatars, that, in our cases, have a limited, if any, autonomous emotional capability (of course, they are autonomous under other aspects). Moreover, in our games the emotion is based also on the fact of being together. Discussing the deep psychological implications between playing and the perception of reality is beyond the scope of this paper, nevertheless for an 'ante litteram' discussion see Winnicott (1982) and for a more specific one, Suler (1998).

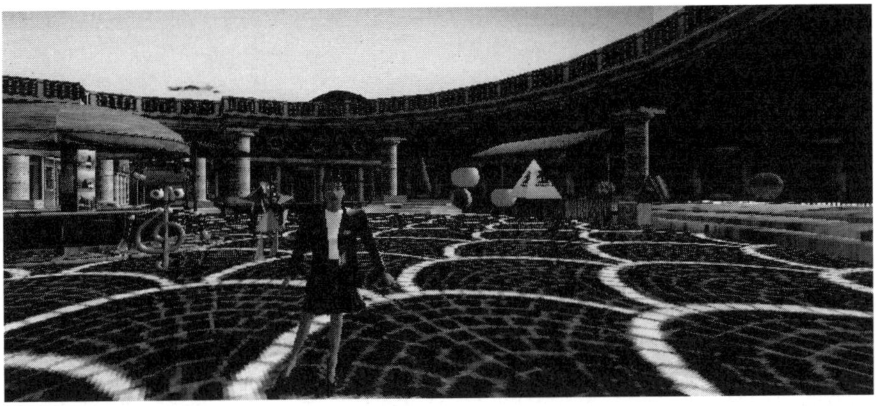

Figure 2. Another view of the virtual piazza

2. Description of the game

The avatar arrives in a certain area where there are many sound-blocks/objects (Figure 2). He may add sound "property" to existing ones. He can add new objects at will. Each object may represent a different sound, they do not have to though. The avatar walks around and chooses which objects he likes. He makes copies of these and adds sounds or changes the sounds on existing ones, then with all of the sound-blocks combined makes his personalized "instrument".

Now any player can make sounds on the instrument by approaching or bumping into a sound-block. The way that the avatar makes sounds on the instrument can vary.

At the end of the improvising session, the 'composition' will be saved on the instrument site, along with the personalized instrument. In this way, each user of the Amusement Center will leave behind him a unique instrumental creation, that others who visit the Center later will be able to play on and listen to. The virtual compositions, along with their relevant 3D environment are broadcasted via Italian RAI3 (freq. 11.534 GHz pol. V) on Hot Bird 1, 13 degree east, and can be received and experienced on PCs equipped with a commercial receiver board. There are, among others, more than four thousand receiver boards in italian schools. The idea of broadcasting interactive virtual worlds has been pioneered by Toshio Iwai (1994) and Lili Cheng. The implementation in the Amusement project is described in Antonini (1999a, b)

The fully creative experience of making a new instrument can be obtained

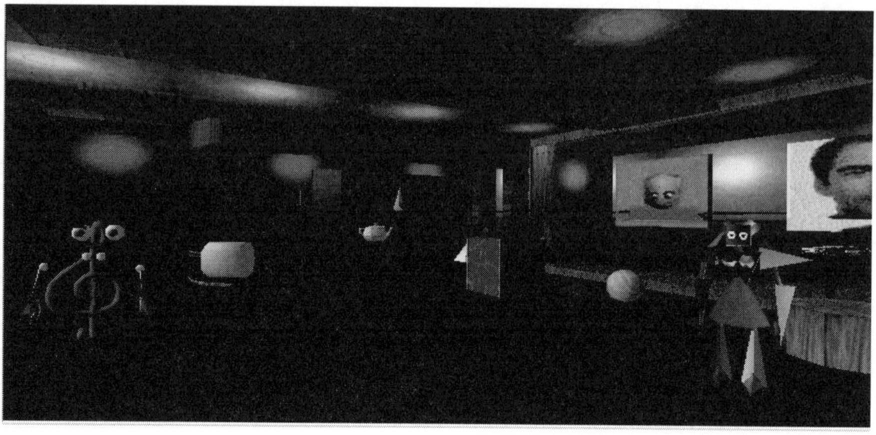

Figure 3. The virtual music club

anyhow also by connecting via Internet to Active Worlds world 'Amuse' (1998a) and 'Amuse2' (1998b) .

Animated colorful sounding objects can be assembled by the user in the Virtual Environment as a sort of sounding instrument (Figure 3). We refrain here deliberately from using the word *musical instrument*, because the level of control we have on the sound in terms of rhythm and melody, among other parameters, is very limited. It resembles instead, very closely, to the primitive instruments used by humans in some civilizations or to the experience made by children making sound out of ordinary objects. The dimension of cooperation is of paramount importance in the process of building and using the virtual sounding instrument. The instrument can be built on one's own effort but preferably by a team of cooperating users. The cooperation has as an important corolary: the sharing of the experience. The shared experience finds its permanence in the collective memory of the sounding instruments built. The sounding instrument can be seen also as a virtual sculpture, indeed this sculpture is a multimedial one. The objects have properties that ranges from video animation to sound to virtual physical properties like solidity. The role of the user representation in the Virtual World, called avatar, is important because it conveys, among other things, the user's emotions. It is worth pointing out that the Avatar has no emotions on its own but it simply expresses the emotions of the user behind it. In a way it could be considered a sort of actor performing the script that the user gives to it in real-time while playing.

Natural *language* is used for the cooperative task of building and experiencing the virtual instrument, but also body language and facial expression are used by our avatars. The user, when building the virtual instrument, uses some skills that, in our view, are closely related to the ones used for expression by means of natural language. We cannot claim to have made a new language in 'Let's Improvise Together', nevertheless, the users, while playing, rearrange not only the layout of the virtual objects and their properties, but also the rules of their use, creating some sort of conventions for their expression.

We tried to organize the game as an improvisation rather than a tight rule based game. The improvisation happens in two steps. First the users organize their virtual space. That means, in practice, that they buid their own virtual instrument. Hence they play with the instrument. The two steps are iterated in a potentially endless process. Since no part of the expression tools is completely determined, the user can, if not build a new language, at least personalise the existing one.

The *vision* is used for the perception of the 3D objects in the virtual space but vision is also used for ex-periencing the virtual instrument. The vision is integrated by some sense of physical feedback given by the objects, for example an object can stop the avatar from going through it and possibly make a sound when bumped into it.

The game, 'Let's Improvise Together,' is mostly related to the experience of sound rather than the experience of *music.* Moreover, the sound is not important *per se* but as an additional dimension to the experience in Virtual Worlds. We have already said that we have deliberatedly circumscribed the acoustic experience to generic sound only. Nevertheless it is possible to have real music pieces as properties of the object constituting the virtual instrument. We have not studied this more complex case thoroughly up to now though.

The other important element of the integration is related to the memory of the experience left by the user in the Virtual World. The new layout is explored and experienced. The layout is a permanent editable memory.

3. Formal definitions

If VR can be regarded as a language as illustrated for example in Matsuba (1999) formal definitions are needed. The formal definition of the language used in the Amusement project game 'Let's Improvise Together' is presented in the following. The goal is to provide a unified formalism for the description of natural language, vision and sound in the framework of this game.

The *lexicon* Γ is constituted by the set of all the objects γ_i

$$\Gamma \equiv (\gamma_i) \quad \forall i \in I$$

I is the set of all integers.

Each object γ_i, in turn, can be built using an *alphabet* Π of properties π_j that last for a given amount of time τ_j

$$\Pi \equiv (\pi_j) \quad \forall j \in Z; \quad Z \subseteq I$$
$$\gamma_i \equiv \{\pi_j, \tau_j\} \quad \forall i \in I; \quad \forall j \in Z_i; Z_i \subseteq Z$$

Permanent properties are

$$\{\pi_j, \tau_j \mid \tau_j = \infty\}$$

Transient properties are

$$\{\pi_j, \tau_j \mid \tau_j < \infty\}$$

The improvisation can be defined in several ways each one reflecting a particular aspect of its creation and/or its fruition. Two possible different definitions that have been used in the Amusement project follows

1. The improvisation can be defined, in a synchronic sense, as a given non ordered sub-set Φ_k of objects γ_i arranged in the 3D virtual space. A sub-set S_k of indexes *i* identifies the subset of objects used in the k-th improvisation. S_k is a non ordered set.

$$\Phi_k \equiv (\gamma_i) \quad \forall i \in S_k$$

To each object γ_i, a triplet Ω_k of cartesian coordinates is associated for each improvisation Φ_k

$$\Omega_k \equiv \{x_i, y_i, z_i\} \quad \forall i \in S_k$$
$$\Phi_k \equiv \{\gamma_i, \Omega_k\} \quad \forall i \in S_k$$

2. Alternatively the improvisation , can be regarded, in a dyachronic sense, as a trajectory, described as a parametric curve Ψ_k in the 3D space as follows

$$\Psi_k(t) \equiv x(t), y(t), z(t)$$

each time

$$\Psi_k(t) = \Omega_k \quad \forall i \in S_k$$

an asynchronous *event* occurs. The former means that the avatar has litterally to bump into the object in order to satisfy it. Another similar condition for proximity can be given defining Ω_k as an interval

$$\Omega_k \equiv \{ x_i, y_i, z_i\} \qquad \forall i \in S_k$$
$$x_{ia} < x_i < x_{ib}$$
$$y_{ia} < y_i < y_{ib}$$
$$z_{ia} < z_i < z_{ib}$$

Now the condition can be written as

$$\Psi_k(t) \subseteq \Omega_k \qquad \forall i \in S_k$$

An event is a sub-set $e_i(t)$ of properties π_j, each one of them becoming manifest at the time t, for a given amount of time τ_j each, if and only if the previous condition is met.

$$e_i(t) \subseteq \gamma_i \qquad \forall i \in S_k$$

we can also have periodic events defined as follows

$$e_i(t + T_j) = e_i(t) \; T_j > \tau_j ; \forall i \in I ; \forall j \in Z_i$$

4. Formal discussion

Now that a formal framework has been defined we will discuss how it has helped us, in our Amusement project, to integrate language, vision and music.

The first observation to be made is that the set Π can be defined as direct sum of sub-sets

$$\Pi \equiv \Pi_1 \oplus \Pi_2 \oplus \ldots \oplus \Pi_h \quad \forall h \in H$$

the sub-sets are Colors, Sounds, Shapes, Texts and many others. The important point is that we can treat them formally, in this framework, in the same way.

The second observation is related to the rhythm or tempo. We have formally defined that

$$\gamma_i \equiv \{\pi_j, \tau_j\} \quad \forall i \in I; \; \forall j \in Z_i ; Z_i \subseteq Z$$

the former means that each property π_j has its carachteristic duration τ_j. Each property becomes manifest at a generic time t and possibly from then on repeats itself every interval T_j as long as the equation

$$\Psi_k(t) \subseteq \Omega_k \qquad \forall i \in S_k$$

is satisfied. When the previous condition is not met any longer the property is switched off. The important point here is that we can treat formally, in the same way, the rhythm of sound and the frame rate at which the animations are rendered.

In this way, for example percussive sound rhythms can be associated to periodic animation of patterns. Their relevant τ_j and T_j need not to be the same and forms of compatibility, if not of harmony, can be experienced.

Note

1. Universidad Politecnica de Madrid, Consorzio Roma Ricerche, Ecole Superieure de Telecomunication Bretagne, Skydata S.p.A., Instituto Europeo de Transferencia de Tecnologia. Amusement — An International Virtual Space for Individual and Collective Presence and Interaction. *i3 Esprit project 25197* http://www.i3net.org/i3projects.

References

Amuse (1998a). http.//193.204.117.70. . (In order to see world download browser from http://www.activeworlds.com. and connect to world).

Amuse2 (1998b). http://www.amuse.roma.ccr.it/amuseaw/. (In order to see world download browser from http://www.activeworlds.com. and connect to world).

Antonini, Riccardo (1999a). Evolvable Believable Agents for Broadcasted Interactive Game Shows. In The Society for the Study of Artificial Intelligence and Simulation of Behaviour (Eds.), *Proceedings of AISB '99–Edinburgh — apr 99* (1–8), http://www.darmstadt.gmd.de/mobile/aisb99/submissions.

Antonini, Riccardo (1999b). Broadcasting Digitally Generated Gameshows. In *2nd International Workshop on Presence — Colchester UK.*

Cheng, L. YORB. http://www.research.microsoft.com/~lilich/.

DOORS OF PERCEPTION 5–Play (1998), http://www.doorsofperception.com/.

Iwai, Toshio (1994). UgoUgoLhuga. In *Fujii Television, Japan* , http://www.iamas.ac.jp/~iwai/ugolhu/index.html.

Kim, Amy Jo (1998). Ritual reality. In CGDC Proceedings, http://www.naima.com/resume.html.

Matsuba, Stephen N. (1999). Speaking Spaces: Virtual reality, Artificial Intelligence and the Construction of Meaning. In Anton Nijholt, Olaf Donk and Betsy van Dijk (Eds.), *Interaction in Virtual Worlds — Entschede Netherland* (127).

Peace World (1999). (In order to see world download browser from http://www.activeworlds.com. and connect to world).

Suler, John (1998). Cyberspace and psycological space, http://www.rider.edu/users/suler/psycyber/psycyber.html.

Winnicott, D. W. (1982). *Playing and Reality.* New York, NY: Routledge.

On tonality in Irish traditional music

Sean Ó Nualláin
Nous Research, Dublin 4, Ireland

1. The quest for celtic fusion

A common complaint made by first-time listeners to Irish traditional music is that the tunes "go nowhere" (I hasten to add that very little of the music associated with the Riverdance show is Irish traditional music). When coupled with the clerical and rural associations of this music, up to the 70's or so, this musical directionlessness provoked a near-hatred among the young. The attempt to produce a musical expression that would be palatable to the record-buying public and true to the roots of the tradition has since the 1970's consumed the musical careers, and in some cases the lives, of some of the most gifted artists in Ireland.

The first band to make a breakthrough was the celtic-rock fusion band, Horslips. They set themselves a gargantuan task; an artistic statement that would integrate authentically-played Irish traditional tunes (on fiddle and concertina), and rock (with a Jethro Tull — like lineup of rock rhythm section, electric guitar, flute and keyboards). Moreover, they sought inspiration for their lyrics in such Irish epics as the Tain Bo Cuailgne, a Gilgamesh-scale creation. Before the tensions inherent in the project wore the band members out, they had become big enough to take out full-page ads in Rolling Stone, after their album charted in Britain. Apart from the occcasional Celtic phrase from the guitar, the fusion in general consisted of Irish tunes played with a rock accompaniment. The ultimate demise of their project has caused their later, more commercially successful followers like U2 to avoid the risk Horslips took in venturing into traditional music. Ironically, Horslips probably could have made more money as a straight rock band.

The current mania for celtic music was not as pronounced in the 70's. In parallel with Horslips, a group of talented folk bands were attempting, against the tide, to create fusions with rock and balkan music using almost solely acoustic instruments. Their material was drawn from various streams of the surprisingly wide Irish folk tradition. Clannad, who later achieved some commercial success (Enya was also, briefly, a member), drew on the song tradition of their native Donegal in such albums as Clannad 2, Fuaim, and Crann Úll. In the latter two, they collected songs from the remoteness of Tory Island and produced breathtaking arrangements with a jazz saxophonist. However, this project, too, collapsed under the strain of attempting to reconcile simple melodies with the rich harmonies often associated withjazz. Obviously, Miles Davis' modal period might have been a worthwhile template, and perhaps a real opportunity was missed here.

Meanwhile, Planxty benefited from the Balkan wanderings of their member, Andy Irvine, as later did Riverdance. Irvine introduced Balkan music, whose ethos resembles Irish music but the harmonic and rhythmic structure of which could not be more different, into the tradition. It is fair to say that Planxty, as represented in such albums as "The well below the Valley" is a fully-realised artistic statement. A celtic-balkan fusion was achieved which, dumbed down, comprises the main attraction of "Riverdance". It may suffice to say that the composer of Riverdance, Bill Whelan, worked with Planxty and produced an Ur-Riverdance called, logically enough, "Timedance", for the 1982 Eurovision song contest interlude. In 1995, he resurrected the genre and, with the help of Michael Flatley, history was created. And so it happened that a group of Irish and Irish-American musicians became millionaires by the exploitation of Balkan music.

In the quarter-century that has passed since the seminal statements of Clannad and Planxty, the exploration of Irish music has continued at a much slower pace. A certain consensus has emerged about how to accompany Irish traditional tunes on chordal instruments (see below) . The music has become so popular that any moderately competent Irish traditional group can make a living on the US college and Irish emigrant circuit. Yet, having established a consensus on how to communicate with an audience that now, disillusioned with the over-commercial nature of corporatist rock and pop, hungers after the authenticity of folk, the question has shifted to how to combine celtic music and jazz. To do this, we need to explore its harmonic structure. There are several cultural hurdles to be overcome.

The first is that jazz was labelled "The devil's music" by the Irish Catholic Church as far back as the 1920's and they deliberately promoted an asexualised version of Irish dance music to compete with it. Instead, then, of risking their immortal souls (as a contemporary politician put it) listening to big bands, the faithful were urged to dance to "céilí" bands in a manner that pre-empted physical contact. The main positive contribution of Riverdance has been to counteract this; however, the cultural split between Irish music and jazz has never been healed. There are very few musicians in Ireland who can play both. Secondly, the fact that jazz is a fortiori an American music makes Irish jazz musicians unwilling to risk what has usually been a hard-won reputation in the field by attempting fusion.

However, some progress has been made. The director of the portentously-titled Irish world music centre, Michéal O Súilleabháin, was developing a wonderful celtic modal jazz piano style, represented in some tracks on his "Dolphin's Way" album, before developing the less successful "hiberno jazz ensemble". Melanie O'Reilly (see www.mistletoemusic.com), a jazz chanteuse who has played, inter alia, the Lincoln Centre and been invited to play the Blue Note, has returned to her native Ireland and is producing a new fusion genre with the poet Nuala ni Dhomhnaill, whose oeuvre is solely in Gaelic.

Celtic-jazz fusion can use a variety of different techniques. One is quite simply to take the harmonic structures that have been agreed on for Irish music and improvise on the chords. A second is to return, as suggested above, to Miles Davis' modal period. Coincidentally, Miles felt drawn to two of the main modes of Irish music i.e. Dorian and Myxolydian. Therefore, in tunes like "So What?" (Dorian) and "All Blues" (Dorian and Myxolydian), an aspiring fusion artist can find material for his project. This is all the truer for Miles' partial eschewing of blues roots in the former piece. Finally, both African and Irish musicians were sufficiently impoverished to develop a "mouth music", called "Scat" by jazzers, and "Lilting" by Irish musicians. Archival material reveals remarkable resemblances between the two, which O'Reilly, in particular, exploits.

2. Tonality and harmony

Let us now formalise some of the discussion above. That Irish traditional music is radically different from "climactic" diatonic music is indeed true. By "diatonic" here, I mean music that relates to a tonic, leading to the kind of patterns of tension and release thereof we can justly call "climactic". Irish music, by contrast, is in general modal. Instead of implicitly referring continually to a triad of 1–3–5, i.e. a major or minor chord, it relates to a single note, i.e. a centre of tonality. Modal music, classically considered, uses the standard major scale but starts it from different points. If we consider the scale C-D-E-F-G-A-B, then the mode beginning at C and ending at C is Ionian; D to D is Dorian; and so on for Phrygian, Lydian, Myxolydian, Aeolian and Locrian. Better to characterise the modes, we can in general point to an harmonic tension between two chords which also gives hints about the emotional flavour of the mode. The exception to this rule is the Aeolian, where the 6th note seems to play the same role, if played on top of a minor chord with its root as the centre of tonality of the mode. Interestingly, this note is often omitted from Irish "minor" tunes. Due to historical reasons, the laboured elucidation of which is an enormous Irish-American academic industry, Irish music remained frozen at, or sometimes indeed regressed into, the modal state.

I do not wish my Stateside colleagues to forego the pleasure of their annual summer trips to Ireland, but here in short is the story: From the end of the 17th century until 1829, Irish Catholics were subjected to laws of such repressive rigour that they were known simply as "The Penal Laws". Immediately following their repeal in 1829, a major cull of the Irish Catholic population took place between 1845 and 1850. At a very conservative estimate, 1 million died and 1 million emigrated during this period. The pretext for the cull was the failure of the potato harvest, due to blight. However, the accounts from the major Irish harbours during this period show massive exportation of food occurring. It is fair to say that the English dream, originating with Edmund Spenser, of solving all Anglo-Irish difficulties by ensuring a massive population disparity between the two islands had been achieved. Indeed, it is fair to say that, since Oliver Cromwell's mid-seventeeenth century visit, the killing-off of a third of the Irish population was a once-a-century obligation for the English, until the Irish took the hint and began to emigrate in sufficient numbers. During the Penal Law period, Catholics were prohibited from living in incorporated towns and either attending or teaching school. It goes without saying that they were denied access to the professions. Irish musicians were like archaeologists picking shards in the ruins of an ancient civilisation in an attempt to reconstruct it. Nor were Irish musicians able to emulate Welsh choirs in polyphonic experiments; in a country where free assembly is prohibited, no such genre can exist. (The Victorian British went on to repeat the social engineering in others of their colonies, as described by Mike Davis in "Late Victorian Famines" — Verso 2000)

The contemporary of Geminiani, Turlough O' Carolan, wrote some tunes in which the tension between modal and diatonic is almost painful in that we can see how a normal Irish classical music might have developed. However, there is no Mozart or Beethoven, let alone Wagner or Schönberg in the Irish musical pantheon. Harmonic development stops at a level corresponding to early mediaeval Europe. Similarly, for all the 7:8 and other Balkan borrowings in Riverdance and its clones, Irish music is in general rhythmically simple with 4:4 and 6:8 tunes predominating over the very occasional 9:8 or 12:8. Getting the accents right is altogether another matter, which is the first area of complexity we find.

In order to sustain the idea of a universal grammar of music, with equally complex "native" musics throughout the world, we need to find other such areas. We shall certainly not find it in textbook treatments of the modes. Normally, we are exposed to a sol-fa introduction in such treatises, with Irish music introduced as belonging to the do, re, sol, la modes. To give them their Greek tags, we can call these Ionian, Dorian, Myxolydian and Aeolian. Let us look at examples from each mode, and indicate in outline how each tune might be harmonised. Ionian, as was mentioned, has its centre of tonality at the first note of the major scale which is used in the piece. It is thus quite easy to confuse, say, D ionian with D major. However, any attempt to harmonise a D Ionian piece with the standard artillery of D major chords quickly comes to grief. In the following tune (an English rendering of the title is "Lord Gordon's"), harmonisation of the first 16 bars is best achieved by establishing a tension between a D major chord and A dominant 7th with a fourth suspended (Figure 1).

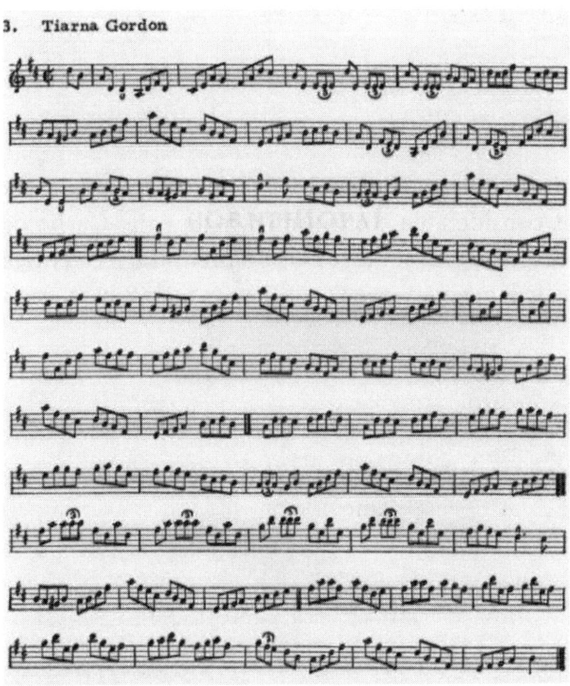

Figure 1.

Let us now look at a tune in A Dorian. This uses the scale of G, but with a center of tonality of A. Similarly, G dorian will use the scale of F but with a center of tonality at G. Miles Davis produced two musical phrases which will help us understand how modality, and in particular Dorian modality, works. The first is the bassline introduction to "Autumn Leaves" on the "Somethin' Else" album (Figure 2).

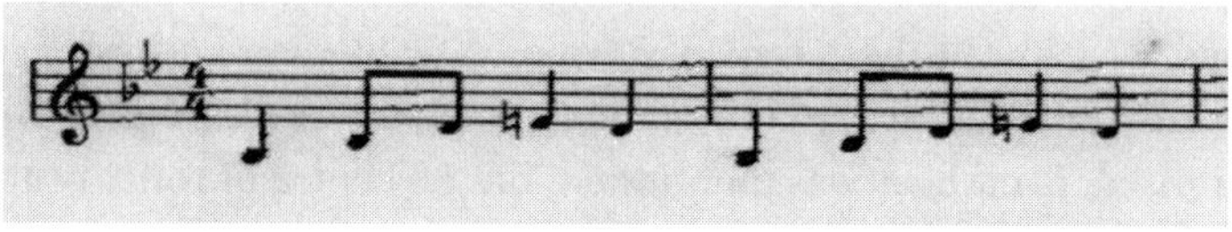

Figure 2.

The second will allow us to understand what we mean by "harmonic tension". Corresponding to the bass line above, we can play these two chords (Figure 3).

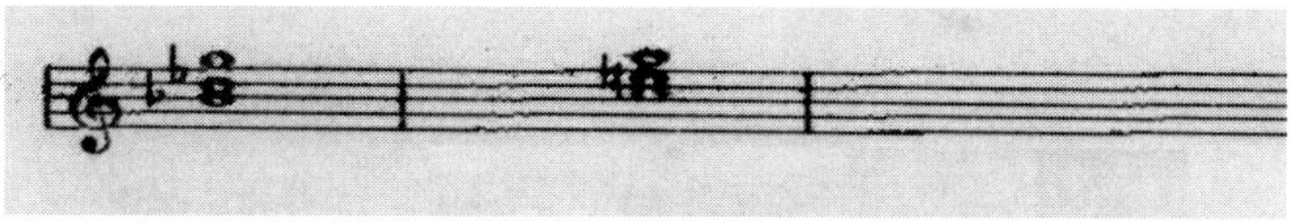

Figure 3.

Now let's look at that A Dorian Irish tune. "The maids of Mount Cisco" (it is a matter of considerable contention whether the Gaelic or English titles should take precedence, as some feel that Irish music is essentially a reaction to losing the Gaelic language) is a classic 3-part reel (8 bars, each played twice) (Figure 4).

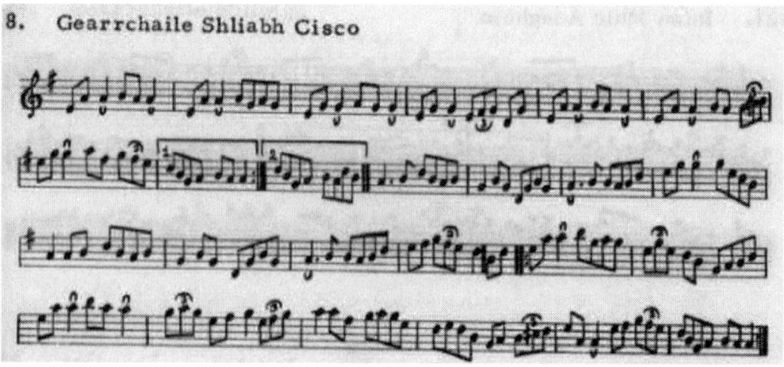

Figure 4.

Again, accompaniment is structured by tensions between the A minor, E minor and G major chords.

Myxolydian was most famously used by Miles is his piece “All Blues”, where he explores the modal consequences of the use of the flattened 7th in blues. Briefly, the first part of the tune is in G myxolydian, corresponding to the scale of C and neatly defined tonally by the G dominant 7th chord; the bridge is in G dorian, whose tonality can be suggested in the context by C dominant 7th. It is Miles at his most playful; a modal exercise in 6:8 is yet “All Blues”. (I fear the copyright repercussions of reproducing my “real book” rendering of this piece, the only accurate one I know, here; jazzers will sympathise). The stunning “Wheels of the world” reel, the definitive version of which was recorded by Tommy Peoples, follows. The key is G; however, harmonisation is achieved by contrasting the D major of the first bar with the C major (alternated with by A minor) of the second bar (Figure 5).

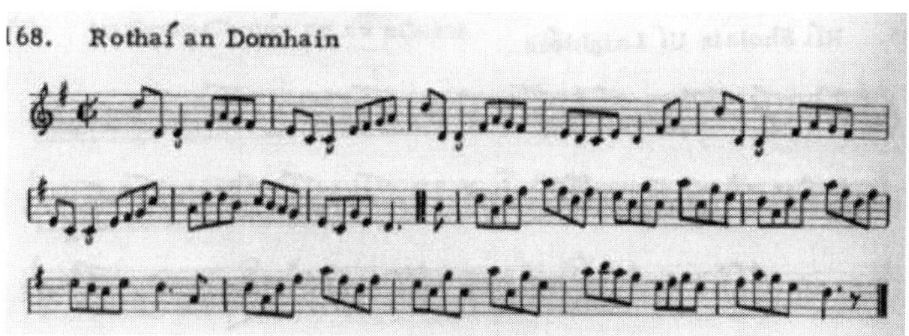

Figure 5.

Aeolian tunes are hard to come by in Irish music. The first movement of Gorecki’s “Symphony of sorrowful songs” is mainly Aeolian; jazz musicians have also used this mode. Morrison’s jig is a fine example of an Aeolian Jig, despite the incidental sharpened c’s; E minor is at the core of any prospective harmonisation (Figure 6).

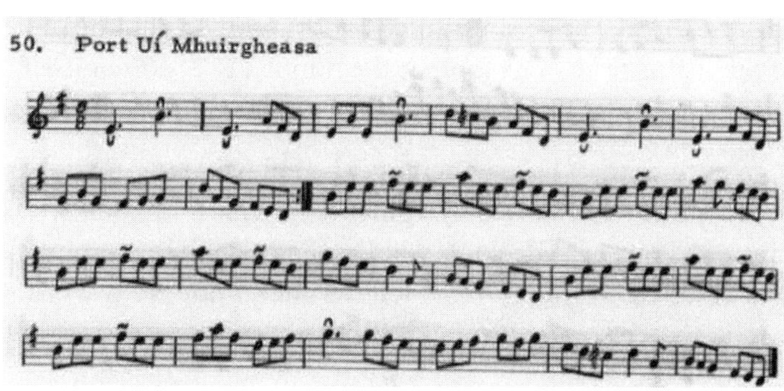

Figure 6.

However, the story may be a deal more complicated. In the past fifty years or so, the Irish have been able to afford chordal instruments: pianos, guitars, and, remarkably enough, mandolas, citterns and bouzoukis. (The Irish-Balkan musical link is worth a book in itself, as may by now be clear). Many folk guitarists, in particular, have been presented with the problem of how to apply their craft to Irish music. Lacking any signposts, many saw their task as finding the chords already there, as they were expert in doing in learning Neil Young and Bob Dylan songs from LPs. Their experiences indicate there may be order in the chaos. The results may be surprisingly sophisticated and I summarise them below. Others, perhaps the majority, bowed to the inevitable and tuned their guitars to a major or (suspended) fourth chord, seeing their task as essentially that of providing a drone.

3. Rules for accompaniment of Irish music

Standard modes; Ionian, Dorian, Mixolydian, Aeolian.
Standard Progressions;

1. Tonic |dominant| tonic (I V I)
2. Tonic| sub dominant |dominant (I IV V)
3. Relative minor to tonic '| dominant| relative minor to tonic (VI m V VI m)

Rules for substitution in traditional music

1. The minor chord corresponding to the centre of tonality can be substituted for by
(a) the subdominant Major or sub dominant major 7th
(b) The relative minor or minor 7th to this sub dominant
For example, E minor can be substituted for by C major or Cmajor 7th, the other natural intervals like the 11th and 13th, and A minor or A minor 7th
2. Any minor chord can be substituted for by a minor 7th, the minor 7th of the 6th of the major scale of its toot, or the minor 11 version of itself.
3. For major modes; suspended 2nd, 4th, and 6ths can be substituted

However, many guitarists have undergone the following traumatic experience; a simple-sounding tune is started by a piper or fiddler (both difficult specimens of humanity) and our hero decides "Ah! Dorian". There is an immediate clash and he switches to Myxolydian. What follows after is not pretty. What seems to be the case is that in searching for full musical self-expression in a modal framework, Irish and Scottish musicians found the plagal modes, hypomyxolydian in particular (I am open to dialogue on what exactly these modes are!). An example follows. For the first two bars, "Rakish Paddy" seems a straightforward A Dorian tune; then, however, the C becomes sharpened, leaving the accompanist stranded. The solution is to regard the tune as harmonically A myxolydian, with the harmonic tension being between an A suspended fourth chord and G major. So we now have the following scenario; scale is G, centre of tonality is D (note that's where the first part of the tune ends), and the harmonic tension is A suspended 4 and G major (Figure 7).

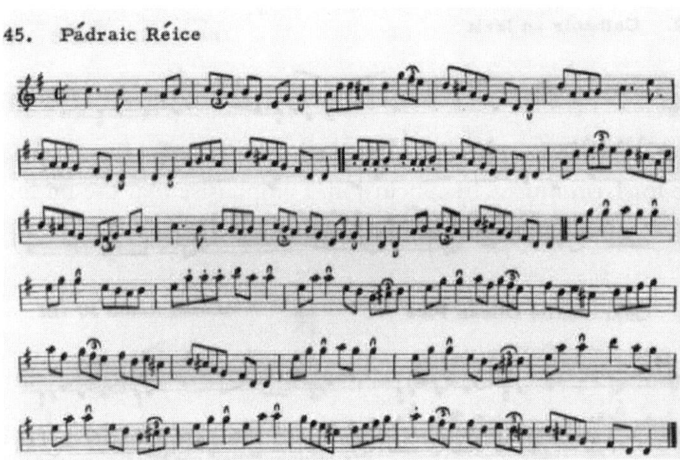

Figure 7.

A related scenario is one in which the accompanist plays a "modal" drone like accompaniment over a tune like the "Salamanca" or "Charles O'Connor", both of which were obviously written with very clear chord changes. The "Salamanca", written in honour of a seminary in that city which trained many Irish priests during the period of the penal laws, must be harmonised after the two lead-in notes as two bars D major, 2 bars E minor, 1 bar B minor, etc. (Figure 8).

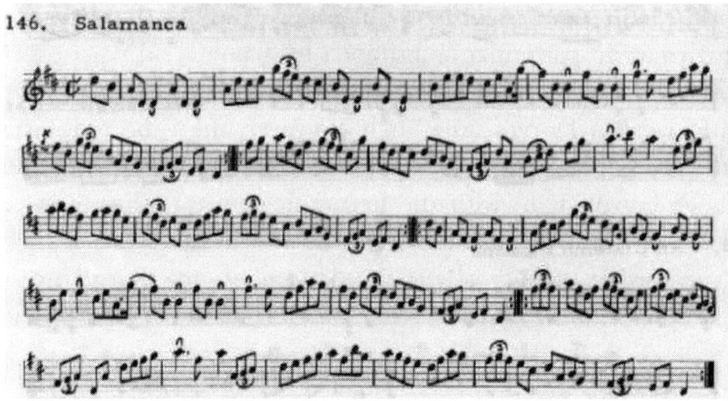

Figure 8.

This is the type of knowledge we will need to create a proper improvisational structure for Irish music. In conclusion, I emphasise that the findings of this short paper about the hidden complexities of Irish music just scratch the surface.

Further reading

Breathnach, Breandan (1971). *Folk music and dances of Ireland.* Cork: Mercier Press.

Vallely, Fintan (Editor) (1999). *The companion to Irish traditional music.* Cork: University Press.

The relationship between the imitation and recognition of non-verbal rhythms and language comprehension

Dilys Treharne
University of Sheffield, England

1. Introduction

The young child learns language through the interaction of his personal attributes, such as memory, attention, reception of sensory information, with those of the environment, such as social interaction, stimulating experiences and language model. If his personal development allows him to receive and use information and opportunities as they occur in his environment, further development can take place. In this way a matrix of communication skills evolves, involving spoken language, concept development, motor skills, social skills, script knowledge etc. The child receives the information through his sensory receptors, all of which contribute in some way to his language development, although for the majority of children the auditory channel is the most important for language.

The communication matrix has a driving force of maturation to propel it but must also have some form of scaffolding to enable the child to structure his experience. It is proposed that the rhythmic pattern that underlies all human behaviour is the basis of one form of scaffold. Using a rhythmic pattern of movement enables a person to master complex motor tasks and long strings of numbers, syllables or instructions are easier to recall if memorised in a rhythmic format.

Rhythm is the relative timing between adjacent and non-adjacent elements in a behaviour sequence (Martin 1972). It is hierarchical and temporal, the place of each element in time being relative to the place of all others. A rhythmic pattern is a sequence in which some elements are accented and some unaccented. The accents occur regularly producing a basic tempo, the rate of which may be changed. The number and length of stimuli and intervals between stimuli vary in a complementary manner between the accents. For example, in music, a basic 4/4 time can be realised in a number of ways, although the relative time to produce each bar or pattern remains the same, being determined by the basic tempo at which the piece is played. The pattern, marked by the accents is recognisable at fast or slow speeds. In music variations in pitch and volume add tune, quality and expression.

(1) 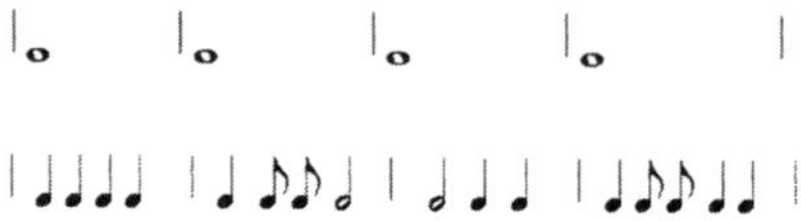

The same applies to human language. It is hierarchically organised with rules governing its structure at all levels. Spoken language, the medium through which most children acquire their linguistic knowledge is characterised by a rhythmic pattern peculiar to each language. Babies rapidly learn to recognise the rhythm of the language spoken around them and respond positively to it. Certain languages such as English are stress-timed, which means that the time between stressed syllables is roughly equal. However as in music the number of events or syllables between stresses, may vary. Consider the sentence

(2) - | - - | - | - | - - | - | - | |
The children are making fruity buns, and the cook is making fruit pies

The periods between the stresses, referred to as feet,[1] are roughly equal in real time, yet | *children are* | contains three syllables and |*making* | just two, | *fruity* | has two syllables in the foot and | *fruit* | has one. The syllables are lengthened or shortened to accommodate the differing number within the foot in order to maintain the same overall time per foot.

It would seem then that the rhythm of language is potentially important to verbal expression and comprehension at least in stress timed languages. Certainly listeners perceive and respond to rhythm and their body movements synchronise with the speech rhythm they hear (Condon 1986). This is evident even in the baby listening to his carer. Clearly then the child is aware of speech rhythms from an early stage. Indeed it appears to be one of the first aspects of speech to which the child responds.

Crystal (1987) states that "stress, duration, pause and especially rhythm" are relevant "to the expressive organisation and decoding of speech". The hierarchical nature of rhythmic patterns may allow processing of information at many different levels; from the rhythmic beats we hear to the rhythms of neuronal transmissions. Once a pattern is known it may be remembered, stored and retrieved at a *suprarhythmic* level and only if this results in failure will a more detailed analysis be needed.

Children with specific language difficulties frequently have disordered rhythmic patterns in their speech output. This poses the questions as to whether a poor rhythmic output reflects an inability to appreciate rhythmic patterns and whether children use rhythm in learning and decoding language. French which is regarded as a trailer-timed language, the stress occurring only at the end of a syntactic or semantic group, will provide different information to the learner and listener from a stress-timed language such as English. The French child acquires the syllable structure and trailer timed rhythm of his language before the middle of the second year whereas children in different more complex linguistic rhythmic environments master the rhythmic patterns of their language later (Konopczynski 1999).

Martin (1972) noted that segmentation of language into decodable units is guided by rhythmic expectancy. Studies investigating young children's ability to segment utterances into words indicated that rhythmic patterns may be used by some children to identify unknown sound sequences as words and that this usage increases between the ages of 5 and 7 years (Bialystok 1986). These studies explored the awareness and use of natural rhythms of language. Other studies have been concerned with the relationship between non-speech rhythmic awareness and language.

Lea (1980) and Shields (1981) both found a significant link between poor non-verbal rhythmic ability and language in children with specific language disorder. Both used tests of rhythmic ability that included perception of a change of rhythm, imitation of rhythmic patterns and synchronisation of a drum beat with a rhythmic pattern. Lea included a test of auditory memory and found significant correlation between rhythmic ability and auditory memory, rhythmic ability and language and language and auditory memory.

Organising material to be remembered into rhythmic chunks increases memory capacity. It is possible that recognition of the metrical patterns of speech allows more information to be stored in a working memory for decoding. Shields' (1981) study found a highly positive correlation between language comprehension and rhythmic ability and a less strong positive correlation between language expression and rhythmic ability. She also found that in children with normal language development the ability to imitate, detect change and synchronise rhythms increased with age.

The studies cited demonstrate a relationship between rhythmic ability and language but do not throw much light on the nature of the relationship or whether training in rhythmic tasks will improve language skills. Normally in spoken English the content or information carrying words are marked by stress. The young child's decoding mechanisms are limited and stress may alert the child to the important elements for decoding. A recognition and memory of the rhythmic pattern may facilitate his memory for the utterance while he decodes it. Rhythmic patterns may also facilitate predictions of aspects of language realisation (Giegerich, 1992).

In expression, children in their third year frequently use a 'ragbag' schwa to substitute for function words, the exact nature of which they are uncertain, but which they seem to know should be present to maintain the sentence rhythm. Jackson, Treharne, and Boucher (1997) reported an increase in the production of syllables in one and two word utterances in children with moderate learning difficulties when attention was drawn to the rhythm of the utterance and the child was required to clap the rhythm.

The study reported here attempts to investigate the relationship between a general appreciation of rhythm and the extent to which a child is able to use rhythm to interpret utterances and which aspects of rhythm, pattern or number of beats, is most important.

2. The study

Subjects

123 children from the reception, years 1, 2 and 4[2] of two local authority schools participated in the study. All the children in years 1 and 2 participated, a random selection from the reception class and the youngest children in year 4.

School pc is situated in a city suburb and draws mainly from social classes 3, 4 and 5. School wl is in a small town adjacent to the city and draws mainly from social classes 1, 2, and 3.

Table 1. Gender and number of children in each school in each year

	gender		school	
	male	female	pc	wl
year 0	5	8	6	7
1	24	16	27	13
2	31	22	19	34
4	11	6	8	9

Procedure

All children completed the PICAC (Porch 1974) Advanced tests of auditory function (vc), a test of rhythm imitation, rhythm matching and the comprehension of rhythmic substitution in sentences. The testing was carried out in a quiet room in the child's school.

Test of rhythm imitation (Figure 1)

A recording of a simple rhythm played on the piano using one note in the mid-frequency range was played to the child once. He was required to tap out the rhythm on the table. The response was marked in three ways:

i. according to the number of beats correct (rhybeats)
ii. whether the child recognised a change or not in the value of each beat (rhypatt)
iii. accuracy (beats and pattern) of the whole (rhyall).

Ten items were presented in this way ranging from simple two beat patterns to four beat patterns.

	Copying Rhythms	
♩ ♩	♪♪ ♩	♪♪ ♩ ♩
♪♪	♩ ♩ ♩	♩ ♪♪

Figure 1. Sample of rhythms presented for rhythm imitation task

Test of rhythm matching (rhysimil) (Figure 2)

A simple rhythm from the imitation test was played to the child, the tester attempted to tap it out and the child was required to say whether the tester was right or wrong. Five items were presented.

Judging sameness

	On tape	*tester taps*	*answer*	*child's response*
1.	♩♩	♩ ♩	right	
2.	♩ ♪♪	♩♩♩	wrong	
4.	♩ ♪♪ ♩	♪♪ ♩	wrong	

Figure 2. Sample of rhythms presented in rhythm matching task

Comprehension of rhythm substitution (compmiss)

The task was presented as an alien trying to learn English. When the alien did not know the word he substituted his own language which has the same tune as English but uses only the syllable *uh.* The task used the child's recognition of the stress and syllable pattern of the prepositions *on, under, in front of,* and *behind.*

The child was presented with a page of coloured pictures (Figure 3) depicting two objects in each of the listed relationships. Four sets of objects were used and the page was turned for each item to maintain interest. Before commencing the test the prepositions were elicited from the child in response to the pictures. The target sentences were presented on tape together with the pictures. Eight items were presented.

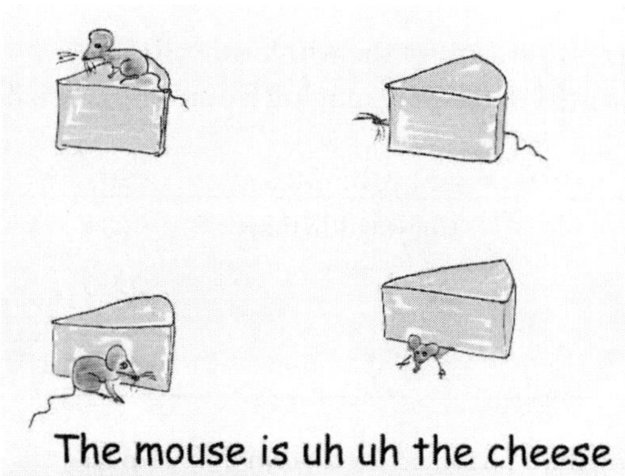

Figure 3. Sample page from the rhythm substitution test

Results

Table 2. Mean scores for each task for each year group

Year	CA(yrs)	VC	rhybeats	rhypatt	rhyall	rhysimil	compmiss
0 reception	5.22	13.06	5.58	4.92	4.23	3.07	2.46
1	6.32	13.77	7.93	7.9	7.38	3.25	3.5
2	7.22	14.22	9.4	9.07	8.77	3.87	3.9
4	9.14	14.49	9.8	9.88	9.76	4.17	5.3
Max score		15	10	10	10	5	8

The performance of the children from school wl was compared to the performance of the children from school pc on all measures. There was a difference in auditory verbal comprehension (VC) sig 0.004. There was no significant difference on any other measure.

A linear correlation was found between chronological age and the ability

i. to imitate rhythms: in terms of the number of beats (rhybeat), pattern (rhypatt) and totally correct in terms of number of beats and pattern (rhyall),
ii. to judge similarity (rhysimil) between rhythms,
iii. to understand spoken verbal instructions (VC)
iv. to correctly interpret missing words in a sentence frame from the rhythmic pattern of that word (compmiss).

All correlations are significant at the 0.01 level.

As may be expected the number of beats correctly identified and the patterns perceived are both highly correlated with the total rhythm scores (rhyall). Therefore only total scores (rhyall) will be reported further.

In order to examine the relationship between rhythmic ability and comprehension more closely a partial correlation was computed controlling for CA. A positive correlation was found between auditory verbal comprehension (VC) and copying rhythms (rhyall) and VC and judging similarity of rhythms (rhysimil) ($p=0.000$). A slightly less marked correlation was found between auditory verbal comprehension (VC) and the ability to infer correctly missing words (compmiss) (p0.001).

A further partial correlation was computed to enable a judgement to be made concerning the relationship between the different rhythmic skills and the ability to interpret incomplete sentences (compmiss). When auditory verbal comprehension (VC) was controlled there was still a positive correlation between imitation of rhythmic patterns and interpretation of missing words (p0.002) and a weaker positive correlation between judging similarity of rhythms and comprehension of partial sentences ($p=0.078$).

Graph 1 shows the direct relationship child by child for year 2 for the three measures of auditory verbal comprehension (VC), copying rhythmic patterns (rhyall) and comprehension of missing words from the rhythmic pattern (compmiss).

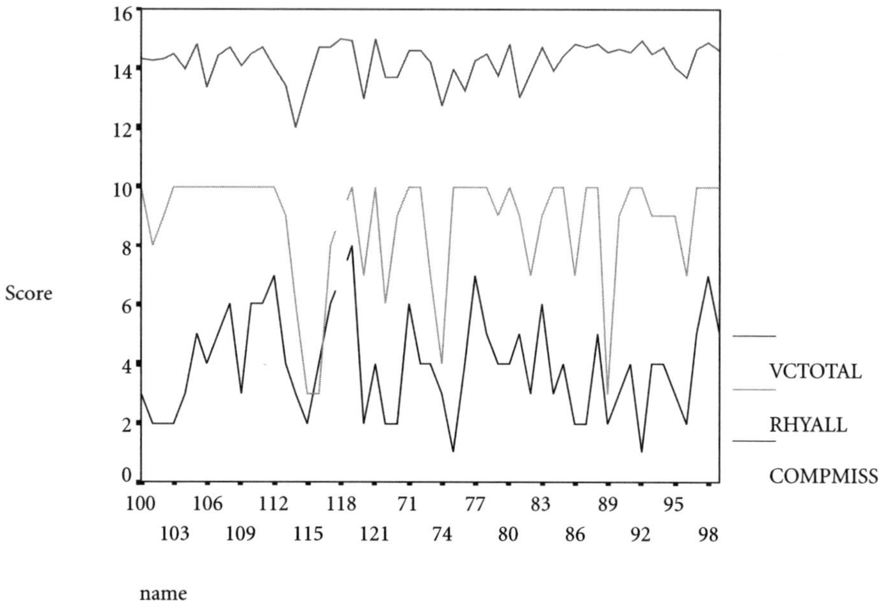

Graph 1. The relationship between the ability to copy rhythms (RHYALL), comprehend incomplete sentences using the prosodic pattern (COMPMSS) and verbal comprehension (VCTOTAL) in year 2 children

3. Comment

The ability to copy simple non-verbal rhythmic patterns, as measured in the current study, appears to develop most rapidly in the majority of children during their fifth year. Some children master the skill a little later and there may be minor errors persisting up until at least 9 years. The greatest difference in performance in this study was between the reception and year 1 children (4/5 and 5/6 year olds). The greatest variability in performance between children in a single year group was in the reception class (standard deviation 3.3949) followed closely by the year 1 children (SD 2.5288). By year 4 the majority of children were able to imitate patterns of two to four beats correctly (mean 9.76 SD .5623). The majority of children were able to indicate the number of beats before the pattern although a small number were aware of a change in pattern before they were able to reproduce either this or the number of beats accurately. This may have been due to a production difficulty rather than a perceptual error.

The ability to judge similarity between patterns showed very slow improvement over the four classes tested. This may have been due to the fact that many children were able to perform this task even in the reception class adding some weight to the notion that production problems may have interfered with performance on the imitation task.

Many children were still having difficulty in year 4 in using the rhythmic pattern of words to identify the word. Many of the errors made at this stage were related to the lack of perception of the stress pattern, that is <u>un</u>der or be<u>hind</u>. A number of children in spite of the preparatory check on vocabulary changed the target words associated with the picture to approximate the pattern e.g. -l- *(in front of)* was interpreted as *on top of.* Nevertheless there is a steady progression of ability between reception and year 4. This is a similar age range for development to that found by Bialystok 1986 concerning the ability to use natural language rhythms to segment utterances. The task in the present study requires the child to match the heard rhythm with his knowledge of the rhythmic pattern of the four possible words or phrases. Counting the number of beats can eliminate 50% of the possible words but the final selection must be made on the pattern of stressed and unstressed beats. The task requires development of auditory memory, prosodic knowledge and matching. The added complexity of the task may account for the slightly later development of this skill compared with Bialystok's task and simple non-verbal rhythmic matching. It may also account for the fact that many errors were due to mis-matching of the stress pattern i.e. children selected <u>un</u>der (l -) instead of be<u>hind</u> (- l) and vice versa.

The results of this study indicate that there is a developmental progression in the ability to copy and match simple non-verbal rhythmic patterns and that this parallels the development of verbal comprehension. Children who performed well on the rhythm tasks were more likely to have high scores on the verbal comprehension task, which required a good working memory for processing complex series of instructions. It is possible that working or processing memory was the link between the two tasks. If this were the case similar results would be found in cross-linguistic studies. Alternatively or in addition the rhythmic pattern of spoken language may alert the child to syntactic or semantic frameworks in which case similar results would be expected in languages using different rhythmic patterns such as French.

The final task given to the children required a different skill, that of using information that was always present but normally redundant, the rhythmic pattern, to comprehend statements. This type of knowledge is language specific. It is more complex in stress-timed languages such as English than in syllable-timed or trailer-timed languages such as French. Konopczynski (1999) notes that French and Spanish children start to use the rhythmic patterns of their language during their second year whereas English children do not until after 2 years. With the increased complexity of English rhythms comes more information, both the numbers of syllables and word stress pattern. Rhythms of syllable-timed languages would provide information on only the number of syllables in the missing word. In fact the findings of this study show that the younger children and those with lower verbal comprehension scores relied more on the number of syllables and the more advanced children were able to add the stress pattern into the processing task.

4. Conclusion

Language received through the auditory channel is processed temporally. Speech can be understood at a rate of 20 phonemes per second (Harley 1995). The acoustic properties of phonemes vary with their context and speech is a continuous changing stream of sound. Syllable boundaries and stress segmentation or rhythm facilitates recognition of sound patterns in continuous speech, providing a structure or scaffold within which the individual may move freely between fast track processing and detailed analysis as needed.

In many situations in which spoken language is used it is heard imperfectly for a number of personal and environmental reasons. However there are many redundant cues which enable the listener to interpret the meaning. Some of these redundancies are syntactic and semantic. When these are not present it is possible to use alternatives such as prosodic features. This study found a correlation between auditory verbal comprehension, non-verbal rhythmic awareness and the ability to understand incomplete sentences using rhythmic aspects of prosody.

It is possible that children who have good rhythmic ability are able to retain a sentence more completely in their working memory because their working memory is better or because using the rhythmic pattern gives them more processing time or more rapid processing ability than children who need to rehearse the whole sentence in order to process it. Those who are more advanced in their development of comprehension are more aware of and able to use a wider range of information cues including prosody and so are able to process incompletely heard sentences.

A second explanation may be that the children who have better rhythmic skills are then able to retain and use prosodic patterns, specifically rhythm in their decoding of imperfectly heard sentences.

Children who have a language disorder affecting their ability to learn and process syntactic and semantic information may be able to use prosodic features as a cue following training even if they do not naturally use prosody in decoding. Research has shown that drawing attention to the rhythmic pattern of words and phrases improves the production of single words and two word phrases (Jackson, Treharne and Boucher 1997). The current finding that children who can imitate rhythmic patterns are better at using rhythmic cues to complete incomplete sentences suggests that developing rhythmic awareness may be a valuable tool to facilitate comprehension.

Notes

The author would like to express her gratitude to the staff and pupils of Parson Cross and William Levick Schools without whose tolerant co-operation the research would not have been possible. Thanks are also due to Karen McCall, research assistant, who tested many of the children.

1. The foot begins with a stress and contains everything that follows that stress, up to, but not including the next stress. Abercrombie 1964.

2. Reception class- age 4 years plus. Children reach their 5th birthday in the reception class

Year 1–5 years plus. Children reach their 6th birthday in this class.

Year 2–6 years plus. Children reach their 7th birthday.

Year 4–8 years plus. Children reach their 9th birthday.

References

Abercrombie, D. (1964) Syllable Quantity and Enclitics in English. In Abercrombie, Fry, McCarthy, Scott and Trim (Eds.), *In honour of Daniel Jones.* (216–222). London: Longmans,

Bialystok, E. (1986) Children's concept of word. *Journal of Psycholinguistic Research 15,* 13–32.

Condon, W. S. (1986) Communication: Rhythm and Structure in Evans, J. and Clines, M. (Eds.), *Rhythm in Psychological, Linguistic and Musical processes.* Springfield, Ill: Thomas.

Crystal, D. (1987) *Clinical Linguistics.* London: Whurr.

Giegerich, H. J. (1992) *English Phonology:An Introduction.* Cambridge: Cambridge University Press.

Harley, T. (1995) *The Psychology of Language: from Data to Theory.* Psychology Press.

Jackson, S., Treharne, D., Boucher, J. (1997) Rhythm and language in children with moderate learning difficulties. *European Journal of Disorders of Communication 32,* 99–108.

Konopczynski, G. (1999) The acquisition of prosody in the light of the interactive developmental intonology(I. D.I) theory. *Paper presented at the 1st Bisontine Conference for Conceptual and Linguisitic Development in the Child Aged from 1 to 2 years. Besançon, France.*

Lea, J. (1980) The association between rhythmic ability and language ability. In F. M. Jones (Ed) *Language Disability in Children.* Lancaster: MTP Press.

McClave, E. (1994) Gestural Beats: The Rhythm Hypothesis. *Journal of Psycholinguistic Research 23* 45–66.

Martin, J. G. (1972) Rhythmic and segmental perception. *J. Acoustical Society of America 65* 1286–1297.

Porch, B. (1974) *PICAC Porch Index of Communicative Ability in Children.* Consulting Psychologists Press.

Shields, J. R. (1981) A study of the rhythmic abilities and language abilities in young children. *First Language Vol 2 Part 2 No. 5* 131–140.

Tunmer, W. E., Bowey, J. A. (1981) cited in Gombert, J. E. 1992 *Metalinguistic Development* Harvester Wheatsheaf.

Rising-falling contours in speech

A metaphor of tension-resolution schemes in European musical traditions? Evidence from regional varieties of Italian

Antonio Romano
Università di Lecce, Italy

1. Introduction

In the literature on music and speech, we are often faced with the idea of a correspondence between the general rising-falling pitch contour in spoken sentences and the classical subdivision of melody in western European music into two parts: a "proposal", generally ending on a fifth, and a "response", following a resolutive pattern towards the tonic.

On the one hand, we find a number of references showing how intonative contours can vary dramatically across languages; nevertheless, in most cases they tend to appear in accordance with a "rising-falling pattern". On the other hand, as recently shown by the music theorist Eugene Narmour (1990) and further discussed by Russo & Cuddy (1999), there are patterns of melodic motion that appear to transcend many musical styles and that seem to be an extension of common vocal melodic patterns.

Local contours as well as overall contours appear to differentiate question sentences from statements: interrogative patterns in many languages tend to show a final rising of the vocal pitch, while affirmative clauses tend to "precipitate" on the tonic. Now, dialectal varieties of Italian, as well as Romance dialects scattered throughout the Peninsula, may present different intonative contours, and yet, something like a relative "fifth jump" can be almost always recognised in the *catastasis* of question sentences where a local contour marks a melodic movement rising different kind of expectation.

The data discussed in this contribution derive from field enquiries held in Aosta Valley, Apulia Region, Südtirol and Abruzzi Region. Other results are provided by a pilot study carried out on the perception of melodic contours of sentences from different western European languages. They show the presence of (a) a suspension in the melodic contour of sentences according to the theory of "suspended meaning", valid both in music and language; (b) native speakers of different varieties recognise these patterns just listening to partial intonation contour of synthetic stimuli.

Rise and fall in music

A classic subdivision of melody in western European music tradition usually distinguishes two parts in melodic phrasing: a first part, called "proposal" (or "question"), generally ending on a fifth, and a second part, called "response" (or "answer"), following a resolutive pattern that tends to globally fall towards the tonic.

It is a common experience to listen to structuring melodies with increasing expectations in the first part, finally resolved with a final concluding tune. A brief passage of D. R. Hofstadter clearly resumes this kind of experience:

> " [listening to music] we maintain a mental stack of keys, and [...] each new modulation pushes a new key onto the stack [...]. Any reasonably musical person automatically maintains a shallow stack with two keys. In that "short stack", the true tonic key is held, and also the most immediate "pseudotonic" (the key the composer is pretending to be in). In other words, the most global key and the most local key. That way, the listener knows when the true tonic is regained, and feels a strong sense of "relief". The listener can also distinguish [...] between a local easing of tension — for example a resolution into the pseudotonic — and a global resolution. " (Hofstadter 1979: 129).

This sense of fulfilment or finality in falling pitch is also described by Cooke (1959: 104) whereas in Meyer (1956) we find accounts for a distinct consideration of such a sensation related to an affective response but dominated by a conscious expectation.

> " Whether a piece of music gives rise to affective experience or to intellectual experience depends upon the disposition and training of the listener. [...] Thus while the trained musician consciously waits for the expected resolution of a dominant seventh chord the untrained, but practiced, listener feels the delay as affect " (Meyer 1956: 40).

As a consequence of affect or rationality, we could see that, in any way, expectation in music involves a high order of mental activity. The fulfilment of a habit response, in art as well in daily life, requires judgement and cognition both of the stimulus itself and of the situation in which it acts.

Thus, an immediate correspondence of this sensation has to be searched for in the structure of the stimuli themselves but also in the way how we perceive the melodic stimulus within the frame of our experience and our personal taste.

A general metaphor linking pitch and suspense could be seen in the fact that pitch is felt by everyone to be an 'up-and-down' dimension. It could be claimed that there is no reason for calling notes with more vibrations per second 'higher', except in so far as they have always been written higher on stave. In answer to this, Cooke (1959) points out the connections between the following facts: (1) by the law of gravity, 'up' is an effort for man, 'down' a relaxation; (2) to sing 'high' notes, or play them on wind, brass, or string instruments, demands a considerable effort; (3) to tune a string 'upwards', one screws 'up' its tension; (4) scientists, talking of 'high' notes, speak of a 'high' number of vibrations per second.

Another possible explanation is given by I. Fónagy: "*Cette projection spatiale du ton est justifiée par le fait qu'il est plus facile de produire une note élevée en levant la tête, et une note plus basse en baissant le menton*" (Fónagy 1983: 121).

Rise and fall in speech

In speech we observe very common patterns of suspension which leave interrogative sentences (and, to some extent, also declarative not concluded) open towards a possible way of integration — expected by the listener — or introducing a possible continuation in the linguistic program of the speaker. These suspensive patterns succeed in the generation of a tension by means of a tonal rise. Only a declining contour allows the satisfaction of this strong feeling by producing the resolution of the mental tension.

An extended sample of languages can be described as having a globally rising-falling pitch movement in the single intonation unit of a simple unemphatic declarative utterance — where the overall pattern generally finishes on an extreme low pitch.

Exceptions to the general rule are mentioned for dialect variants as in some Midland and Northern dialects of British English, as well as in Estremadura dialect of Spanish and in the Corfou dialect of Greek, where declaratives are said to end with a rised final pitch (Hirst & Di Cristo 1998: 19). But we would easily add in this list, without hesitation, Venetian dialects and north-eastern regional varieties of Italian, whose declarative sentences are often perceived as questions by other Italian people.

2. Downtrends and uptrends

Physiological explanations in terms of universal constraints have been proposed for the declination of F_0 within affirmative sentences in a number of languages.[1]

The movement in the fundamental contour, accounting for accent components and sentence mode components, would be globally characterised by a downtrend whose mean slope is defined as a consequence of the programmed sentence length and of the number of *downsteps* or *upsteps* marking accent realisation. At this purpose one can observe how a declination of smaller units is reset into declination of larger units (*declination within declination*, also see Ladd 1996).

The overall *downward sloping* is described as a relaxation gesture in Lindblom (1968) and as a principle of articulatory laziness in Ohala (1990). In Vaissière (1983) we found that the overall tendency to the declination may be disabled, as it happens in question sentences. There the trend is reversed, and an uptrend appears at the end of the sentences. Lieberman (1967) studies the final rising of questions within breath groups and describes it as a product of an increased activity of larynx muscles, but several other approaches attempted to give full explanations of this phenomenon.

Independently from the original reasons of such overall trends, we can model them from the functional point of view, by analysing each typical prosodic configuration as a result of the recursive implementation of similar patterns. Therefore, the basic rise-fall pattern would be determined on biological bases and as an effect of the phonologisation of the archetype "conventionalised" as the phonetic marker of the completeness of an utterance in many languages. Instead, in this framework, all the non-fall patterns would have psychological and ethological explanations as well as in the phonologisation of the contrast (see Vaissière 1995). J. Ohala defines an "ethological frequency code" and observes that "low frequencies signal domination: so a person making a statements uses a low frequency. High frequencies signal submissiveness. A person asking a question [...] tends to use a high pitch voice." (Ohala 1984). Moreover, as it is clearly discussed by Vaissière (1995), regardless of size, each constituent tend to conform the shape of a common archetypal (rise-fall) contour and a few derived contrastive (rise-non fall contour, whose characteristics may be motivated on biological, psychological and/or ethological grounds).

Declination in Italian

Classic reviews on the prosodic characterisation of standard Italian describe a final declination for assertive utterances and a rising movement (global or at least at the end of the sentence) for yes/no-questions, regional varieties seem to have recourse instead to alternative patterns to differentiate questions from statements in spontaneous speech.

Instrumental evidence of rising-falling contours signalling questions comes from various researches carried out by various authors and accounting for Sicilian Italian of Palermo, southernmost Sallentinian, different varieties of Sardinian, Apulian Italian of Bari as well as for some francoprovençal varieties of the Aosta Valley. The auditive impression deriving from the observation of patterns in Neapolitan or, within a different rhythmic framework, in some Italian varieties spoken in Piedmont or even in Tuscany, suggests the existence of more varieties in which this principle of distinctiveness needs more accurate study. Further studies should be also devoted to the intonative system of Venetian (showing a declarative scheme always tending to rise at the end) in order to investigate the way how it has been redesigned to maintain the statement-question opposition.

As a by-product of a fieldwork in some apparently homogeneous Italian linguistic areas, we detected different ways to signal question in terms of specific local contours — as geographical distinctive features — but we observed the same underlying melodic strategy: creating a tension and resolving it. Yet, the communication between people coming from areas where different prosodic sub-systems are widespread is not prevented by these cues.

Therefore we tried to observe how the rising is really implemented and how people behave in front of musical stimuli presenting these different situations.

The real implementation of a rising to signal interrogation

We considered sentences from two Italian speakers marked by a different use of melodic contour (but with the same rhythmic properties). As we showed in previous publications, though sharing the same overall linguistic system, Sallentinian speakers, have recourse to prosodic systems mainly differing on the final contour of y/n question which is rising-falling for speakers of the southernmost area (as the male speaker FC29 here considered, see Figure 1). and always rising for speakers of the central-northern area (as the female speaker FM28, see Romano, 1997).

Both contours in 1a. and 2a. are characterised by a rising-falling movement ending towards a low pitch (–1 tones compared to the mean pitch values just before the last stressed vowel).

A final rise is realised upon the last stressed syllable in 1i. (+2 tones) followed by a fall-down on the post-stressed ones (–1÷2 tones) vs. a final global rise in 2i. mainly involving the final unstressed syllables (about +1 tone).

As we can resume, apparently no fifth jump seems to be regularly realised: but for speaker 1 two different movements are opposed upon the last stressed syllable generating a gap of at least 3 tones; for speaker 2 a gap becomes sensible only upon the post-stressed phase and reaches its maximum at the end of the sentence (hence only about +2 tones, even if this gap has been observed spanning up to +4 tones in more emphatic sentences).

So, the claim that standard Italian has a rise to a fifth, in common with musical works, can only be a statistic reference in view of the wide differences in pitch range found between speakers on the one hand, and between utterances of one person in different states of mind and different communicative situations.[2]

Nevertheless, as different contours are used by speakers geolinguistically distant to realise the "same" message, within their own intonative codes, slightly different aesthetic preferences appear in the perception of "foreign" prosodic features and both scientific and popular terminology on these patterns refer to a musical setting and to singing.

As highlighted by I. Fónagy, evident analogies do exist between melodic patterns in emotional speech and traditional schemes in European music. Intonation brings us towards the separation phase between speech and music, to an hypothetical ancestral language, whose unique function was the resolution of biological and mental tensions (Fónagy 1983: 149).

We claim that, independently from the selection of a different final contour, relevant acoustic cues of an interrogative characterisation of the sentence are given by the realisation of an unresolved tension in the first part of the utterance and by a functionally distinctive way to oppose a resolutive asserting pattern to a suspending one: at any rate the tension generated at the end of a question contains marks signalling that the question is achieved.[3] Our claim seems to be supported by the results of the perceptual test described below.

1a.

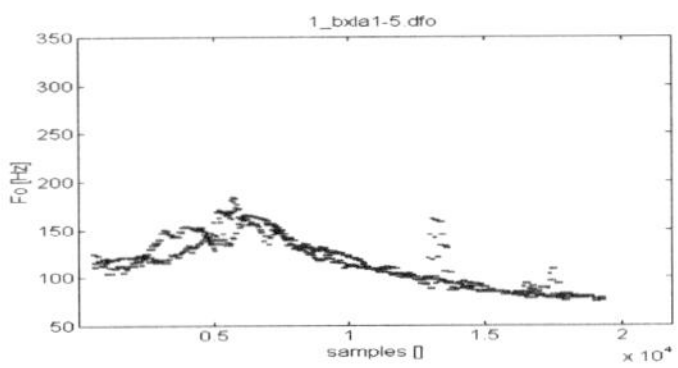

[labambi:navwɔlelabam b ola .]

2a.

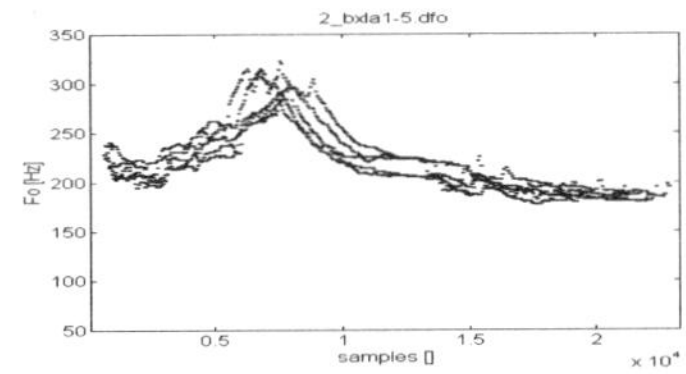

[la bambi:navwɔlelab am b ola .]

1i.

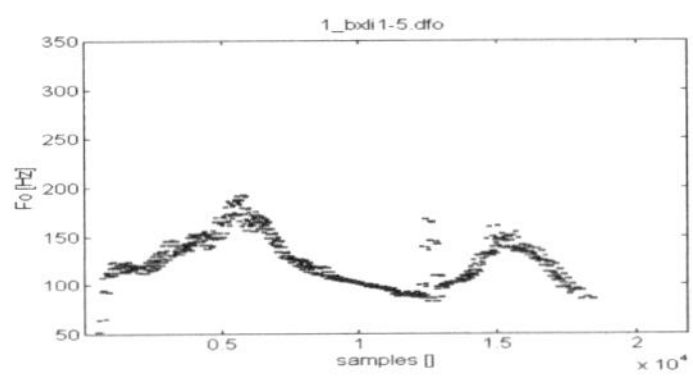

[labambi:navwɔlelabambola ?]

2i.

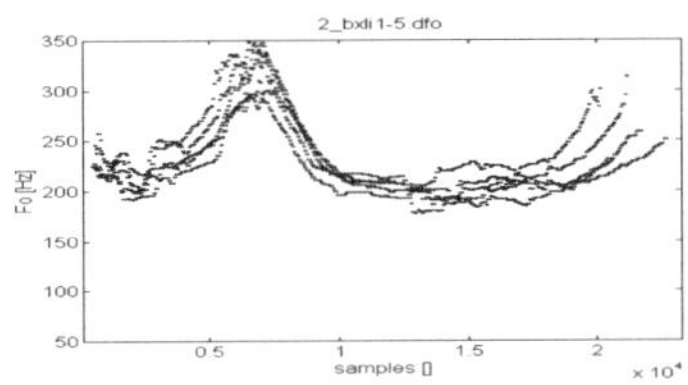

[labambi:navwɔlelab ambol a ?]

Figure 1. Pitch contours of 5 realisations of 2 sentences (declarative and interrogative, corresponding to the same order and organisation of speech units) uttered by two Italian speakers (1a. and 1i. by a 29 years old, male speaker of a southern Sallentinian variety; 2a. and 2i. by a 28 years old female speaker of a northern Sallentinian variety). The sentence in 1a. and 2a. is *La bambina vuole la bambola.*, "The child wants the doll". The same sentence is realised in two distinct ways in 1i. and 2i. at the interrogative mode, with the same meaning nuance and the same information distribution (narrow focus on the last constituent). The question is *La bambina vuole la bambola?*, "The child, she wants the doll? (or something else?)".

3. A perceptual experiment

As for the principle of pattern perception, L. Meyer said that

> "To assert that incompleteness gives rise to expectations of completeness is tantamount to tautology. For things seem to be incomplete only because we entertain definite feelings, latent expectations, as to what constitutes completeness in a given stimulus situation" (Meyer 1956: 128).

Our sense of completeness or incompleteness is also a product of those patterns or sound terms which become established as more or less fixed, given parts of a particular work. That is, once a sound term has been established as a coherent, though not necessarily as a complete or closed unit, then part of the series taken by itself will, generally speaking, seem to be incomplete, particularly if the fragment occurs in the earlier parts of the total work. Thus repetitions of the beginning of a well-shaped pattern already heard several times will arouse expectations that it will be completed as it has been in the past (see Meyer 1956: 128–129).

The perception of different ways to realise such an expectation in speech has been investigated by trying to evaluate the rate of identification of speech contour segments.

We carried out the experiment with listeners who had an active competence of one of the two intonative sub-systems analysed by asking them to express a judgement of completeness and sentence mode on musical stimuli obtained from such segments of both varieties (cf. Ohala & Gilbert 1979).

Stimuli

We selected three declarative-interrogative pairs of utterances as the ones reported in Figure 1, and we prepared a series of 12 stimuli randomly organised to be used in the perceptual testing of one sample of listeners. The task of identifying the completeness of the sentence being easy enough in the case of natural utterances containing verbal information, only the melodic information was taken into account. The stimuli were sequences of pulse trains generated on the base of the rhythmic and melodic organisation of the contours extracted by an electronic pitch analyser and used to generate synthetic stimuli by means of software developed at the purpose. The original sentences were one declarative-interrogative pair pronounced by the two speakers (4 utterances) and another pair of longer sentences uttered by only one speaker (the southern one). The sentences were cut into two pieces after the point where the highest tension was reached. Then the test sequence was made by 6 initial and 6 final portions randomly ordered.

Procedure

Every subject listened to the random sequence of stimuli in isolation with headphones and was free to hear the stimulus whenever he/she wanted by clicking on a computer screen. The stimuli, corresponding to each of the 12 sentence portions of the corpus, were presented to the listener in random order asking him/her to freely rate them by clicking on one of 4 buttons proposing an answer such as "1st part of a declarative sentence", "2nd part of a declarative sentence", "1st part of an interrogative sentence" or "2nd part of an interrogative sentence". A first test, with free listening of the stimuli, was aimed at training the listener to the test conditions.

Subjects

Twelve subjects were drawn from various places of the region and included undergraduate and graduate students, school teachers and local travellers which had or not experience of different varieties. They were organised into two groups after their original geolinguistic competence: 6 listeners were from the southern area (sub-system 1.) and 6 from the northern one (sub-system 2.).

Results

Results are resumed in the tables below organising data in confusion matrices.

As a general trend, none or only a few of the non-final segments of a sentence are rated as final question contours and this for both groups. First parts of a question can be confused with first parts of an assertion and vice versa, but they are rarely misperceived as final parts (resolutive or not).

The two groups of listeners did not show significant differences in the way they distinguish a question from a statement or they rise expectations or fulfil them listening to different stimuli marked by slight geolinguistic diversity. Segments of a declarative sentence have been correctly identified in 75% of stimuli. The same score has been reached for interrogative stimuli. A suspensive initial contour seems to have been perceived in 85% of the cases in which the stimulus was really incomplete but initial. For stimuli coming from the last incomplete part of a question the identification rate has been slightly lower (81%). These results do not support a pretended innate experience of variable tension-resolution schemes — a passive competence of "foreign" patterns could give relevant cues at this purpose. Such an evidence may come instead in other ways. A pilot experiment is currently being carried out on several European languages with a group of subjects having no experience about them, as opposed to a group of subjects who learned or who were studying them. The two groups did not show significant differences in the way they distinguish a question from a statement in a foreign language on the basis of their melodic contour alone.

Table 1. All the stimuli (declarative and interrogative sentences) and both groups.

Rated as	Stimuli: Statement 1st part	Statement 2nd part	Question 1st part	Question 2nd part
1st part of an incomplete statement	47%	11%	36%	6%
2nd part of an incomplete statement	28%	64%	3%	6%
1st part of an incomplete question	22%	8%	64%	6%
2nd part of an incomplete question	6%	14%	3%	78%

Table 2. First part vs. Second part of a sentence

Rated as	Stimuli: 1st part	2nd part
1st part	85%	15%
2nd part	19%	81%

Table 3. Statement vs. Question

Rated as	Stimuli: Part of a statement	Part of a question
Part of a statement	75%	25%
Part of a question	25%	75%

4. Conclusions

In this paper we resumed some elements of the correspondence between general rising-falling contours in speech and the classical European musical schemes proposal-response.

As already stated in a number of different works, intonative contours of sentences tend to appear, across languages, cultures and dialects, in accordance with a rising-falling expectation pattern. As a matter of fact, in questions the "falling" has generally to be seen as an actual overall rising in pitch differently shaped from one variety to another.

We analysed dialectal varieties of Italian, as well as Romance dialects spoken in Italy, which may present slightly different intonative contours in question sentences, and yet, a relative "fifth jump" has been often recognised in the *catastasis* of the sentence while a local contour appeared at the end of the sentence marking a complete melodic movement in terms of the listener expectations but referring to an incomplete knowledge of the speaker that needs for a response.

In several field enquiries we observed that people tend to associate emotional or stylistic or geolinguistic labels to different patterns, but in most cases they correctly identify a broken contour from a final rising or rising-falling interrogative contour, probably thanks to something like a feeling of fulfilment, exactly like if it were music.

We claimed, and outcomes from our experiments partially proved, that a common experience of rising-falling pattern as well as of tension-resolution schemes provides solid cues to the listeners in view of the identification of semantic completeness. Our first findings agree, under certain conditions, with the conclusions of Meyer who guessed "expectations based upon learning" prior to the natural modes of thought. The expectations which are entertained on these basis are actually associated to structural gaps to be filled; but what constitutes such a gap depends upon what constitutes completeness within a particular system (Meyer 1956: 43). At this stage, it becomes uncertain to consider rising-falling contours in speech as a metaphor of tension-resolution schemes in singing or to see both of these schemes on a common level of structural derivation from more basic (universal), possibly semiotic, principles.[4]

A common semiotic function might be a product of signature properties of more primitive motoric or limbically controlled events. A parallel may be seen in the temporal structuring of music and speech, where phrase final lengthening, while undoubtedly having an important signalling function, is a product of all motor controlled sequencing activities (as it has been suggested by our anonymous reviewer).

Notes

1. This phenomenon is investigated in the literature, including the research of Lieberman (1967), and the models developed by Gårding (1979). Further details about these topics are also in Bruce (1982), Bertinetto & Magno-Caldognetto (1993) and Ladd (1996).

2. Nevertheless, other structural elements across languages contribute to reinforce this model: listings, for example, have recourse to melodic elements intended to generate a

strong "suspended meaning" just before the last item of the list, the penultimate item being realised with an overall upward and the last one within the frame of a downward.

3. At this stage, two types of incompleteness can be distinguished: one which arises in the course of the pattern because something was skipped over; another one in which the figure, though complete so far as it goes, simply is not felt to have reached a satisfactory conclusion, is not finished. The first type of incompleteness may be seen as a "structural gap", the second type, as a product of a delay in the need and desire for "closure". And if, for the latter we can assume a linguistic learned competence, for the former, we suspect a "competence" related to music and to the experience of natural laws.

4. The emergence of singing has been related to melodies with a given meaning, a power to communicate but also, maybe, a distinctive power for the personality of the singer or speaker: a mark of his/her originality (Collaer, 1965: 625). The origin of mymesis, language gestures and human expressions, as a communication medium, are probably related to an evolution stage preceding the emergence of the articulated languages. Like in some *apothropaic* songs, these gestures may respond to the idea of the imposition of human will (cf. the *respite from death gained by a tale* in Abry, 1997).

References

Abry, Christian (1997). Pour une Histoire Naturelle de la Parole dans la "Théorie de l'Esprit". *Thèse d'habilitation*, Univ. de Grenoble (France).

Bertinetto, Pier Marco & Emanuela Magno Caldognetto (1993). "Ritmo e intonazione". In A. A. Sobrero (Eds.), *Introduzione all'italiano contemporaneo. Le strutture.* Bari, Laterza, 141–192.

Bruce, Gösta (1982). Developing the Swedish intonation model. *Working Papers in Linguistics*, Univ. Lund, 22, 51–114.

Collaer, Paul (1965). "Il mondo della musica". In V. L. Grottanelli (Ed.), *Ethnologica. L'uomo e la civiltà.* Milano, Labor.

Cooke, Deryck (1959). *The Language of Music.* Oxford University Press, London & New York.

Fónagy, Ivan (1983). *La vive voix.* Paris, Payot.

Gårding, Eva (1979). Sentence Intonation in Swedish. *Phonetics*, 36, 207–215.

Hirst, Daniel. & Albert Di Cristo (1998). "A survey of intonation systems". In D. J. Hirst & A. Di Cristo (Eds.), *Intonation Systems: a Survey of Twenty Languages.* Cambridge Univ. Press, 1–40.

Hofstadter, Douglas R. (1979). *Gödel, Escher, Bach: an Eternal Golden Braid.* New York, Basic Books.

Ladd, D. Robert (1996). *Intonational phonology*, Cambridge, Cambridge Univ. Press.

Lindblom, Bjorn (1968). Temporal organisation of syllable production. *Quarterly Progress Status Report of the Speech Transmission Laboratory*, Stockholm, 2, 1–15.

Lieberman, Philip (1967). *Intonation, Perception, and Language.* Research Monograph No. 38, Cambridge, Mass, MIT Press.

Meyer, Leonard B. (1956). *Emotion and Meaning in Music.* Chicago, University of Chicago Press.
Narmour, Eugene (1990). *The analysis and cognition of basic melodic structures: The implication-realization model.* Chicago, University of Chicago Press.
Ohala, John (1984). An ethological perspective on common cross-language utilization of F0 of voice. *Phonetica*, 41, 1–16.
Ohala, John & J. B. Gilbert (1979). Listeners ability to identify languages by their prosody. *Studia Phonetica*, 18, Ottawa, Didier, 123–131.
Romano, Antonio (1997). Persistence of prosodic features between dialectal and standard Italian utterances in six sub-varieties of a region of Southern Italy (Salento): first assessments of the results of a recognition test and an instrumental analysis. *Proc. of EuroSpeech'97*, Rhodes 1997, 175–178.
Russo, Frank A. & Lola L. Cuddy (1999). Motor Theory of Melodic Expectancy. *Proc. of the Acoustical Society of America — ASA/EAA/DAGA '99 Meeting* (Berlin, 1999).
Vaissière, Jacqueline (1983). Language Independent Prosodic Feature. In A. Cutler & D. R. Ladd (Eds), *Prosody: Models and Measurements*, Berlin, Springer, 53–66.
Vaissière, Jacqueline (1995). Natural Explanations for prosodic cross-languages similarities. *Proc. of ICPhS 95,* (Stockholm, 1995) 654–657.

Part III
Creativity

Conn Mulvihill
National University of Ireland, Galway, Ireland

Creativity is highly valued but badly understood. This section presents a number of views on what creativity is all about. The views are drawn from a broad spectrum of interests, reflecting the fact that creativity seems to be found in some form in almost all human activities.

First, we have a summary of the panel session on creativity which was held in the afternoon of the solar eclipse on Inis Mór (Big Island), the largest of the Aran Islands. Of course to be any use at all in human terms, any type of computation that involves creativity has to be efficient. Klein takes an overarching viewpoint and looks backwards into human history to find evidence of the emergence of an efficient model for human computation. He also suggests that human consciousness will continue to change due to the increasing use of analogical iconographic reasoning inherent in computational media, which is an interesting speculation on a creative link between humans and their environment.

A view on creativity from Economics is provided by Rickards. He finds no universally accepted definition of creativity but does suggest that creativity can be stimulated. Rickards posits that teams face two barriers to creative performance: a weak inter/intrapersonal barrier and a strong barrier that involves breaching acts of conventional expectations. This 'twin' characterisation of creative barriers is quite interesting. Rickards also cites historical visions of creativity and concludes by suggesting links between consciousness and creativity.

A cultural vision is offered by Lonergan. Lonergan examines the Tarahumara Indian and mestizo culture in Northwest Mexico. She discusses their history and beliefs, citing the centrality of humour in religious wakes or Tesgüinadas. She cites several examples of Mexican metaphors that illustrate the tragicomic nature and hidden information content of the humour. This use of multiple meanings in humour is in itself a noteworthy example of human creative activity.

A computational perspective is found in the last paper. Whether creativity is to be found in machine activities, or ever could be, is a point taken up by Mulvihill and Colhoun. The authors speculate on what characteristics might be present in any algorithm that was considered creative.

Plenary panel session: What is creativity?

Riccardo Antonini, Michéal Colhoun, Sean Day,
Paul Hodgson, Sheldon Klein, Julia Lonergan,
Paul Mc Kevitt, Conn Mulvihill, Stephen Nachmanovitch,
Francisco Camara Pereira, Gérard Sabah,
and Ipke Wachsmuth

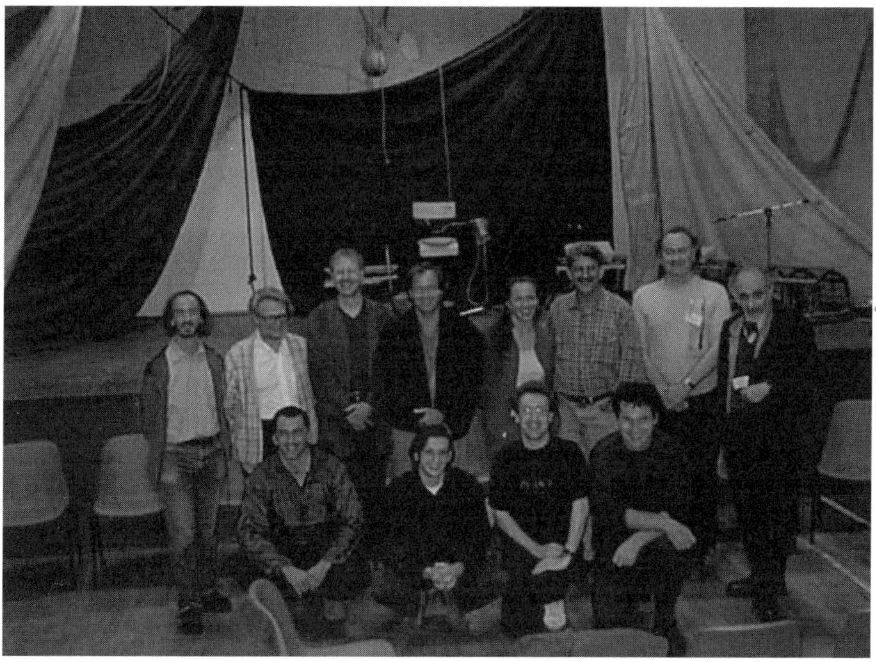

Plate 1. "What is creativity?"
Panel-members: Back row (left to right): Sean Day, Gérard Sabah, Ipke Wachsmuth, Paul Hodgson, Julia Lonergan, Stephen Nachmanovitch, Paul Mc Kevitt, Sheldon Klein, Front row (left to right): Riccardo Antonini, Francisco Camara Pereira, Michéal Colhoun, and Conn Mulvihill.

Conn Mulvihill asked a number of questions on creativity in the call for papers, as given in the introduction to this book, the central one being, what is creativity? He also contributed a paper on creativity and asked the question, is creativity algorithmic? Conn also used these two questions to kick off the panel discussion as well as singing the song "Raglan Road" the words of which were written by the poet Patrick Kavanagh and the tune of which is "The dawning of the Day".

Conn's paper points out that any language is taken to be characterisable through form and content and creativity activity occurs where form and content mix. Paradoxes mix form and content in a special way and ambiguity and diagonalisation appear where form and content mix whereas algorithmic studies are mainly concerned with space/time metrics and not with form/content interplay. It is posited in the paper that any language supporting creativity should mix form and content and be marked by ambiguity and reflective arguments and hypertext might be an example.

Riccardo Antonini said creativity is, in his view, a form, a very special one indeed, of mastering a given language. Triviality is on the contrary the common use of such a language. For example, in his game "Let's compose together" there is a language whose lexicon is the set of all the possible objects (and their attributes: colours, sound etc.).

The syntax, that in Greek means "putting things together", is very loose there, but still there is one, since there are only some ways to compose the objects together, while some others are not possible. For example, we cannot overlap objects one inside the other (we may of course, but we do not allow the people to do it). With such a lexicon and syntax, a trivial game is putting objects together at random. A creative way of putting them together is, on the contrary, for example, creating an alley, in which while you walk you listen to music, and watch the pictures and animations associated. The syntax is a constraint, the lexicon is the raw material, and the creativity is the capability of building non trivial phrases in this (or any other) language.

Sean Day said: as to whether an algorithm could be written for "creativity", I would have to say "No". It is possible to write algorithms that produce creative things — this is done all the time. Likewise, it is possible to be creative via algorithms — such is virtually a basic requirement of being creative. However, "creativity" in of itself is, by definition, un-bounded, infinite. "Creativity" is the essence of Gödel's Theorem — there will always be something, undefined and perhaps eternally indefinable, beyond the realm, transcending it. Thus: It is possible to shape algorithms for a computer/robot/android who could become highly creative, and quite probably could eventually (self?)-evolve creativity in wholly non-human forms. However, neither this nor any other entity nor algorithm can encompass the whole of "creativity", which is infinite.

Sheldon Klein commented: I think of creativity in the context of the cognitive worlds created collectively by groups of humans some 40,000 years ago, at the onset of the Upper Paleotlithic, when, after an archaeological record of more than a 150,000 years of unchanging technology, humanity embarked upon the exponential growth of creativity in the arts, technology and social organization that continues to the present day. I suggest that the source was in the invention of global classification schemes, in combination with analogical modes of reasoning. Semantic features may be viewed as an alternate notation for class or category memberships. If complex set memberships are represented by boolean feature vectors, the vectors may also be interpreted as binary integers, and the minimum number of features needed appears as the number required to give a unique identifier to every element in the cognitive universe. If a 'hashing collision' occurs when a new entity is encountered, then adding a single new feature to the category system system can remove the ambiguity. But this addition doubles the size of the potential universe, and creates a vast domain of potential concepts that may be explored, at low cost, by analogy. The process can accelerate the discovery of new phenomena and the need for more features, with the result that exponential growth of the cognitive universe becomes a self-sustaining process.

Julia Lonergan said that Creativity and Natural Language Processing (NLP) have an objective in common, both seek for ways to represent meaning outside of natural language. Machine Translation has as its aim the representation of the meaning in natural language in an alternative form, usually called an interlingua. This form consists of defining the computational elements of language with a system of language independent symbols. In the case of famous literary works, such as Finnegans Wake, James Joyce relied on metaphorical extensions of meaning, idiomatic comparisons, and phonetic similarities to create riddles that also encode meaning in language. In both cases, the meaning is hidden in the deep structure and relies on the background knowledge of the recipient to decode the content. Theatrical compositions function similarly. In dance, for example, mime, gesture, music, and movement convey a story independent of language.

Thus, as a lexicographer, who has been trained to transfer the English language into its interlingual symbols NLP, and as an artist, writer, and dancer, who has given language related realities a form of expression outside the use of natural language, she finds that NLP and creativity converge at the point that both seek to capture and represent human expression in alternate ways.

Paul Mc Kevitt said that Conn asked two questions and with respect to the first one (what is creativity?) Geraint is right (Geraint Wiggins, a workshop attendee had made a point about creativity and the unexpected), in that the unexpected or surprise is interesting and hence creativity is surprise and in particular creativity is an emergent property of Free Play; Paul then played "The dawning of the day" on Ipke's tin whistle.

Stephen Nachmanovitch responded: Can creativity be taught? Are there algorithms for creativity? This is a very a important question, but it is important to turn it upside down. What one can teach is not creativity but the disinhibition of creativity. Every human being is born creative, is potentially creative all the time. Every one of us has created several billion cells just today. We are talking together in this room thanks to the creativity of the settlers of this island, of the people who built this building, of the people who evolved our languages. We exist in an environment of overwhelming, continuous, all-around creativity. Creativity is never a problem. The problem is the inhibition of creativity, which usually comes about through fear. Fear of embarrassment, fear of not being in control, etc. The algorithm that most affects my creativity is other people. That's why it's great to be speaking together today. I think that the formula for changing one's creativity is inviting another human being, with a somewhat different mind, into your creative space, and - boom! something will happen. If beings are brought into apposition with other beings, who have other operating systems and other biases, and if you cross the biases, bringing together what James Joyce called their intermisunderstanding minds, then powerful combinatorial and synergistic effects take place. This can be done with ideas, even machines. My preference is to do it with other human beings. They're the most fun.

Francisco Camara Pereira pointed out that there are two issues upon which he'd like to state some comments. Sometimes, he sees much confusion among them: Creativity with Computers and Computational Creativity. The first one, very common, is mainly Human Creativity — one uses a program to create and develop his/her ideas. The major parts of the process are controlled by the Human (specially, the evaluation). The second issue, to which he (and others) call Computational Creativity, is indeed a very interesting subject of study. It centers mainly in the quest for methods/frameworks that accomplish in some way the task of automatic resolution of problems in a creative fashion.

He sees this "creative fashion" as the way we tend to solve problems when common or routine solutions don't work. Although vague this may seem (isn't any definition of creativity?), he believes we can (and will eventually) develop models that can be considered creative in that sense. Such a system would be able to generate its ideas and be able to evaluate them at some degree of complexity. He believes this can be a very important path in AI, and we still have much to learn from Psychology and Philosophy.

Inspired by the place, Ipke Wachsmuth, from Bielefeld University, took a creative approach to express his sentiment about ingredients of creativity. He took:

'C' for Compassion, to say that it needs a sympathetic attitude for creativity, that feels for a matter in devotion;
'R' for Rhythm, to say that creativity often leaps in alternating periods of tension and relaxation;
'E' for Exposure, since he thinks a system can only be creative when opening up to, and interchanging with, its environment;
'A' for Art, to say that as much as art is an expression of creativity, enjoying art fosters creativity;
'T' for Travel, to say that it needs to go and see persons and places to enrich your creative pool;
'I' for Impulsiveness, to say that a creative act often springs from the minute idea;
'V' for Vitality, saying that as much as a vital system is necessary for a creative act, vitality also grounds on creativity;
'I' for Imagery, to make the point that, more than reasoning, it needs imagery to conceive the new;
'T' for Tree, to refer to the impact of a creative idea that has the potential to have many branches, like a tree;
'Y' for Yi-jing, leaving it to the audience to understand in which way this should be relevant.

The analogical foundations of creativity in language, culture & the arts: "The Upper Paleolithic to 2100CE"

Sheldon Klein
Computer Sciences & Linguistics,
University of Wisconsin-Madison, USA

1. Toward a unified theory of multi-model human behavior

For 150–200,000 years, the material culture of anatomically modern humans showed little or no change. The techniques of stone tool manufacture remained static, there was no representational art, and no unequivocal symbolic behavior (Mellars 1989, 1991; Mellars & Stringer 1989). However, about 40,000 years ago, quite abruptly, the creative behavior of modern humans entered upon an exponential pattern of growth that continues through the present day. The best evidence seems to indicate that, over a 10,000 year period, modern humans emerged from their place of origin in Africa, and populated the globe. New forms of material and symbolic culture appeared, including representational iconography in 2 and 3 dimensions. No theory of human cognition is truly adequate unless it can account for the changes in human cognitive behaviour that began in the Middle to Upper Paleolithic transition. This is a tough constraint; yet, I would add one more:

Few researchers outside of the field of computational linguistics and artificial intelligence are aware of the tremendous ambiguity that is implicit in the phonology and syntax of natural language, unless powerful computational models of behavioral context are brought to bear. Seemingly powerful experimental results based on limited subject matter are, essentially, unproven. Almost every aspect of the problem space is subject to combinatorically increasing demands on computation time, or, in the case of massively parallel computing, combinatorically increasing demands on connectivity.[1] Though computers compute a million times faster than humans, human computation succeeds where computers fail. Any theory of human cognition that cannot account for this difference is also inadequate.

There are a number of theories in each of several disciplines that are concerned with human cognitive behavior that have contradictory premises. I'd like to consider the evidence for a theoretical model that is consistent with at least one theoretical approach in each of them.

2. Boolean groups and the computation of analogies

Exclusive OR and hidden layers

For a connectionist network to learn the exclusive-OR logical operator, it is necessary to introduce at least one hidden layer (Elman, Bates, Johnson, Karmiloff-Smith, Parisi, Plunkett 1996: 60–65). This is also true for its symmetric counterpart, the strong equivalence operator (Table 1).

Table 1.

Exclusive Or
"a or b, but not both"

a	b		a	b	
T	T	F	1	1	0
T	F	T	1	0	1
F	T	T	0	1	1
F	F	F	0	0	0

Strong Equivalence
"a if and only if b"

a	b		a	b	
T	T	T	1	1	1
T	F	F	1	0	0
F	T	F	0	1	0
F	F	T	0	0	1

If T is replaced by 1, and F by 0, then the exclusive-OR is defined by the arithmetic operation of mod-2 (non carry) addition, and the strong equivalence operator is defined by the rules for multiplying the signs, + and – (Table 2).

Table 2.

Mod-2 addition (non-carry)	**Mod-2 subtraction** (non-borrow)
a+b	a–b
1+1=0	1–1=0
1+0=1	1–0=1
0+1=1	0–1=1
0+0=0	0–0=0

If one creates a 4–valued truth table using binary integers, and the logic of either operator, one obtains a mathematical object called a Klein-4 group (after Felix Klein), which plays a major role in the theories of Piaget (1953), and Topology, an field devoted to the study of the properties of geometric objects that are independent of spatial transformations. Table 3 contains a version derived with the strong equivalence operator.

Table 3. Boolean Klein-4 Group

	00	01	10	11
00	11	10	01	00
01	10	11	00	01
10	01	00	11	10
11	00	01	10	11

3. Analogical Transformation Operators (ATOs)

$$*ab = *ba \quad *a*ab = b \quad *b*ba = a$$

Example using the strong equivalence operator:

$$a{=}101,\ b = 011,\ *ab = 001$$
$$*b*ab = *011\ 001 = 101$$
$$*a*ab = *101\ 001 = 011$$

If the binary notation is used to indicate features, then the truth table for either exclusive-OR, or strong equivalence may be used to compute analogical operators that can be used to derive new analogies on the basis of prior examples.

Visual Analogies (binary features, strong equivalence truth table)

Abstract

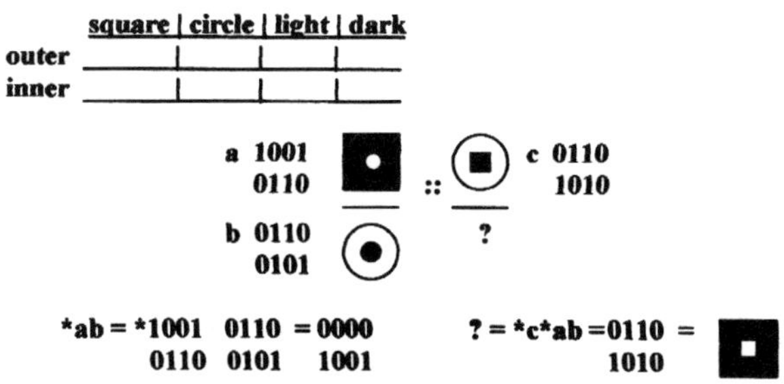

Figure 1. Abstract visual analogy

Iconographic

The analogical computation in Figure 2, is derived from an ATO analysis of a traditional classification of the 64 hexagrams of the I Ching, a Chinese divination system (Klein 1983: 151–180). I substituted arbitrary visual elements for each of six lines which might be either open or closed, and represented by 0 or 1,a notation used by Leibniz (1968).[2] The original of A in Figure 2 would have appeared as:

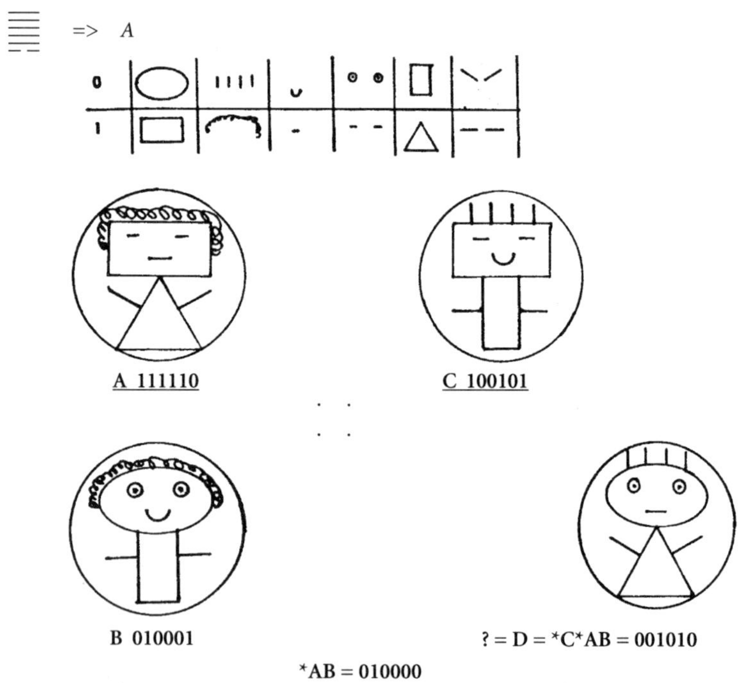

Figure 2. Iconographic Analogy & the I Ching

4. Analogy and Language

ATO logic can model context free phrase structure grammar in the notation of categorial grammar (Klein 1989, 1996). Categorial grammar reformulates phrase structure rules as if they were algebraic equations. A rule $S \rightarrow Y\ Z$ could yield S/Z as the grammatical category of Y, and a sequence $Y\ Z$ would be parsed to $S/Z\ Z$, and then to S, after cancellation of the Zs. The same result can be

achieved by assigning Boolean integers to *Y* and *Z*, and a derived Boolean integer for *S*:
Let $Y = 10101$, and let $Z = 11001$, Then, using the strong equivalence operator truth table, $*YZ = 10011 = S$. $*SZ = Y$, and $*SY = Z$. Assigning and computing boolean integers for the morphological and syntactic units of a context-free phrase structure grammar can be accomplished by partial selection of values, computation of others. There are several rather interesting consequences:

a. Grammatical categories appear to be analogical operators.
b. ATOs can be interpreted as functors.[3]
c. Syntactic rules specify the formation of hierarchies of analogies.

Categorial grammars that include semantic features and phonological features as part of their data can also be implemented by the use of ATO logic. If each element of the morphological database is represented by three Boolean vectors, (for phonological features, morphological codes, and semantic features), then versions of categorial grammar more powerful than context-free phrase structure may also be modelled. Any analogy one may posit about relations among phonological units can be computed by ATO logic, using Boolean vectors of either articulatory features or acoustic distinctive features. It thus becomes possible to compute phonological changes, including temporal changes, by ATO logic.

5. Unifying visual & verbal analogies

Consider the following verbal example (Klein 1983). The features, 'male', 'female', 'young', 'adult', 'love', 'hate', 'light', 'dark' are sufficient to formulate the verbal analogy in Table 4.

Table 4. Verbal & visual analogy

X = Boy loves light :: Z = Woman hates dark
Y = Girl hates light ?

M F Y A L H Lt Dk where **M** = male, **F** = female, **A** = adult, **L** = love, **H** = hate, **Lt** = light, **Dk** = dark.

X = 10101010 :: Z = 01010101 ***XY = 00110011**
Y = 01100110 ?

? = *z*xy = 10011001 = Man loves dark

Also, consider the visual/verbal examples in Figure 3 (Klein 1983: 152, [Figures 1 & 2]).

The Boolean vectors and computations are identical in both examples. If they are combined, the visual and verbal interpretations of the features seem to

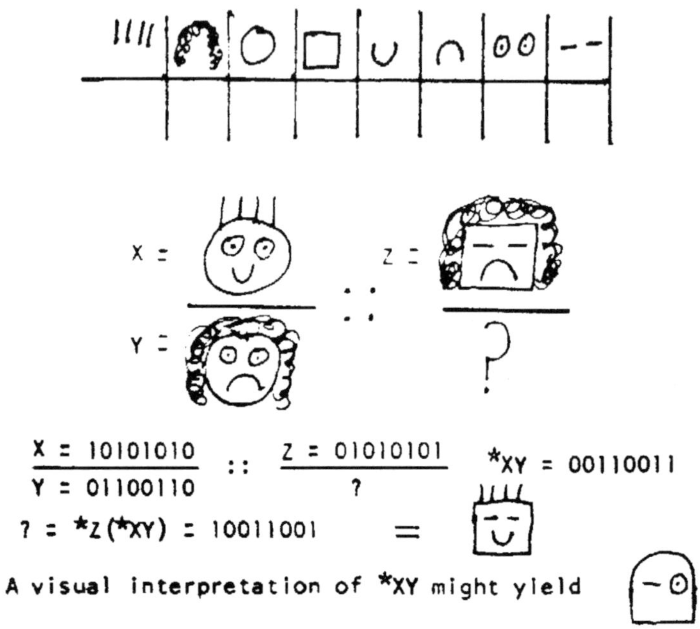

Fig. 1. Calculation of a pictorial analogy.

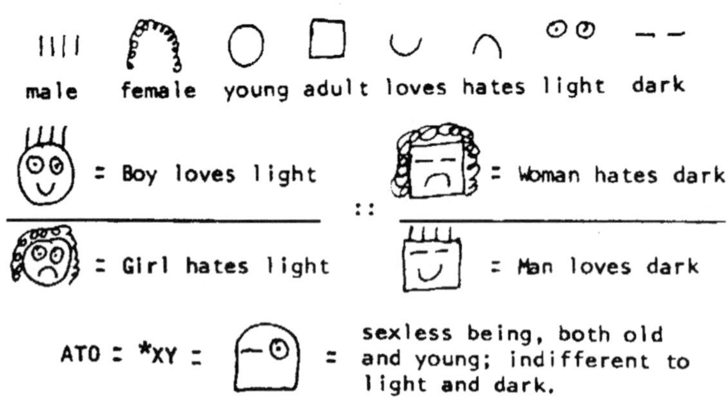

Fig. 2. The Pictorial analogy with a natural-language interpretation.

Figure 3. Visual/verbal analogy

belong together. Why they seem to combine in a natural way can be explained by interpreting each feature vector as a path down a binary decision tree. The trees for the components of the combined example in Figure 4 are isomorphic, (Klein 1983: 154–155, [Figures 7 & 8]).

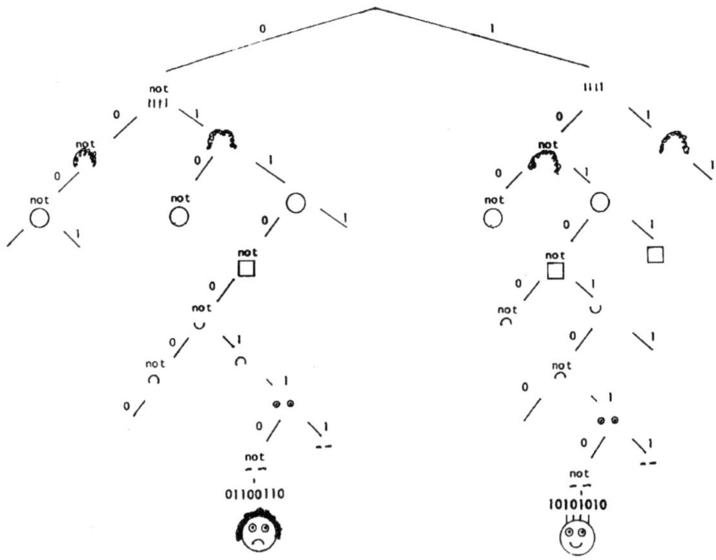

FIG. 8. Partial portrayal of independent feature tree (pictorial).

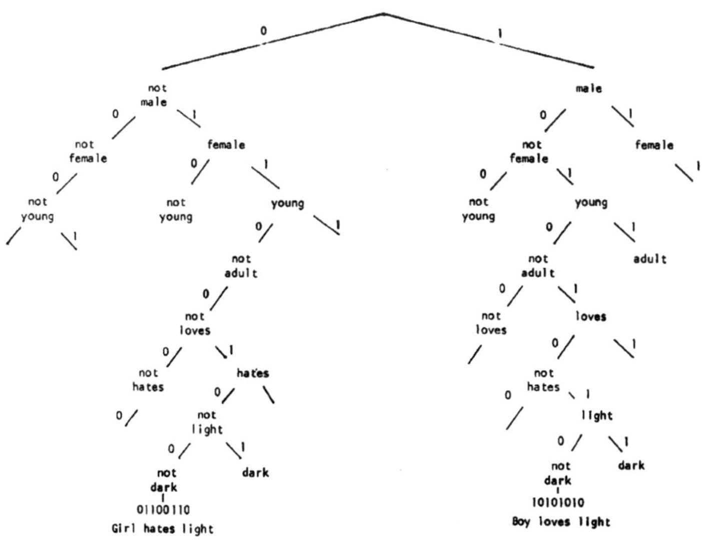

FIG. 7. Partial portrayal of independent feature tree (verbal).

Figure 4. Isomorphic visual & verbal binary trees

The number of terminal elements of such a tree is equal to the number of features of a decision path. If the terminal elements of that tree are projected onto the vertices of a hypercube of dimensionality equal to the number of terminal elements, the analogical relations of the original are present as spatial analogies among edges of the hypercube projection. The unity of the conceptual domains is made especially apparent if the Boolean vectors that were interpreted as paths down the binary decision trees are used to label the associated vertices of the hypercube (Figure 5).

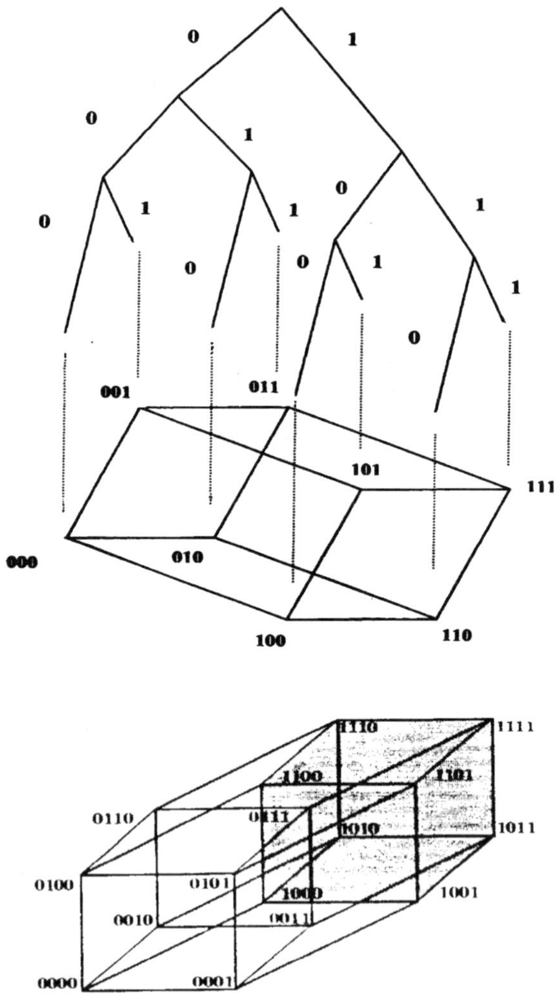

Figure 5. Projections of 3 & 4 feature binary trees onto 3-dimensional & 4-dimensional cubes

Boolean vectors of n features may also be considered coordinates of concepts in an n-dimensional space, where distance is a measure of concept similarity, and where symmetries in the patterning of lines that connect concepts, reflect analogies that are valid in other notational representations.

6. Behavioral-iconographic analogy

Figures 6a, 6b, 6c & 6d illustrate a combined Behavioral-Iconographic analogy (Klein 1983: 153–154, [Figures 3–6]).

Complex analogies may also be computed, as in the following abstract example:

If ((X :: Y) :: (Z :: W)) :: (P :: ?), then

? = *P(*(XY) (*ZW)).

A concrete illustration of this abstract example is as follows:

X
A loves B, has no \$, and is not married. B loves A, has no \$, and is not married. C loves no one, has \$, and is unmarried.

→

Y
A loves B, has no \$, is married to B. B loves A, has no \$, is married to A. C loves no one, has \$, and is unmarried.

Where La = "loves A," etc., \$ = "has money," and Ma = "married to A," etc., the X and Y states may be represented as follows:

	La	Lb	Lc	\$	Ma	Mb	Mc
A	.	1	0	0	.	0	0
B	1	.	0	0	0	.	0
C	0	0	.	1	0	0	.

X ⇒ **Y**

	La	Lb	Lc	\$	Ma	Mb	Mc
A	.	1	0	0	.	1	0
B	1	.	0	0	1	.	0
C	0	0	.	1	0	0	.

Y

***XY**

.	1	1	1	.	0	1
1	.	1	1	0	.	1
1	1	.	1	1	1	.

If we depict "loves" as a nose pointing at the beloved (in between, if two loves), if a noseless state means "loves no one," if holding hands depicts "married to," and if a "\$" indicates "has money," we can obtain the visual interpretation of figure 3.

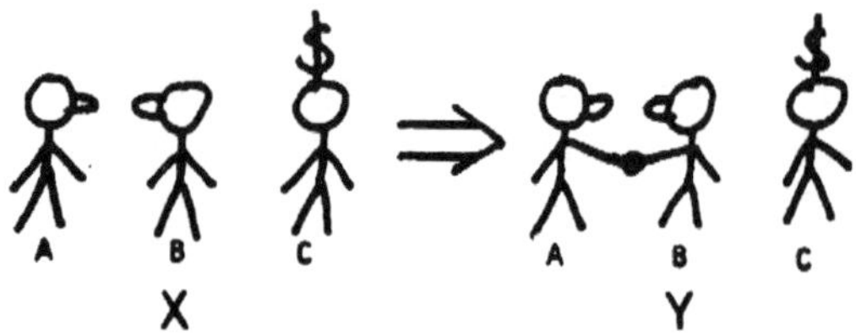

Fig. 3. A visual interpretation of X→Y, where X is "A loves B, has no $, and is unmarried. B loves A, has no $, and is unmarried. C loves no one , has $, and is unmarried" and Y is "A loves B, has no $, and is unmarried to B. B loves A, has no $, and is married to A. C loves no one, has $, and is unmarried."

Figure 6a. Behavioral-iconographic analogy

Continuing with this complex example:

Z

A loves no one, has no $, and is married to B. B loves A, has no $, and is married to A. C loves A, has $, and is unmarried.

⟹

W

A loves no one, has $, and is married to C. B loves no one, has no $, and is unmarried. C loves A, has $, and is married to A.

Z

	La	Lb	Lc	$	Ma	Mb	Mc
A	.	0	0	0	.	1	0
B	1	.	0	0	1	.	0
C	1	0	.	1	0	0	.

⟹

W

	La	Lb	Lc	$	Ma	Mb	Mc
A	.	0	0	1	.	0	1
B	0	.	0	0	0	.	0
C	1	0	.	1	1	0	.

***ZW**

.	1	1	0	.	0	0
0	.	1	1	0	.	1
1	1	.	1	0	1	.

This yields the visual interpretation of figure 4.

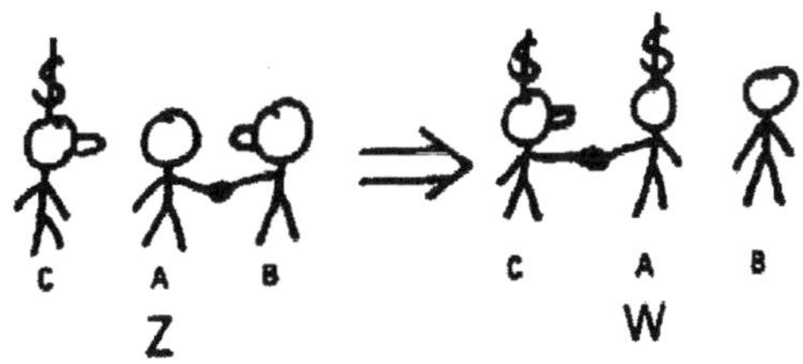

Fig. 4. A visual interpretation of Z → W, where Z is "A loves no one, has no $, and is married to B. B loves A, has no $, and is married to A. C loves A, has $, and is unmarried" and W is "A loves no one, has $, and is married to C. B loves no one, has no $, and is unmarried. C loves A, has $, and is married to A."

Figure 6b. Behavioral-iconographic analogy (cont.)

*(*XY) (*ZW)								"surrealistic" interpretation
.	1	1	0	.	1	0		A loves B and C, has no $, and is married to B. B loves C, has $, and is married to A and C. C loves A and B, has $, and is married to B.
0	.	1	1	1	.	1	=	
1	1	.	1	0	1	.		

The visual interpretation obtained is that in figure 5.

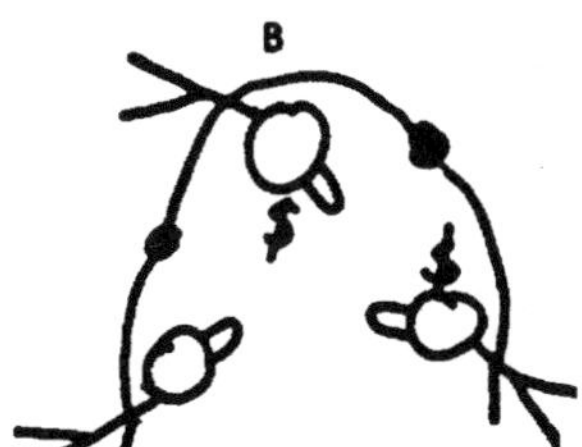

Fig. 5. A visual interpretation of the "surrealistic interpretation" *(*XY) (*ZW): "A loves B and C, has no $, and is married to B. B loves C, has $, and is married to A and C. C loves A and B, has $, and is married to B."

Figure 6c. Behavioral-iconographic analogy (cont.)

If we then postulate a situation P,

	La	Lb	Lc	$	Ma	Mb	Mc
A	.	1	1	0	.	0	0
B	1	.	0	0	0	.	0
C	1	0	.	1	0	0	.

= **A loves B and C, has no $, and is unmarried. B loves A, has no $, and is unmarried. C loves A, has $, and is unmarried.**

we can compute its successor state by analogy with the combinded results of X — Y and Z — W by solving

$$((X :: Y) :: (Z :: W)) :: (P :: ?),$$

where ? = *P(*(*XY) (*ZW)), which can be represented as follows:

	La	Lb	Lc	$	Ma	Mb	Mc
A	.	1	1	1	.	0	1
B	0	.	0	0	0	.	0
C	1	0	.	1	1	0	.

= **A loves B and C, has $, and is married to C. B loves no one, has no $, and is unmarried. C loves A, has $, and is married to A.**

This yields figure 6.

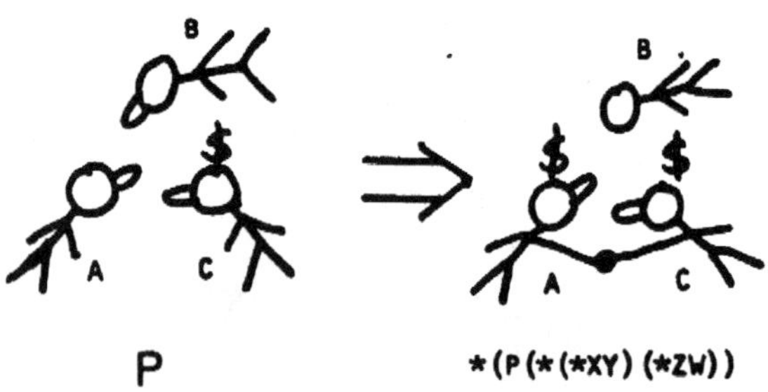

Fig. 6. A visual interpretation of P → *P (*(*XY) (*ZW)), where P is "A loves B and C, has no $, and is unmarried. B loves A, has no $, and is unmarried. C loves A, has $, and is unmarried" and *P (*(*XY) (*ZW)) is "A loves B and C, has $, and is married to C. B loves no one, has no $, and is unmarried. C loves A, has $, and is married to A."

Figure 6d. Behavioral-iconographic analogy (cont.)

7. Stone tools and language

Are motor skills associated with the origins of language? The view that they are is one associated with Piaget, but which remains controversial (Gibson & Ingold 1993). However, none of the arguments in the debate actually touches upon any of the formal syntactic or semantic aspects of language, nor do they recognize that there can be different types of language and that these can have rather different cognitive prerequisites, e.g. languages describable by finite-state grammars, context-free phrase structure rules, or context-sensitive, nor do they comprehend the cognitive computational requirements each entails, requirements that may be inherent, whatever the brain architecture, and whatever the cognitive model. The importance of language is in what it has enabled its users to do. For that reason, of utmost importance is the Middle to Upper Paleolithic transition, the moment when anatomically modern humans, after more than 150,000 years of behavioral banality, began to do rather interesting things.

The evidence of Boker Tachtit

Astounding as it may seem, it is possible to examine the cognitive processes of individual humans in 20 to 60–second bursts of time, in a collection of events that took place from 38,000 to 47,000 years ago. The hard evidence is recorded in stone, in the form of refitted cores from the archaeological site of Boker Tachtit in the central Negev Desert of southern Israel (Klein 1990: 551):

> The site was excavated by A. Marks in the 1970s, and revealed a sequence of four superimposed occupation levels, separated by intervening sterile deposits (see Marks 1981, 1983). The results of both uranium-thorium and radiocarbon dating indicate that the occupations took place between c. 47,000 and 38,000 BP, placing the site clearly within the conventional time-range of the Middle-Upper Paleolithic transition in the Near East. As Marks point out, one of the most valuable aspects of this sequence is that it represents a series of relatively short-lived episodes of human occupation and tool manufacture in a clear chronological succession (Marks 1983: 68): '...each occupation surface appears to have been lived on only briefly, as shown by the spatial distributions of reconstructable cores (Hietala and Marks 1981), and, therefore, each assemblage was produced during only a minute portion of that time. The assemblages taken together, however, should reflect accurately technological and typological patterns at specific intervals during this time span'.

A 'refitted core' represents the reconstruction of the original block of flint from which a tool, or sequence of tools was produced. The refitting process is one of reassembling a 3-dimensional puzzle from the debitage (the remaining flint fragments). An artifact of the refitting process is the knowledge of the exact sequence in which the various flint fragments were detached. The refitting work was accomplished by P. Volkman (1983), and he produced a tabulation of the various alternative sequences of flint removal that were actually found at each level of the site. These tabulations were for the final sequences of removal that predetermined the production of opposed-platform points at Boker Tachtit. When I saw Volkman's charts, I realized that they reflected the logic of a Klein-4 group, and were amenable to reformulation in a Boolean group notation and analysis for analogical patterning (Klein 1990: 502–506). The diagram in Figure 7 is Volkman's, and the labeled lines with numbered arrows represent the order and direction of the final detachments of flint in preparation for the final detachment of points (arrows labeled 'P').

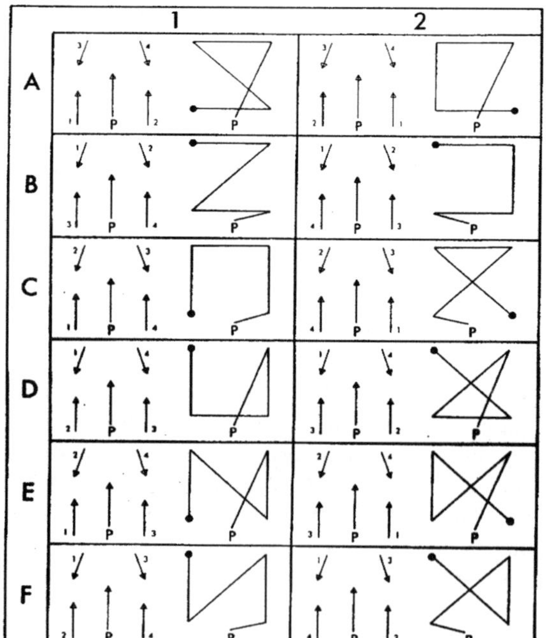

Figure 7. Illustration reproduced from Volkman 1983: Figure 6–25, to show schematic representation of the blade removal sequence variations that predetermine the removal of the opposed-platform Levallois Points at Boker Tachtit.

Table 5 indicates the different patterns of point production found at the various levels of the Boker Tachtit site (Level 1 is the earliest).[4]

Table 5. Data reproduced from Volkman (1983: Table 6–3), showing frequenciesof Levallois Points produced in the reduction sequence types shown in Figure 7.

Sequence Type	A1	A2	B1	B2	C1	C2	D1	D2	E1	E2	F1	F2	Totals
Level 1	1		1	1	1	3	1	2			2		12
Level 2			6	3	3	3	3		4	2	3	1	28
Emireh, Level 2			1		1	1	1	1					5
Level 3			1										1
Subtotal	1		9	4	5	7	5	3	4	2	5	1	
Totals	1		13		12		8		6		6		46

Table 6. (Klein 1990: 506 [Table 18.3])

							1	2	3	4
*A1B1	10	10	10	10	<	A1	01	11	00	10
						B1	00	10	01	11
*C1D1	10	10	10	10	<	C1	01	00	10	11
						D1	00	01	11	10
*E1F1	10	10	10	10	<	E1	01	00	11	10
						F1	00	01	10	11

	1	2	3	4						
A2	11	01	00	10	>	*A2B2	00	00	00	00
B2	00	10	11	01						
C2	11	00	10	01	>	*C2D2	00	00	00	00
D2	\`00	11	01	10						
E2	11	00	01	10	>	*E2F2	00	00	00	00
F2	00	11	10	01						

*A1A2	01	01	11	11
*B1B2	11	11	01	01
*C1C2	01	11	11	01
*D1D2	11	01	01	11
*E1E2	01	11	01	11
*F1F2	11	01	11	01

Table 6 contains my reinterpretation of the information contained in Volkman's Figure 18.2 in terms of binary semantic features representing left '0'/right '1', distal '0'/base '1' locations, in the order the detachments were made. The table also contains computed ATOs for Volkman's grouped sets of sequences. *I was able to derive the new sequences that appeared on level 2* (E1, E2 & F2) *using analogical ATO computations among just the sequences that occurred on level 1 of the site.*

Non-human use of tools and analogy

The use of tools is not limited to humans. Chimpanzees have been observed to use tools, and even to smash rocks to obtain useful fragments. Sea otters use rocks to open crustacean shells. The process is taught to their young — routinely, a sea otter will swim to the bottom and bring back both a crustacean and a rock, and then, use the rock to open the shell, while floating on its back, with the rock and the crustacean on its belly. There are numerous other examples, where the tool usage appears as learned behavior limited to specific groups of the same species.

Wynn (1991) has shown that tools made by very early humans reflected 4–fold symmetry. However, reconstructions of cores that might show varied sequences that form a Boolean group seem unavailable. Nevertheless, it seems likely that ATO type logic, which has been shown to be closely related to context-free phrase structure grammar, is part of the cognitive functioning not just of primates, but of most mammals. Consider the cognitive requirements for the young of a species to learn by imitation. The observed behavior must be seen as a kind of generalized script with roles that may be taken by participants other than just the performer of the moment. Moreover, as part of the imitative process, the pupil must place itself in the role of the teacher in order to perform the observed behaviour, an action usually requiring mirror-image reversal. Also required is an implicit recognition that the teacher and itself are members of a set that can quantify the role in a complex, goal-directed sequence of tasks. Accordingly, the use of ATO logic alone is not enough to account for the changes in human behavior that began in the Middle to Upper Paleolithic transition.

8. Behavioral rules and logical quantification by analogy

ATO logic can be used to predict plausible social behavior using examples in the form of situation descriptions in a binary feature notation (Klein 1983,

1988). Patterns of behavior in one domain can be extended to new situations in other domains. The process involves elevating the objects and relations in one context to a superset status, then computing the equivalence connections of the elements across each domain. The process is facilitated when a society has an active global classification scheme as part of its cosmology. China (Table 7) and India, for example, currently have active systems, and anthropologists have provided ample evidence of the prevalence of such systems in North and South America, and Australia, to name but a few. I believe it is fair to suggest that every society in the world has a global classification scheme in its history, even if its present day usage is limited to artifacts in grammatical categories. This seems to imply an origin in the Upper Paleolithic, and it would have been an invention that made it possible to compute the logical quantification of analogical extensions of behavior to novel situations in novel domains in real time (Klein 1990). The essential requirement for complex social organization to function is that the participants can predict the behavior of others. To use one's own behavioral schema to model the behavior of others requires a reassignment of characters to the roles in a particular scheme. Without the existence of a system of constraints, the computation can involve calculations of combinatoric complexity. A global classification scheme provides such a system of constraints, and it permits the computation of analogies by 'table-lookup', rather than by a combinatoric analysis.

Table 7. Chinese global classification system linked to the trigrams of the *I Ching*.

SOME TRIGRAM CORRESPONDENCES

	001 thunder	110 wind	101 fire	100 mountain	000 earth	111 heaven	011 lake	010 water
Element	wood		fire	earth		metal		water
Direction	East		South	Center		West		North
Color	blue		red	yellow		white		black
Season	spring		summer	*"fang"*		autumn		winter
Climate	windy		hot	humid		dry		cold
Planet	Jupiter		Mars	Saturn		Venus		Mercury
Sound	shouting		laughing	singing		weeping		groaning
Musical note	*chüeh*		*chih*	*kung*		*shang*		*yü*
Emotion	anger		joy	sympathy		grief		fear
Animal	dragon	fowl	pheasant	dog	ox	horse	sheep	pig
Family	1st son	1st da	2d da	3d son	mother	father	3d da	2d son
Body part	foot	thigh	eye	hand	belly	head	mouth	ear
Attribute	movement	penetration	brightness	standstill	docility	strength	pleasure	danger

SOURCES: Blofeld (1978:190–91), Wilhelm (1967 [1923]:1–11, 310), Legge (1964 [1899]:xliv–v), Legeza (1975:11), Fung Yu-lan (1953 [1934]:40–42, 86–132).

Linear computational efficiency

The behavioral analogy computation, given in an earlier example, implied a binary decision tree, composed of unary features, that resulted in $2^{15} = 32{,}768$ terminal elements as situation descriptions (Klein 1983: 155):

> "The tremendous computational advantage of ATOs applied to situation descriptions now becomes clear. To make such calculations it is *not* necessary to specify [and search] the entire feature tree; rather, one need only enumerate the sets of features relevant to the analogy."

As the number of features in a system increases, the computation time, in the worst case, increases only linearly, as opposed to the exponential or combinatorically increasing processing time typical of other methods of computation. If a cognitive system uses n features, it can account for 2^n concepts. If changing circumstances require just *one* additional feature to account for some new distinction, the size of the potential cognitive universe doubles, and it can be explored, by ATO logic with only a linear increase in computational effort.

9. A unified computational model

Consider the following factors:

1. Hidden layers in neural nets were required in order to model the **exclusive-OR** logical operator, one of the ATO alternatives.
2. Every new analogy requires a change in a category system. Consider the following analogical computation:

The small mouse fears a lion. ::	**The new student fears an exam.**
The large mouse likes a lion.	**?**

This can be computed by an ATO approach using syntactic trees in categorial grammar notation. Consider the dual-notation grammar in Table 8.

Table 8. Dual-notation grammar

LEXICON								
Det		*Adj*		*N*		*V*		
the	011011	small	001111	mouse	000011	fears	110110	
		large	001100	lion	111000	likes	110000	
		new	011001	student	011000			
		old	000110	exam	011110			
CATEGORIES								
Det	10011	Adj	11111	N	01111	V	11001	
NPP	01111	NP	00011	VP	00101	S	11001	
SYNTAX								
N	= Adj N		VP	= V NP		S	= NP VP	
01111	=*11111, 00011		00101	= *11001, 00011		11001	= *00011, 00101	
NP	= Det N							
00011	= *10011, 01111							

Figures 8 to 12 contain the categorial grammar trees used in the computation of the analogy.

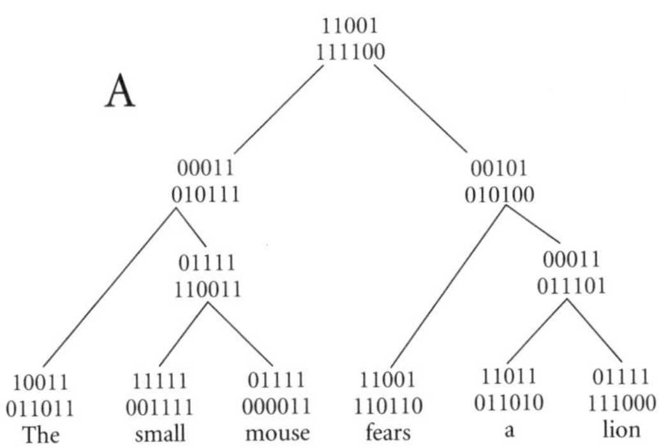

Figure 8. Boolean categorial grammar analysis of the first sentence in the analogy

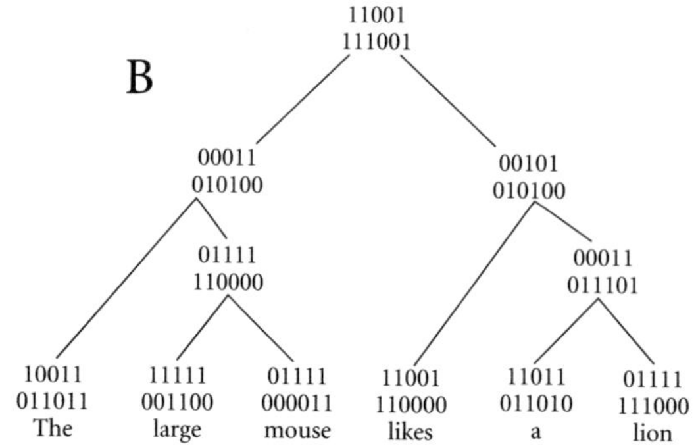

Figure 9. Boolean categorial grammar analysis of the second sentence in the analogy

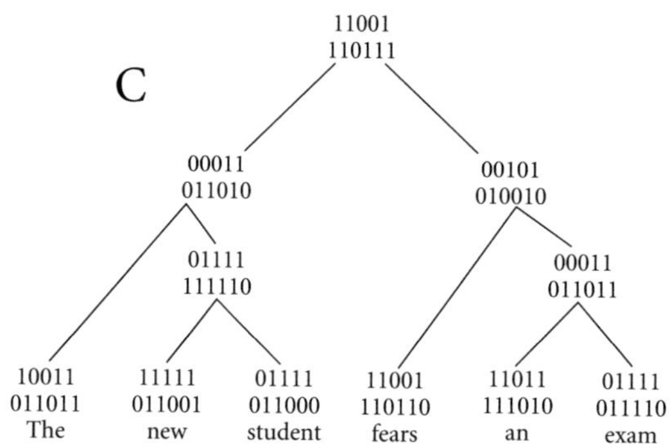

Figure 10. Boolean categorial grammar analysis of the third sentence in the analogy

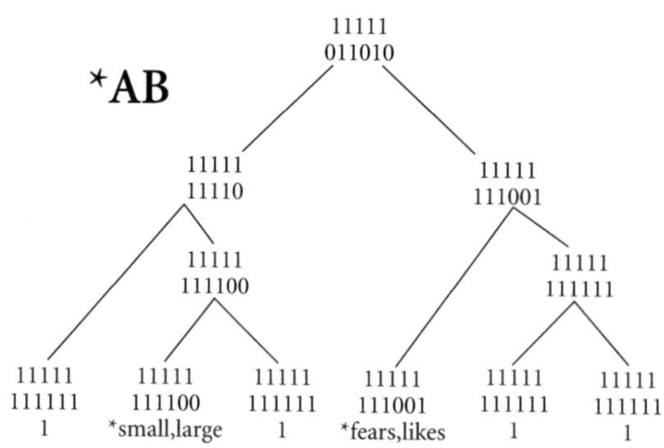

Figure 11. ATO tree, ***AB**, derived by applying the strong equivalence version to corresponding nodes in trees **A** and **B**

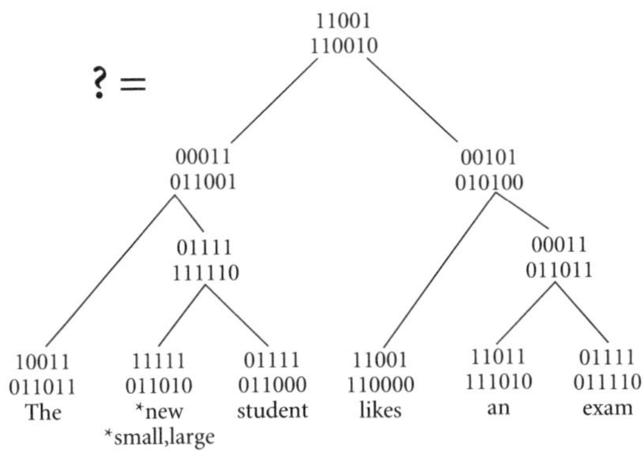

Figure 12. The result of applying the ATO tree to the Boolean categorial grammar analysis of the third sentence in the analogy

Table 9. Resolving the ambiguity by adding a new analogy,

$$\frac{\text{small } 001111}{\text{large } 001100} :: \frac{\text{new } 011001}{\text{old } 000110}$$

*small, large
= 111100

*new, old
= 100000

* *small, large, *new, old
= *111100, 100000 = 100011

But, *011010, 100011 = 000110 = **old**

The *?* tree, computed by ATO logic applied to each node of trees *A* and *B*, yields an ambiguous result that can be resolved by the positing of an additional analogy, (**small** :: **large**) :: (**new** :: **old**), which could form the nucleus for an additional pair of categorizations (Table 9).

3. Every act of learning a general case from a specific instance involves a new analogy, and either the creation of a new category, or the extension of an existing one.
4. ATO logic makes it possible to plan by analogy, at a computational cost that increases only linearly with the number of states in the plan sequence. Given a sequence of situations in a feature array notation, **A => B => C => D**, governed by an ATO transformation sequence, ***AB** => ***BC** => ***CD**, one may create a series of events to change the final state from D to E by replacing the first state, A, with *A*DE which would then yield the a new sequence, ***A*DE** => ***B*DE** => ***C*DE** => **E** :

```
*AB    *BC    *CD              *AB          * BC        *CD
 / \   /  \   /    \             /    \        /    \     /    \
A     B     C      D   *A*DE    *B*DE      *C*DE    E
```

If unary features are used, the resulting goal-directed sequence may contain 'surrealistic' or contradictory elements.

5. A culturally-based set of behavior patterns that persists across generations implies the existence of a hierarchy of ATOs that has remained stable at its higher levels (Table 10).

Table 10. ATO Hierarchy

```
      *AD       = pattern governing "pattern governing 'pattern governing event sequence'"
      /  \
  *AC    *BD      = pattern governing 'pattern governing event sequence'
   / \   /  \
*AB  *BC *CD     = pattern governing event sequence
 /  \ /   \ /  \
A    B     C    D  = event sequence
```

This can be interpreted as mechanism for the theory presented in Shore (1996): higher level operators are multiply encoded, through the medium of global classification schemes, in diverse domains of behavior including architecture, music, mythology, religious iconography and ritual, and in *language.*

With such a model, existing high-level structural patterns of behavior in a society can be applied to new domains, without necessarily modifying any ATOs, by extending the scope of pre-existing global classification schemes (Klein 1983). It is worth noting that this view also suggests that it might serve as a model interpretation for Spengler's theories regarding temporal structure of civilizations (1926–28).

A post-post Structuralist model

The *post-Structuralist wing* of the *post-Modern* movement in anthropological & archaeological theory rejected the Structuralism of the 1960's for a number of reasons, among which was its apparent static nature. The theory I have proposed uses the techniques of structuralist analysis for the collection and analysis of data, but makes use of implied logical relations as data for dynamic models of complex social behavior and change. *The result is that a structuralist methodology is used to derive the conclusions of post-structuralist theory, and that the structuralist models of Claude Lévi-Strauss appear to have a broad empirical foundation* (Lévi-Strauss 1962, 1964–71).

Do ATOs cccur in nature?

The answer is yes, and in the most fundamental processes of life and evolution on the planet. The relationship between DNA and RNA appears as a mirror image reversal if coded in a Boolean group notation:
If each DNA nucleotide base is named by a two place binary integer,

DNA	a	c	g	t	
	00	01	10	11	
					> ATO =00
	11	10	01	00	
RNA	t	g	c	a	

Why this is so is rather simple. Boolean group reversibility is a fundamental component of self-reproducing machines. It is the principle by which positive images are recorded as negatives, which are then turned into positives. It is the principle of digital image recording and reproduction.

And it has the properties of an encryption technique that adds a code book text to a message text using non-carry addition, and which returns the original if the code book text is subtracted from encrypted message by non-borrow subtraction. *But in binary arithmetic, these two processes are identical.* This *involutive* property has profound consequences:
The Transmission of Language, Culture and DNA, involve a single process, that of information transfer in a noisy channel, with the only difference being that of medium and time scale, implying that language, language change, and language variation are, ultimately, the same phenomena as their genetic counterparts.

10. 2100CE

The title of this paper promises a statement about the future of the human mind during the next century. Let me close by calling your attention to Terrence Deacon's book, *The Symbolic Species* (1997). Deacon's views on language evolution are ones I share: that the genetically determined innate capacities required in either Chomky's or Pinker's version of such theories is unnecessary. Observed linguistic universals appear because the architecture of the brain makes some language structures computationally inefficient. The languages of the world, which have real functions as communicative devices, have developed in configurations that prevent them from being computationally inefficient. Deacon also describes in considerable detail the mechanisms and the evidence of changes that can take place in brain structure functionality in a single individual in a single lifetime. This suggests to me that the nature of human consciousness may change in significant ways during the next century simply because of the shift to analogic iconographic reasoning that seems inherent in the use of computational media. For a speculation, it is unusually testable, and on a continuing basis, through the use of functional magnetic resonance imaging (fMRI) of the brain.

Notes

1. If the problem domain requires combinatorically increasing demands on resources, f(n!), where n is the number of entities involved in the required computations, then even adding an entire computer for each element of n will not help, for f(n!)/n = f((n-1)!), a saving that becomes meaningless as n becomes large.

2. Leibniz was made aware of the I Ching when a Jesuit Missionary in China wrote to him noting that a sequential arrangement of its 6 line figures seemed equivalent to a sequential listing of binary integers, from 0 to 63 .

3. Curry (1961) has sanctioned the use of the term '*functor*' for grammatical categories in categorial grammars, rather than the term, '*operator*'.

4. Tables 5 and 6 are corrected versions of the ones that appeared in Klein (1990).

References

Blofeld, John (1978). *Taoism: The road to immortality.* Boulder: Shambhala.

Curry, Haskell B. (1961). Some logical aspects of grammatical structure. In R. O. Jakobson (Ed.), *Structure of Language and Its Mathematical Aspects* [Proceedings of Symposia in Applied Mathematics Vol. XII] (56–68). Providence: American Mathematical Society.

Deacon, Terrence (1997). The Symbolic Species. New York: W.W. Norton & Co.

Elman, J.L., E.A. Bates, M.H. Johnson, A. Karmiloff-Smith, D. Parisi, K. Plunkett (1996). *Rethinking Innateness: A connectionist perspective on development.* Cambridge, MA: The MIT Press.

Fung ,Yu-lan (1953 [1934]). *A history of Chinese philosophy*, Vol. 2, translated by Derk Bodde. Princeton: Princeton University Press.

Gibson, Kathleen R. and Tim Ingold (Eds.) (1993). *Tools, language and cognition in human evolution.* Cambridge: Cambridge University Press.

Hietala, H.J. & A.E. Marks (1981). Changes in spatial organization at the middle to upper paleolithic transitional site of Boker Tachtit, central Negev, Israel. In J. Chauvin and P. Sanlaville (Eds.) *Préhistoire du Levant* (305–318). Paris: Centre National de la Recherche Scientifique.

Klein, Sheldon (1983). Analogy and mysticism and the structure of culture. *Current Anthropology* 24, 151–180.

Klein, Sheldon (1988). Reply to S.D. Siemens' critique of S. Klein's 'Analogy and mysticism and the structure of culture (Klein 1983)'. *Current Anthropology* 29, 478–483.

Klein, Sheldon (1990). Human cognitive changes at the middle to upper Paleolithic transition: The evidence of Boker Tachtit. In P. Mellars, (Ed.), *The emergence of modern humans: An archaeological perspective* (499–516). Edinburgh: Edinburgh University Press.

Klein, Sheldon (1991). The invention of computationally plausible knowledge systems in the upper paleolithic. In R. Foley, (Ed.), *The origins of human behaviour* (67–81). London: Unwin Hyman.

Klein, Sheldon (1996). Grammars, the *I Ching* and Lévi-Strauss: More on Siemens' 'Three formal theories of cultural analogy'. *Journal of Quantitative Anthropology* 6, 263–271.

Leibniz, G. W. (1968 [circa 1696–1698]). *Zwei briefe über das binäre zahlensystem und die Chinesiche philosophie.* Belser: Belser Presse.

Legeza, Laszlo (1975). *Tao magic: The Chinese art of the occult.* New York: Pantheon Books.

Legge, James (translator) (1962 [1899]). *The Yi King.* New Hyde Park, N.Y.: University Books.

Lévi-Strauss, Claude (1962). *La Pensée sauvage.* Paris: Plon.

Lévi-Strauss, Claude (1964–71). *Mythologiques* [4 volumes.]. Paris: Plon.

Marks, Anthony E. (1981). The middle paleolithic of the Negev. In J. Chauvin and P. Sanville (Eds.) *La préhistoire du levant* (287–298). Paris: Centre National de la Recherche Scientifique.

Marks, Anthony (1983). The middle to upper paleolithic transition in the Levant. In F. Wendorf and A.E. Close (Eds.), *Advances in world archaeology* [Vol. 2] (51–58). New York: Academic Press.

Mellars, Paul (1989). Major issues in the emergence of modern humans. *Current Anthropology* 30, 349–85.

Mellars, Paul (1991). Cognitive changes and the emergence of modern humans. *Cambridge Archaeological Journal I*, 63–76.

Mellars Paul & Chris Stringer (Eds.) (1989). *The human revolution: Behavioural and biological perspectives on the origins of modern humans.* Edinburgh: Edinburgh University Press.

Piaget, Jean (1953). *Logic & Psychology.* Manchester: Manchester University Press.

Volkman. Phillip W. (1983). Boker Tachit: core reconstructions. In A. Marks (Ed.) *Prehistory and paleoenvironments in the Central Negev, Israel* [Vol. 3: *The Avdat/agev Area* (Part 3)] (127–190). Dallas: Southern Methodist University Press.

Wilhelm, Richard (Translator) (1967 [1923]). *I Ching* [3rd edition] . English transl. by Cary F. Baynes. Princeton: Princeton University Press.

Wynn, Thomas (1991). Archaeological evidence for modern intelligence. In R. Foley, (Ed.), *The origins of human behaviour* (52–66). London: Unwin Hyman.

Creativity in humans, computers, and the rest of God's creatures

A meditation from within the economic world

T. Rickards
The Manchester Business School, England

Creativity has attracted attention as a contribution towards achieving individual and organisational innovations. Using the textual form of a personal meditation, this economic perspective is examined in the context of current research into the nature of work teams. This economic view is then extended to considerations of the nature of discovery processes in various domains of arts, science, and everyday life. Extensions of the concept of creativity are considered from its early metaphysical applications, to secular creativity, animal creativity, and computer creativity. A conjecture is offered on the relationship between various constructions placed on notions of creativity, and recent awaking of interest in the phenomenon of consciousness.

1. Introduction: Common sense perceptions of the creative individual

Inspired by the ecumenical goals of the conference, I determined to escape from the conventional bounds of academic rigour by offering a piece of work in progress. In this way I hope to contribute to dialog in a conference that seems to tolerate both the practical and the conceptually oriented, in domains as diverse as computer science and creativity. I thank one of the anonymous reviewers whose remarks encouraged me to persevere with this somewhat unorthodox approach. However, given further encouragement I might be tempted to provide the finished article with more conventional academic cladding.

After too many years cramped into an academic posture, I have not found this stretch for freedom particularly easy. However, in what follows, I have attempted a form of free-association around the topics of creativity and computers. In doing so, I began by reflecting on the question of individual creativity. 'Who', I asked myself 'would be generally regarded as creative?' When I pose this to business people and MBA students, Einstein usually gets a mention, as does Newton, and the great generalist Leonardo. Picasso is a clear favourite among modern painters; Mozart gets the nod among musical geniuses perhaps still a tad ahead of John Lennon.

I recently asked the question to a group of students taking a combined science with business studies degree. Most of these old favourites were again suggested by the group. There were also some unexpected nominations. One student voted for Mr Dyson, celebrated for his invention of an improved vacuum cleaner. Another suggested the footballer Maradonna. I am still pondering on this one. Perhaps the respondent saw creativity as a way of succeeding through an unexpected way of cheating and beating the system. That would be consistent with a response given by managers who give up on some Lateral Thinking task they have been set. ('It's a con'). Another student came up with a previously unremarked financial wizard — George Soros. I don't think he had been suggested before, although there have been quite a few mentions of Richard Branson, whose case has undoubtedly been helped by his flair for self-publicity. Finally, and also unusually, someone offered Armani, a modern designer and founder of a fashion house.

When I have my list of nominations, I like to discuss the absentees. Why are there so few women nominated? 'They have only just been liberated' one student suggested. That's a distinct possibility, and at least as convincing as the 'women have no Freudian need to displace their generative powers'; or the 'women can't do original research' views. Also, why are visual artists more frequently mentioned than are poets and novelists? Why no chess players? Or, for that matter chat-show hosts, or TV cookery pundits? Despite the gaps and absences, the list does support the more formally stated view of the creative individual as one who generates unexpected ideas appreciated for their potency in challenging and replacing the older existing set of related ideas. However, even among my business samples, business professionals tend mostly to be ignored. Can we conclude that most cognitive maps locate business and creativity in different territories?

2. The unfinished theoretical investigation of creativity

The nature of creativity continues to fascinate and frustrate in many walks of life. My interest in the subject has primarily been economic. In what follows, I will first report from that perspective, and then examine other issues that fall beyond the economic sphere. To arrive at a simplification of the field, I recently resorted to taking a selected 'handful of books' for study, extracting from them what seemed to be the dominant themes and theories (Rickards 1999). The following notes derive from that study. An immediate observation is the lack of consensus regarding the nature of creativity. One leading authority introduced an influential text with the words: 'The concept of creativity may trail clouds of glory, but it brings along also a host of controversial questions. The first of these is: What is it?' (Boden 1994: 1). Another wrote: 'The jury is in on the current state of creativity research and the verdict is — case dismissed for lack of evidence' (Ford 1995: 13). These views are shared by one of the best-known writers on stimulating creative ('lateral') ideas: 'The real reason we have done so very little about creativity is very simple. We have not understood it at all' (De Bono 1990: 218).

Creativity has been studied from a wide range of disciplines including psychology, philosophy, education, and business studies. This helps explain a lack of consensus, and indeed there are plenty of disagreements, even within each discipline 'Research in creativity has taken on the role of a prodigal stepbrother to research on intelligence..because although it is in the same family, it never quite seemed to those who follow it, to measure up… The stepbrother is prodigal because of his tendency to go beyond accepted bounds, and even at times to be grandiose. Some have wondered if it exists as a single entity or class of entities, aside from in name' (Sternberg 1988 vii).

These expert views can hardly be discounted. They constitute a case for giving up, or looking for some new approach to make progress. Wisely or not, I wish to pursue the second course. I will be approaching the subject as if it were a very difficult puzzle. A review of received wisdom helps us to gain understanding of the most important 'bits of the jigsaw', or what might be called the prevailing 'platform of understanding' (Rickards 1999). This also indicates missing and ill-fitting bits of the jigsaw.

3. A platform of understanding of creativity

Among theorists and practitioners alike, there is a view that creativity is 'something to do with' processes that produce new and valued ideas. The novelty and value may be primarily an assessment by the person doing the thinking and creating. Or it may be an assessment by wider social groupings. There is also mostly agreement that the process is complex and multi-facetted. Most authorities agree that there is no universally agreed creativity test, nor is there a universally agreed definition. The processes are regarded as partly unconscious, and may leap into consciousness as a moment of inspiration or insight. Even here, however all is not lost. The very large number of definitions are not particularly divergent in character. Rather, they reveal partial views from various perspectives. Some of the heat was taken out of the definitional problem through a meta-analysis that showed them to collapse into four overlapping components of 'person, product, process and press (i.e. environment).

Research suggests that the processes can be deliberately actuated, just as they can be attenuated by environmental factors. There are many accounts of the special and idiosyncratic conditions required for a particular person to 'settle down' to the creative process. For some, this involved occupying a favoured location. Others, needed special stimuli (one author, for example, required that his writing desk was full of ripening apples). Controversially, alcohol and various mind-influencing drugs have been mentioned in this connection.

We have begun to revisit animal rights as an ethical issue. What is consciousness, and do animals have it in a way that grants them ethical equivalence with humans? There is an echo of the debate regarding the creativity of animals. The gestalt scientist Köhler was confined to Tenerife during World War one. As he watched the apes of Tenerife he found many examples of what the Gestaltists referred to as insight closure. One ape, Sultan, in particular seemed able to change his behaviours consistent with gestalt theory. Sultan was filmed while he appeared to be solving problems by discovering a new use for a stick, or a box, to enable him to reach his favourite food of bananas. The process had the characteristics of a sudden unexpected discovery considered to come from a Gestalt reconfiguration or switch of perceptual frame. Some years later the artistic efforts of another chimp were displayed at an exhibition of modern painting. This year we learned that a captive elephant had produced a modernistic painting working from an artist's palate, with the brush held in its trunk.

4. Dispatches from the economic world

The commercial world has, in general, treated creativity at arms-length. With few notable exceptions, economists have found no place for creativity in their mathematical constructions. Practical business folk are inclined to the view that creativity — if it exists — is innate. They are, however, willing to concede that new ideas are valuable, and that specialists such as 'boffins' and advertising agents are good at coming up with clever ideas which eventually contribute to a firm's well-being. However skeptical, business supports the kind of research aimed at 'taming' creativity and generating new and better ideas to order. There has thus been some encouragement for techniques that stimulate creativity. There is a practical advantage for studying these issues at the level of the team rather than the individual. Team members try to communicate and exchange ideas, so that inter-personal exchanges are easier to track. In contrast, introspective studies of individuals engaged in creativity, although fascinating, have not been so revealing of the inner mental processes involved.

Before considering the nature of creative teams, however, we need to touch on the 'platform of understanding' of the creative individual. We can get at this by trying to tease out the implicit theories of creativity held across various domains. One leading figure, Professor Mark Runco, has done just that (Runco 1990). The approach draws on social validation theory (Wolf 1979) for its legitimization, and has been tested and discussed in investigations of related fields such as intelligence (Sternberg 1985). The contributions from the 'everyday' study above indicate tacit theories of creativity. The stereotypic creative individual has been summarized as someone whose characteristics include a 'heightened sense of identity' (Albert 1990: 21); strong ego strength; and effective operation within certain kinds of psychopathology and early life experiences. This stereotype, like that of the great leader, has been challenged as dangerously culture-bound. Furthermore, there has been a tendency to concentrate on 'virtuous success', so that the overall set of features may underplay the malevolent, and deviant. Indeed, the innocuous appearance of the word 'effective' actually hides quite severe technical difficulties in research studies (Sutton & Hargadon 1996). It has typically been associated with exceptional talent at solving socially valued problems.

When we move from the level of the individual to that of the group, one point should be made, as it is not immediately obvious. Let us define a creative team as one that achieves unexpectedly new and valuable results. They break new ground in what they do, and in how they do it. However, the team is far more than a collection of creative individuals. There is some experimental evidence that a collection of so-called 'high creatives' rarely work well as a functional unit (Belbin 1981, Tjosvold 1992).

Studies at the level of the group have assumed that creativity is a valued, perhaps necessary, characteristic of teams generating new and valued outputs. However, an important issue has remained largely unexplored, namely the features that might differentiate creative teams from others that achieve 'standard' or expected outputs. The creative problem-solving literature suggests that the creative performance of such teams is enhanced by leadership interventions. The literature has indicated a leadership role of a facilitative kind, that provides a team with procedures or protocols for generating new ('creative') outputs.

Based on our experiences with teams attempting to develop innovative products, we considered two critical questions to be 'what mechanisms are at play when a team fails to achieve expected performance?' and 'what mechanisms lead to outstanding performance? The posing of these questions followed from our own experiences of some teams that never seemed to achieve a satisfactory level of coherence. We had also found some teams that exceeded expectations. We called these 'dream teams', and the under performers 'teams from hell' (Rickards & Moger 1999). The performance of dream teams seemed to us to exemplify the processes of creative team-work.

We concluded that the teams had to deal with barriers of some kind. Such considerations led to a two-barrier model to creative performance in teams. The first barrier represents the inter-personal and intra-personal forces that have to be overcome prior to norm formation. We assume that the barrier is weak, in the sense of providing only a temporary obstruction, which most teams overcome. In contrast, again drawing on general understanding of the rarity of outstanding performance, we assume that the second barrier is a more difficult one for teams to pass through. It represents the forces that are overcome when a team breaks out of the conventional expectations within a particular social context such as a corporate culture. These two assumptions lead to our two-barrier hypothesis of team development. This can be formally stated as follows:

'The performance characteristics of a comparable set of teams operating with common tasks can be accounted for in a developmental process that encounters two successive constraints or barriers to excellence. The first is a weak barrier through which most teams pass to achieve a shared standard of performance. The second is a strong barrier through which few teams pass'.

Leadership was identified as an overarching feature of exceptional teams. These teams also showed differences on various observable characteristics. It has been suggested that creative leadership impacts on a set of team factors, which can be studied as predictors of exceptional performance.

Factor 1: Platform of Understanding. The creative leader explains that at the start of any creative effort, a team benefits from exploring shared knowledge, beliefs, and assumptions. These elements comprise a 'platform of understanding' from which new ideas develop.
Factor 2: Shared Vision. The platform of understanding suggests perspectives. A dominant perspective amounts to a shared view. The standard view is one mostly constrained by habit and assumptions.
Factor 3: Climate. The team leader emphasizes the importance of a positive climate. Various studies have demonstrated that a warm and supportive climate is associated with innovative outcomes from group activities
Factor 4: Resilience. The team leader emphasizes the principle of dealing with dashed expectations by seeking alternative perspectives. 'There must be other ways…there may even be better ways'
Factor 5: Idea Owners. Efforts are made to build commitment to ideas. The team leader encourages deliberations designed to align the ideas within regions over which team members have know-how and control
Factor 6: Network Activators. This factor was derived after interviewing a sample of participants who were successful executives outside the creative problem-solving exercises. It retained the managerial vocabulary of someone able to create additional team resources through external networking.
Factor 7: Learning From Experience. The creative leadership interventions have been explained as a means of achieving experiential learning.

Benign structures
To date the two barrier hypothesis is pointing to a creative process in teams that can be directly influenced by the team leader introducing procedures we have called benign structures. The team, in following the benign structures, is better able to pass through the proposed two barriers to excellent (i.e. creative) performance.

5. Implications of the two-barrier hypothesis

We have tested the two-barrier hypothesis in various kinds of innovation teams, and the first qualitative results of the two-barrier hypothesis are promising. However, the studies have been deliberately restricted to project teams. These have special characteristics. They have a reasonably well defined commercial goal or objective. They are relatively stable over time. In our studies, we were even able to find multiple teams working on similar or identical tasks, again making comparisons easier. Most importantly, we had special sets of teams for which we introduced carefully designed structures for supporting creativity — the so-called creativity techniques. For such reasons we have made some progress in identifying the 'benign structures' that supported exceptional performance.

The performance of exceptional teams is regarded as indicators of the teams' creative competence in action. Self-nominations may not match the more clinical observations of independent observers. However, this kind of self-report has been found a good predictor of tangible innovative outputs from various studies of innovative teams. Overall, the two-barrier hypothesis has some promise for speculations regarding the nature of creativity in a wider set of domains.

6. Extrapolating the experimental results to natural systems

To understand the implications of the hypothesis we need to take the pieces of the jigsaw and make more sense of them. The factors all seem to have something to do with what Stafford Beer has called a viable system (e.g. Beer 1981). In dysfunctional teams, the factors lead to a non-viable system, a team from hell. In functional teams, the factors all work together in the interests of producing a fully-functioning system. Viable systems theory 'works' in explaining how and why systems (including organisations and cultures) are self-structuring, mostly resulting in standard performance. It is rather good at suggesting restructuring of elements of the system (particularly its communication and control channels) to induce viability in dysfunctional systems. Our work suggests ways of dealing with the barrier to dysfunctionality, and the tougher barrier to exceptional performance.

That is not to say that viable systems theory is unable to accommodate major restructuring. Beer tells a tale of explaining Chile as a viable system to the late President Allende. His elegant exposition shows how the system (in accord to the theory) develops its structures for viability. The theory has provision for a 'systems 5' intervention that permits such changes. Beer would have indicated how such a change comes from the Chief Executive Officer. Allende, the model communist leader, anticipated the point. 'Ah, yes, *The People!*' he remarked. In principle, 'The Leader' or 'The People' can find ways of transcending mere viability and of reconstructing reality by intervening across all the various elements within the system.

7. A meditation on creativity in humans, computers, and the rest of God's creatures

The ethos of this conference seems to invite a wide view that transcends the economic paradigm. I would like to seize the opportunity thus offered. In doing so I find myself wondering along these lines;. What are we to make of creativity over these few days together, as a community containing, among its ranks great artistic talents, scientifically brilliant individuals, computer whizz-kids, educationalists, philosophers, and theologists? Can we arrive at any satisfactory shared understanding of an utterance such as '*That*'s creative, but *that* on the other hand isn't ?' For sure, we are some way away from a general all-purpose definition. Are we content with a term that covers a wide-range of phenomena from the performance of computer programmes, to the actions of apes, and the words of poets? Are we comfortable with the notions of a creative individual, a creative team, a creative organisation, and even a creative culture?

My meditation takes me back to the activities of academic who had formerly held at post at the Victoria University of Manchester. David Jenkins, one of the University's more notorious clerics, became appointed to the post of Bishop of Durham. From that position, he engaged in a debate that challenged the very core of religious beliefs. One of his epithets was to suggest that Christianity could move on from a belief in miracles. He described miracles as 'conjuring with bones'. Was David Jenkins being creative? Or was he attempting to eliminate a belief in creative works that had sustained itself for two Millenia? Whatever the intent, his behaviours contrasted with a little incident in which I was more directly involved. Some years earlier I had been appointed as lecturer in creativity at that same University. It was alleged that the news of the appointment was met with wrath by none other than the Professor of Divinity. He scrawled an irate message across the memorandum announcing the appointment, and returned it to the Registrar's office. '*Lecturer in Creativity!*' he had scribbled, '*Does **God** know?*'

I suppose these anecdotes indicate one component in any consideration of creativity. Where does the concept square (or fail to square) with our notions of a supreme being? There are certainly people who regard themselves as Creationists. For them, the world and all that is within it was created by God. Huw Wheldon, a BBC broadcaster, (and not a Creationist in that sense, as far as I know) once remarked that he could not see any merit in the idea of creativity. 'All *that* ended on the seventh day' he commented dismissively. 'Since then, there has only been imitation and recombination.'

The term creativity in use today has a lot of historical baggage. In earlier days, creativity was a term with strictly sacred connotations. Sacred art reflected the one and only Creator. The creative impulse was an inspiration. The metaphor here is of that of the artist as vessel or receptacle, receiving the gift of knowledge as the sacred breath of God. Representations of nature were representations of the creations of the Almighty. A creative picture meant no more than one which held up the world created by God to further His glory. Perhaps unsurprisingly, one tradition in creativity is to treat the process of discovery with reverence. The 'magic, mythic and mysterious' approach is still one that has appeal. Quite a few creative artists are suspicious of attempts by psychologists to 'get into their heads'. They have a fear that to know more about the origins of their inspiration would risk them losing it.

The Enlightenment rejected theological authority, and replaced it with the authority of scientific reason. What seems to have happened is a refusal by the pre-modern notions to go away quietly. The 'magical, mystical, and mysterious' notions persist, supported by the 'stories' of inspiration told by creative artists and others. Nevertheless, modernism was itself to become open to attack. The post-modernists have gone further, and have rejected all forms of authority, including that of science (see, for example, Boje, Gephart, & Thatchenkery 1996).

Once the 'ghost in the machine' was exorcised, it became easier to examine machines as a source of creativity. This has led to interest in computer creativity, championed among others by no less a figure than Herbert Simon (1986) . Other studies have indicated that musical 'fingerprints' can be constructed that accurately predict a composer from a fragment of music; and that music, poetry, and mathematical pieces can be generated by computer. Researchers have indeed shown that interesting mathematical relationships exist after content analysis and coding of poetic samples (Martindale 1990).

Here the issue is not whether computers are creative, but rather whether the use to which they have been put can shed light on the creative process. These are big and difficult questions indeed. We are finding renewed efforts to 'get at' the deepest and oldest mysteries through connecting metaphysics with neuroscience (Churchland 1995; Crick 1995).

I find some encouragement in the possibility that there will be a growth of interest in creativity aligned to a growth of interest in consciousness (Block, Flanigan, & Guzeldere 1997). The history of consciousness research has some parallels with that of creativity as is seen from my concluding quotation: 'Consciousness, as a subject matter of research in philosophy and in science, has a fascinating history. [It has been] taken to be the "starting point of all psychology," only a few decades before it was condemned as being part and parcel of superstition and magic".' (Block et al. Ibid: xi). Perhaps a symposium on creativity and consciousness might be a way of bringing the two fields a little closer together.

Postscript

Timeless as I fondly believed these meditations to be, I now feel the need to speak from a later point in time. Since the original notes were assembled, the model of leadership, team factors and outputs has been tested in assorted publications and doctoral research dissertations. The work has to compete for survival in the Darwinian jungle of academia. More consistent with the theme of the original contribution, I wanted to comment on one highly interesting development. The work on the creative leader had turned into a study of trust. Ironically, the connection was made through encounters with the movement for pain-free horse training, associated with the legend of Monty Roberts and horse whispering. With colleagues, I have become encouraging meditations on trust-based relationships, in the factory and board room, but also in events at which attempts are made to gain the trust of untamed or badly treated horses. Inevitably the basic proposition has attracted the distortions of multi-media journalists enthusiastic for a story involving business leaders and bucking broncos. The basic proposition has also met with the scorn and rejection as well as fulsome signals of encouragement to continue. At very least, the experience confirms my initial notion that there is much to be learned about humna creativity from considerations of the ways we relate to other creatures.

References

Albert, Robert S. (1990). Identify, experiences, and career choice among the exceptionally gifted and eminent. In M. A. Runco, Mark (Ed.). *Theories of creativity* (13–34). Newbury Park (Cal): Sage.

Beer, Stafford (1981). *The brain of the firm.* Chichester: J. Wiley.

Belbin, Raymond M. (1981). *Management teams: Why they succeed or fail.* London: Heinemann.

Block, N., O. Flanigan, & G. Guzeldere (1997). *The nature of consciousness.* Cambridge: MIT Press.

Boden, Margaret A. (Ed.) (1994). *Dimensions of creativity.* Cambridge, Mass: The MIT Press.

Boje, David M., R. P. Gephart Jr., & T. J. Thatchenkery (Eds.) (1996). *Postmodern management and organization theory.* Thousand Oaks: Sage.

Crick, Francis (1995). *The astonishing hypothesis: The scientific search for the soul.* London: Touchstone.

De Bono, Edward (1990). *I am right You are wrong.* London: Viking.

Ford, Cameron M. (1995). In C. M. Ford, & D. A. Gioia (Eds.), *Creative actions in organizations: Ivory tower visions and real world voices.* Thousand Oaks, Ca: Sage

Martindale, Colin (1990). *The clockwork muse: The predictability of artistic change.* NY: Basic Books.

Penrose, Roger (1989). *The emperor's new mind.* Oxford: Oxford University Press, Vintage Edition.

Rickards, Tudor (1999). *Creativity and the management of change.* Oxford: Blackwells.

Rickards, Tudor, & Susan T. Moger (1999). *Handbook for creative team leaders.* Aldershot, Hants: Gower.

Runco, Mark A. (1990). Implicit theories and ideational creativity. In M. A. Runco, (Ed.), *Theories of creativity* (234–252). Newbury Park(Cal): Sage.

Simon, Herbert A. (1986). What we know about the creative process. In R. L. Kuhn (Ed.), *Creative and innovative management* (3–22). Cambridge, Mass.: Ballinger.

Sternberg, Robert J. (1985). Implicit theories of intelligence, creativity and wisdom. *Journal of Personality and Social Psychology, 49*, 607–627.

Sternberg, Robert J. (1988). *The nature of creativity.* Cambridge, Cambridge University Press.

Sutton, R. I. & A. Hargadon (1996). Brainstorming groups in context: Effectiveness in a product design firm. *Administrative Science Quarterly, 41*, 685–718.

Tjosvold, Dean (1992). *Team organization: An enduring competitive advantage.* Chichester: Wiley.

Wolf, M. M. (1979). Social validity: The case for subjective assessment, or how applied behavior analysis is finding its heart. *Journal of Applied Behavior Analysis, 11*, 204–214.

The origins of Mexican metaphor in Tarahumara Indian religion

Julia Elizabeth Lonergan
New Mexico State University, USA

1. Introduction

The Tarahumara, or "Pillars of the Sky," are the indigenous people of northern Mexico occupying the southwest corner of the State of Chihuahua. They believe that they are a chosen people who are charged with the role of serving *Onorúame* (God the Father) through religious wakes called *tesgüinadas. Tesgüinada,* means "beer-drinking wake," after *tesgüino,* or corn-fermented beer. Two of the most important religious wakes are performed for the *Semana Santa* (Holy Week), or the 7-day Feast of Unleavened Bread (Passover) in April, and for the Feast of the Harvest, or *Dia de los Muertos* (Day of the Dead) in November. *Tesqüinadas* are also given for the purpose of healing, and deterring misfortune brought by the *mal ojo* (evil eye) (Palma 1992). Humor and beer-drinking is intimately connected with religion. Joking and laughter are the critical venues used to maintain the cosmic balance between good and evil on the earth. During Tarahumara holidays, humor is elicited from violations of the norm, contrary behavior, and *cómico sexual* (humor on the subject of sex). This paper makes references to the function of humor in Tarahumara religious ritual and compares the indigenous mythologies with the linguistic metaphor used by the Mexican *mestizos.* The Tarahumara have three major annual *fiestas,* or *tesgüinadas.* They perform *tesgüinada* for the New Year in April, the feast of the first fruits in August, and the feast of the harvest in November (Bennett & Zing 1935).[1] The paper entertains the notion that the mechanisms of metaphorical speech used characteristically by the Mexican *mestizo* allude to having origin in indigenous Mexican Indian mythology and religious ideology. The contradictions between: (1) the Tarahumara people believing themselves to be of a chosen priesthood, (2) the observances of sacred Holidays with beer-drinking, and (3) their usage of joking and *cómico sexual* as the instruments for confronting and evading harm and misfortune, all blend together to form a strange and contradictory union. These contradictions form the interesting paradox which provides a baseline for understanding the Mexican peasant and the *mestizo* sense of humor.

2. Mexican linguistic strategies

Tragicomic humor, or humor that manifests both tragic and comic elements, is prevalent in the speech of the Mexican *mestizos* who reside along, farm, and emigrate across the river systems that delimit the frontier between northern Mexico and the southwestern United States. Within the peasant population, the degree of language-related humor is extensive. Their world view is full of idiomatic proverbs and metaphors that speak from a kind of collective pessimism. This includes the attitude of suffering, where "Mexicans know that life is worthless" (Guillermoprieto 1994). Mexicans have a strong tendency to elevate and transform pain into laughter by contrasting an obsessive rhetoric regarding death, loss, and tragedy, against an uncontrollable and unrelenting passion for weeping through laughter (Guillermoprieto 1994). To express pain, they use laughter instead of tears. This use of language is grounded in a strong oral history. Tarahumara is a native Uto-Aztecan language of Chihuahua, Mexico, that until recently had no writing system. Tarahumara is an oral rather than a written language, and Tarahumara society is oral rather than a literate one. This has a strong influence of the population of Chihuahua. Ninety-seven percent of Tarahumara are *mestizo* with the Chihuahueñse population (Levi-Meyer 1993).[2] The criteria for distinguishing the population between *mestizo* (W. European-Indian/mix) and *indígena* (indigenous) is the ability to speak the indigenous language (Gonzáles et al. 1994). Of the total population of 300,000 inhabitants living in the Sierra Tarahumara, between 229,500–247,534 are *mestizo*-Tarahumara and only 50,226–60,000 are *Rarámuri*-Tarahumara (González et al. 1994). *La primaria* is the basic educational instruction that is given to all Mexican children from the age of 6 until the age 14. In 1990, more than half of the Chihuahueñse population was at "educational risk" and did not complete basic education (Garcia et al. 1995). And Mexico's Federal programs for indigenous children provide only two years (K-1–2) of bilingual education (Tarahumara — Spanish) to elementary level Tarahumara children. With little access to new communication technologies and standardized education, the *mestizo* and Rarámuri populations, continue to maintain a strong mode of verbal communication and metaphorical speech. The "civil" language has not been cleansed of its persuasive and figurative elements through exposure to the rationalist ideal of "emphatic iconoclasm." Emphatic iconoclasm calls for a literal, metaphor-free language to distinguish between proper academic language and figurative, improper everyday language (Debatin 1997). Modern philosophies of education, which critique colloquial language as imprecise and figurative, have failed to eliminate, control and discipline the "magic thinking" that governs peasant perception and consciousness. The language remains metaphorical and full of figurative elements.

3. Metaphors: An instrument of humor

Mexican culture displays extremely contradictory and opposing values. The norms and values that run through the culture are expressed in superstition and folklore, which in turn, predisposes the Mexican language to contradiction and metaphor. Metaphors are complex linguistic constructions for interpretation and understanding. What is metaphorical can not be literal. Metaphor is understanding and experiencing one kind of thing in terms of another by bringing forward aspects that might not be seen through another medium. Metaphors acts an communicative processes in which metaphorical meaning and its validity claim are negotiated (Debatin 1995). Often, they are instances of coherence, distinguished by the presence of a relevant analogy. Coherence is the synergism of knowledge, where synergism is the interaction of two or more discrete agencies to achieve an effect of which non is individually capable (Fass 1988). According to Debatin (1997), reflection upon metaphor does not entail converting metaphorical meaning into literal meaning, but instead it requires a determination to decide its validity. At the earliest moments of comprehension of a metaphorical utterance, listeners project two conceptual domains linguistically represented by the source and target terms onto each other to arrive at a metaphorical meaning that highlights the emergent similarities (Gibbs 1994). Metaphors must prove themselves in the light of critical reflection when necessary background knowledge related to a conceptual framework is mapped onto a target framework, and validity is derived from inferences on conceptual relatedness. Metaphorical tension arises from the literal incompatibility, and the listeners experience some aesthetic delight when they discover the hidden meaning of metaphor (Gibbs 1994). The effect of metaphor can be described as an "as-if" prediction that comes true only in the light of anticipatory evidence and reflective metaphoization (Debatin 1995). From a postmodernist perspective, the mind is not a mirror of reality, but instead knowledge corresponds to the nature of the epistemic justification of dominant beliefs at a given moment. Where are the minds of the ones who speak an endangered language? The language shows the dominant beliefs of what given moment? Mexican metaphor renders visible the indigenous cultural images that are most deeply anchored in tradition and makes them accessible to our reflection.

4. Developing the joking relationship

Tarahumara use of humor in the celebration of High Holy Days (*tesgüinadas*) provides source knowledge for understanding some details of Mexican metaphor. The Tarahumara possess patterned joking associated with the *tesgüinada* (Kennedy 1970). *Tesgüino*, or the corn-fermented beer that is brewed by the Tarahumara, is central to every Tarahumara *fiesta*. Joking relationships are established in these regular beer drinking parties where the most extroverted, exhibitionistic, and dynamic personalities are the protagonists, leading the humorous discourse (Kennedy 1970). Tarahumara culture encourages drunkenness and attaches no shame or disgrace to it (Fontana 1979). The most important social entities in Tarahumara society are *compadres* and *comadres* (closest friends) who are defined by reciprocal invitations to beer parties (Kennedy 1970). The Tarahumara *mestizos* living in the *pueblos* call everyone that they are close friends with "*compadre.*" *Compadre* is also the term that a *mestizo* calls the Tarahumara-Rarámuri when they visit their house asking for "*kórima*". Asking for *kórima* is a basic indigenous notion that all the Rarámuri have the right to ask someone in a better economic situation than they are in to give them food, money, shelter, or water (González et al. 1994). Their economic system is cooperative and reciprocity defines their morality structure. Beer is the national drink and the medium for reciprocity and interchange. The *tesgüinada* is the most centrally defining element of the Tarahumara social structure (Fontana 1979). The Tarahumara hold humor in high esteem. It is this network of people, who customarily drink corn-beer together and the pattern of word-plays that unfold, that outlines the Tarahumara social and political life. The following Mexican metaphors are a constitutive model for thought which assume significance by virtue of their rhyme and their correspondence to something else.

(1) *Nadie sabe lo que traí el morral, nomas el que lo carga.*
[Nobody knows what is in the bag, except the one that carries it.]

Sentence (1) contains a semantic relation between a "*morral*" and "the outward appearance of a man." In the source domain, knowledge surrounding the *morral*, which is a back-pack bag carried by the Tarahumara around their waist that contains supplies for their foot journeys, is mapped onto the target domain of the outward appearance of a person. Specifically, each Tarahumara man packs his own *morral* and unless one looks inside, there is no way to determine what is in there. Similarly, when one sees a Tarahumara man with his *ropa de manta* (loin cloth) and *morral*, one tends to believe that they are poor and ignorant people, still wearing linen breeches from their loins to their thighs. It is easy to judge such a person by the outward appearance, not really knowing what the inward man represents. The contradiction in this metaphor is that the Tarahumara believe that their clothing identifies them as the people following "the Pillars of the Sky."[3]

The Rarámuri are considered by the Roman Catholic Tarahumara to be pagans because they refused "Catholicism" and instead escaped into the Sierra Madre Mountains on foot. They translate that they originated from the location on the earth where the pillars existed that touched the sky, where the columns reached the heavens (Gonzáles & Palma 1985). *Onorúame*, or God the Father, was at the "pillars." For this reason, there was a strong resistance to Catholic integration and they refused to bow before the Catholic imagery. The Tarahumara-Rarámuri escaped the Spanish mission reduction in order to maintain their customs. The Rarámuri are distinct in that they baptize their own children. They bury their dead in caves and they believe in God (the Father), not in the Catholic Virgin, and not in the Roman Catholic mass (Levi-Meyer 1993). Of the *mestizos* of Chihuahua Mexico, ninety-seven percent are of Tarahumara descent, and they became the Mexican farmers of the Sierra Valley in Chihuahua (Bennett & Zing 1935). Cultural differences have not been found to be very great between the Rarámuri and the other *mestizo*-Tarahumara (Pastron 1977). The *mestizo* accept the imagery of the Catholic Church and Catholicism, they bury their dead in the *campo santo* (cemetery), they live in the *pueblos* (mission centers), and they dance all the Catholic *fiestas* (holidays). Still, the "Christianized" Tarahumara retained nearly as much of aboriginal religious customs as their more rebellious counterparts (Kennedy 1978).

(2) *Cuando el río suena, es porque agua lleva.*
[When the river sounds, it is because it carries water].

In (2), the statement of "the sound of the river being produced by the water it carries," is used to conceptualize the semantic properties of "rumor being produced because of the truth they carry." It calls on the listener to consider their pre-existing knowledge surrounding the analogous example and to observe its relations and correspondence with the properties of the rumor assertion. The metaphor is invoked when the one suspects something is going to happen, or is about to learn about something that has already happened through rumor.

The Tarahumara are superstitious about living near the many river systems and waterways in the valley. There are rumors that the river has a spiritual force that can trap the soul of a person and cause death. Witchdoctors travel in dreams to locate and release the soul from the river and cure to the sick. They also resisted the mission integration established by the Catholic Church at the base of the mountains for fear of the "flooding." They say that their ancestors were the survivors of a great flood. As the survivors of the great flood, they must continue to act as "pillars" to keep the sky from falling in. Erasmo Palma, a native of the *Sierra Tarahumara*, provides this statement given by his grandmother:

> the indigenous ancestors narrate that in the past the water covered the whole world; it was a punishment sent by God because the people were behaving badly; and for this same reason, the Tarahumara never want to make their houses close to the river, but instead they make them in the highest mountains (1992, p. 48, author's translation).

There are an estimated 50–65,000 Tarahumara Indians currently scattered in the canyons of the *Sierra Tarahumara*. Until 1781 there existed laws in Chihuahua which sanctioned the forced removal of the Tarahumara from their settlements to work on Spanish *haciendas* and laws which allowed impressing them to work in mining operations (Kennedy 1978). Only three percent of Tarahumara resisted *pueblo* migration and managed to isolate themselves during the Spanish Conquest by hiding in the deep gorges of the canyons of the *Sierra Tarahumara*. The most famous of these is the Copper Canyon; it is the largest in the world. The *Sierra Tarahumara* is four times the size of the Grand Canyon in acreage (Levi-Meyer 1993). Their continued residence, isolated in the highland cliffs of the *Sierra Madre* Occidental Mountains above the river valley, reinforces their ancient superstitions and beliefs.

(3) *El que siembra su maiz, que se come su pinole.*
[Whosoever grows corn, let him drink *pinole*.]

There is a metaphorical relation between "growing corn" and "drinking *pinole*" in (3). *Pinole* comes only from *maiz* (corn); similarly, the situations that encompass an individual come only from his own actions. *Pinole* is a powder-like corn substance that is dissolved in water and consumed as a beverage. It is a high calorie energy source necessary for foot racing. The Tarahumara-Rarámuri have a strong tradition of running. Rarámuri means "those who run well." They are famous for their foot racing abilities in which they kick a small wooden ball and race. Rarájipame means "runners with the ball."

The most gifted runners can run for 6–8 hours non-stop, sometimes covering over 40 miles in a single race (Fontana 1979). They start training for races as soon as they are old enough to walk. Even the women can run for more than six hours straight (Fontana 1979). They were participants in the 1928 Olympic Games. And when the Tarahumara governor learned that the race in Amsterdam was to be a mere 26 miles, he sent three girls to run it (Fontana 1979). The religious altars of the Tarahumara are earth and stone piles before which they prostrate themselves as preparation for footraces. Earthen and stone mounds are scattered throughout the trails in the Sierra Tarahumara, and they serve as altars, even for a certain few who live in the mission center.[4] The Mexicans are very fearful of the indigenous who use these ancient altars believing that they are tools for creating *brujerías* (witchcraft). The Tarahumara men that were captured during the 1650–1850 campaigns to dominate them, were condemned for their *hechiceros* (those who can make magic happen) *y brujerías* (witchcraft) and after confessing their sins, they were condemned to death (Gonzáles 1991).[5]

(4) *Mejor tortilla dura que ninguna.*
[Better hard tortilla, than no tortilla at all.]

In (4), "eating a hard tortilla" is metaphorical for "farming an arid plot of land." Farming is the primary source of livelihood for the Tarahumara; and tortilla is the primary food. When you are dependent on agricultural yield, even a parcel of waterless land that produces, it is better than having no land at all. The best lands of the indigenous have been taken, and they have been forced into the mountains to farm the arid, highland soil. Despite this, their land continues to yield the corn. Without the corn harvest, the people would starve. The Feast of the Harvest (Day of the Dead) is the mechanism by which the harvest is safeguarded. From corn, the Tarahumara make all their basic foods: *tesgüino, pinole, tamales, menudo,* and *tortilla.* Corn is a native food of the Americas, not imported from Spain.

The "Day of the Dead," or the Feast of the Harvest, and is observed so that harm does not come to the crops. The "Land of the Dead" is viewed as a land of opposites, where in the night, the dead awake. After death, the dead do not leave the premises immediately, and if they are not carefully waked, they will not travel to the "Land of the Dead." The days before the first *tesgüinada* fiesta are days in which the soul likes to wander around at night. Three *tesgüino* fiestas are held for a deceased man, and four *fiestas* for a deceased woman or else the soul will remain on earth as a ghost (Bennett & Zing 1935). Four *fiestas* over a year's period are danced for a female, because it is believed that women travel slower than men at traveling. If *fiestas* are not performed, it is believed that the dead soul will return to harm the people or crops (Bennett & Zing 1935). After the *tesgüinadas,* the dead person is thought to have reached his destination from where he can no longer return. The Mexican celebration of the "Day of the Dead" is kept annually in November throughout Mexico, and it is literally a party in the cemetery with the dead. The cemetery is cleaned and decorated once a year, and provides the picnic grounds for a daylong visit with the dead. It is a hybrid between the ancient Feast of the Harvest and the beliefs surrounding death. There is a link between the *tesgüinada* and the rituals preformed at the grave. Humor to the extreme of laughing at death is an explanatory source of humor.

(5) *El muerto y el harrimado, a los tres dias apestan.*
[The dead and the guest, both stink after three days.]

In, (5) the "the smell of a corpse" is used to describe the feeling towards "guests that overstay their welcome." This metaphor relates a "body left in the home more than three days" with "guests staying your home more than three days." This brings the listener's imagination to evoke the sensory perception of death, and it articulates a practical model of action.

The death ritual in Mexico is called a *velorio*, or the night *vigil*. The *velorio* is a funeral that begins with the lighting of a fire near the head of the deceased. The body is left in the home, in the bed, surrounded by personal belongings. The family members take turns staying awake, sitting with the corpse all night; and the body is not left alone for 24 hours. During this time, the whole village visits the deceased. They ensure that someone is always with the deceased because during this time, there takes place a battle for the soul of the individual between *Onorúame* and the Devil. Those in the joking-relationship with the deceased laugh as they dig the grave. The superstition is that the one closest to the deceased in a drinking and joking relationship, is the one who is not endangered by the power of the soul of the dead, and thus the least likely to be harmed (Kennedy 1970). After three days, the *Mutcímuli* leave food for the dead, three of each item, believing that he returns to eat. Three crosses are erected, ashes and water are sprinkled and beer is offered as a drink offering. If it was a woman who died, a race us run with the men dressing in women's clothing (Fontana 1979). This creates such laughter that the deceased travels safely to the land of the dead. *Mutcímuli* is a term applied to what Kennedy called "those in the joking relationship." The *mutcímuli* are the most boisterous characters who perform at the *tesgüinadas* to the delight of the watchers. The Tarahumara view of death is interesting, as the emphasis is not on death and mourning, but on beer-drinking and laughter.

(6) *Febrero loco y Marzo un poco.*
[Crazy February and March is a little crazy.]

Before the festival of Passover in April, the Indians say that the Devil is loose and creating the high winds characteristic of February and March. The Devil is in the air of the earth and preparing for the yearly battle against the sons of *Onorúame.* The semantic relation between "Crazy February/March" and "Devils power" is anomalous. This is because there is no relevant analogy between "the behavior of a Time-Object" and the "behavior of a Mythological-Object." This violated semantic restriction indicates a metaphorical relation. The correspondence between two properties is that "the winds stop after the month of March," and "the Devil is stopped after the festival of Passover." It is the responsibility of the Tarahumara to keep the *Semana Santa* (Holy Week) which strengthens GOD and perpetuates life for one more year.

The purpose of the *Semana Santa* (Holy Week) is to strengthen *Onorúame* (God the Father) so that He can continue to oppose the Devil, thus allowing the animals and the people to survive another year (Kennedy 1989). It is a symbol of the Passover, which is observed year to year, until God overcomes the Devil. During this *tesgüinada* (beer-drinking wake), called the "*baile de los fareseos,*" or "*Norírahuachi,*" the Tarahumara mimic the anarchy created by the ancient Hebrew sect called the Pharisees. Those who protect the earth are the Rarámuri soldiers who enact the mythological battle between the sons of the Devil, called the "*fareseos*" or "Pharisees," and the sons of *Onorúame*, or the Tarahumara soldiers (Bonfiglioli 1995). Beginning on Thursday at sunset, three days before the 7-day feast ends, the Tarahumara paint their bodies white and transform themselves into *fareseos.* While dancing, dressed in loin cloths, and with staff in hand, all Tarahumara men unite and move together in one great "snake-like" entity that unendingly extends itself in parallel lines. The dancers travel and weave synchronized circles throughout the entire village of Norógachi, Chihuahua to the sound of the *tambor* and flute. The uniting of good (the "Pillar of the Sky") with the entity of evil (Tarahumara *fareseos*) in one being, and the accompanying ritual of servitude in beer-drinking expresses the utopian idea of establishing brotherhood between all men. *Norírahuachi* is representative of the existing world that suddenly becomes alien and that needs to be destroyed so that it may be regenerated and renewed. While dying it gives birth. On the final Sabbath day of the *Semana Santa*, a symbolic reincarnation of evil (a stuffed doll called Judas) has his guts pulled out by Rarámuri soldiers and then is burned. On this day, the Tarahumara *fareseos* remove their white paint and transform themselves into Tarahumara soldiers. The embodiment of evil and its transformation through a triumphant killing brings the flowering of the New year. The dancing of *Norírahuachi* is the victory over supernatural awe, over death. The vigil is observed annually, until *Onorúame* awakens to take revenge on the fallen Angel. This is done annually, and it represents the *inicio del año* for the Rarámuri, the New Year celebration (González et al. 1994; Bennett & Zingg 1935).[6]

(7) *Un clavo saca otro clavo.*
[One nail takes out another nail].

Sentence (7) contains a simple form of metaphor as a semantic relation between two phrases: "another nail" and "another lover." In the domain, the listener is asked to compare the properties of a nail acting as a swift and sure instrument used in replacing or removing another nail and the use of a new lover acting as a swift and sure instrument used to immediately forget the lost love. Aesthetic delight comes from deciding if a new lover should be used as a tool to solve the problem just as fast.

Ritual humor on the subject of sex is held in high esteem by the Tarahumara society. Comedians, called *mutcímuli*, represent the behavior and disgrace of the transgressions by violating the norm through reference to sexual sin (*cómico sexual*). The humorist reenacts the behavior of the transgressor (the Devil who introduced sexual sin) and the disgrace of those violators (the *mestizo* compatriots) through *comicó sexual*, or repeated reference to sexual violations of the norm. During the *fareseos* (Pharisees) dances performed at Easter, the sons of the fallen Angel, have bad intentions which the Tarahumara demonstrate through sexual jokes and nonverbal sexual activities. During *tesgüinadas*, "*cosas malas no son malas*" (bad things are not bad) and they indulge overtly in illicit forbidden behaviors (Bonfiglioli 1995). The Tarahumara assumes the identity of the mythological characters in alliance with the Devil and performs all sorts of disruptive antics and create disorder. The more *tesgüino*, the more explosions of laughter. These humorists do the opposite of the norm and have the freedom to depart from conventional behavior. The behavior creates the disorder that sustains laughter throughout the night. The laughter of the ritual ceremony serves to communicate to the supernatural mythological beings that a "watch" is underway, where the "sons of God" are waiting, watching, and prepared to ward off the "sons of the Devil." Bernard Fontana (1979) vividly describes the feeling of his observance of *tesgüinada*:

> the night's observance was marked by hilarity. A large group of men sat just outside our door and spent most of the night, or so it seemed to me, laughing. In a strange way, I was transported to my childhood in northern California. I could remember falling asleep in my bed, warm and content beneath the covers, listening to the laughter of my parents…far from keeping me awake, that happy laughter was the greatest reassurance a child could have that all was right with the world (p. 149).

Joking is the cosmic mediator. The Tarahumara do not place themselves above the deity of evil, but themselves become the deity of evil. The men, through the application of white paint to their loin-cloth covered bodies, do not place themselves above the object of their mockery, but become the object of mockery. In this way, the people temporarily suspend the hierarchic distinctions and barriers of certain traditions norms and prohibitions of their usual life. There is use of obscure language and free play with words and colloquialisms. It is unlike the tongue of the upper-class, and its rich and colorful comic nature is outside of official speech. For the purpose of *tesgüinada*, laughter has a regenerative power.

(8) *Nunca digas de esa agua no beberé.*
[Never say "from that water I will never drink."]

Finally in (8), the listener is asked to derive the validity of "never drinking from that water" by comparing to the properties of knowledge in the target analogy of "never being in that bad situation." The nonliteral mapping has the effect of directing the listener into inferring the following relation: water is needed by every living creature to survive, one must drink water, water is common to all, and all have to partake, eventually, in the same bad situation. Water is necessary for life; similarly, witchcraft is can be accessed by anyone because it is believe to be worked by sheer thought. Tarahumara view all negative effects as precarious and beyond their control (Pastron 1977).

The Tarahumara attribute all bad situations personal illness, personal tragedy, suffering, misfortune, and loss to *brujería* (witchcraft). Sorcery, or witchcraft, is worked by sheer thought; and superstitions beliefs in witchcraft dominate Tarahumara culture. Malicious intent is a necessary ingredient of witchcraft (Pastron 1977). By coveting, or "*hechando ojo*" (putting the "wanton eye") on something or someone, a jealous neighbor can cause *mala voluntad* (bad intent or sickness leading to illness, misfortune, etc.). If one does not share, the person that was impoverished can bewitch the one who refused to share (Passin 1911). Thus, hospitality to strangers, brotherhood and sharing food are sacred duties in Mexican culture. Among the worst sins against the moral code of the Tarahumara is the impoverishment of another through an unwillingness to share. Individual accumulation and ambition are threats to their egalitarian lifestyle (Jessen 1996). The *tesgüinada* and its central joking element are used to prevent "mal ojo" and the fear of witchcraft. *Tesqüinadas* are given for the purpose of healing illness, suffering or misfortune brought by the *mal ojo* (evil eye) (Palma 1992). "Putting the eye" is equivalent to "coveting."

5. Conclusions

We can find traces of Tarahumara mythology in the linguistic strategies employed by the Mexican *mestizo.* Their metaphors assume significance by virtue of their rhyme and their correspondence to something else. Their purpose is to provoke humor. They are a possible design for concealing meaning rather than revealing it. Many are sexually suggestive. A good metaphor established correspondence between very apparently dissimilar objects or events. The objects and events used for metaphorical comparison come directly from mythologies and rituals native to the Tarahumara indigenous population. Humor is central to indigenous Mexican religion, and joking plays a central role in Tarahumara Indian *tesgüinadas.* The same mythologies pervade the orientations of the peasant class. In the villages of Mexico, the mestizos continue to practice indigenous methods of waking the dead, visiting the cemetery, taking their children to *curanderos* (those who cure with magic) for illness related to "evil eye," and participating in communal labor projects in exchange for beer. The people continue to choose *comadres* and *compadres* based on the joking relationships between them. These people promise to care for their children in the case of death and they are repaid with gifts, food, and beer parties. When we were children, our favorite game was "playing comadres." In Chihuahua, the terms "compadre" and "comadre" are synonymous with "Tarahumara Indian." The Tarahumara are still a marginalized people who use oral and visual means as modes for the transmission of language. Metaphor serves as the linguistic basis for the encapsulation and dissemination of their cultural beliefs. Joking and laughter are critical venues used in the cosmic balance maintained by the "Pillars of the Sky" who believe that they have the role of serving *Onorúame* on earth. Laughter functions as a magical incantation. Fear is seen as a travesty of seriousness which is defeated by laughter. The cultural and historical context of Tarahumara humor and laughter provides insightful background knowledge for understanding the basic cognitive schemes by which native Mexican people conceptualize their experience and external world. So important are the indigenous mythologies that to ignore or underestimate their influence on metaphorical speech would also be to distort the picture of Mexican cultural development.

Notes

1. The old testament also dictates in Exodus 34:22–23, "And thou shalt observe the feast of weeks, the feast of the first fruits of wheat harvest, and the feast of ingathering at the year's end… Thrice in a year shall all your men children appear before God."

2. There is a misconception that the conquest and the forced Catholic conversions and the resultant gene-mixing occurred entirely between Spanish and (native) Mexican Indian. The Jesuit Order of Christ, a dominant Catholic institution responsible for sending missionaries into New Spain in the 17th century, was centered in Bohemia (Germany) and included missionaries from all over South-Central Europe, including Bohemia, Germany, Italy, Portugal, Prague, Austria, Belgium, France, and Croatia, as well as Spain.

3. After the Exodus, "the Lord went them by day in a "pillar of a cloud" to lead them, and by night in a "pillar of fire" to give them light." The Book of Exodus 13:21.

4. The book of Exodus makes reference to the earth and stone altars. "An altar of earth shall though make unto me. And if thou wilt make me an altar of stone, thou shalt not build it of hewn stone." See Exodus 20:24–25.

5. On the Day of the Annunciation of the Virgin Mary (21 of March, 1698) captive Tarahumara gentiles were baptized and then their heads were cut off and put on tall poles to serve as an example to the others of what would happen if they rebelled (González 1991; García 1992; Kennedy 1978). This violence set off the bloodiest rebellion throughout the whole northern Tarahumara country. The Tarahumara surrounded the buildings, battered upon the doors of the church. They climbed upon the altars, tore from their places the images of the Mother of God and of the saints, rent them asunder, and cast the pieces into

the river that flowed close by. They smashed the altars and the baptismal font,[...]and laid hands on everything else, destroying and ruining all (Dunne 1948). The infamous Spanish Army General Retana then moved from Parral and with the approval of Jesuit priest Joseph Neumann he beheaded 30 Tarahumara men and posted their heads along the road near Cocomórachic (Kennedy 1978 ; Jessen 1996). Captain Retana continued to behead another 33 men, placing their head on poles near Sisoguíchic (Kennedy 1978; Jessen 1996).

6. The Easter celebration which takes place in April, according to Old Testament law, is the New Year observance. "This month shall be unto you the beginning of months. It shall be the 1st of the year to you." Exodus 12:2.

References

Bennett, Wendell C & Robert M. Zing (1935). *The Tarahumara: An Indian tribe of northern Mexico.* Chicago: University of Chicago Press.

Bonfiglioli, Carlo (1995). *Fariseos y matachines en la sierra tarahumara: Entre la pasión de Cristo, la transgresión cómico-sexual y las danzas de conquista.* [Pharisees and Matachines in the Sierra Tarahumara: Between the temptation of Christ, the transgression through sexual humor, and the dances of the conquest.] Mexico City: Instituto Nacional Indigenista.

Contreras, Guillermo (1999). Volunteers struggle just to reach Indians. *The Sunday Journal,* Albuquerque, Nov. 28, 1999.

Dunne, Peter Martin (1948). *Early Jesuit missions in Tarahumara.* Los Angeles: University of California Press.

Debatin, B. (1995). *The rationality of metaphor: An analysis based on the philosophy of language and communication theory.* Berlin: De Gruyter.

Debatin B. (1997). Metaphorical Iconoclasm and the Reflective Power of Metaphor. In B. Debatin, Jackson T. R. & Steuer D. (Eds.) *Metaphor and Rational Discourse.* Tübingen: Niemeyer, 147–158.

Dunne, P. M. (1948). *Early Jesuit Missions in Tarahumara.* Berkeley: University of California Press, p. 181.

Fass, Dan (1988). An account of coherence, semantic relations, metonymy, and lexical ambiguity resolution. In, S. Small, G. W. Cottrell, & M. K. Tanenhaus (Eds.) *Lexical ambiguity resolution: Perspectives from psycholinguistics. neuropsychology, and artificial intelligence.* San Mateo, California: Morgan Kaufmann Publishers.

Fontana, Bernard L. (1979). *Tarahumara: Where night is the day of the moon.* Flagstaff: Northland Press.

García H. M., & Suárez, M. H. (1995). *Perfil Educativo de la poblacion mexicana,* (4th ed.) [Education Profile for the Mexican Population.] Aguascalientes: Instituto Nacional de Estadistica, Geografia e Informatica.

Gibbs, Raymond W. Jr. (1994). *The Poetics of Mind: Figurative thought, language, and understanding.* Cambridge: Cambridge University Press.

Gonzales, R. L., & Erasmo Palma (1985). Vida y muerte del mundo en el pensamento

Tarahumara. [The life and death of the world in Tarahumara thought.] *Tlalocan, 10,* 189–209.

González, R. L., Gutiérrez, S., Stefani P., Urías, M., Urteaga, A. (1994). *Derechos culturales y derechos indígenas en la Sierra Tarahumara.* [Cultural and indigenous rights in the Sierra Tarahumara.] Juárez: Universidad Autónoma de Ciudad Juárez.

Gonzáles, R. L. (1991). *Historia de las rebeliones en la Sierra Tarahumara (1626–1724).* [History of the rebelliones in the Sierra Tarahumara]. Chihuahua: Editorial Camino.

Grimes, JE, & BF Grimes. (1996)(Eds.) *Ethnologue Language Family Index.* SIL: Summer Institute of Linguistics [online] Available:[http::/ /www.sil.org/ethnologue/countries/ Mexi.html]

Guillermoprieto, Alma (1994). Mexico City, 1992. In A. Guillermoprieto (Ed.), *The heart that bleeds: Latin America now.* New York: Random House.

Jessen, A. R. (1996). *Conflict and Cooperation in the Sierra: Differential Responses to Neo-liberal Policy by Rarámuri Indians and Mestizos in Chihuahua, Mexico.* Thesis Dissertation, Northwestern University.

Kennedy, John G. (1970). Bonds of laughter among the Tarahumara Indians: Toward a rethinking of joking theory. In W. Goldschmidt & H. Hoijer (Eds.), *The social anthropology of Latin America: Essays in honor of Ralph Leon Beals.* Los Angeles: University of California Press.

Kennedy, John G. (1989). *The Tarahumara.* New York: Chelsea House.

Lumholtz, Carl (1894). Tarahumari life and customs. *Scriber's Magazine,* 16 (9), 296–311.

Levi, Jerome Meyer (1993). *Pillars of the sky: The genealogy of ethnic identity among the Rarámuri-Simaroni (Tarahumara-Gentiles) of the northwest Mexico.* Thesis Dissertation, Harvard University.

Palma, Erasmo (1992). *Donde cantan los pájaros chuyacos.* [Where the birds *chuyacos* sing.] Chihuahua: Govierno Del Estado de Chihuahua.

Passin, Herbert (1942). Sorcery as a phase of Tarahumara economic relations. *MAN* (London), 42 (1–18), 11–15.

Pastron, Allen Gerald (1977). *Aspects of witchcraft and shamanism in a Tarahumara Indian community of northern Mexico.* Los Angeles, CA.: University of California Press.

Rapp, Albert (1951). *The origins of wit and humor.* New York: Dutton.

Is creativity algorithmic?

Conn Mulvihill and Micheál Colhoun
National University of Ireland, Galway, Ireland

1. Introduction

Great literature, sculpture, music and painting testify to the creative mark of gifted individuals throughout human history. All of these arts speak to us in their own particular languages. Sometimes, these languages are quite difficult to characterise. They certainly appear to require considerable time and effort before mastery is achieved.

In science as well, there have been many gifted individuals who have contributed fundamentally to our understanding, and who have in fact produced precise languages for representing and communicating this understanding. Typically, students must spend a number of years grappling with the languages of science before being deemed proficient in their understanding and use.

Now a language, perhaps any language, is characterisable in gross terms through the words 'form' and 'content'. We take form to be the medium, as it were, and content the message. Where the two remain separate, one tends to associate form with the rules that govern the shape of the language, and content with whatever function the language performs. In linguistic terms, it is even possible to give a gross characterisation of language forms, the well-known Chomsky hierarchy.

2. Language, art, biology

We know that languages appear to have some rules regarding how things can be expressed. Some languages are very fixed in this regard, for example classical Latin, with precisely delineated rules for conjugating verbs and declining nouns etc. (Jones 1986).

However what is expressed in a language varies tremendously: a wish, a command, an observation, a desire and so forth. It may even be a reflection on the form of the language itself! It therefore appears difficult to generally characterise content except in unhelpful terms such as 'anything about anything'. Perhaps the most plastic expression of this difficulty is to be found with literary movements, which not only address content, but also reflect on and manipulate the conventional rules of form themselves (O'Connor 1984; Hyde 1899).

This brings us to an interesting point. Where form and content mix, there appears to be scope for creative activity, at least if driven by a human speaker. The English language in Elizabethan times was very plastic (Halliday 1975). This provided a powerful tool for Shakespeare. Indeed this very ambiguity seems quite important in language, and may be one of the roots of whatever creativity we associate with it.

Let us side-step a little from literature in order to approach creativity through another art. We mentioned that ambiguity in form and content was associated with creativity in literature. Let us now consider the language of art and see if the same can be said to hold.

Perhaps we can gain something here from considering 'modern art'. To many, the language of this art is itself impenetrable, whereas a good old-fashioned landscape painting appears to have a recognisable content even if the agents of form that express it may vary somewhat. The various experimental art forms in the late nineteenth and early twentieth century seem to have addressed in great detail the boundary between form and content. Consider for example the impressionistic use of colour (Gombrich 1978). So once again a very creative period appears to be bound up with the issue of interplay between form and content.

It is interesting to note here as well that biological languages such as DNA display an interplay between form and content, mediated through the processes of meiosis and mitosis. There is certainly scope for creative activity through a genetically driven biological system, as we know from evolutionary studies. Hence language, art and biology all furnish examples that touch on an interplay between form and content as being associated with creativity.

3. Paradoxes

The above examples lead us to think that interplay between form and content is terribly important for the creative process, whatever that in fact is. It is interesting to push the boundaries here, and consider a limiting case, where form and content are as tightly bound together as possible. The example that comes to mind here in linguistic terms is that of a paradox (Sainsbury 1988). The phenomenon of paradoxes has of course been noted since ancient times, and is found in such memorable paradoxes as the Cretan 'I am a liar' paradox. Here, and in similar cases, the binding of form and content is at the heart of the paradox, achieved through a reflective or diagonal argument.

This phenomenon is of course a limiting case. But it provides further evidence that where form and content mix, strange effects follow. It is also interesting in that it represents in some way as it were a self-manipulation without human intervention. This is of course useful from the perspective of self-manipulating formal systems which we need if we are to bind up creativity in some way in computers.

4. Computers: Languages and algorithms

Is there anything to be currently said about form and content in the context of computers? Is there any sense in which form and content mix? Certainly computer science is connected at a fundamental level with language (Fisher 1993). We communicate with computers through rigid languages, and with ourselves through more plastic ones. The computer languages of today have precise rulesets for form. In terms of their content, computer languages are concerned with algorithms, rigid recipes that machines can process in furthering a task. But how do we characterise content, and is there any relationship with form? Can we in fact answer the question 'Is creativity algorithmic?'.

Well, when we as computer scientists consider a particular algorithm, there is much that can be said about it. We can examine it dimensionally — so many lines of code, so many branches, this amount of memory required, this amount of time to compute for that input etc. We can examine it with respect to other algorithms — it belongs in this family, it is better than that one under the following circumstances. Such metrics tend to be quantitative and open to a rational consensus as to their accuracy. Thus we come up with a set of properties at a general level that address algorithmic content in terms of intrinsic and comparative properties.

Analysing an algorithm is not the same as producing it no more than appreciating a work of art is the same as creating it. These words are themselves interesting, as one does tend to say that a work of art is created, whereas there seems to be something more constrained about working with algorithms. To follow on from this(if we cite the experience in other domains), a way must be found to generate some type of interplay between form and content in order for there to be any hope of binding creativity inside a machine.

However it is not usual to consider interplay between form and content during such an algorithmic analysis. It is possible for some discussion to occur in this area — such as for example examining a recursive versus procedural formulation of the same algorithm. Again, in more general terms, one may note that in certain languages such as Lisp, there exists a control/data equivalence such that functions may be manipulated by other functions, a property not normally associated with computer languages. Is such a property a necessary one for creative activity in machines if we accept the centrality of such interplay in the creative process? Let us further this discussion by attempting to characterise the relationship between form and content in computers.

5. Computers: Form and content

In computing, we can actually produce a special type of algorithmic content that directly addresses form — such an algorithm is known as a compiler, and can give a yes/no answer to the question 'is this form correct?'

Put another way, we can produce a connection between a special definition of truth in terms of yes/no answers and a proof mechanism embodied in a compiling algorithm for producing the appropriate truth value. This is a very fundamental connection of great value to computer scientists. We would be in a bad way if we did not have compilers that give us yes/no answers to questions of form.

However it is only because we choose to have a precisely constrained form that we can do this. There can be no surprises. In fact one of the few surprises that can arise, the famous dangling else problem, is handled unambiguously in all compiler implementations. There is no room for ambiguity in the interplay between form and content. Nor is there much in the line of reflective argument.

Would the situation be any better if we produced a special type of algorithmic content that in fact addressed content? The mathematician Lenat devised a special relationship between form and content in his AM and Eurisco algorithms. One addressed primitive concepts in mathematics, the other addressed a variety of domains. Both had rules for algorithmic self-manipulation, and generated some excitement at the time due to their apparently exploratory nature. Control structure manipulation was present in both, perhaps more successfully in the second. Yet it appears to have been the richness of the embedding representational space that led to the apparent successes of the piecewise manipulations, and not the discovery of any type of mechanical creativity.

Whatever the shortcomings of these algorithms in producing mechanical creativity, it is clear at the very least that some interplay between form and content lay at the heart of what was being attempted. Just as in Lisp, there was a control/data equivalence that proved central to the endeavour. This suggests again that achieving some characterisation of the relationship between form and content is important for any hope of machine creativity.

Consider again the compiler — content examining form. Perhaps content can examine content? After all, if computer languages have a restricted form, examinable by machine, perhaps we can also place restrictions on their content. In other words, perhaps we could produce a proof mechanism embodied in an algorithm that would give us yes/no answers with respect to content, an algorithm that examined algorithms in a very general way. This might be slightly better, in that content seems less restricted than form, and so, given both algorithms, we could get closer to understanding and characterising a boundary point where interesting interplay occurs.

We seem to be out of luck here. We know this for the following reason. The foundations of computing are based on work in logic and mathematics. Such work is concerned with the general properties of symbol systems. The logician Gödel addressed a fundamental point about the nature of such systems. He showed that for certain classes of systems truth and proof in the mathematical sense were not in fact co-extensive. So it follows that for many symbol systems we cannot produce a piece of content capable of giving us yes/no answers about all possible pieces of content.

We also have an interesting boundary point in this result. What is remarkable about the result in the context of the current discussion is that it makes use of a special type of form in order to achieve its aim: a reflective form in a diagonal argument that is related to our above discussion on paradoxes. It states in essence 'here is a piece of content that you cannot reach by proof'. Thus in order to generally characterise the scope of content, it was found useful to characterise a very special relationship between form and content, a limiting case involving a reflective or diagonal argument. Intriguingly, this argument structure also appears in art and music, often held to be creative disciplines (Hofstadter 1979).

Thus an attempt to 'close off' content through some algorithm akin to a compiler will not succeed. If there can be no surprises with compilers, can there be surprises with content? The boundary point displayed in the above result is itself very surprising. And it mixes form and content. Perhaps it is itself an example of a creative language phrase, albeit a very special one.

6. Review

Let us attempt to summarise some of the observations to date. In all human activity, we find languages. We characterise languages in gross terms through the convenient vehicles of form and content. Where form and content mix, there appears to be scope for creative activity, and one marker associated with this activity appears to be ambiguity, at least in literature. Turning to art, we again find experimentation on the boundary of form and content in the nineteenth and twentieth centuries. Biological languages also have interplay form and content. Paradoxes are a limiting case in the interplay between form and content, and one marker here seems to involve a reflective or diagonal argument.

In terms of computers, content is characterisable in gross terms, through various algorithmic properties, and form is precisely delineable. However there seems only restricted scope for mixing form and content. Experimental languages such as Lisp allow some mixing of form and content. We can produce an algorithm, a compiler, for giving yes/no answers to questions of form. But this means that there is no ambiguity. Dangling elses are banned.

Mixing form and content was attempted by Lenat, with some limited success. In the general case, we find that it is impossible to produce an algorithm to give yes/no answers to questions of content. So we find that we can give yes/no answers on questions of form in computer languages, but not on questions of content. However, in order to state the latter, it was found useful to consider the interplay between form and content through a reflective or diagonal argument. Such arguments appear in art and music as well, and so it might be that the argument phrase itself is an example of a creative phrase.

In the next section, we will turn to consider what properties a language displaying creativity might be expected to display.

7. Three hypotheses

On the basis of the analysis considered in the previous sections, we posit the following provocative hypothesis at this point:

Creative language hypothesis:
Any language supporting creativity must have the ability to mix form and content. Mixing form and content is marked sometimes by ambiguity and sometimes by reflective activities. Hence ambiguity and reflection function as markers, perhaps necessary ones, for creativity.

Would it be unreasonable to suggest that we are now witnessing a creative surge in the phenomenon known as the Internet/WWW? Consider the above definition. The language of the WWW is hypertext. Does this language mix form and content through the use of hyperlinks? For are hyperlinks form or content or both? Consider an image on a web site. It can be used directly as a point of information, and it can often also be used to proceed to another location. Hence the same formulation is serving two functions, and displays an ambiguity. A web site also might refer to itself, or portions of itself. Is this in some way reflective?

Of course more is needed for a full analysis. For one thing, the above discussion has a lot to say about creativity, but little about the impetus for creativity and subsequent evaluation of the creative process. What would be required in order to further the discussion on impetus and evaluation is first, a mechanism to seed the creative process, and, second, a mechanism to stabilise it.

Although not central to the current discussion, we will now posit two further hypotheses in order to, as it were, complete the creative model. Both of these will be briefly motivated.

One possibility for the creative impetus is random events. Perhaps random events cause languages to configure in novel ways — into highly creative configurations from time to time.

Hence we posit the following:

Random event hypothesis:
Random events cause languages to form from time to time into creative configurations which are marked by ambiguities and reflection.

These configurations are then stabilised through some limiting mechanism that places terminating conditions on their activities. Such a limiting mecha-

nism is a bias factor, and typically might operate through some time, spatial or environmental fitting cut-off mechanism.
Thus we have:

Bias factor hypothesis:
Bias factors are responsible for stabilising a language after it has been formed into a creative configuration through a random event.

Neither of these latter two hypotheses will be developed further at this stage. It is tempting to speculate however that a symmetry of some form may exist between the creative language hypothesis and the bias factor hypothesis. For example, one thinks of ambiguous situations being disambiguated and vice versa, and also of reflective situations becoming linear and vice versa.

8. Conclusions

In this paper, we have begun to explore the characteristics that mark out languages as creative vehicles. It has been seen that ambiguity and reflection appear in creative phases of language activity in several domains — natural language, art, biology. It has been argued that the same two phenomena should be present in a computer language for any hope of giving a positive answer to the inquiry 'is creativity algorithmic?'

Through the mediation of the creative language, random event and bias factor hypotheses, we have also in this paper arrived at an exploratory viewpoint on how to model the creative process. The view presented here is that a language has both stable and creative configurations. A language may pass from a stable configuration to a creative configuration through the mediation of a random event. When in a creative configuration, ambiguity and reflection are present. Bias factors stabilise these creative configurations, placing terminating conditions on their activities, and a stable language state results.

References

Jones, Peter & Keith Sidwell (1986). *Reading Latin.* Cambridge: University Press.
O'Connor, Ulick (1984). *Celtic dawn.* London: Black Swan.
Hyde, Douglas (1899). *A literary history of Ireland.* T. Fisher Unwin (revised edition, 1980).London: Ernest Benn.

Halliday, Frank Ernest (1975). *The excellency of the English tongue.* London: Gollancz.
Gombrich, Ernst (1978). *The story of art.* Oxford: Phaidon.
Sainsbury, Richard (1988). *Paradoxes.* Cambridge: University Press.
Fischer, Alice & Frances Grodzinsky (1993). *The anatomy of programming languages.* Englewood Cliffs, New Jersey: Prentice-Hall.
Hofstadter, Douglas (1979). *Gödel, Escher, Bach: An eternal golden braid.* Brighton: Harvester Press.

Subject Index

N

R

Name Index

In the series ADVANCES IN CONSCIOUSNESS RESEARCH (AiCR) the following titles have been published thus far or are scheduled for publication:

1. GLOBUS, Gordon G.: *The Postmodern Brain.* 1995.
2. ELLIS, Ralph D.: *Questioning Consciousness. The interplay of imagery, cognition, and emotion in the human brain.* 1995.
3. JIBU, Mari and Kunio YASUE: *Quantum Brain Dynamics and Consciousness. An introduction.* 1995.
4. HARDCASTLE, Valerie Gray: *Locating Consciousness.* 1995.
5. STUBENBERG, Leopold: *Consciousness and Qualia.* 1998.
6. GENNARO, Rocco J.: *Consciousness and Self-Consciousness. A defense of the higher-order thought theory of consciousness.* 1996.
7. MAC CORMAC, Earl and Maxim I. STAMENOV (eds): *Fractals of Brain, Fractals of Mind. In search of a symmetry bond.* 1996.
8. GROSSENBACHER, Peter G. (ed.): *Finding Consciousness in the Brain. A neurocognitive approach.* 2001.
9. Ó NUALLÁIN, Seán, Paul MC KEVITT and Eoghan MAC AOGÁIN (eds): *Two Sciences of Mind. Readings in cognitive science and consciousness.* 1997.
10. NEWTON, Natika: *Foundations of Understanding.* 1996.
11. PYLKKÖ, Pauli: *The Aconceptual Mind. Heideggerian themes in holistic naturalism.* 1998.
12. STAMENOV, Maxim I. (ed.): *Language Structure, Discourse and the Access to Consciousness.* 1997.
13. VELMANS, Max (ed.): *Investigating Phenomenal Consciousness. Methodologies and Maps.* 2000.
14. SHEETS-JOHNSTONE, Maxine: *The Primacy of Movement.* 1999.
15. CHALLIS, Bradford H. and Boris M. VELICHKOVSKY (eds.): *Stratification in Cognition and Consciousness.* 1999.
16. ELLIS, Ralph D. and Natika NEWTON (eds.): *The Caldron of Consciousness. Motivation, affect and self-organization – An anthology.* 2000.
17. HUTTO, Daniel D.: *The Presence of Mind.* 1999.
18. PALMER, Gary B. and Debra J. OCCHI (eds.): *Languages of Sentiment. Cultural constructions of emotional substrates.* 1999.
19. DAUTENHAHN, Kerstin (ed.): *Human Cognition and Social Agent Technology.* 2000.
20. KUNZENDORF, Robert G. and Benjamin WALLACE (eds.): *Individual Differences in Conscious Experience.* 2000.
21. HUTTO, Daniel D.: *Beyond Physicalism.* 2000.
22. ROSSETTI, Yves and Antti REVONSUO (eds.): *Beyond Dissociation. Interaction between dissociated implicit and explicit processing.* 2000.
23. ZAHAVI, Dan (ed.): *Exploring the Self. Philosophical and psychopathological perspectives on self-experience.* 2000.
24. ROVEE-COLLIER, Carolyn, Harlene HAYNE and Michael COLOMBO: *The Development of Implicit and Explicit Memory.* 2000.
25. BACHMANN, Talis: *Microgenetic Approach to the Conscious Mind.* 2000.
26. Ó NUALLÁIN, Seán (ed.): *Spatial Cognition. Selected papers from Mind III, Annual Conference of the Cognitive Science Society of Ireland, 1998.* 2000.
27. McMILLAN, John and Grant R. GILLETT: *Consciousness and Intentionality.* 2001.

28. ZACHAR, Peter: *Psychological Concepts and Biological Psychiatry. A philosophical analysis.* 2000.
29. VAN LOOCKE, Philip (ed.): *The Physical Nature of Consciousness.* 2001.
30. BROOK, Andrew and Richard C. DeVIDI (eds.): *Self-reference and Self-awareness.* 2001.
31. RAKOVER, Sam S. and Baruch CAHLON: *Face Recognition. Cognitive and computational processes.* 2001.
32. VITIELLO, Giuseppe: *My Double Unveiled. The dissipative quantum model of the brain.* 2001.
33. YASUE, Kunio, Mari JIBU and Tarcisio DELLA SENTA (eds.): *No Matter, Never Mind. Proceedings of Toward a Science of Consciousness: Fundamental Approaches, Tokyo, 1999.* 2002.
34. FETZER, James H.(ed.): *Consciousness Evolving.* 2002.
35. Mc KEVITT, Paul, Seán Ó NUALLÁIN and Conn MULVIHILL (eds.): *Language, Vision, and Music. Selected papers from the 8th International Workshop on the Cognitive Science of Natural Language Processing, Galway, 1999.* 2002.
36. PERRY, Elaine, Heather ASHTON and Allan YOUNG (eds.): *Neurochemistry of Consciousness. Neurotransmitters in mind.* 2002.
37. PYLKKÄNEN, Paavo and Tere VADÉN (eds.): *Dimensions of Conscious Experience.* 2001.
38. SALZARULO, Piero and Gianluca FICCA (eds.): *Awakening and Sleep-Wake Cycle Across Development.* 2002.
39. BARTSCH, Renate: *Consciousness Emerging. The dynamics of perception, imagination, action, memory, thought, and language.* 2002.
40. MANDLER, George: *Consciousness Recovered. Psychological functions and origins of conscious thought.* 2002.
41. ALBERTAZZI, Liliana (ed.): *Unfolding Perceptual Continua.* 2002.
42. STAMENOV, Maxim I. and Vittorio GALLESE (eds.): *Mirror Neurons and the Evolution of Brain and Language.* n.y.p.
43. DEPRAZ, Natalie, Francisco VARELA and Pierre VERMERSCH.: *On Becoming Aware.* n.y.p.
44. MOORE, Simon and Mike OAKSFORD (eds.): *Emotional Cognition. From brain to behaviour.* 2002.
45. DOKIC, Jerome and Joelle PROUST: *Simulation and Knowledge of Action.* n.y.p.
46. MATHEAS, Michael and Phoebe SENGERS (ed.): *Narrative Intelligence.* n.y.p.
47. COOK, Norman D.: *Tone of Voice and Mind. The connections between intonation, emotion, cognition and consciousness.* 2002.
48. JIMÉNEZ, Luis: *Attention and Implicit Learning.* n.y.p.
49. OSAKA, Naoyuki (ed.): *Neural Basis of Consciousness.* n.y.p.